X/1999

VOL. 4
INTERMEZZO
Shojo Edition

STORY & ART BY CLAMP

ENGLISH ADAPTATION BY FRED BURKE

Translation/Lillian Olsen
Touch-Up Art & Lettering/Wayne Truman
Cover Design/Hidemi Sahara
Graphic Design/Carolina Ugalde
Editor (1st Edition)/Julie Davis
Editor (Shojo Edition)/Julie Davis

Managing Editor/Annette Roman
Editor in Chief/William Flanagan
Director of Licensing & Acquisitions/Rika Inouye
Sr. VP of Sales & Marketing/Rick Bauer
Sr. VP of Editorial/Hyoe Narita
Publisher/Seiji Horibuchi

Printed in Canada

Published by VIZ, LLC
P.O. Box 77010 • San Francisco, CA 94107

1st Edition published 1998

Shojo Edition
10 9 8 7 6 5 4 3 2 1
First printing, June 2003

www.viz.com

X/1999™

Vol. 4
INTERMEZZO
Shojo Edition

Story and Art by
CLAMP

X/1999
THE STORY THUS FAR

The End of the World has been prophesied…and time is running out. Kamui Shiro is a young man who was born with a special power—the power to decide the fate of the Earth itself.

The story opens with Kamui's reappearance in Tokyo after a six-year absence. Almost immediately upon his arrival, he's challenged to a psychic duel by a number of "men in black." These men turn out to be "curse zombies"—psychic constructs sent by a powerful being to spy on Kamui. Kamui defeats the curse zombies handily, but their presence is an uneasy reminder that others recognize something special about Kamui.

At school, one of Kamui's childhood friends, Kotori Monou, recognizes him almost immediately, but Kamui turns her away with a somber warning: "Don't get involved with me. Never talk to me again. Things are different from six years ago."

Heartbroken, Kotori stumbles away crying. Falling unconscious, she sinks into a vision of the End of the World, featuing the world shattering like a glass ball, and Kamui as its destroyer. She awakens in the school infirmary to the news that a young man matching Kamui's description had carried her in. Since Kotori has a heart condition, her brother Fuma is worried by her collapse, and takes her home.

Kamui himself is then injured in a duel—his opponent, Saiki, is rescued by the sword-wielding Arashi, while Kamui is tended to by Fuma and another mysterious young man, the young priest Sorata, who explains much of Kamui's destiny to the confused young man.

Meanwhile, Fuma and Kotori's father, priest of the Togakushi shrine, is confronted by a young man, Nataku, intent on obtaining the sacred sword kept by the shrine. Mr. Monou fights bravely, but in vain—the sword is carried off by Nataku, and Mr. Monou dies in Fuma's arms, whispering a warning about the end of the world. Soon after this, Kamui discovers his mother's sister, Tokiko Magami, working as the school nurse. Tokiko tells Kamui of the strange circumstances surrounding his birth.…

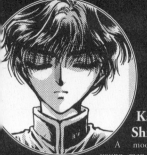

Kamui Shiro

A moody, distant young man, Kamui was taken from Tokyo at a young age by his mother, who wished to protect those closest to them from the fate surrounding Kamui and herself. After six years, Kamui returns to Tokyo in obediance of his mother's cryptic instructions to him, even as she was dying in a mysterious fire that consumed their apartment. Kamui has little understanding of the true nature of his destiny, and despite his powerful psychic abilities, he wants only to live a normal life.

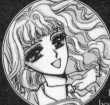

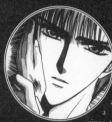

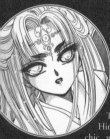

Hinoto

A blind prophetess who lives in a secret chamber underneath Tokyo's Diet building, Hinoto is a powerful psychic whose dreams of the future have never failed to come true. Lately, her dream has been of the world's destruction, and her vision places Kamui at the heart of the cataclysm to come.

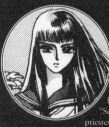

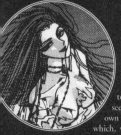

Kanoe

Hinoto's younger sister, Kanoe is also a seeress, but she has her own vision of the future which, with the help of her own group of powerful followers, she plans to bring about.

Kotori Monou

Beautiful, and fragile due to a heart condition, Kotori was one of Kamui's best friends when they were children. In fact, Kamui promised to marry Kotori when they grew up. On occasion, Kotori has had startling visions of the future, and the fate of the Earth.

Fuma

Kotori's brother, Fuma was also great friends with Kamui when they were both children. Fuma and Kotori's mother died in a gruesome incident, and since then, Fuma has been very protective of his fragile sister.

Arashi

A somber young woman who can summon a mystical sword that grows from the very palm of her hand, Arashi is one of the "Seven Seals" surrounding the priestess, Hinoto.

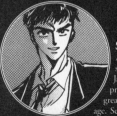

Sorata

A young priest from the shrine at Mt. Koya in Japan, Sorata was raised by priests who recognized his great power from a young age. Sent to Tokyo by his mentor, "Stargazer," Sora has sworn to protect Kamui with his life.

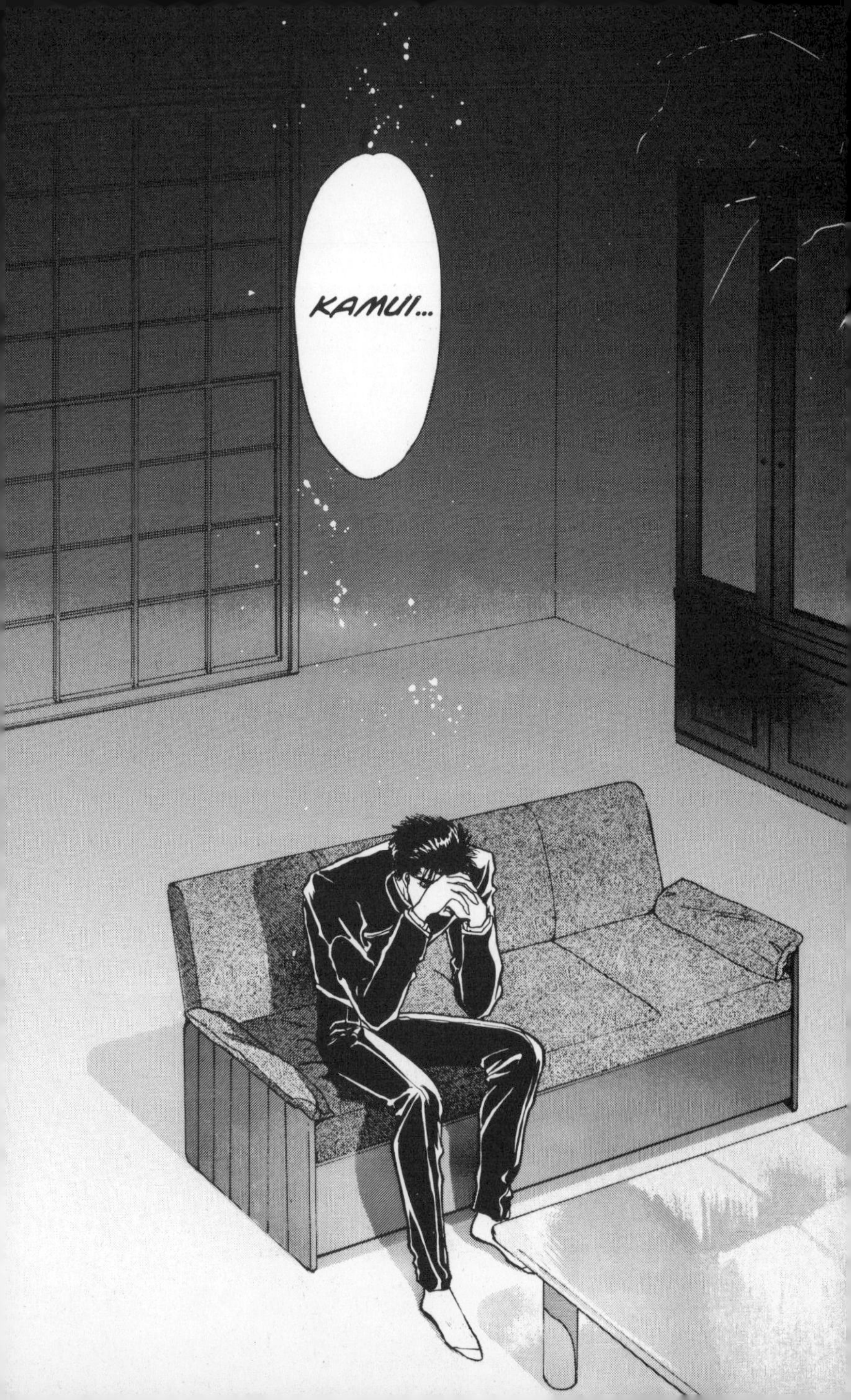
KAMUI...

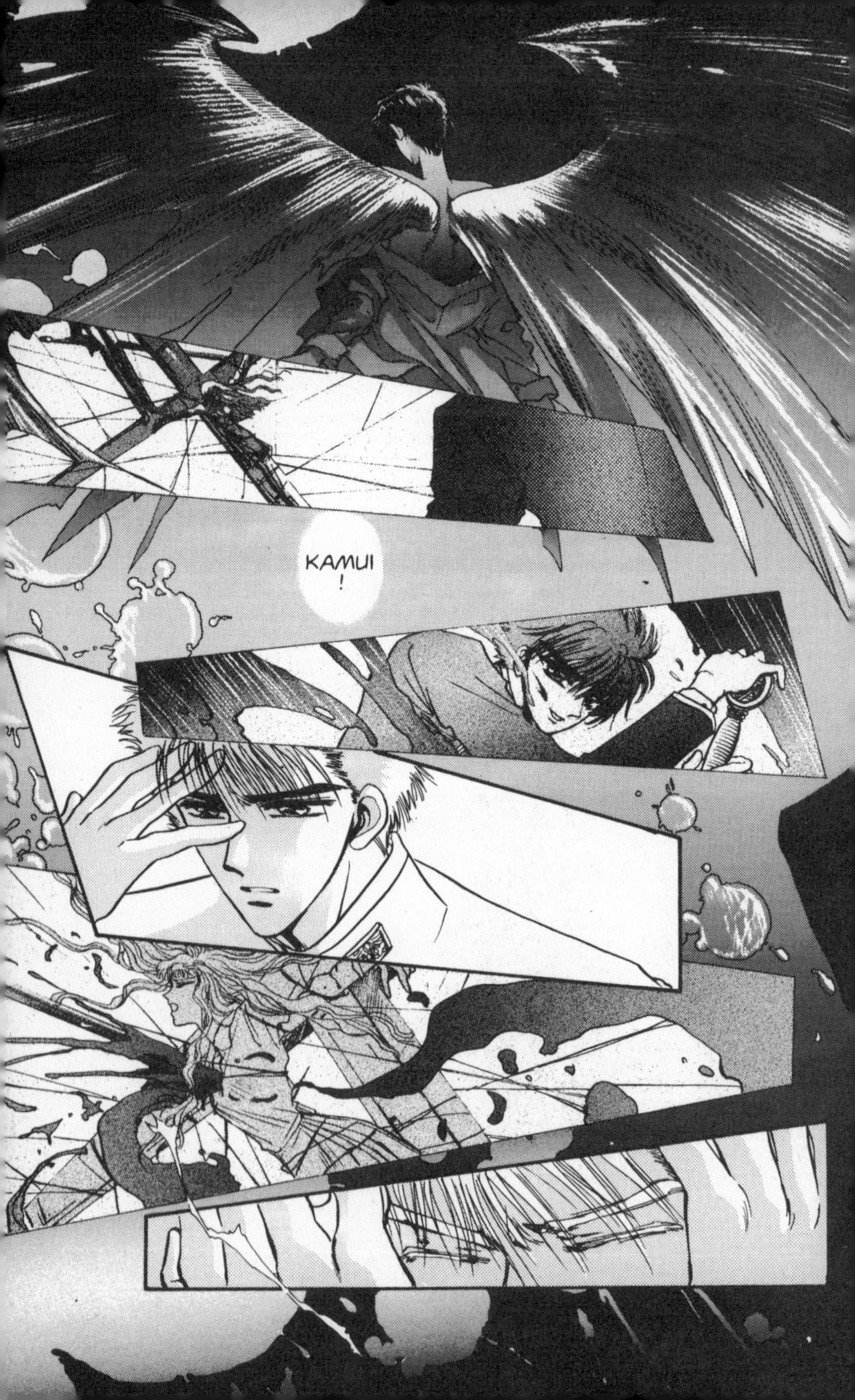
KAMUI!

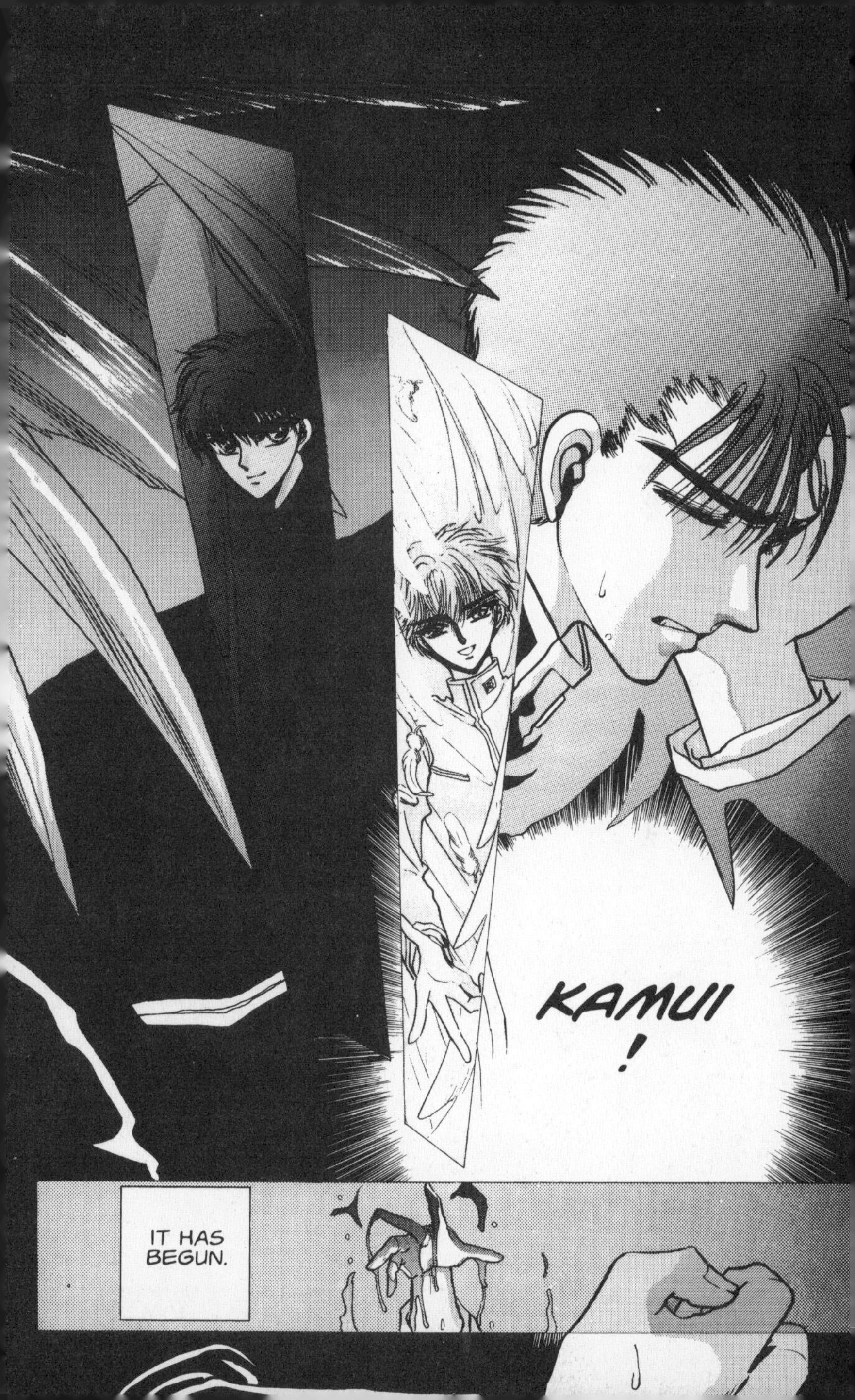
KAMUI
!
IT HAS
BEGUN.

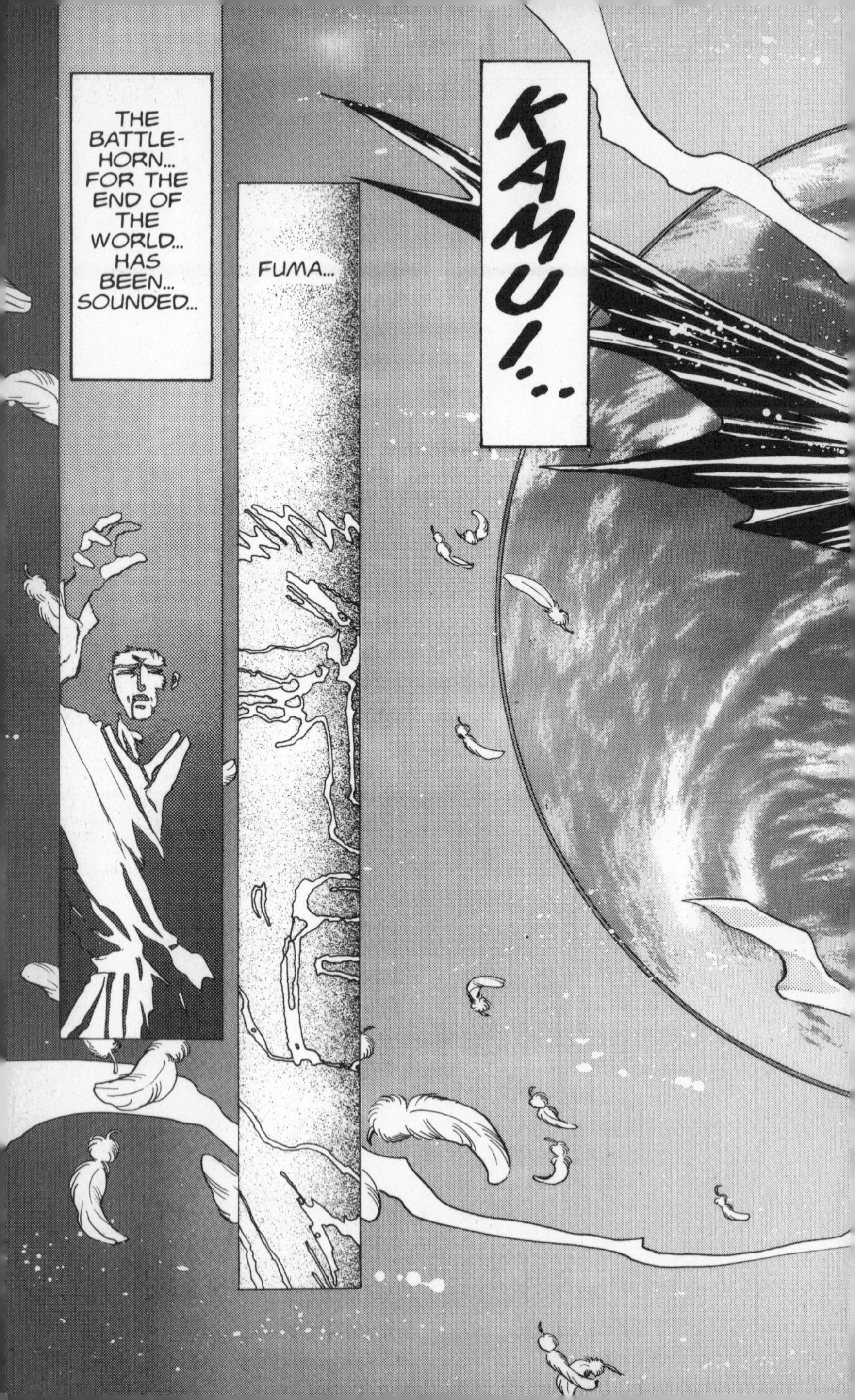
THE BATTLE-HORN... FOR THE END OF THE WORLD... HAS BEEN... SOUNDED...
FUMA...
KAMUI...

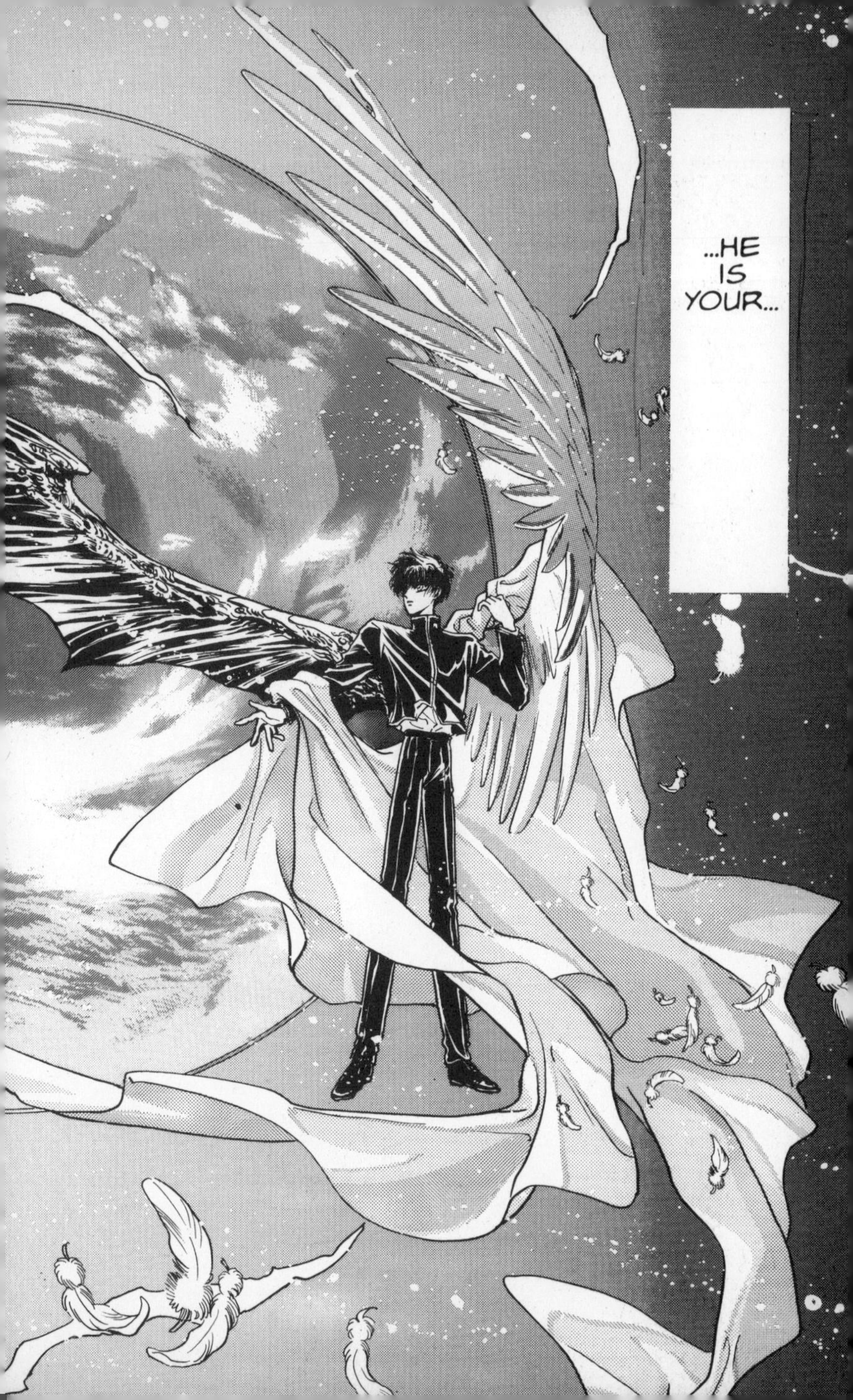
...HE IS YOUR...

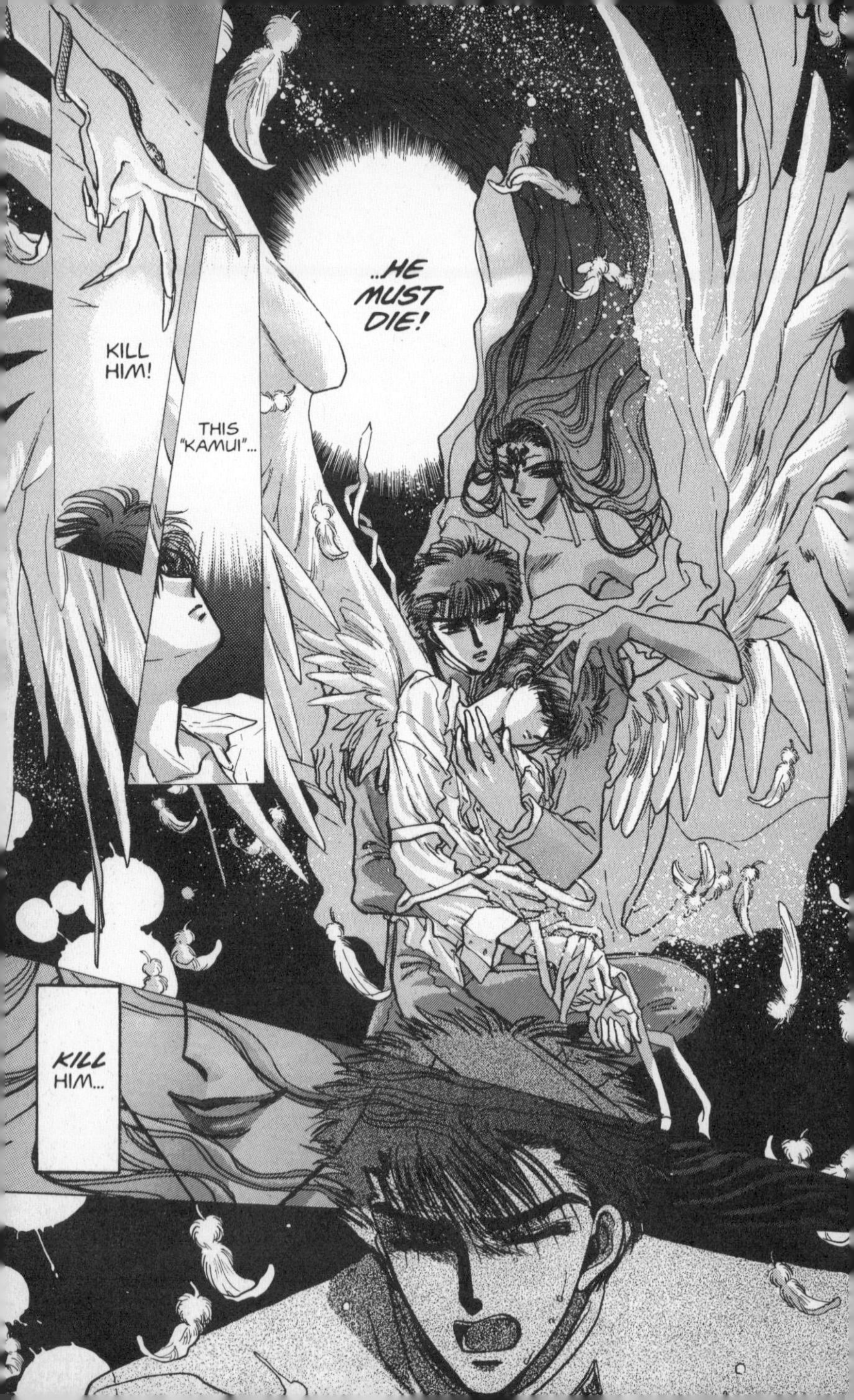
KILL HIM!
THIS "KAMUI"...
..HE MUST DIE!
KILL HIM...

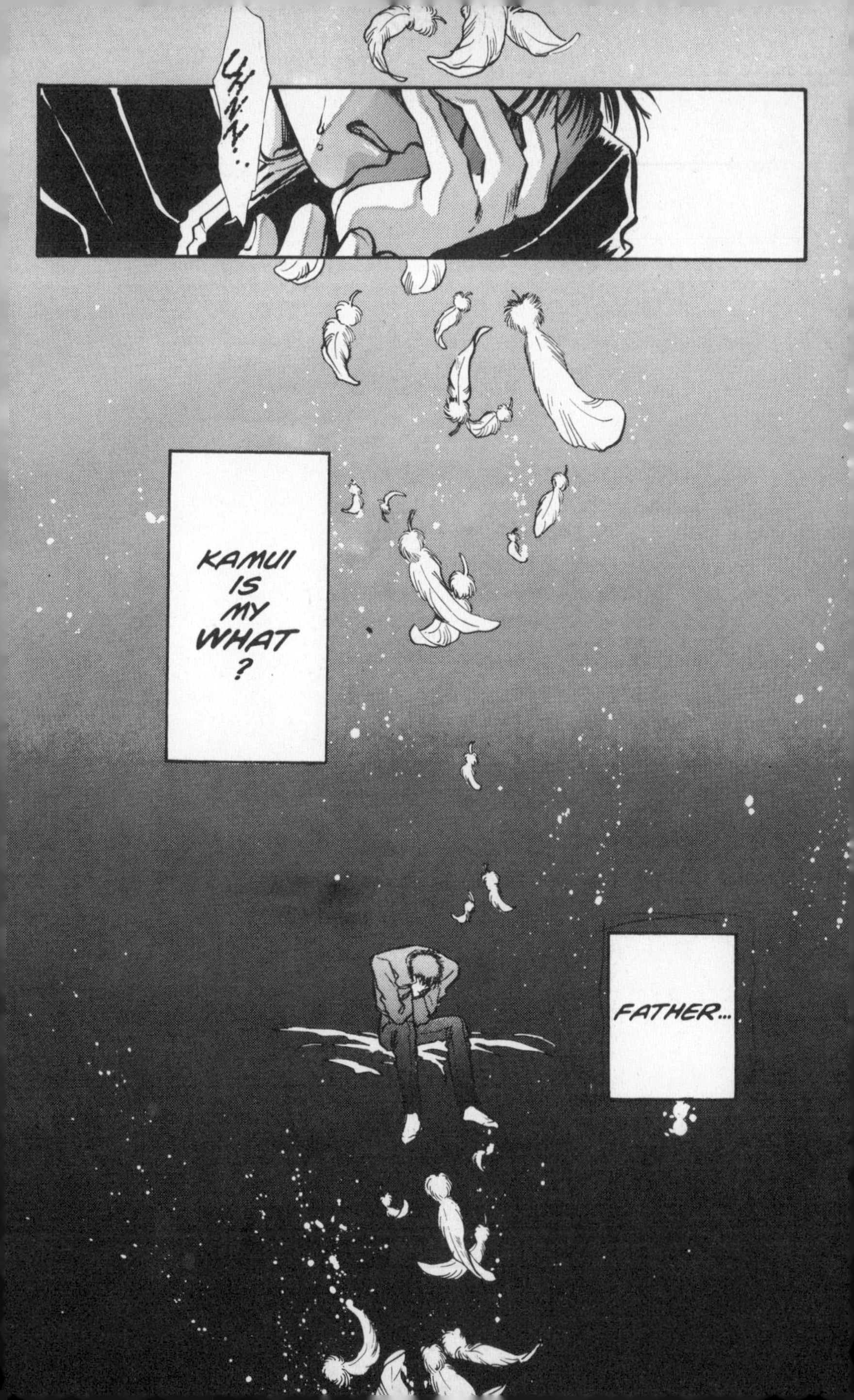
UHNN...
KAMUI IS MY WHAT ?
FATHER...

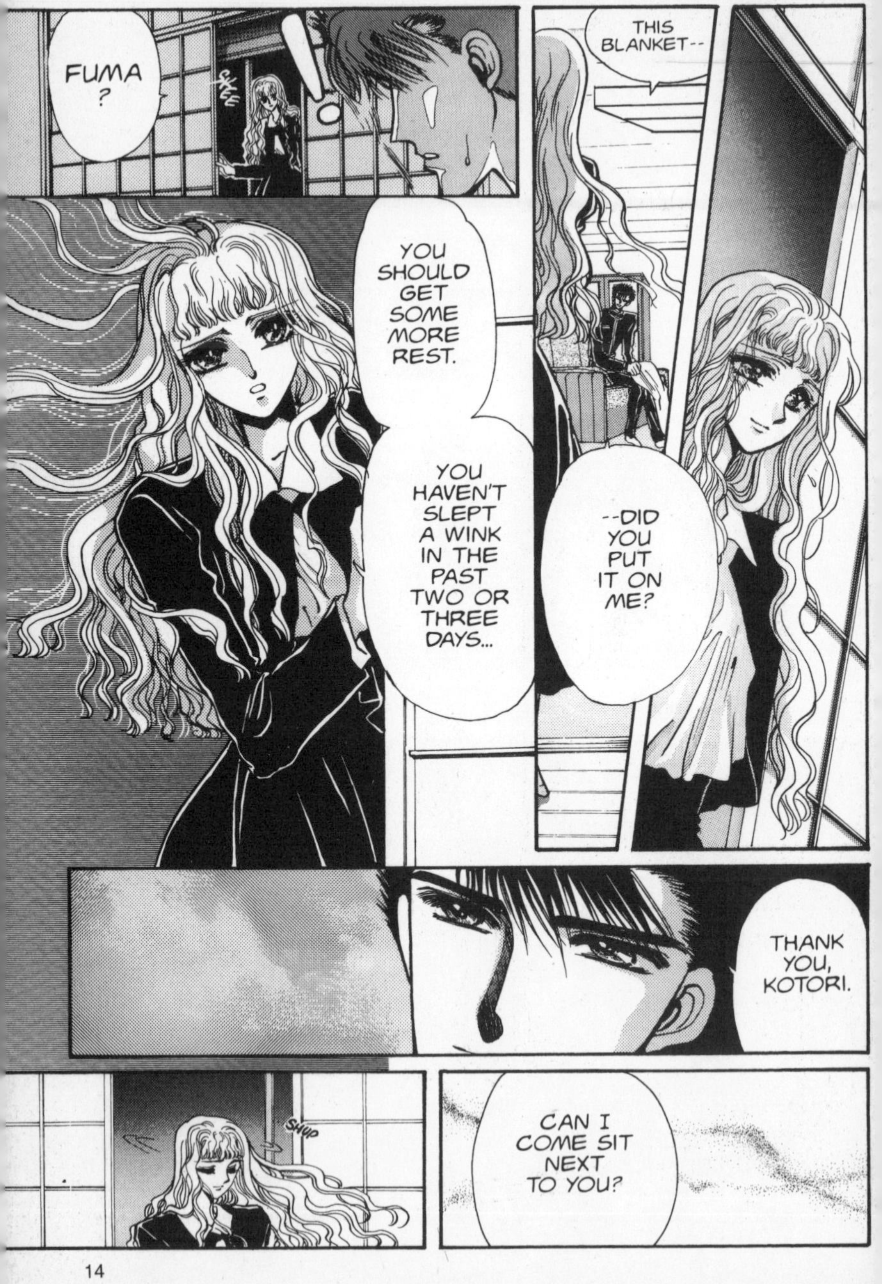
FUMA ?
YOU SHOULD GET SOME MORE REST.
YOU HAVEN'T SLEPT A WINK IN THE PAST TWO OR THREE DAYS...
THIS BLANKET--
--DID YOU PUT IT ON ME?
THANK YOU, KOTORI.
SHUP
CAN I COME SIT NEXT TO YOU?

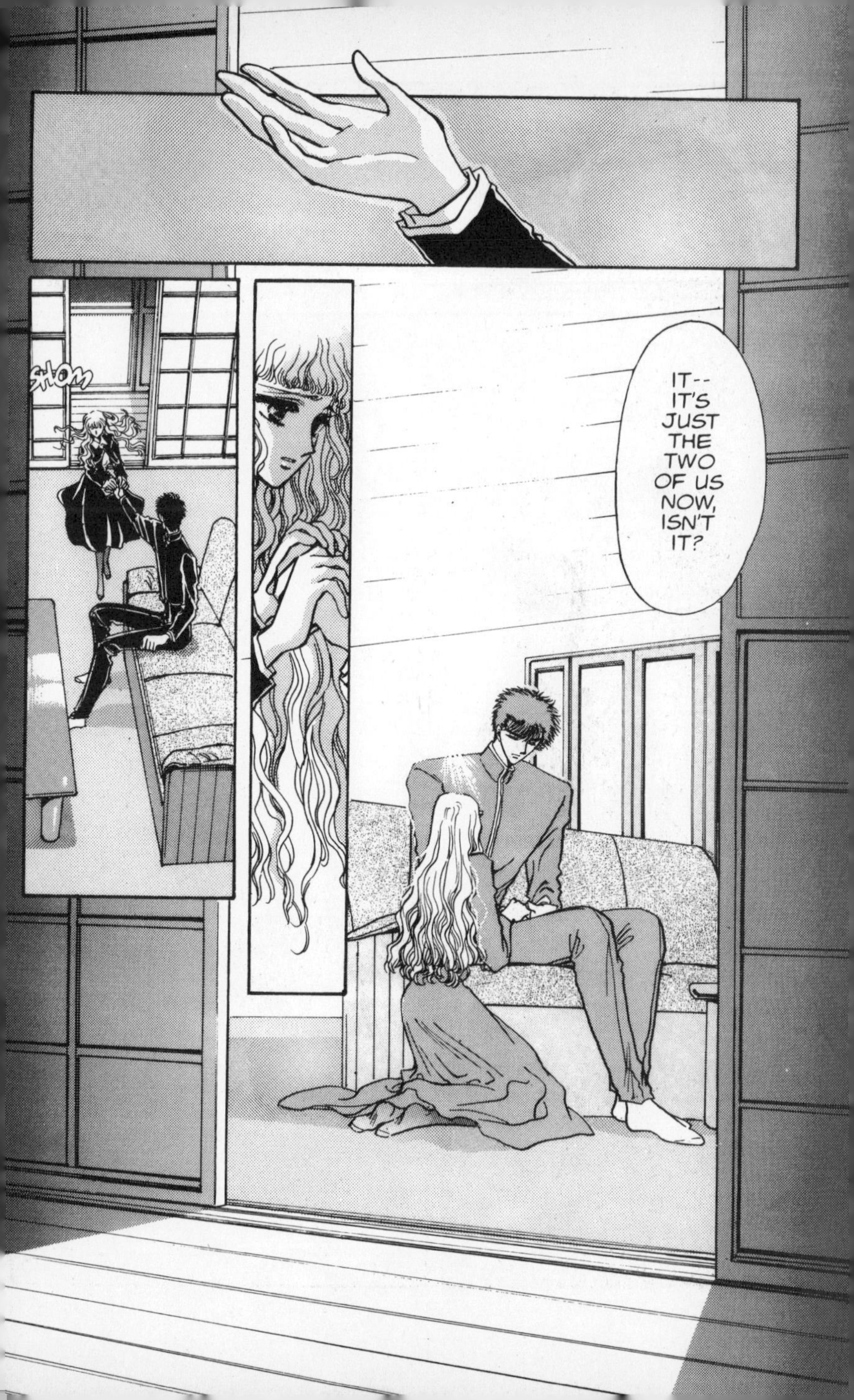
SHOM
IT-- IT'S JUST THE TWO OF US NOW, ISN'T IT?

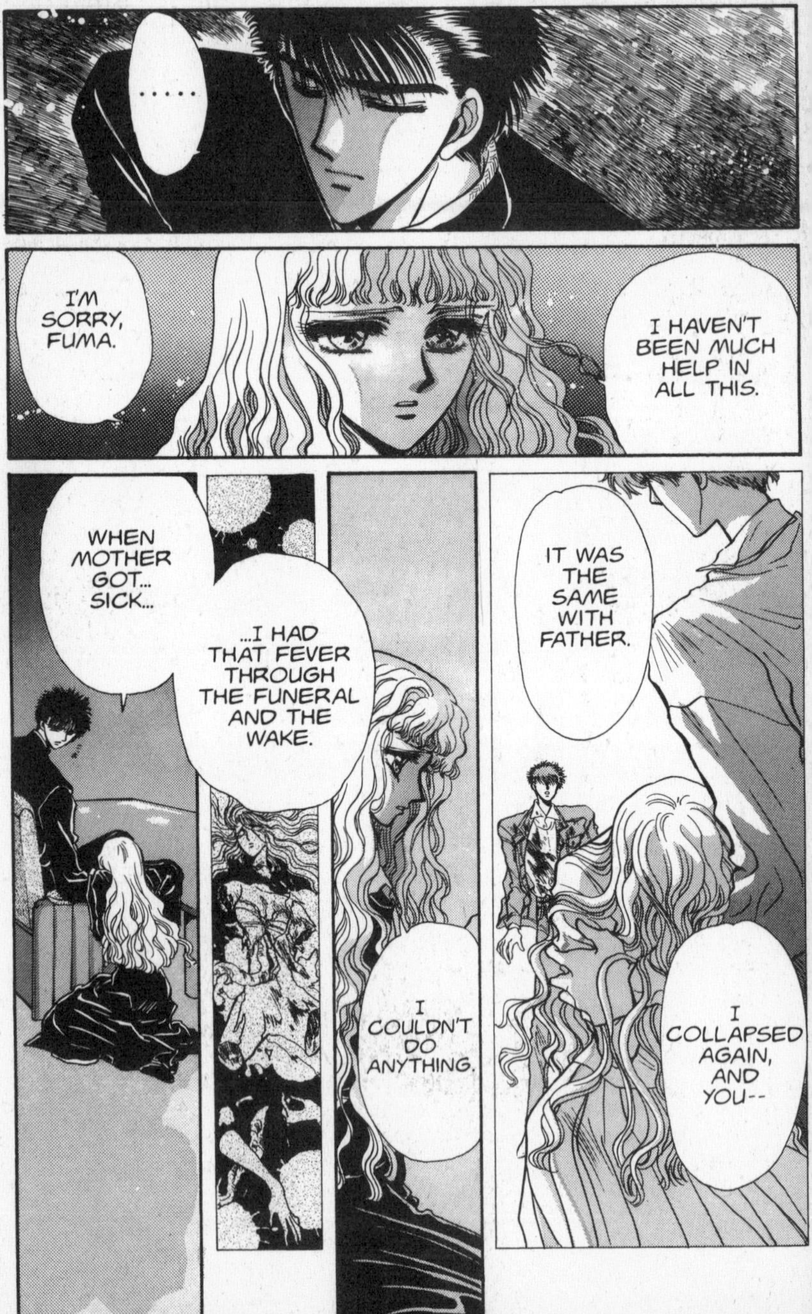
......
I'M SORRY, FUMA.
I HAVEN'T BEEN MUCH HELP IN ALL THIS.
WHEN MOTHER GOT... SICK...
...I HAD THAT FEVER THROUGH THE FUNERAL AND THE WAKE.
I COULDN'T DO ANYTHING.
IT WAS THE SAME WITH FATHER.
I COLLAPSED AGAIN, AND YOU--

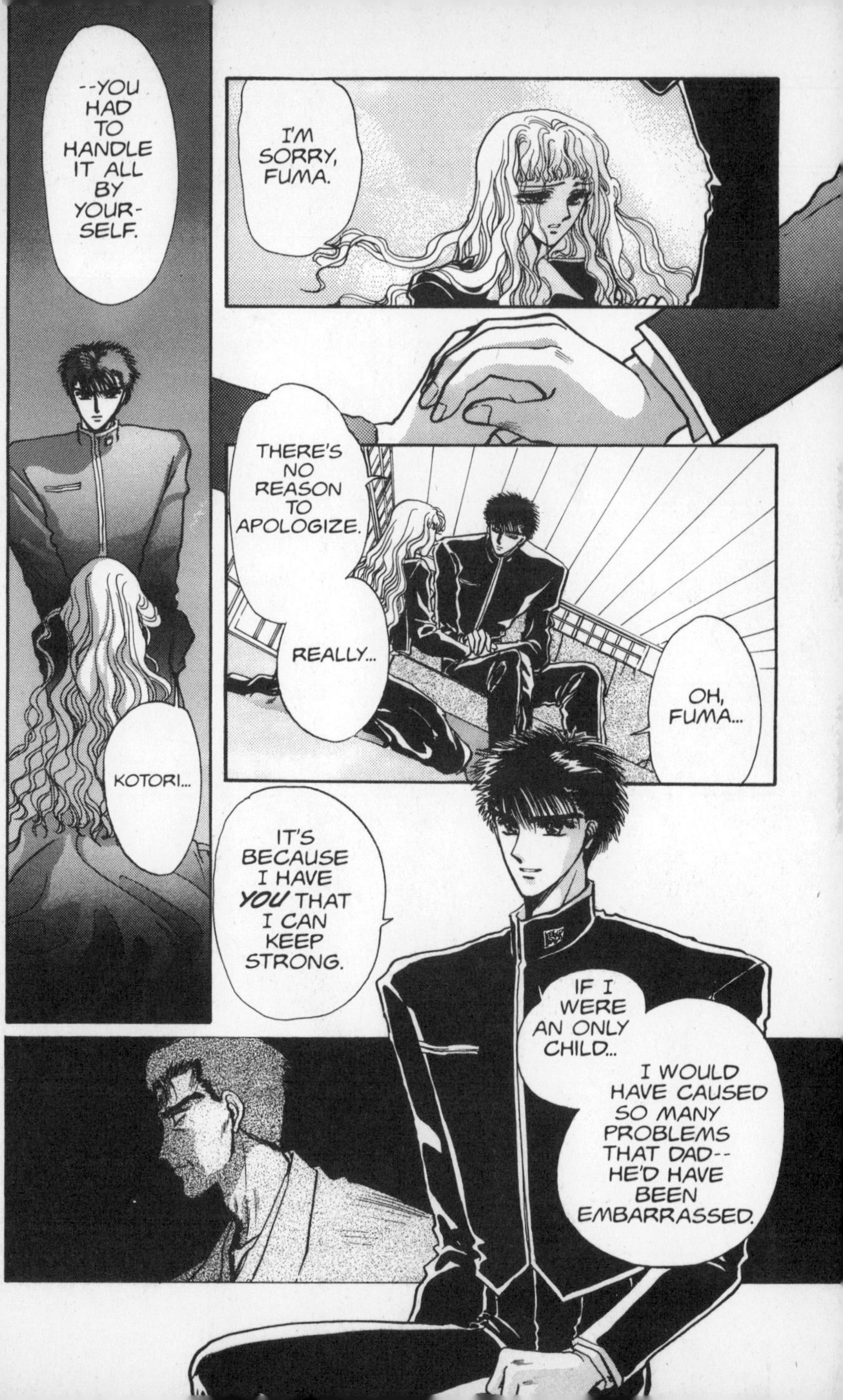
--YOU HAD TO HANDLE IT ALL BY YOUR-SELF.
KOTORI...
I'M SORRY, FUMA.
THERE'S NO REASON TO APOLOGIZE.
REALLY...
OH, FUMA...
IT'S BECAUSE I HAVE ***YOU*** THAT I CAN KEEP STRONG.
IF I WERE AN ONLY CHILD...
I WOULD HAVE CAUSED SO MANY PROBLEMS THAT DAD-- HE'D HAVE BEEN EMBARRASSED.

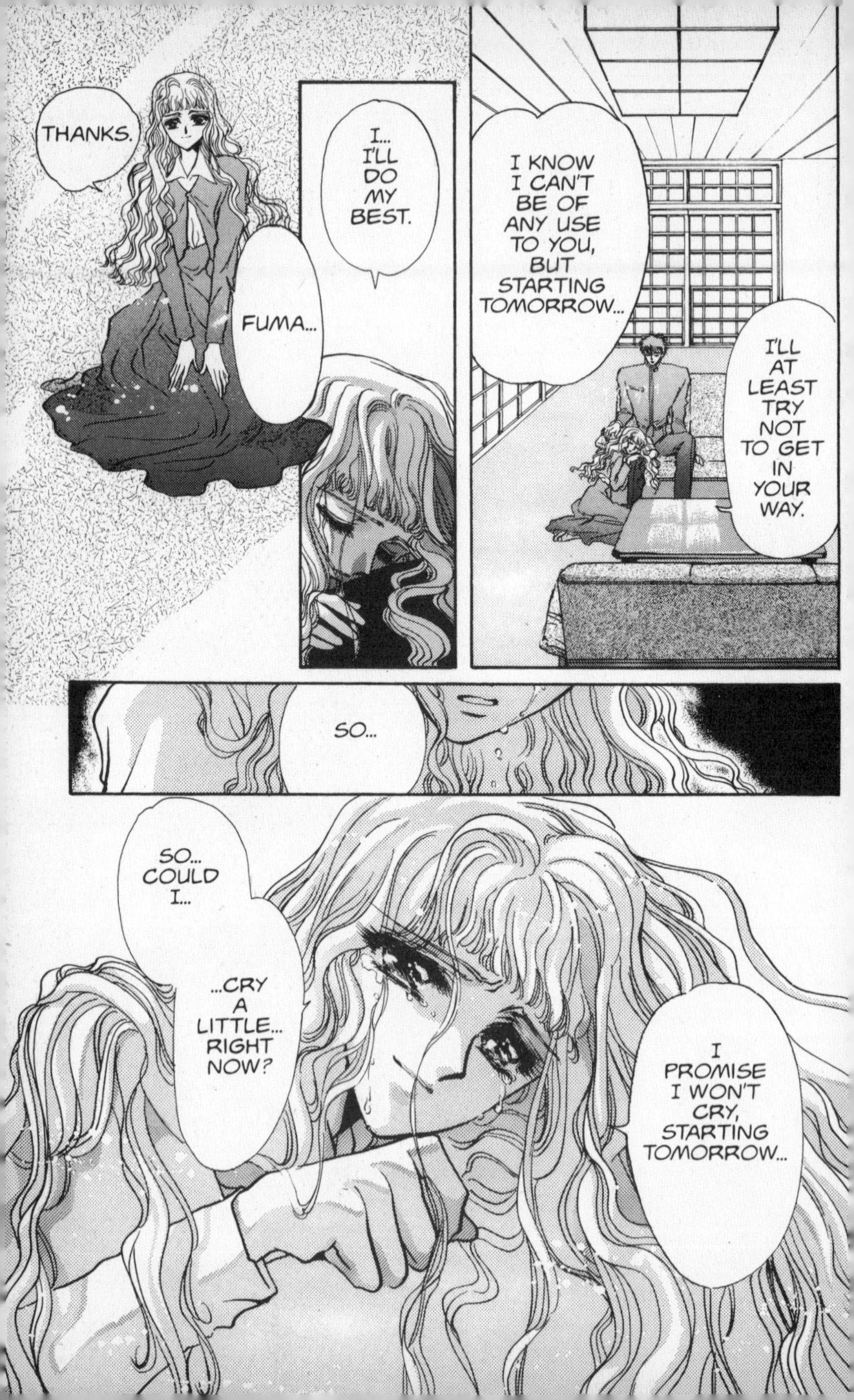
THANKS.
I... I'LL DO MY BEST.
FUMA...
I KNOW I CAN'T BE OF ANY USE TO YOU, BUT STARTING TOMORROW...
I'LL AT LEAST TRY NOT TO GET IN YOUR WAY.
SO...
SO... COULD I...
...CRY A LITTLE... RIGHT NOW?
I PROMISE I WON'T CRY, STARTING TOMORROW...

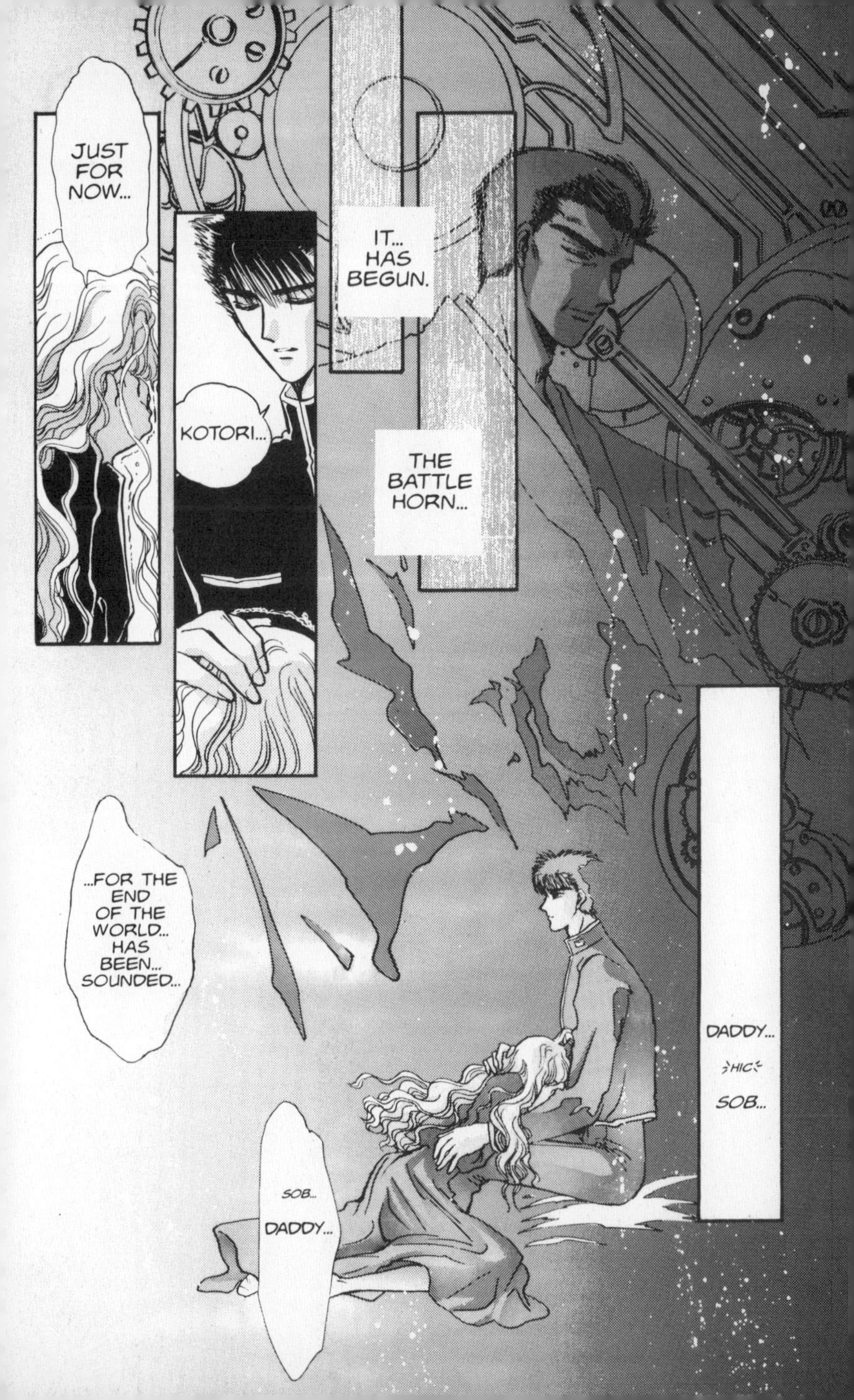
JUST FOR NOW...
KOTORI...
IT... HAS BEGUN.
THE BATTLE HORN...
...FOR THE END OF THE WORLD... HAS BEEN... SOUNDED...
SOB... DADDY...
DADDY...
HIC
SOB...

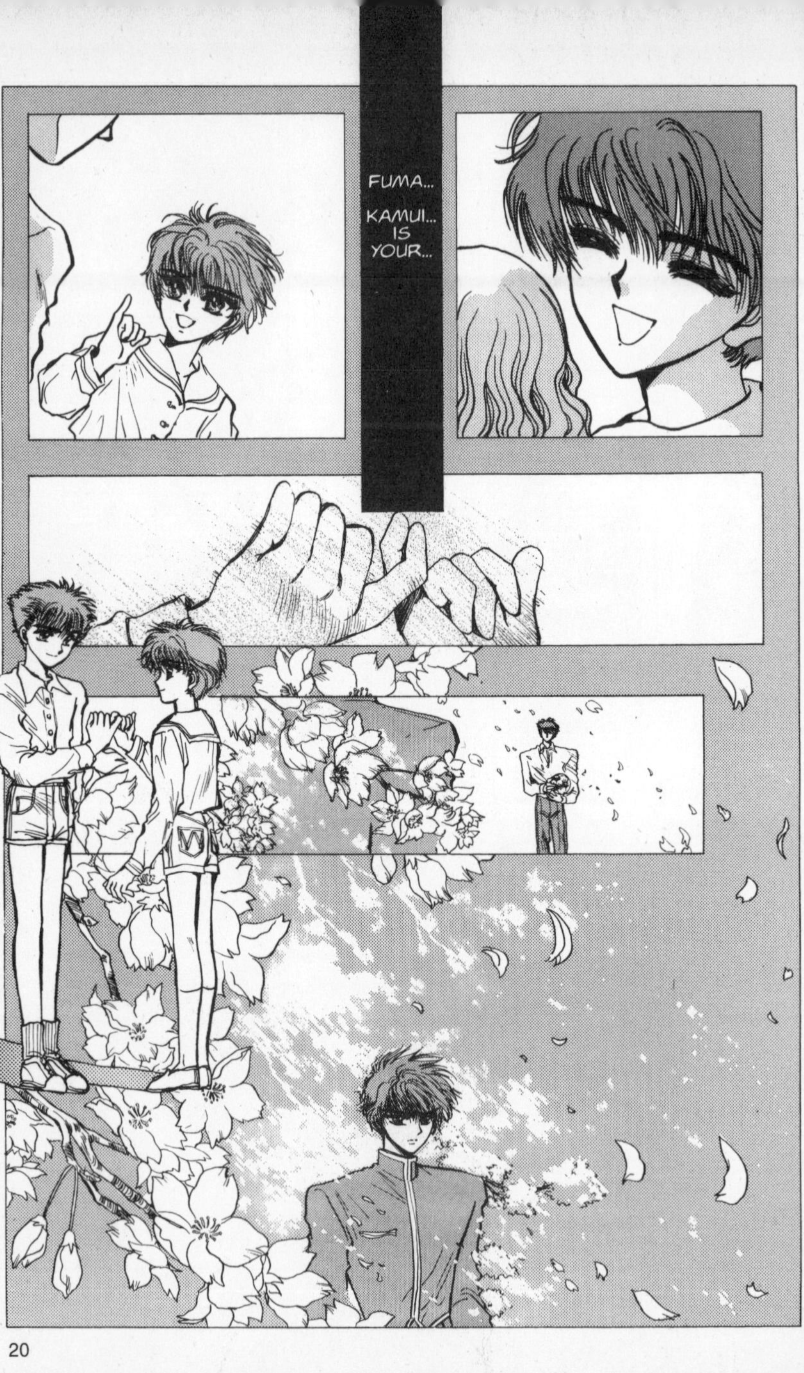
FUMA...
KAMUI... IS YOUR...

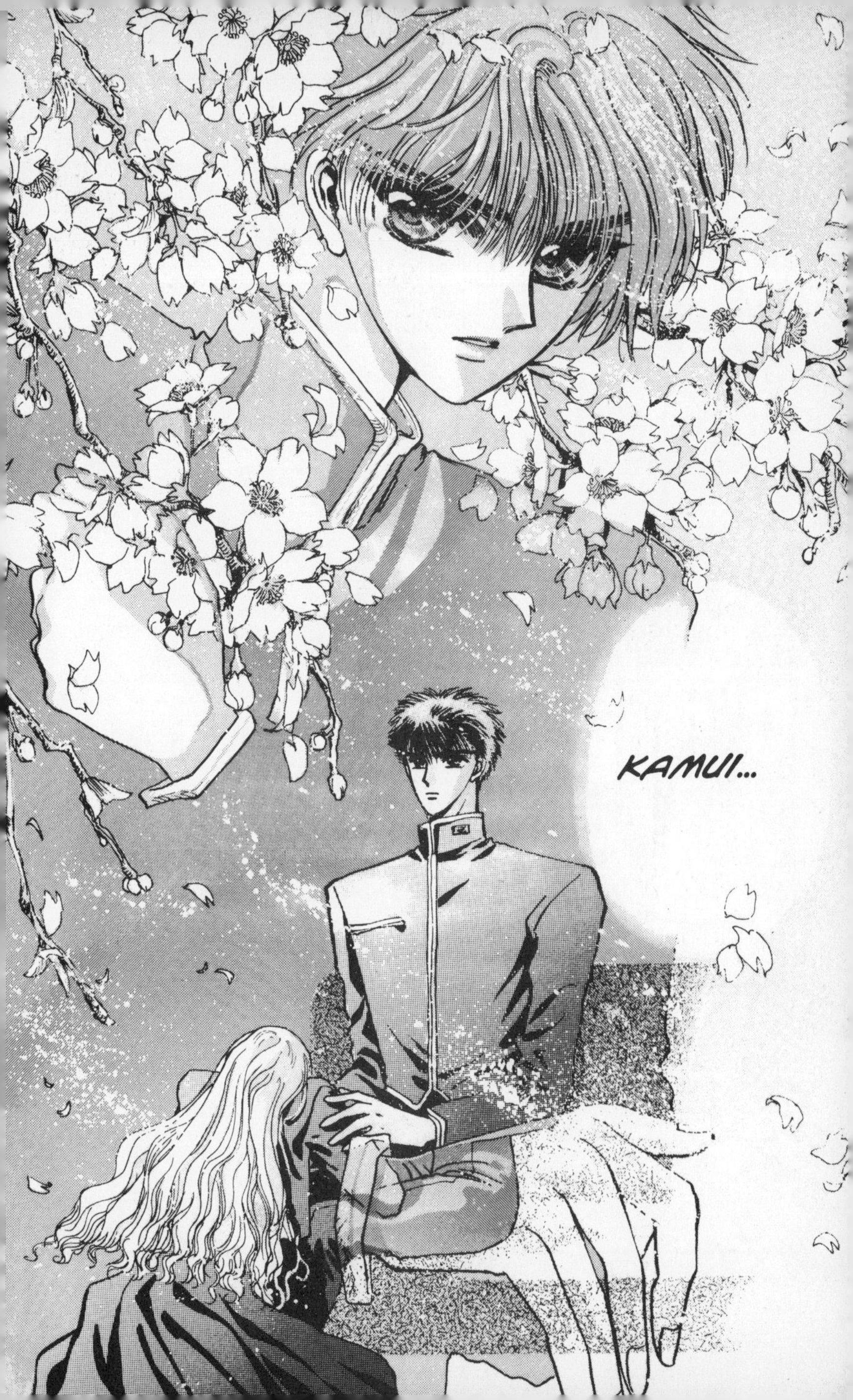
KAMUI...

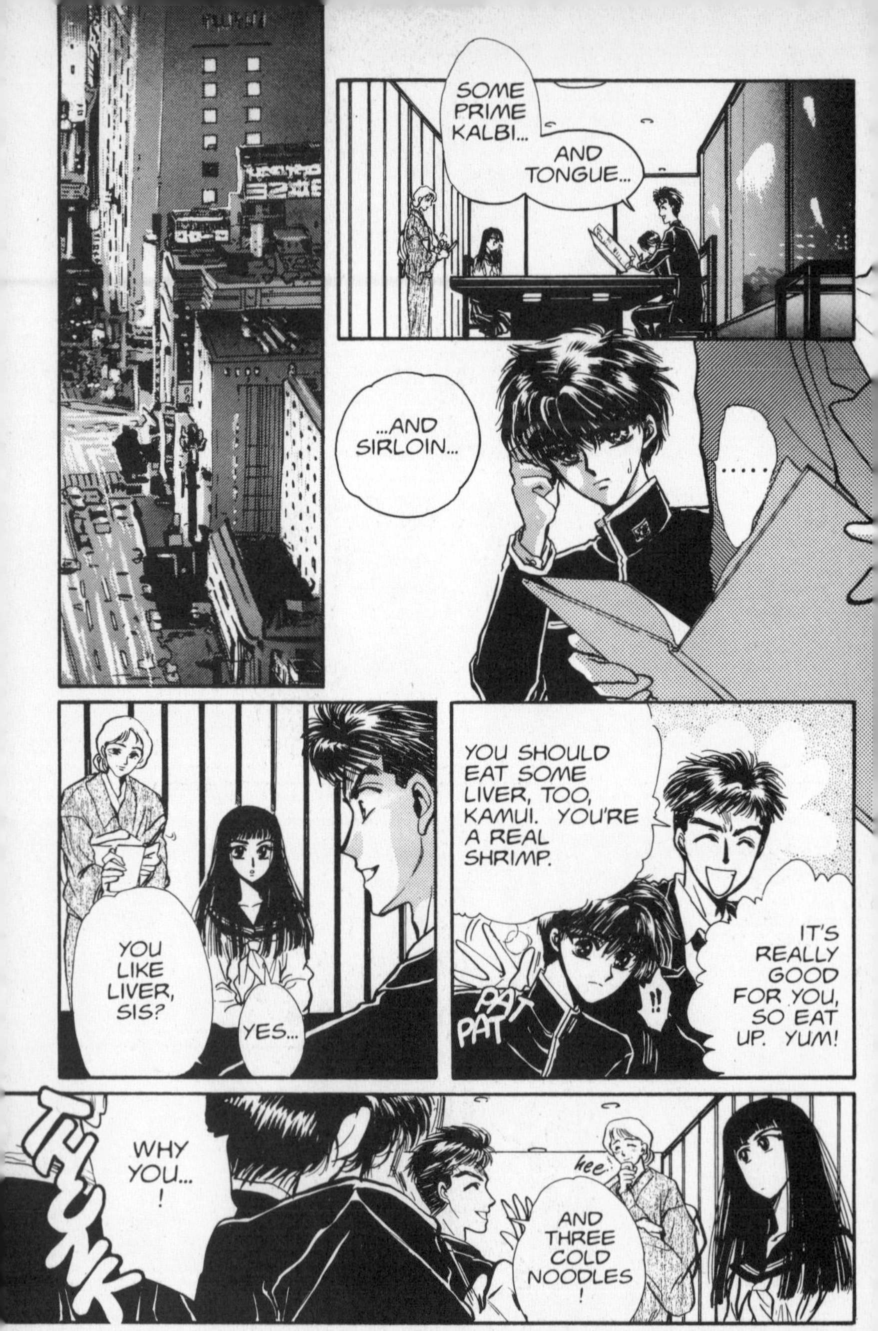
SOME PRIME KALBI...
AND TONGUE...
...AND SIRLOIN...
......
YOU LIKE LIVER, SIS?
YES...
YOU SHOULD EAT SOME LIVER, TOO, KAMUI. YOU'RE A REAL SHRIMP.
PAT PAT
!!
IT'S REALLY GOOD FOR YOU, SO EAT UP. YUM!
THUNK
WHY YOU... !
hee
AND THREE COLD NOODLES !

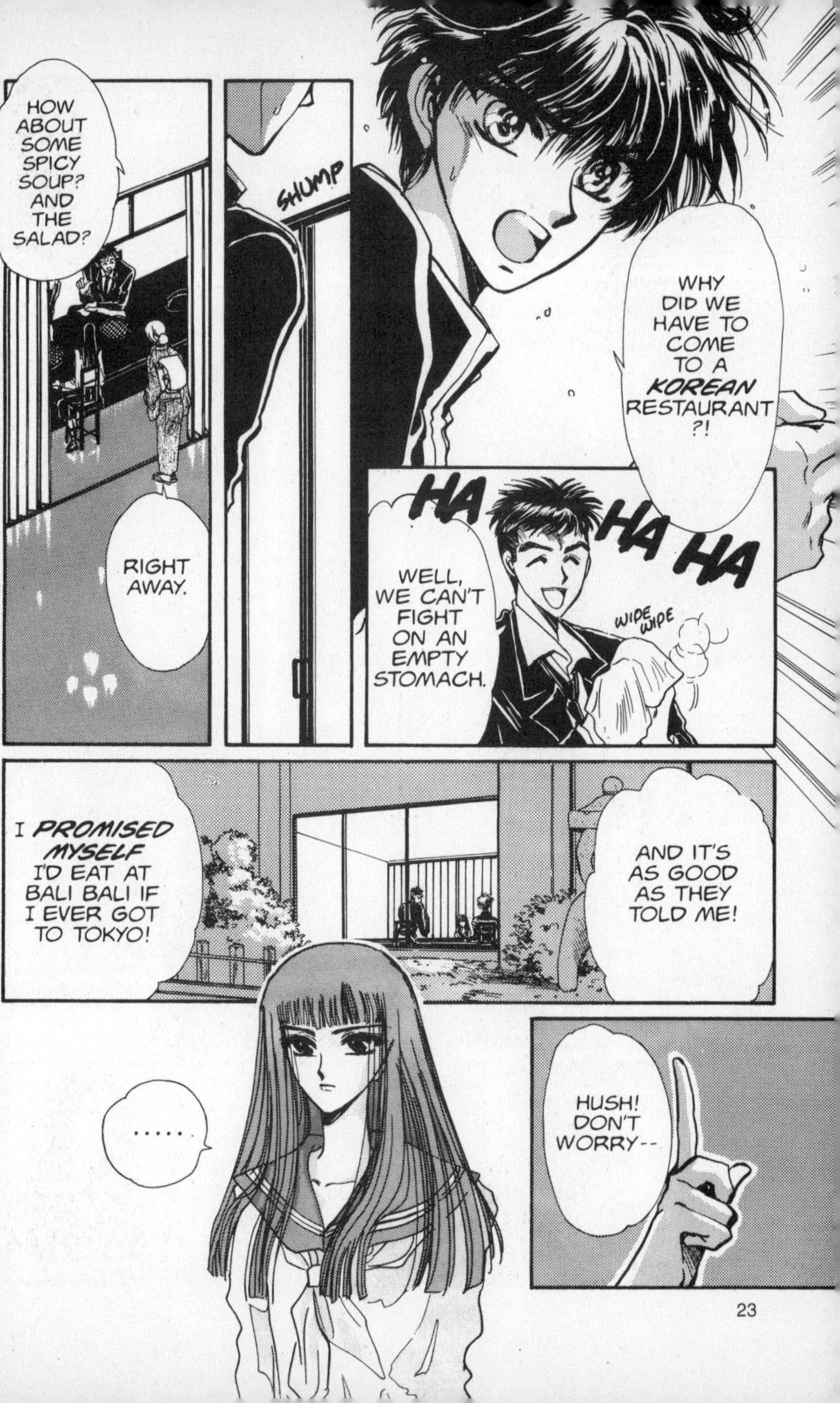
HOW ABOUT SOME SPICY SOUP? AND THE SALAD?
RIGHT AWAY.
SHUMP
WHY DID WE HAVE TO COME TO A *KOREAN* RESTAURANT?!
HA HA HA
WELL, WE CAN'T FIGHT ON AN EMPTY STOMACH.
WIPE WIPE
I *PROMISED MYSELF* I'D EAT AT BALI BALI IF I EVER GOT TO TOKYO!
AND IT'S AS GOOD AS THEY TOLD ME!
......
HUSH! DON'T WORRY--

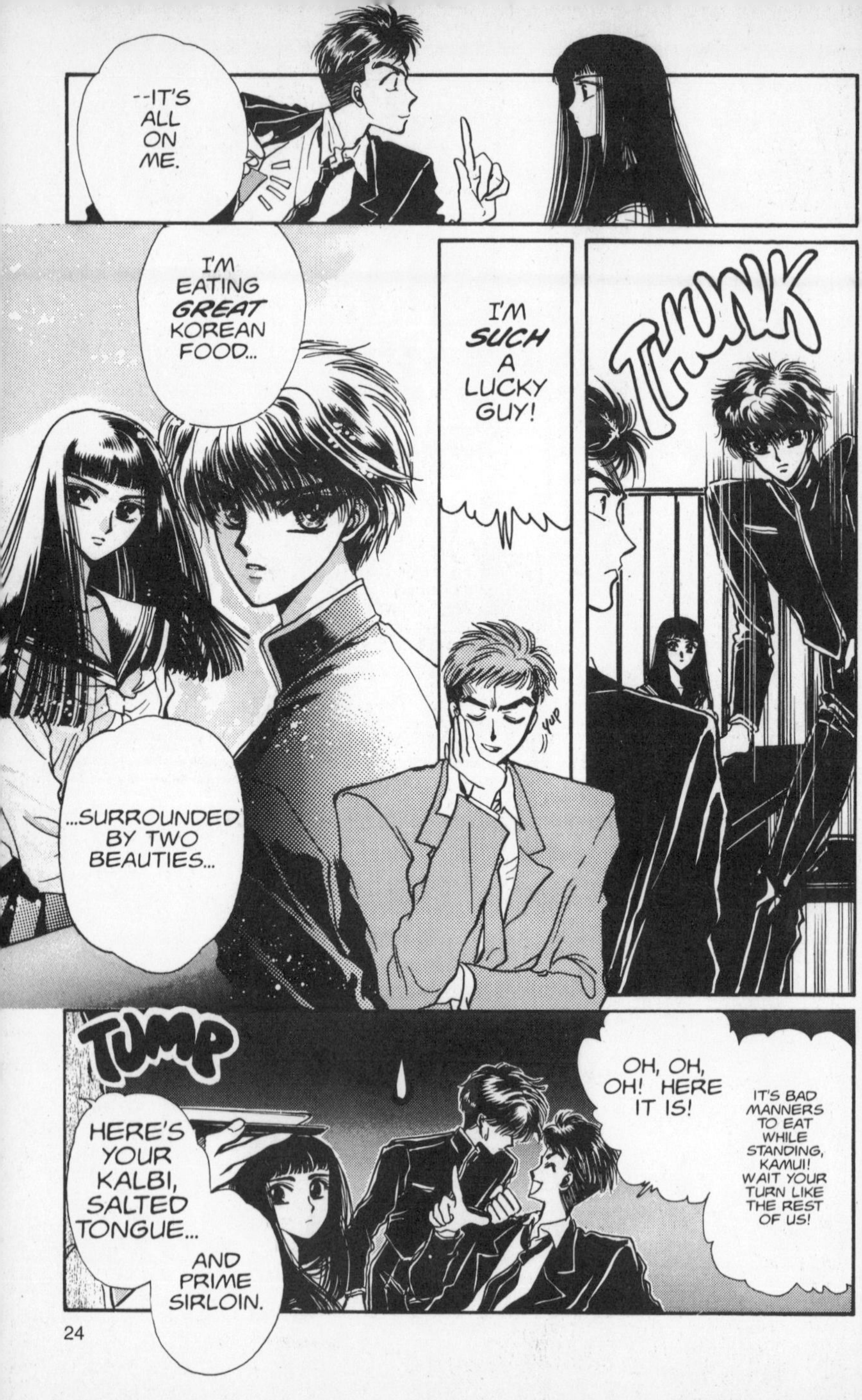
--IT'S ALL ON ME.
I'M EATING GREAT KOREAN FOOD...
...SURROUNDED BY TWO BEAUTIES...
I'M SUCH A LUCKY GUY!
YUP
THUNK
TUMP
HERE'S YOUR KALBI, SALTED TONGUE...
AND PRIME SIRLOIN.
OH, OH, OH! HERE IT IS!
IT'S BAD MANNERS TO EAT WHILE STANDING, KAMUI! WAIT YOUR TURN LIKE THE REST OF US!

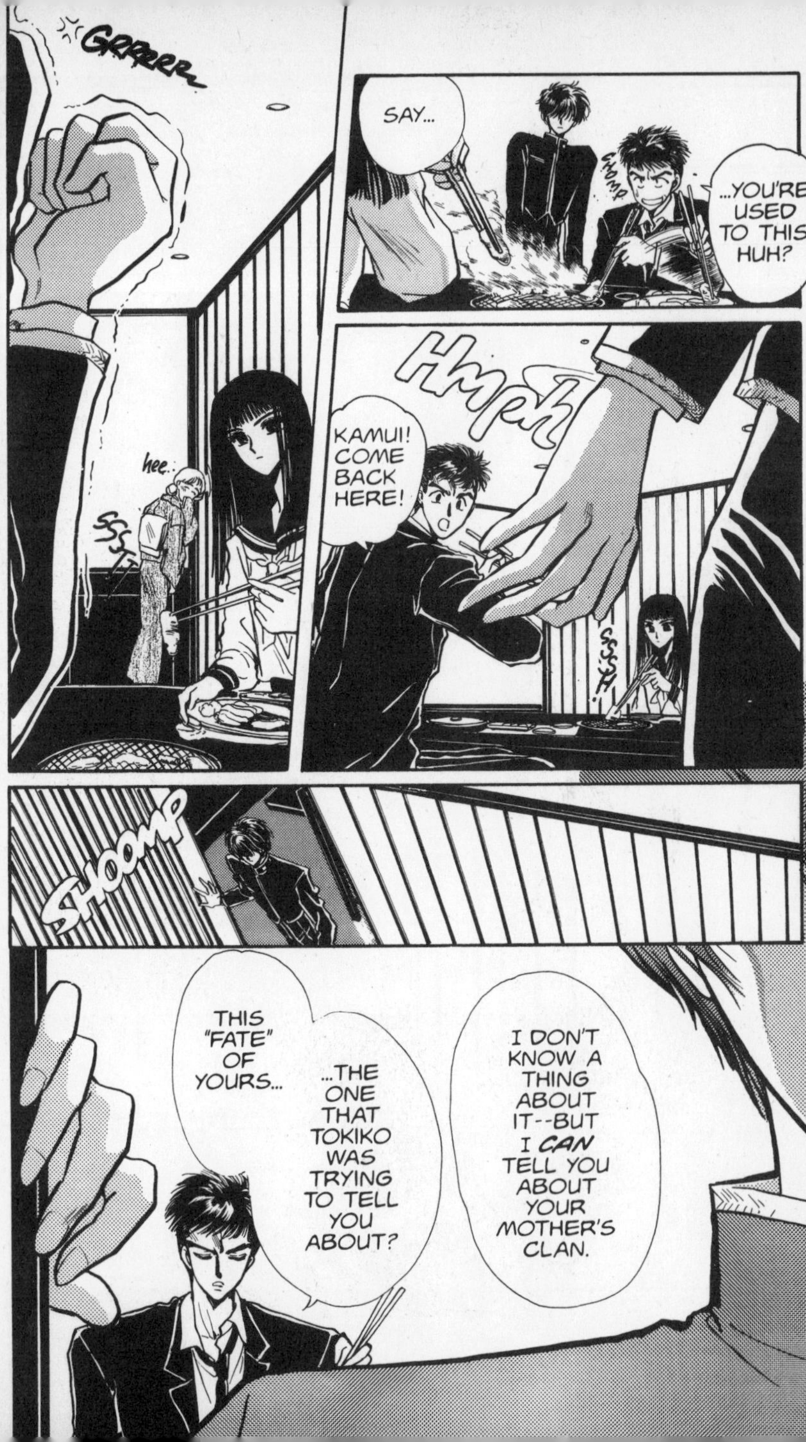
GRRRRR
hee..
SAY...
...YOU'RE USED TO THIS, HUH?
HMPH
KAMUI! COME BACK HERE!
SHOOMP
THIS "FATE" OF YOURS...
...THE ONE THAT TOKIKO WAS TRYING TO TELL YOU ABOUT?
I DON'T KNOW A THING ABOUT IT--BUT I *CAN* TELL YOU ABOUT YOUR MOTHER'S CLAN.

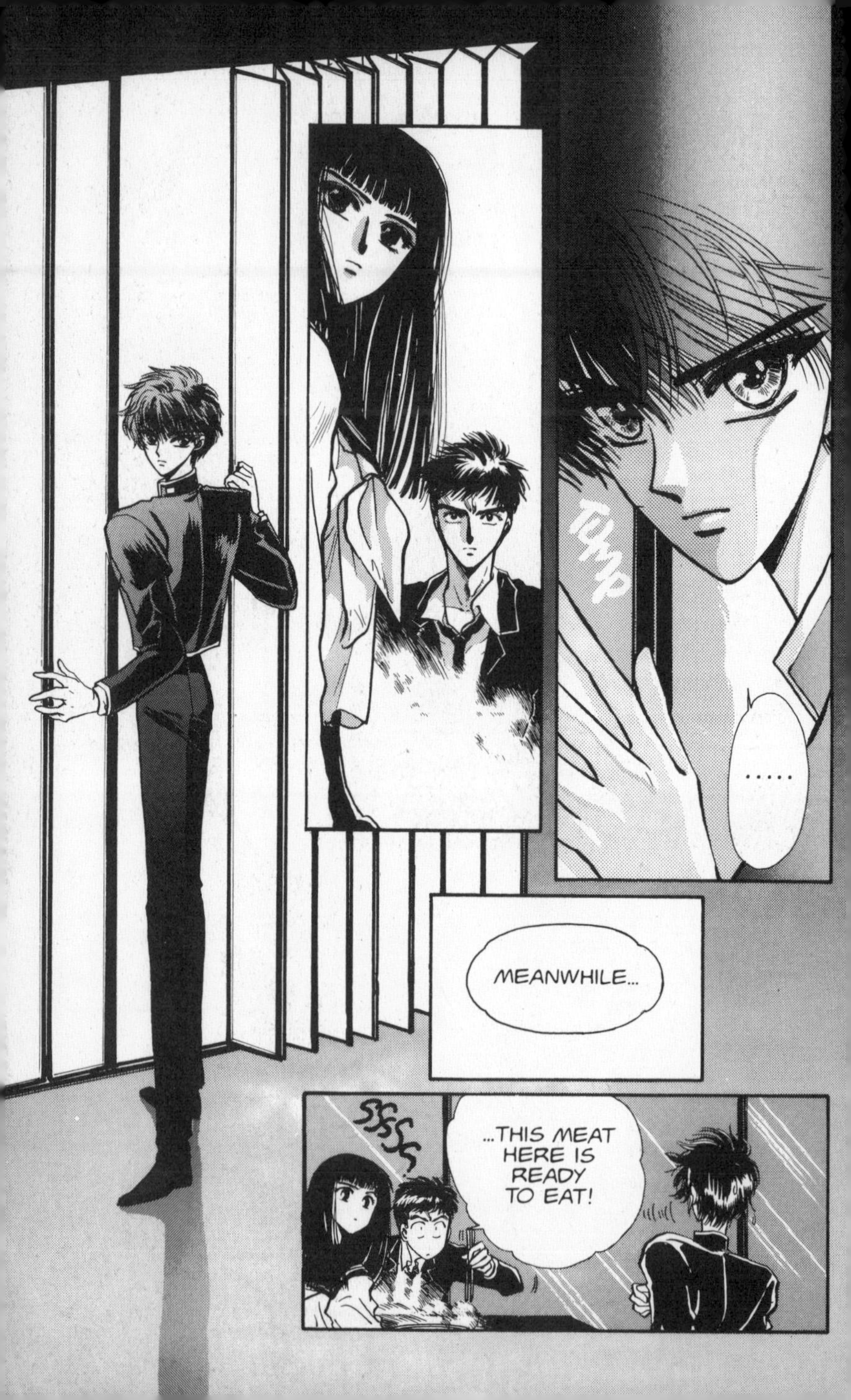
THUMP
.....
MEANWHILE...
SSSS
...THIS MEAT HERE IS READY TO EAT!

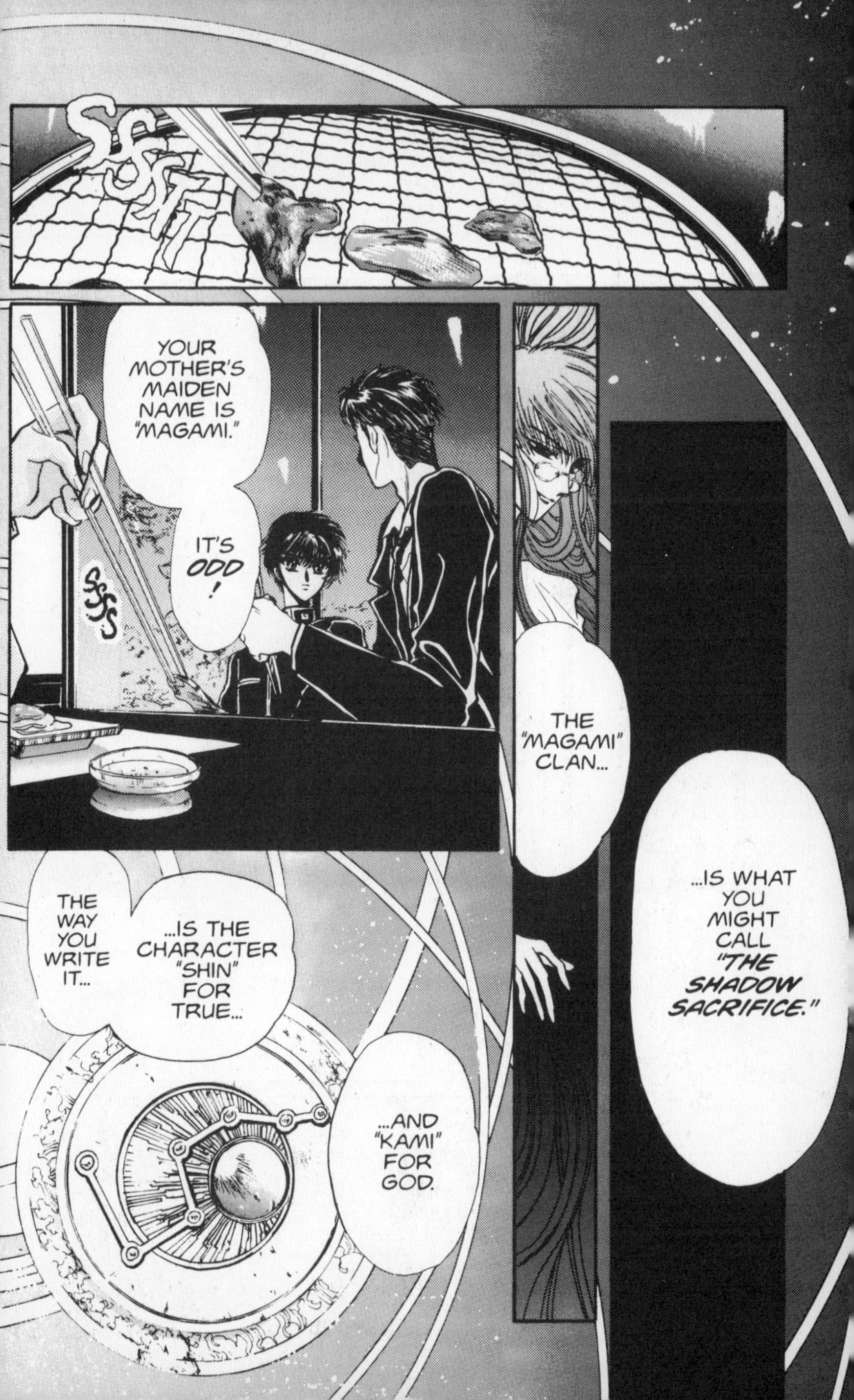
SSSST
YOUR MOTHER'S MAIDEN NAME IS "MAGAMI."
IT'S ODD!
SSSS
THE WAY YOU WRITE IT...
...IS THE CHARACTER "SHIN" FOR TRUE...
...AND "KAMI" FOR GOD.
THE "MAGAMI" CLAN...
...IS WHAT YOU MIGHT CALL "THE SHADOW SACRIFICE."

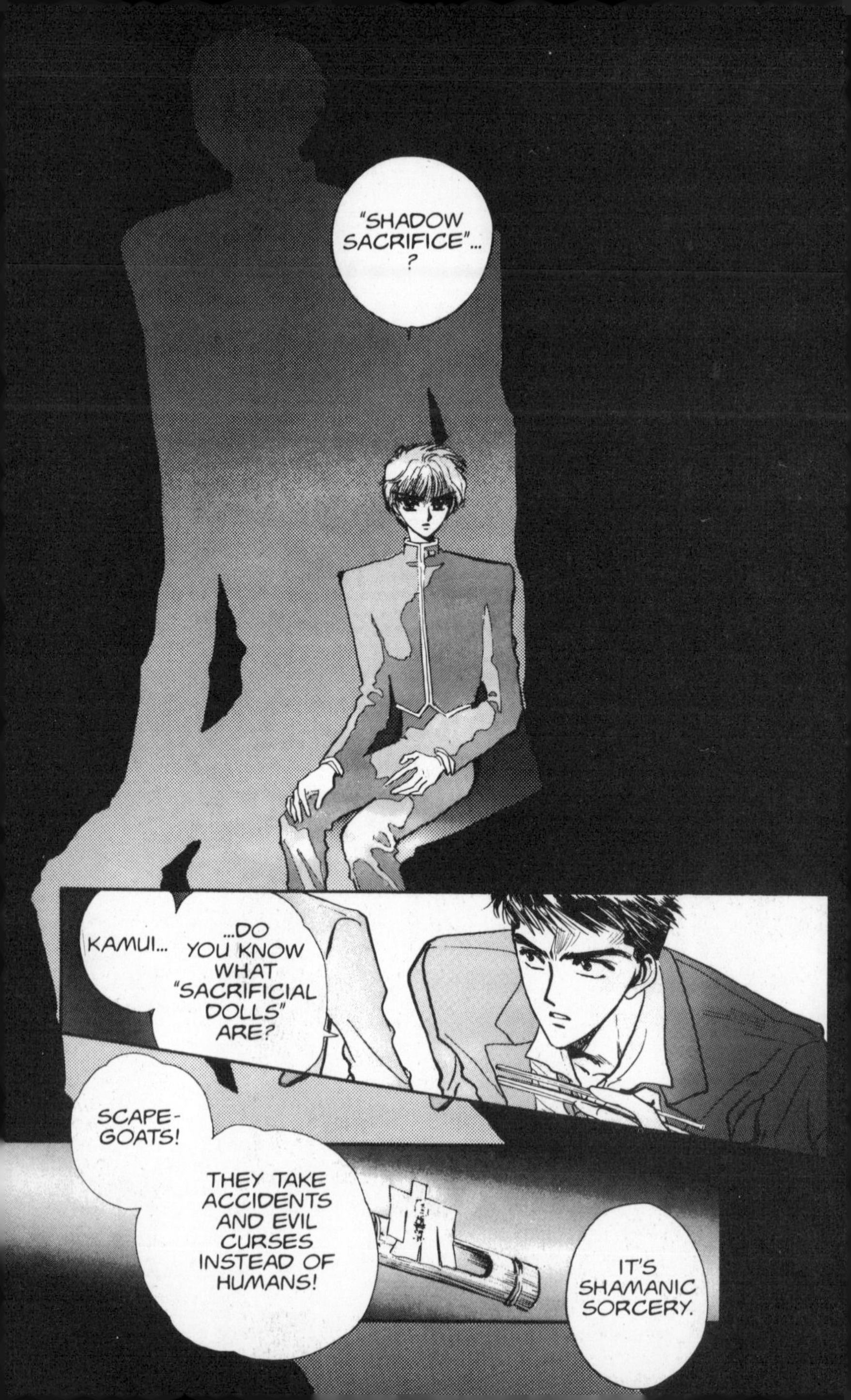
"SHADOW SACRIFICE"... ?
KAMUI...
...DO YOU KNOW WHAT "SACRIFICIAL DOLLS" ARE?
SCAPE-GOATS!
THEY TAKE ACCIDENTS AND EVIL CURSES INSTEAD OF HUMANS!
IT'S SHAMANIC SORCERY.

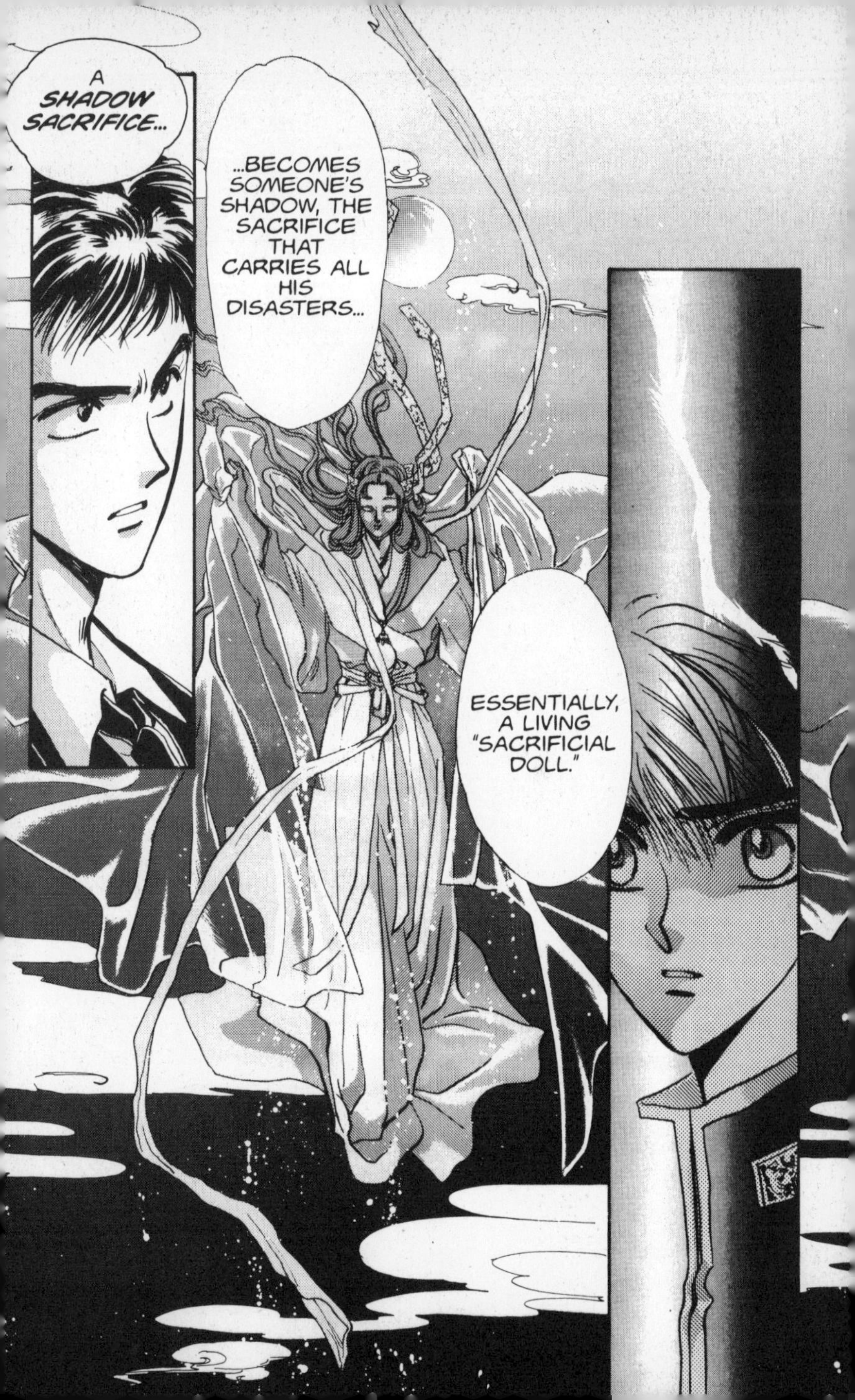
A SHADOW SACRIFICE...
...BECOMES SOMEONE'S SHADOW, THE SACRIFICE THAT CARRIES ALL HIS DISASTERS...
ESSENTIALLY, A LIVING "SACRIFICIAL DOLL."

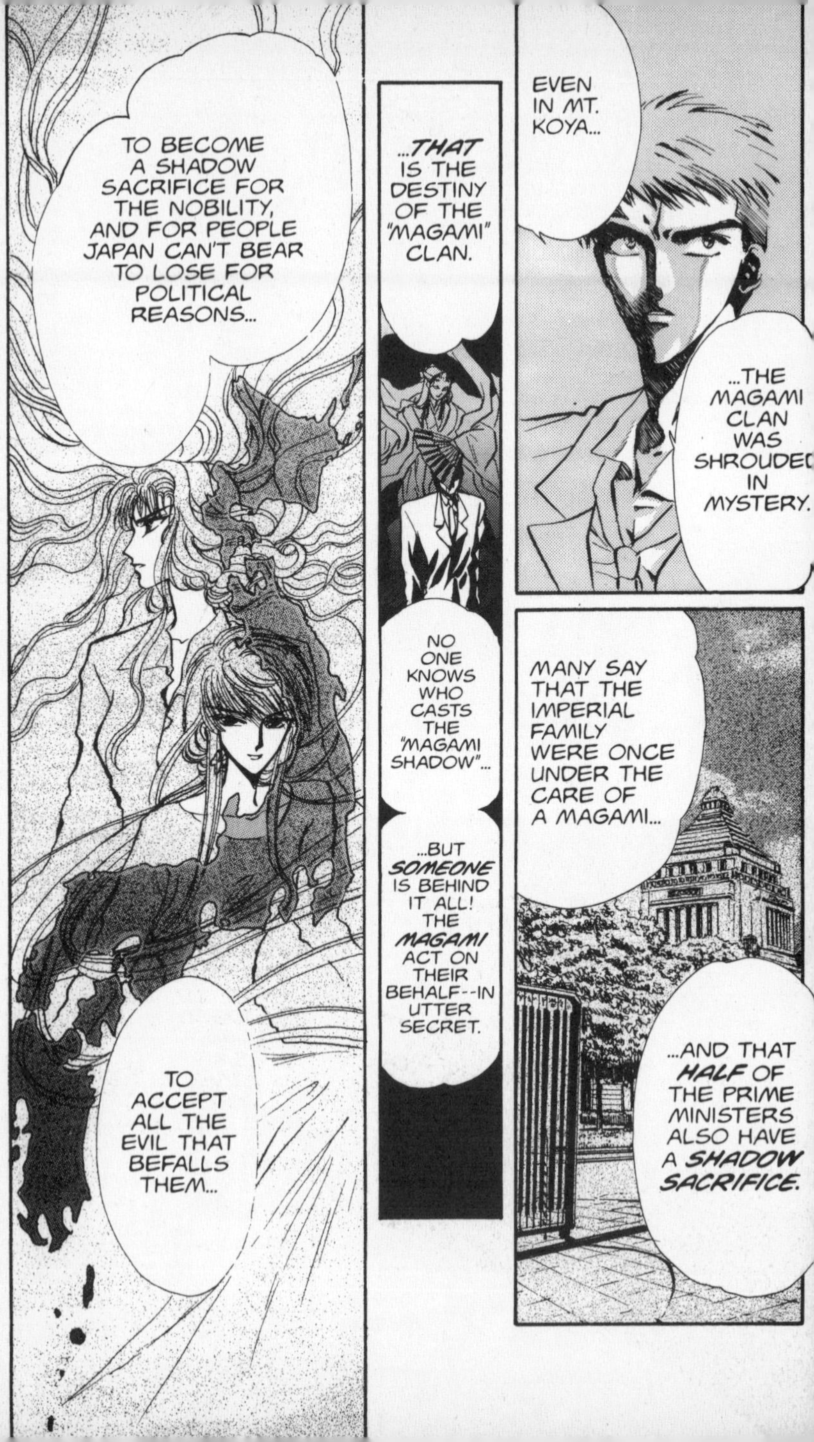
TO BECOME A SHADOW SACRIFICE FOR THE NOBILITY, AND FOR PEOPLE JAPAN CAN'T BEAR TO LOSE FOR POLITICAL REASONS...
TO ACCEPT ALL THE EVIL THAT BEFALLS THEM...
...*THAT* IS THE DESTINY OF THE "MAGAMI" CLAN.
NO ONE KNOWS WHO CASTS THE "MAGAMI SHADOW"...
...BUT *SOMEONE* IS BEHIND IT ALL! THE *MAGAMI* ACT ON THEIR BEHALF--IN UTTER SECRET.
EVEN IN MT. KOYA...
...THE MAGAMI CLAN WAS SHROUDED IN MYSTERY.
MANY SAY THAT THE IMPERIAL FAMILY WERE ONCE UNDER THE CARE OF A MAGAMI...
...AND THAT *HALF* OF THE PRIME MINISTERS ALSO HAVE A *SHADOW SACRIFICE.*

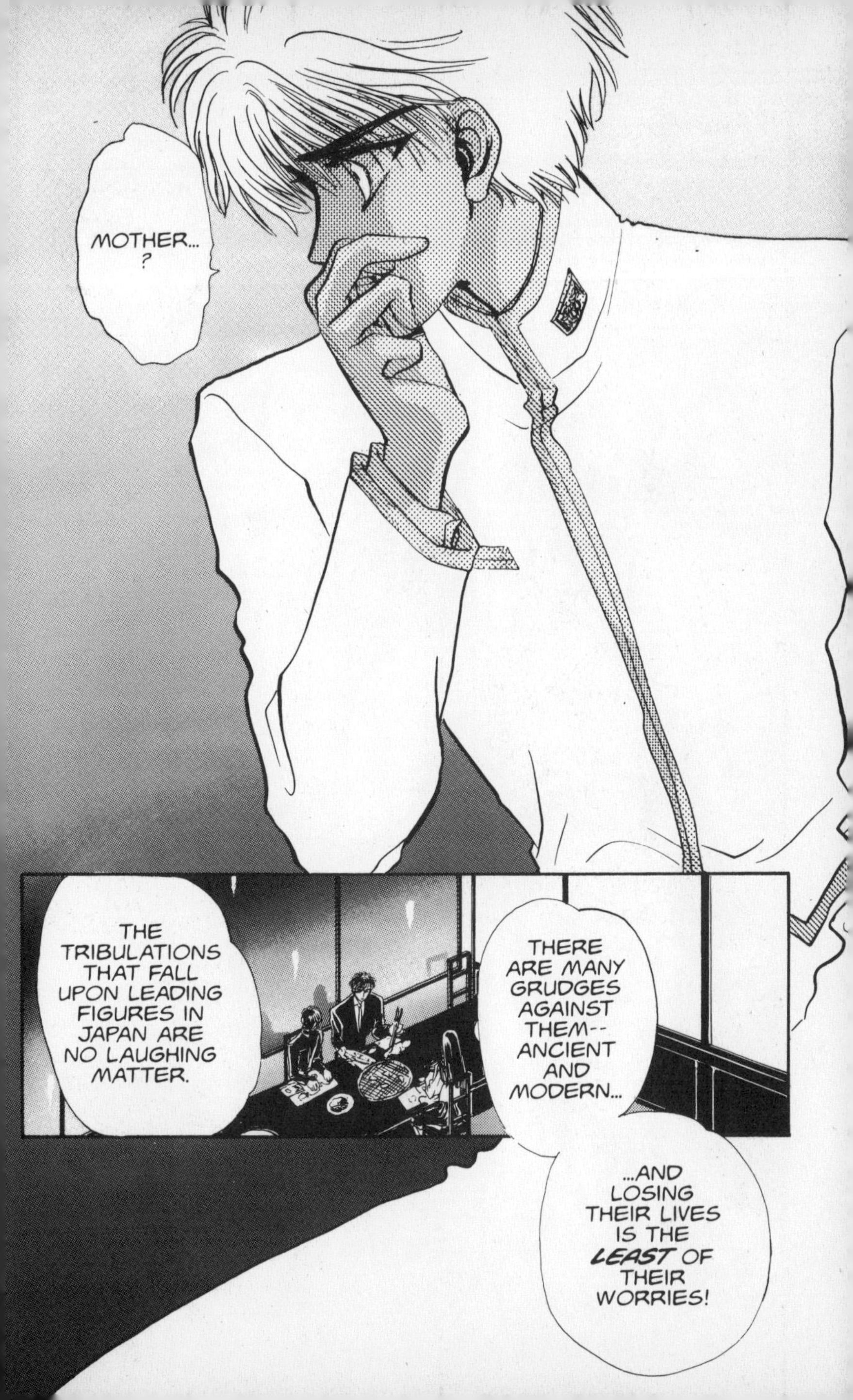
MOTHER... ?
THE TRIBULATIONS THAT FALL UPON LEADING FIGURES IN JAPAN ARE NO LAUGHING MATTER.
THERE ARE MANY GRUDGES AGAINST THEM-- ANCIENT AND MODERN...
...AND LOSING THEIR LIVES IS THE LEAST OF THEIR WORRIES!

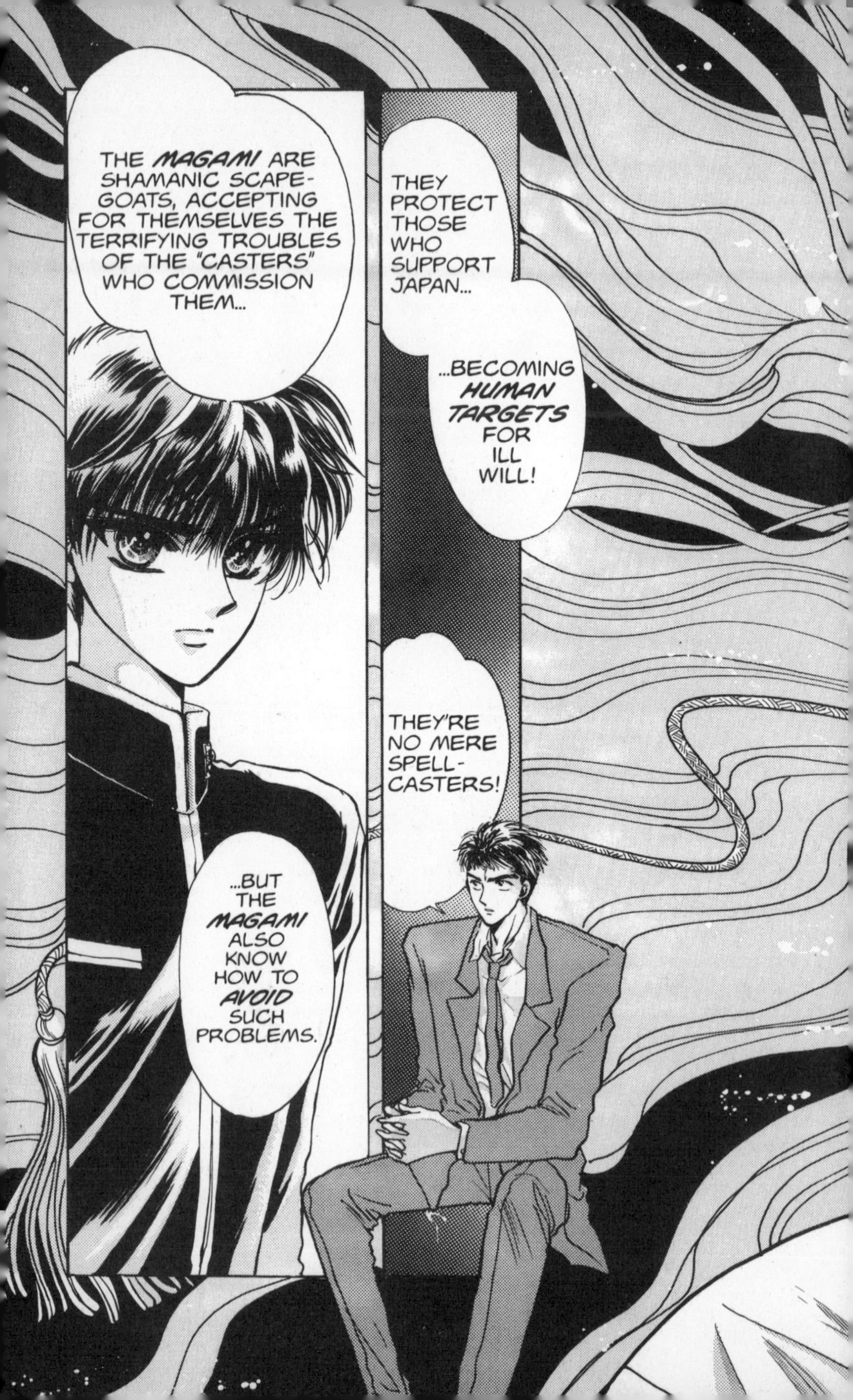
THE *MAGAMI* ARE SHAMANIC SCAPE-GOATS, ACCEPTING FOR THEMSELVES THE TERRIFYING TROUBLES OF THE "CASTERS" WHO COMMISSION THEM...
...BUT THE *MAGAMI* ALSO KNOW HOW TO *AVOID* SUCH PROBLEMS.
THEY PROTECT THOSE WHO SUPPORT JAPAN...
...BECOMING *HUMAN TARGETS* FOR ILL WILL!
THEY'RE NO MERE SPELL-CASTERS!

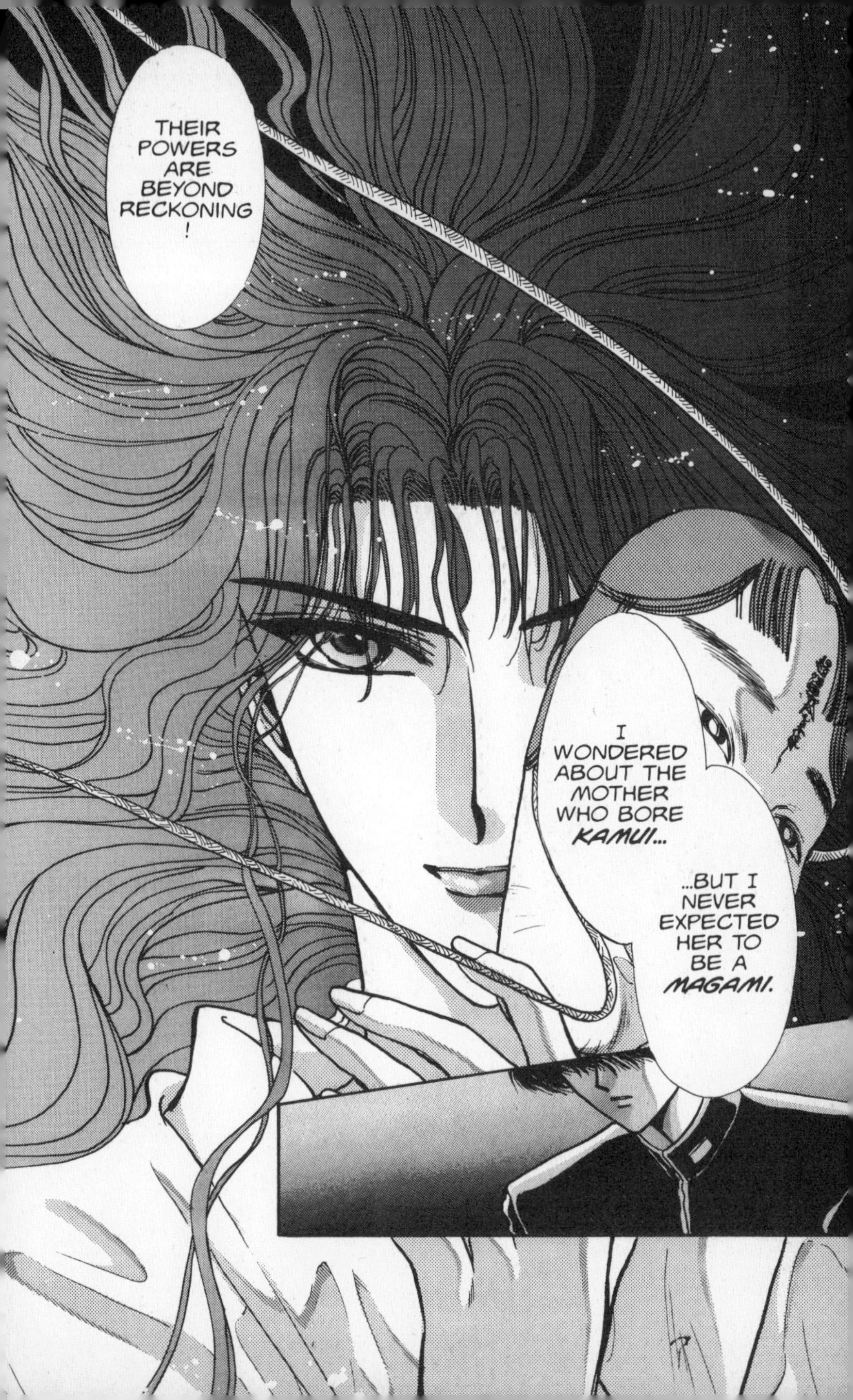
THEIR POWERS ARE BEYOND RECKONING!
I WONDERED ABOUT THE MOTHER WHO BORE KAMUI...
...BUT I NEVER EXPECTED HER TO BE A MAGAMI.

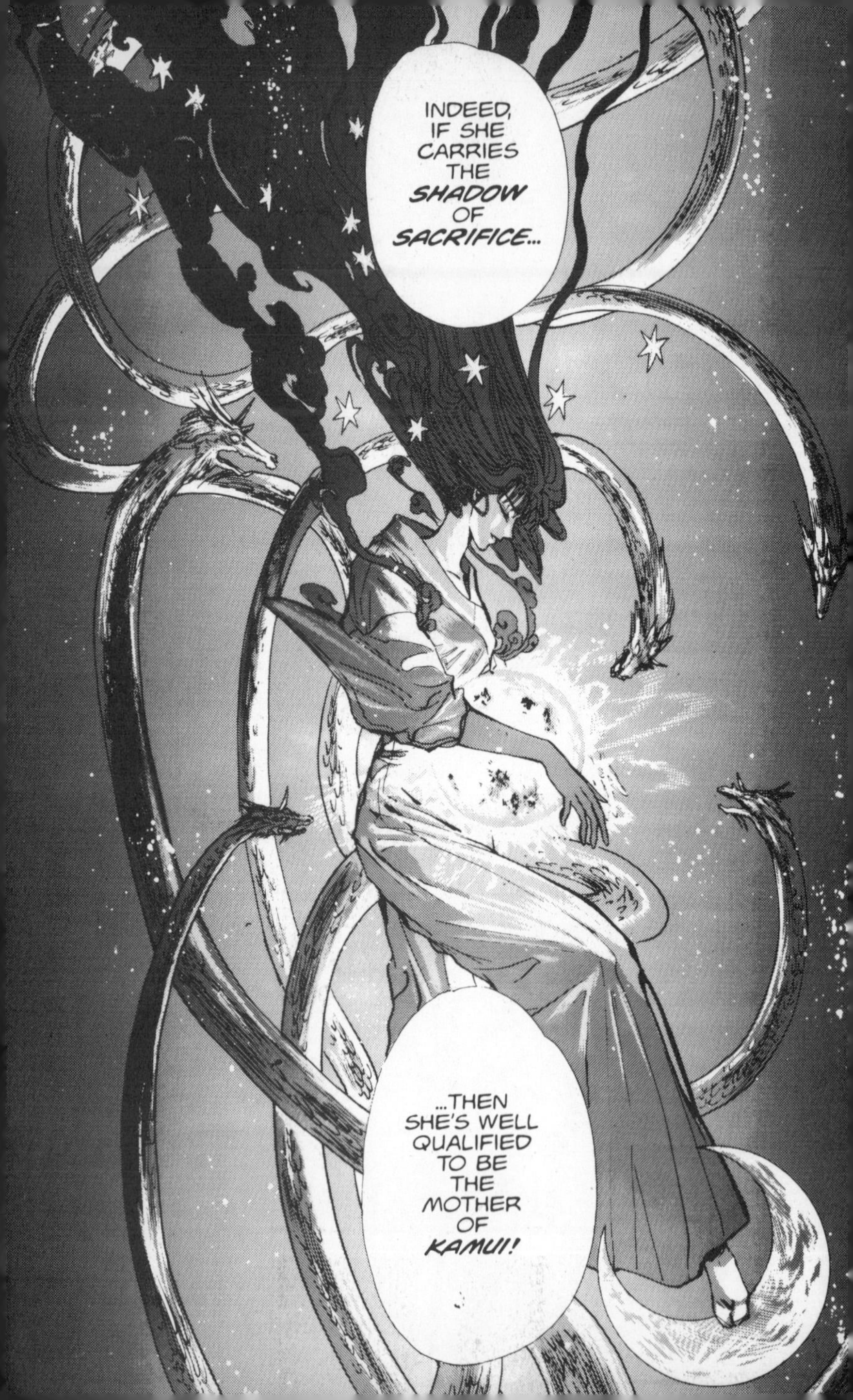
INDEED, IF SHE CARRIES THE *SHADOW* OF *SACRIFICE...*
...THEN SHE'S WELL QUALIFIED TO BE THE MOTHER OF *KAMUI!*

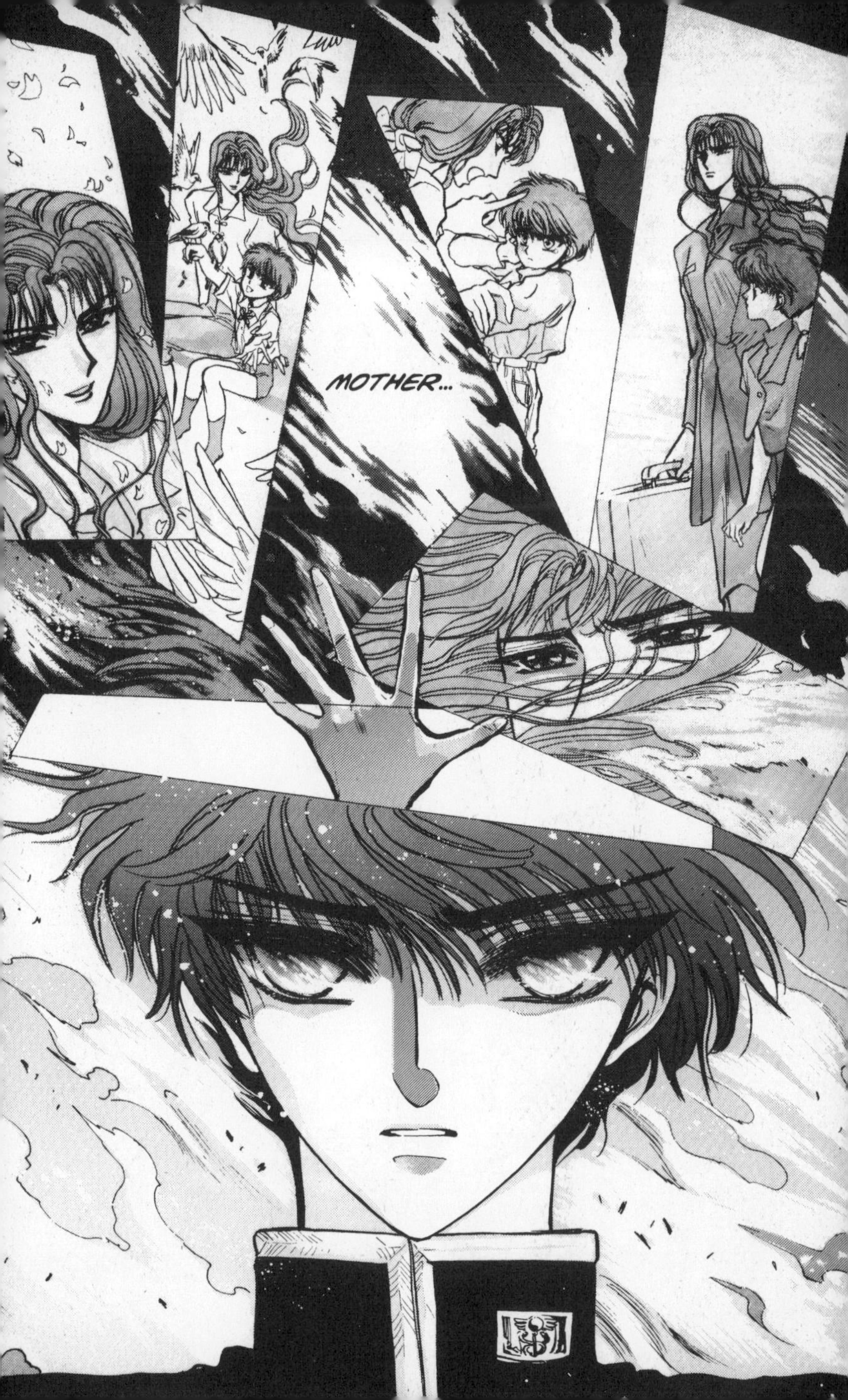
MOTHER...

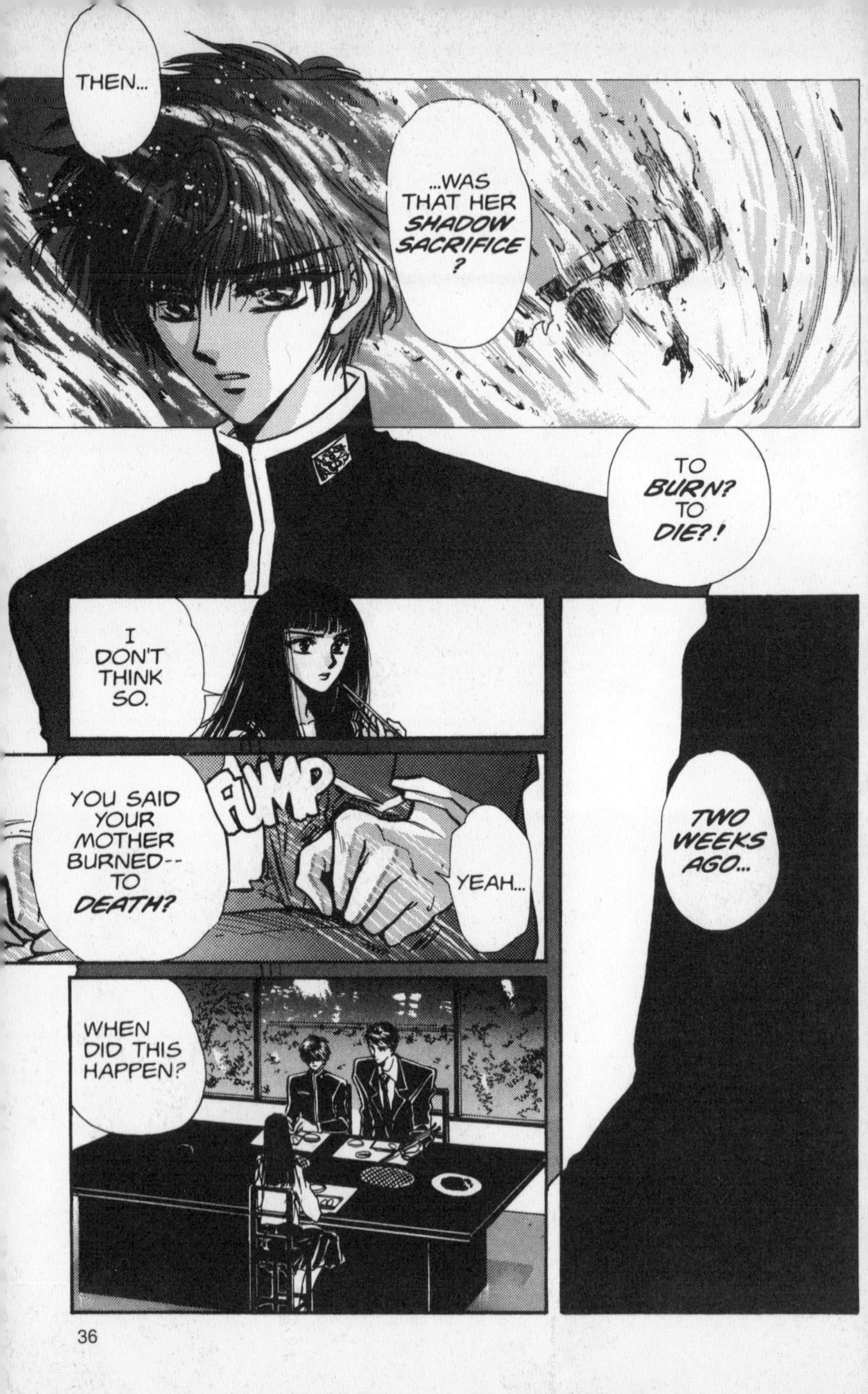
THEN...
...WAS THAT HER SHADOW SACRIFICE ?
TO BURN? TO DIE?!
I DON'T THINK SO.
YOU SAID YOUR MOTHER BURNED-- TO DEATH?
FUMP
YEAH...
WHEN DID THIS HAPPEN?
TWO WEEKS AGO...

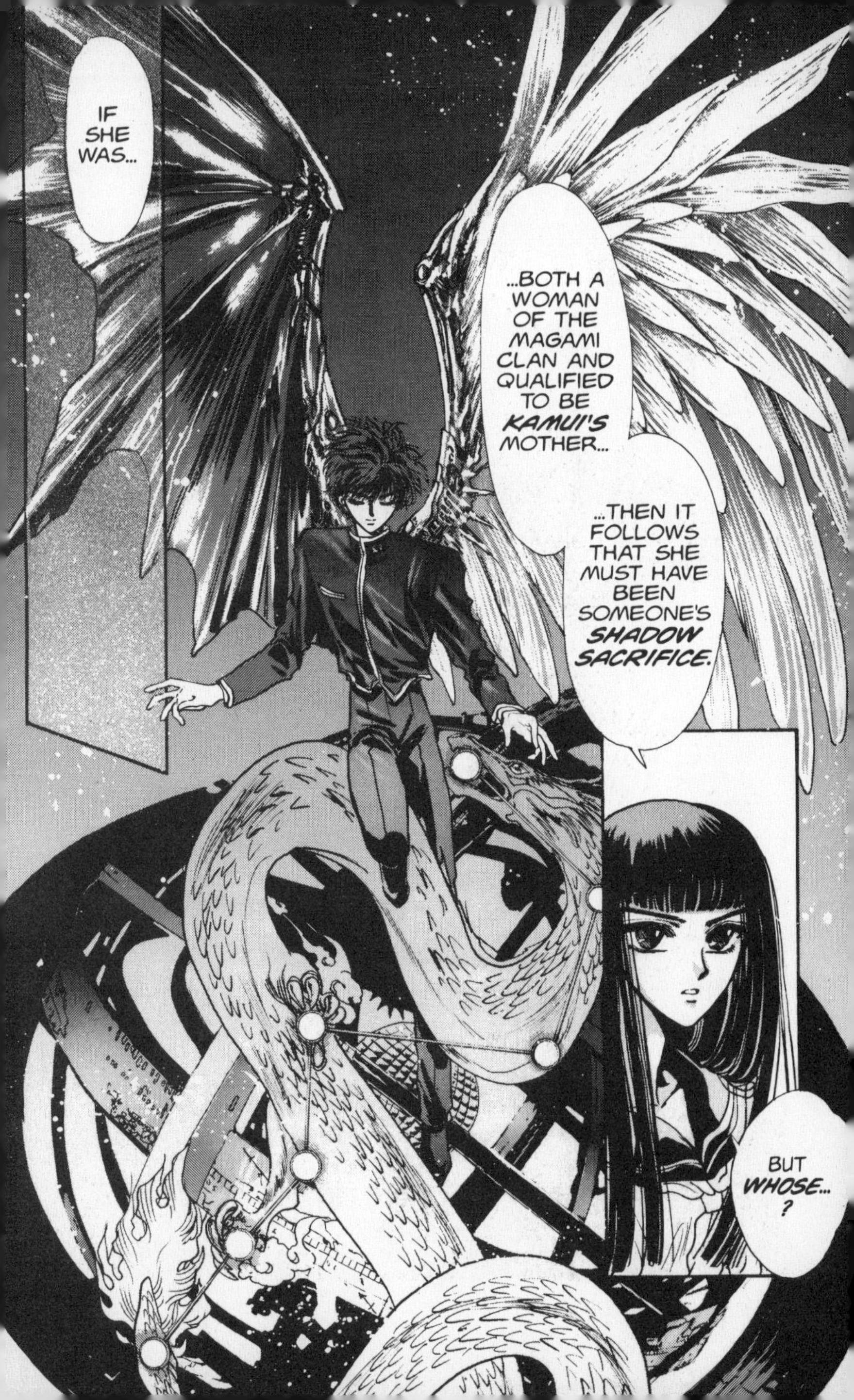
IF SHE WAS...
...BOTH A WOMAN OF THE MAGAMI CLAN AND QUALIFIED TO BE KAMUI'S MOTHER...
...THEN IT FOLLOWS THAT SHE MUST HAVE BEEN SOMEONE'S SHADOW SACRIFICE.
BUT WHOSE... ?

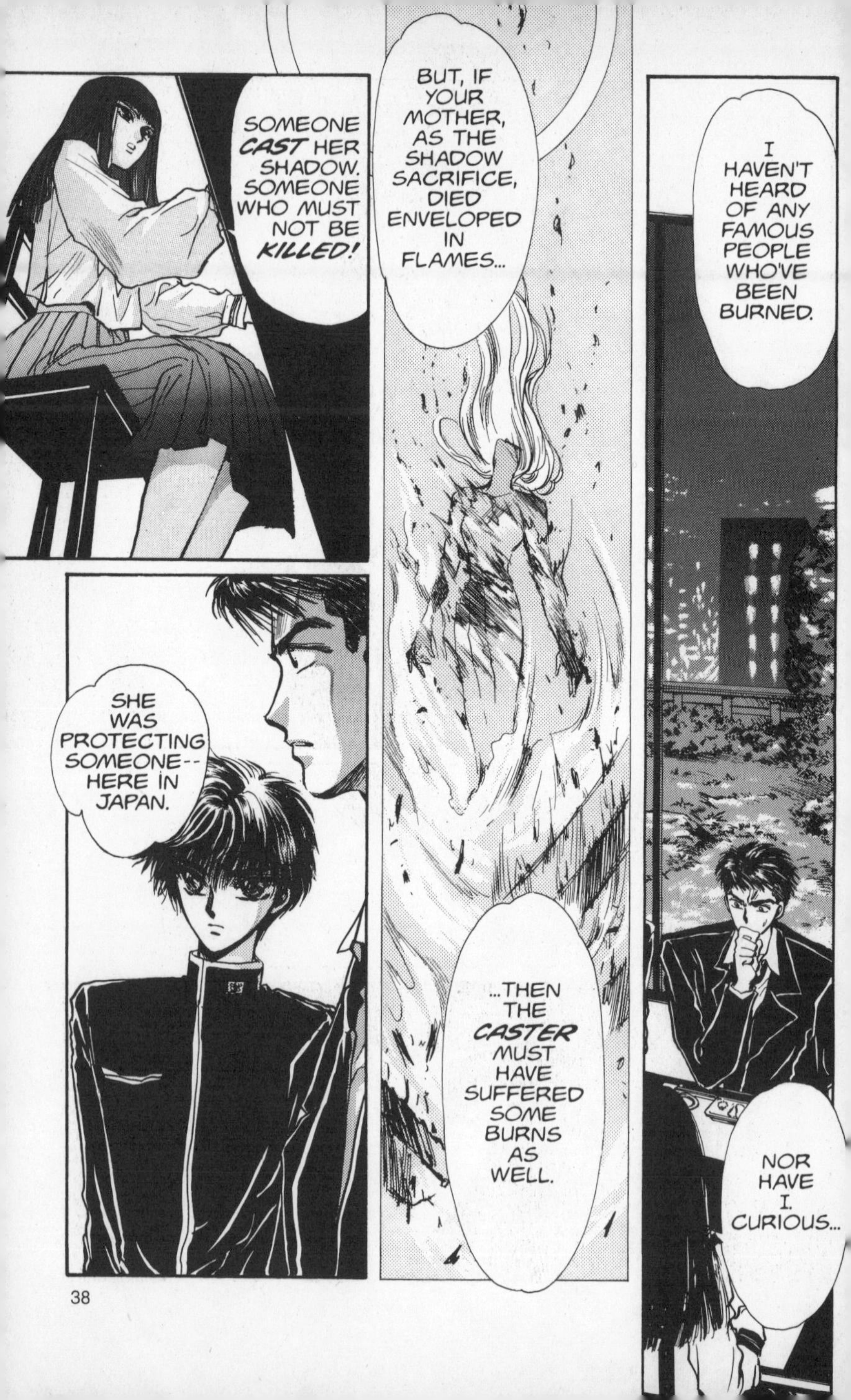
SOMEONE CAST HER SHADOW. SOMEONE WHO MUST NOT BE KILLED!
SHE WAS PROTECTING SOMEONE-- HERE IN JAPAN.
BUT, IF YOUR MOTHER, AS THE SHADOW SACRIFICE, DIED ENVELOPED IN FLAMES...
...THEN THE CASTER MUST HAVE SUFFERED SOME BURNS AS WELL.
I HAVEN'T HEARD OF ANY FAMOUS PEOPLE WHO'VE BEEN BURNED.
NOR HAVE I. CURIOUS...

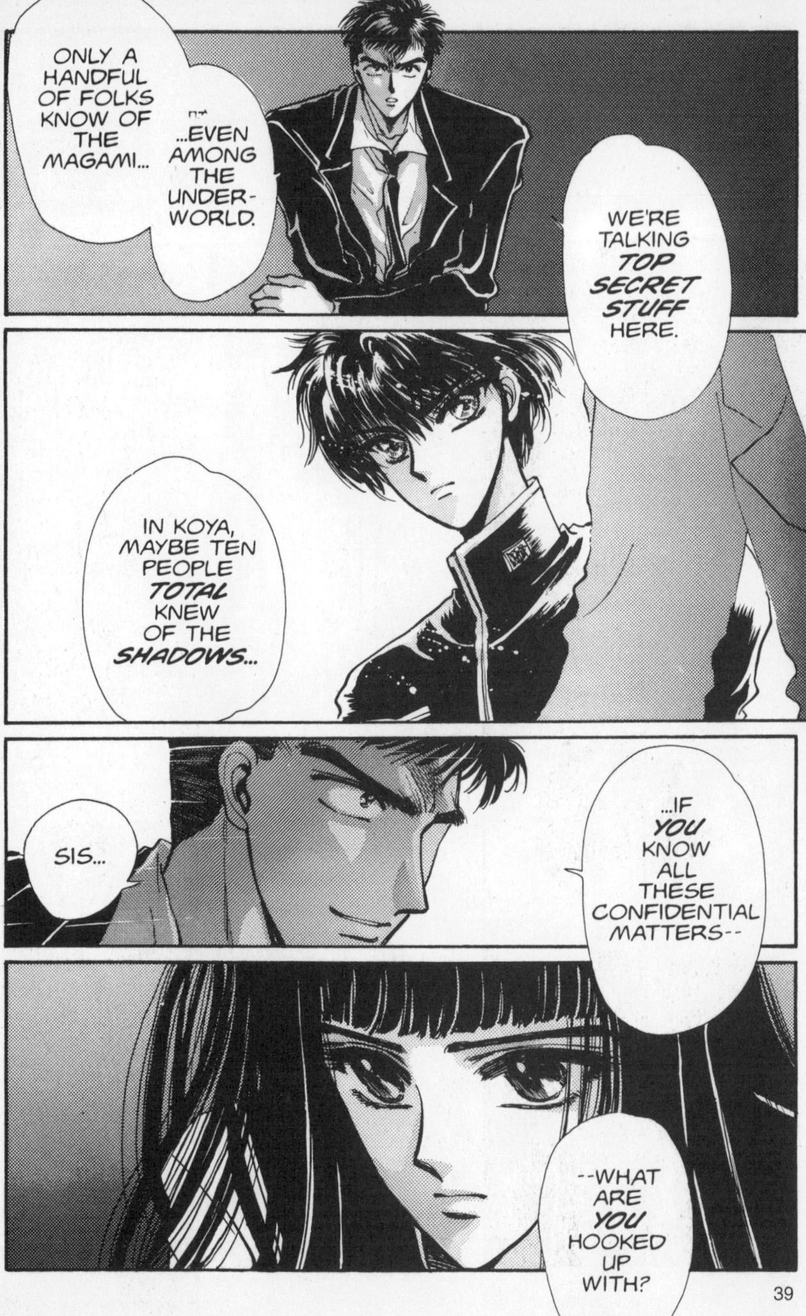
ONLY A HANDFUL OF FOLKS KNOW OF THE MAGAMI...
...EVEN AMONG THE UNDER-WORLD.
WE'RE TALKING TOP SECRET STUFF HERE.
IN KOYA, MAYBE TEN PEOPLE TOTAL KNEW OF THE SHADOWS...
SIS...
...IF YOU KNOW ALL THESE CONFIDENTIAL MATTERS--
--WHAT ARE YOU HOOKED UP WITH?

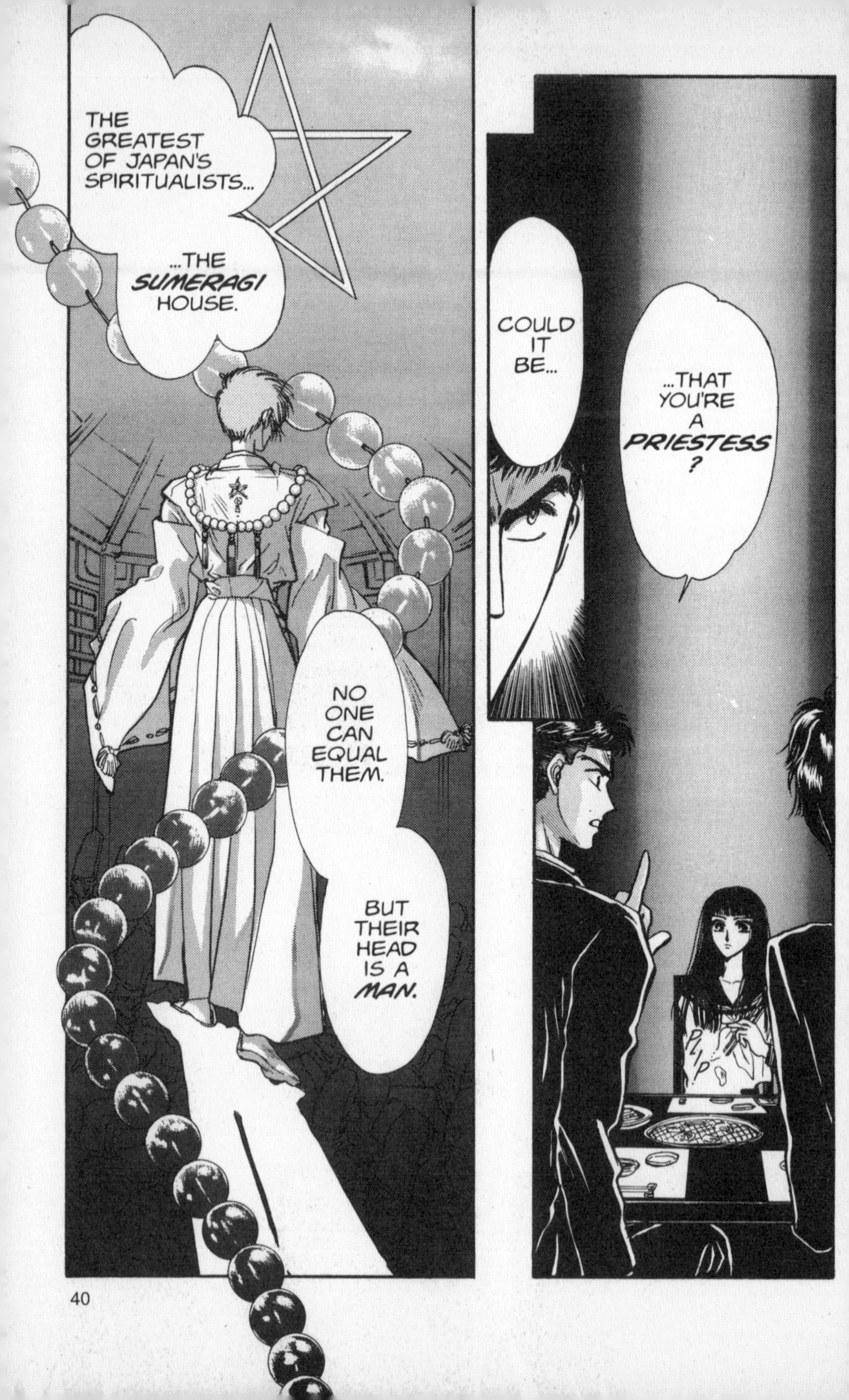
THE GREATEST OF JAPAN'S SPIRITUALISTS...
...THE SUMERAGI HOUSE.
NO ONE CAN EQUAL THEM.
BUT THEIR HEAD IS A MAN.
COULD IT BE...
...THAT YOU'RE A PRIESTESS?
PLIP

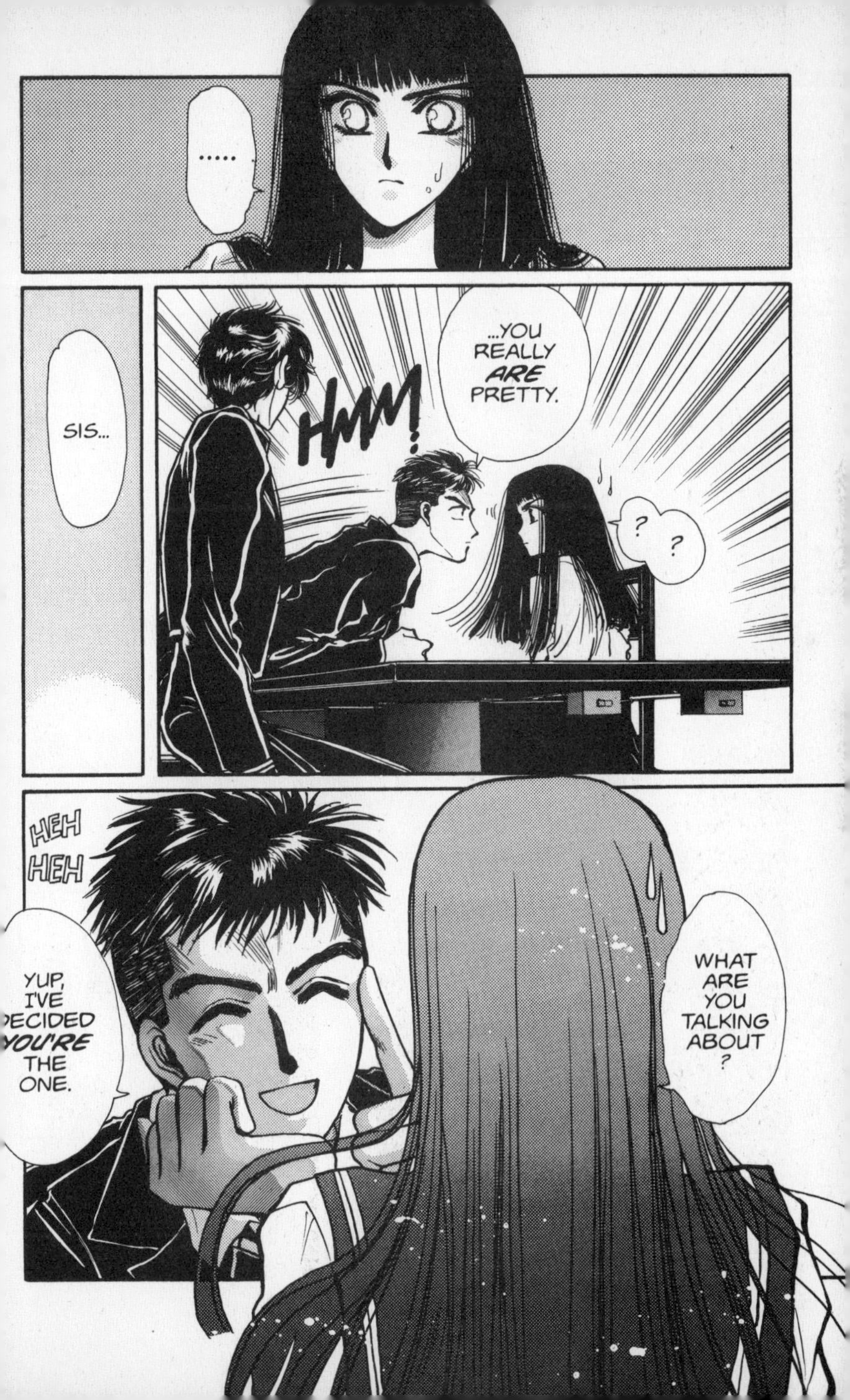

......
SIS...
HMM!
...YOU REALLY ARE PRETTY.
? ?
HEH HEH
YUP, I'VE DECIDED YOU'RE THE ONE.
WHAT ARE YOU TALKING ABOUT?

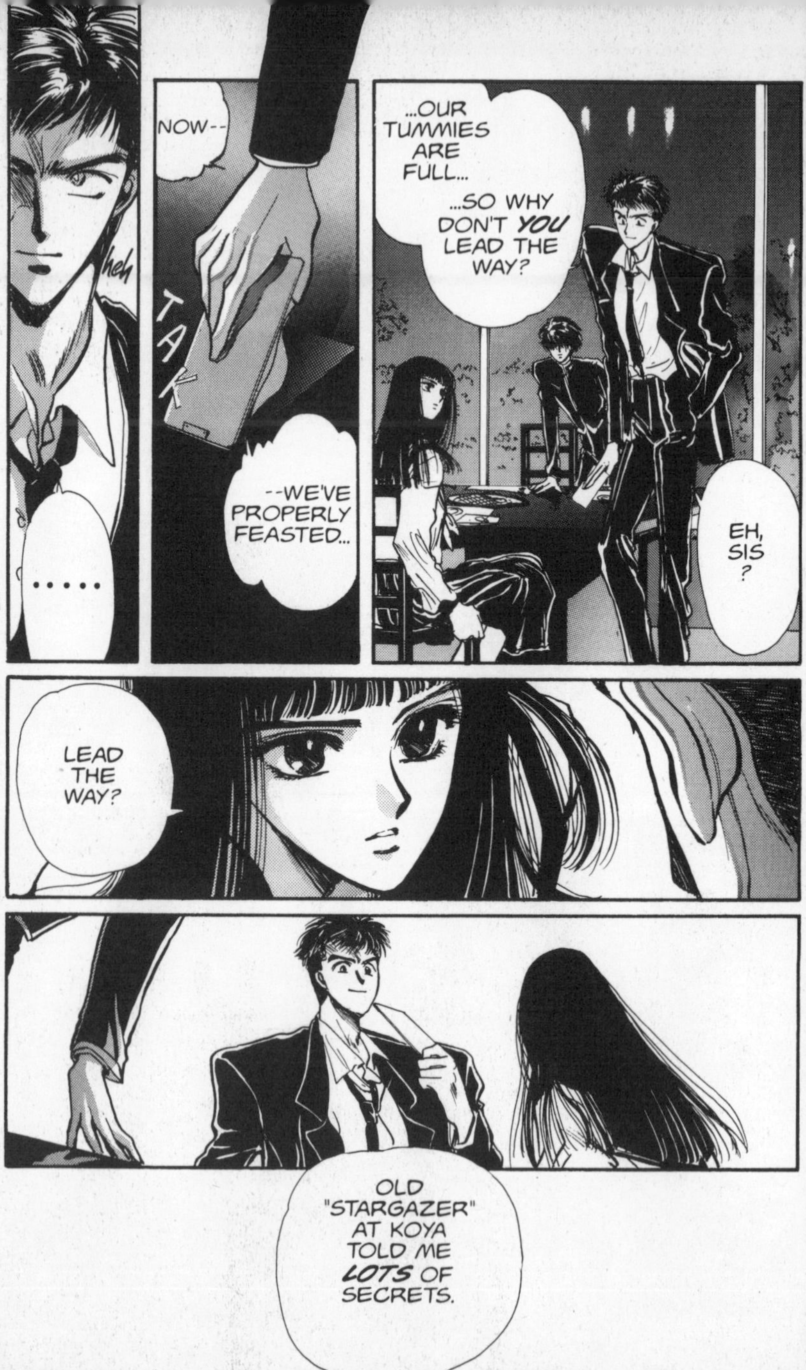
heh
.....
NOW--
TAK
--WE'VE PROPERLY FEASTED...
...OUR TUMMIES ARE FULL...
...SO WHY DON'T YOU LEAD THE WAY?
EH, SIS?
LEAD THE WAY?
OLD "STARGAZER" AT KOYA TOLD ME LOTS OF SECRETS.

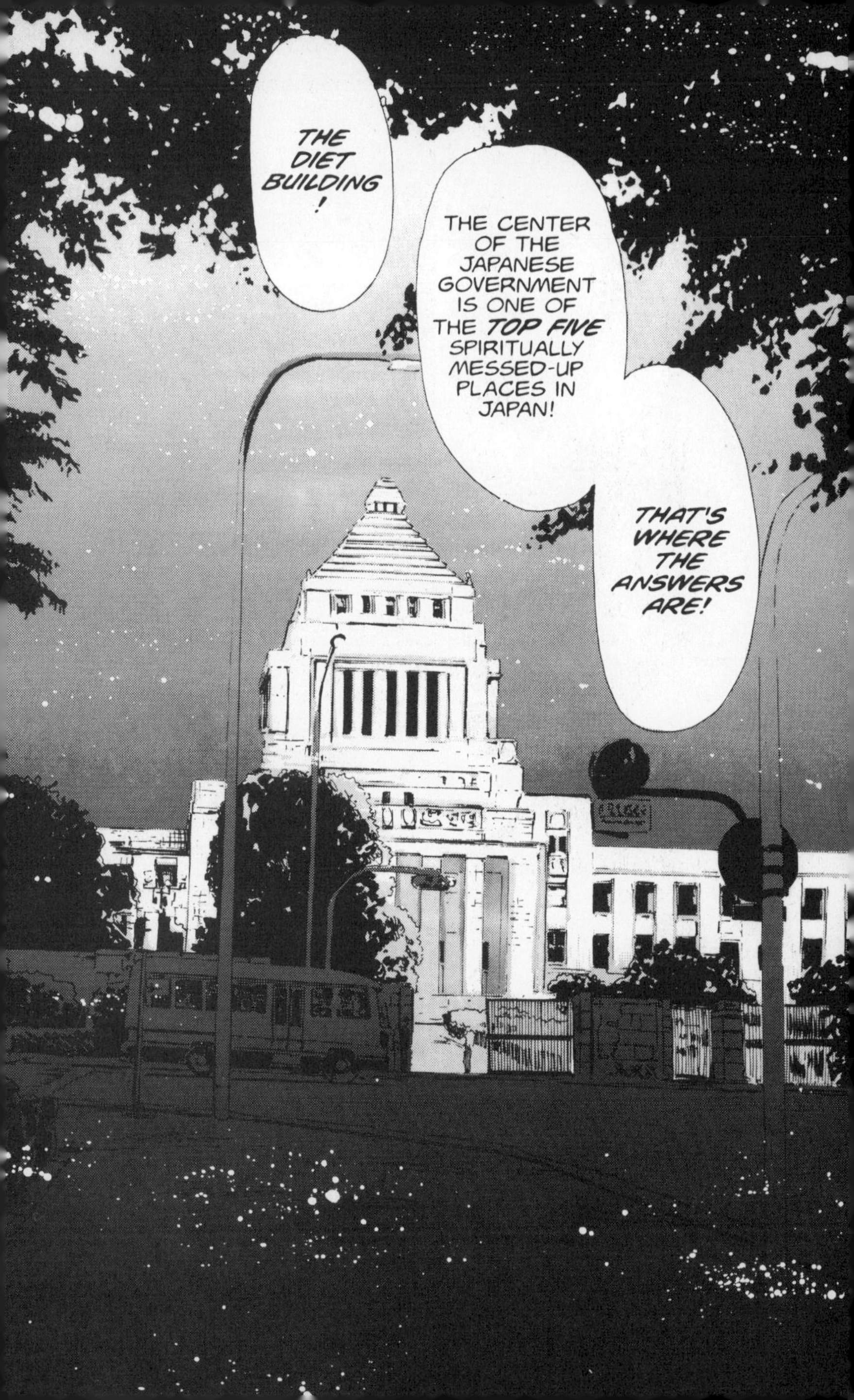
THE DIET BUILDING!
THE CENTER OF THE JAPANESE GOVERNMENT IS ONE OF THE ***TOP FIVE*** SPIRITUALLY MESSED-UP PLACES IN JAPAN!
THAT'S WHERE THE ANSWERS ARE!

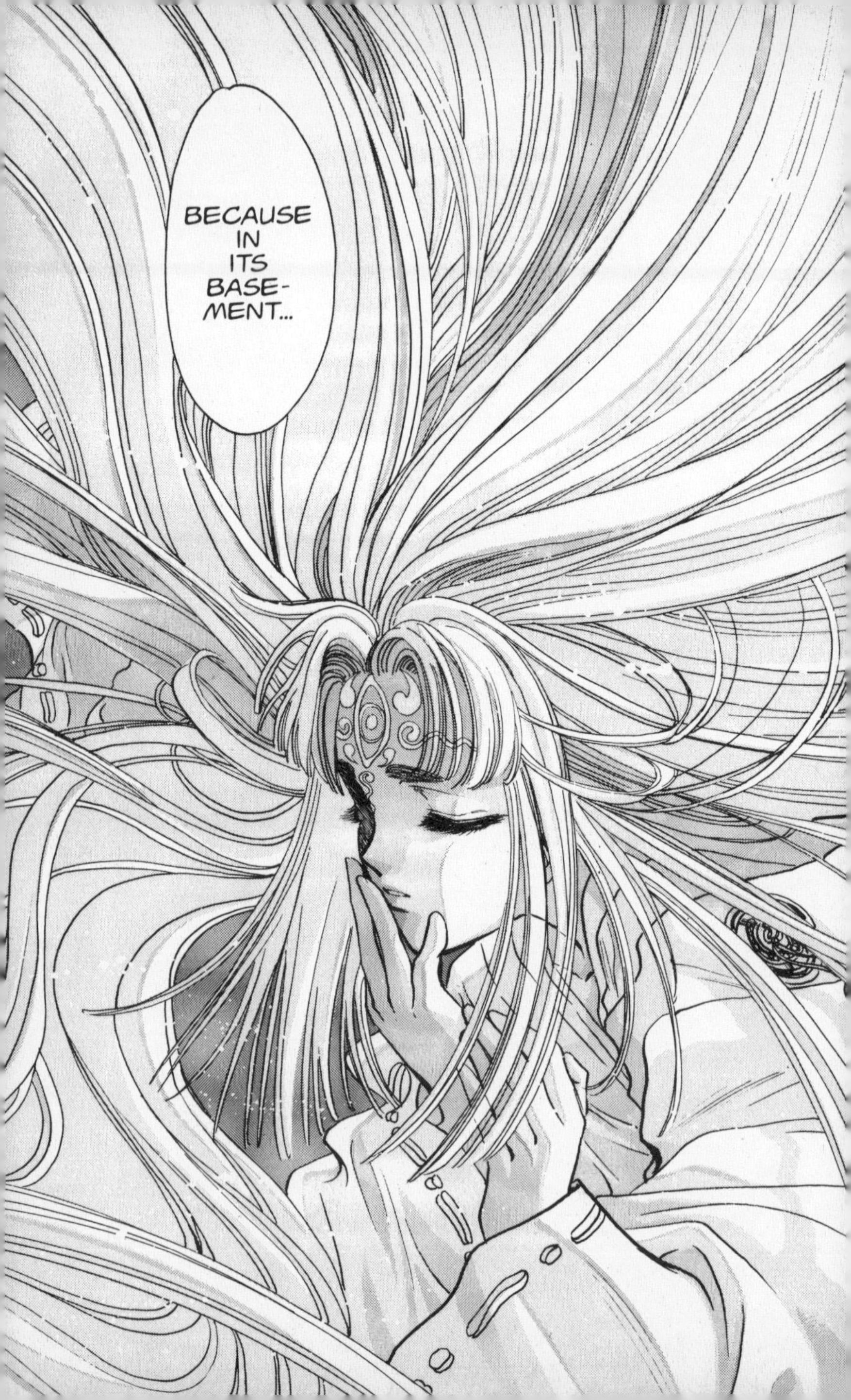
BECAUSE IN ITS BASEMENT...

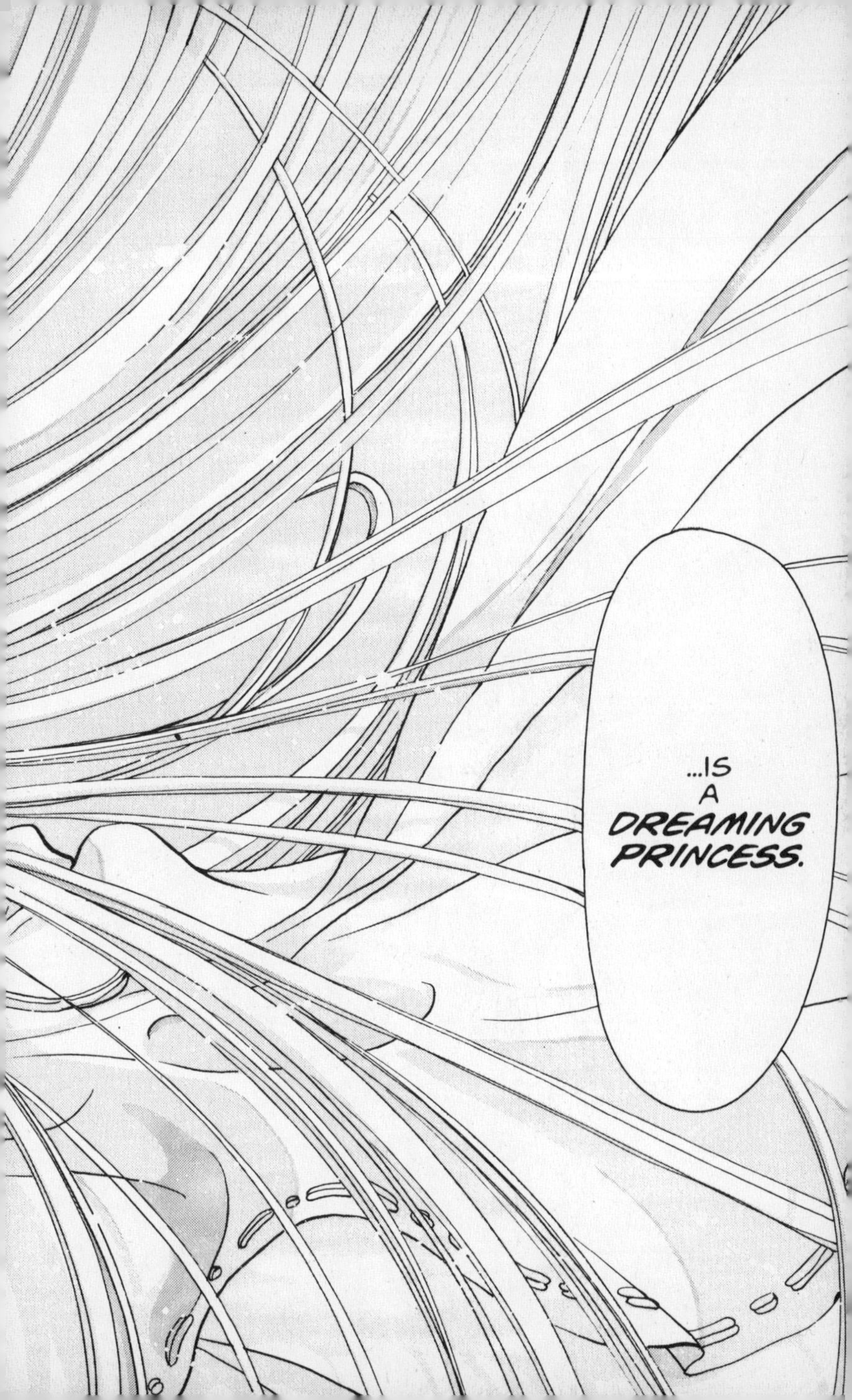
...IS A DREAMING PRINCESS.

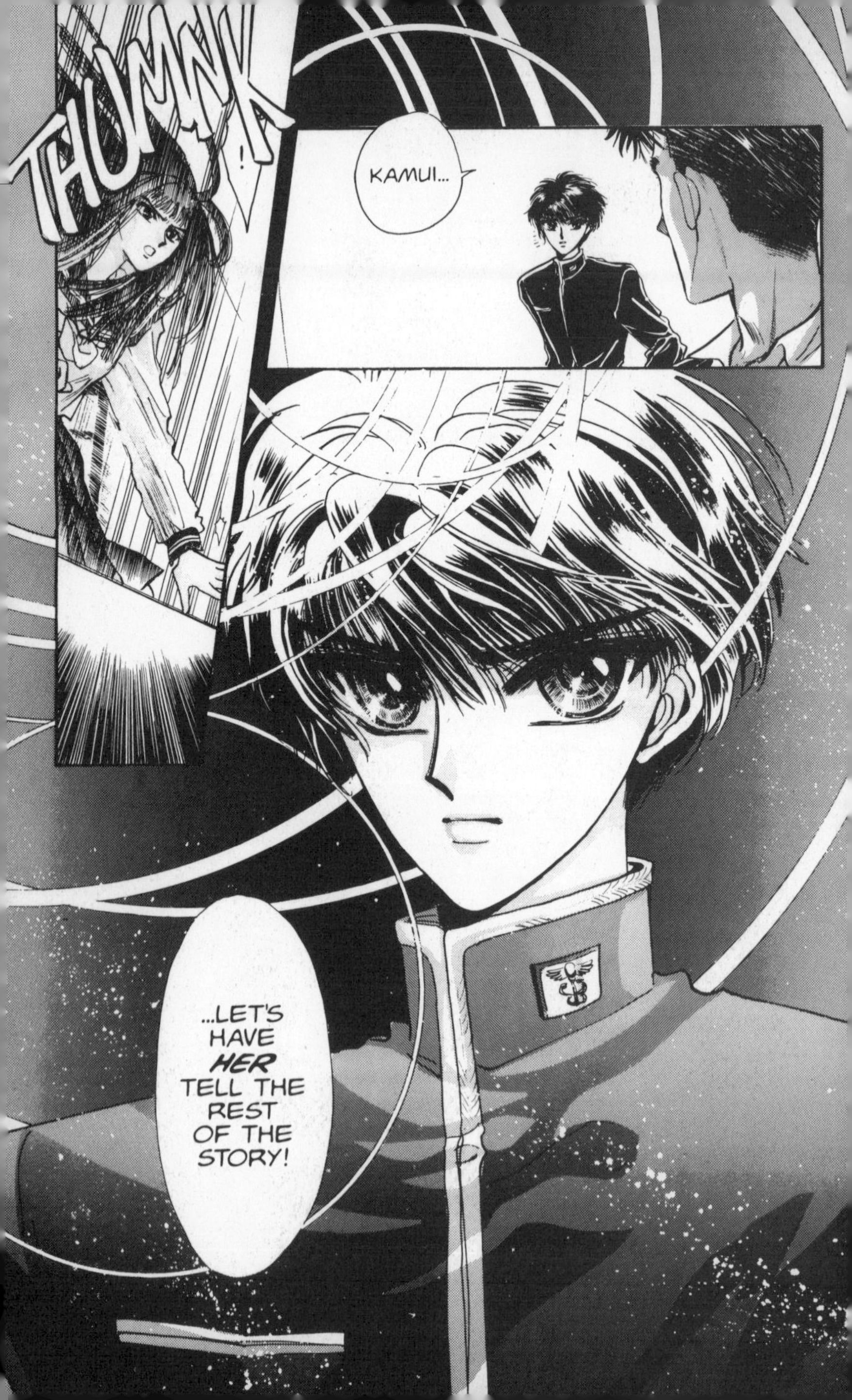
THUMP
!
KAMUI...
...LET'S HAVE *HER* TELL THE REST OF THE STORY!

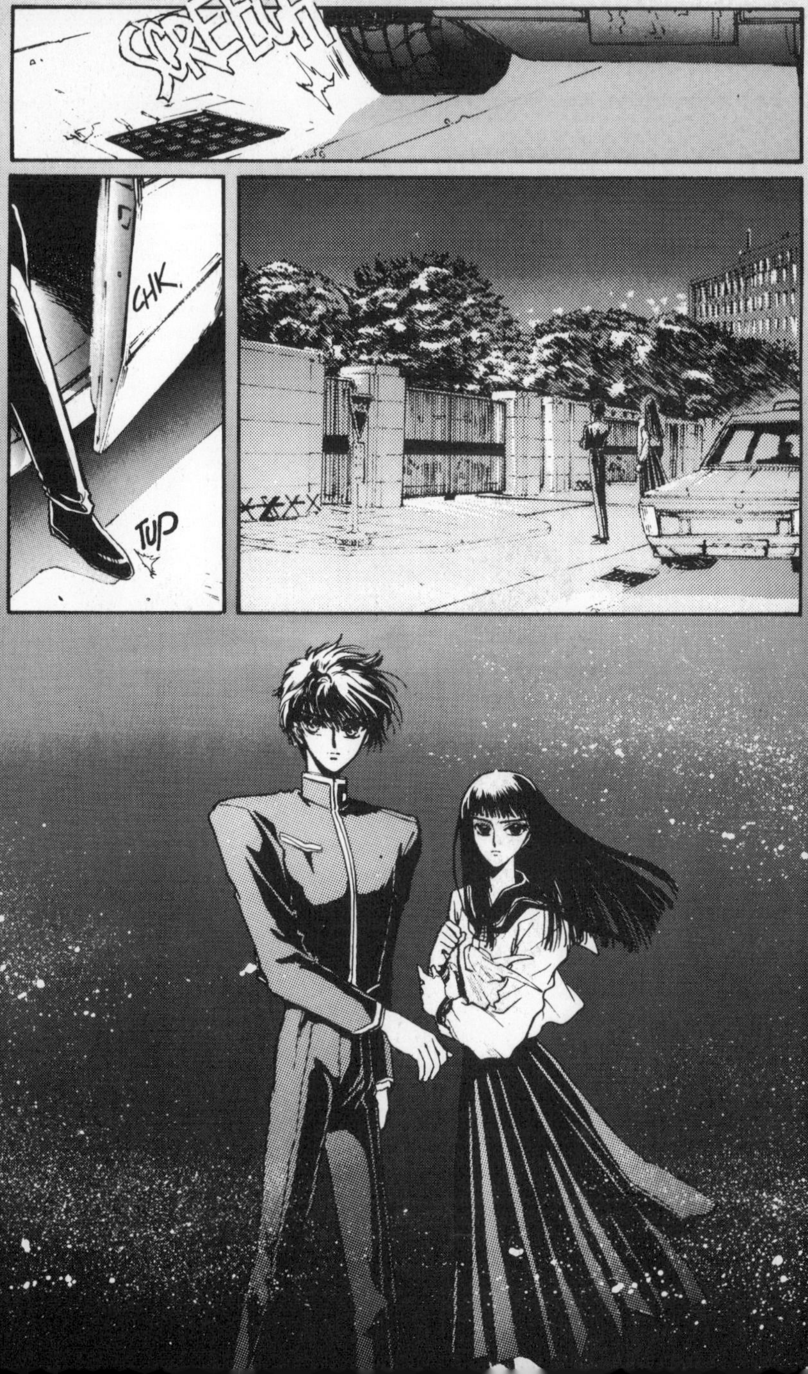
SCREECH
CHK.
TUP

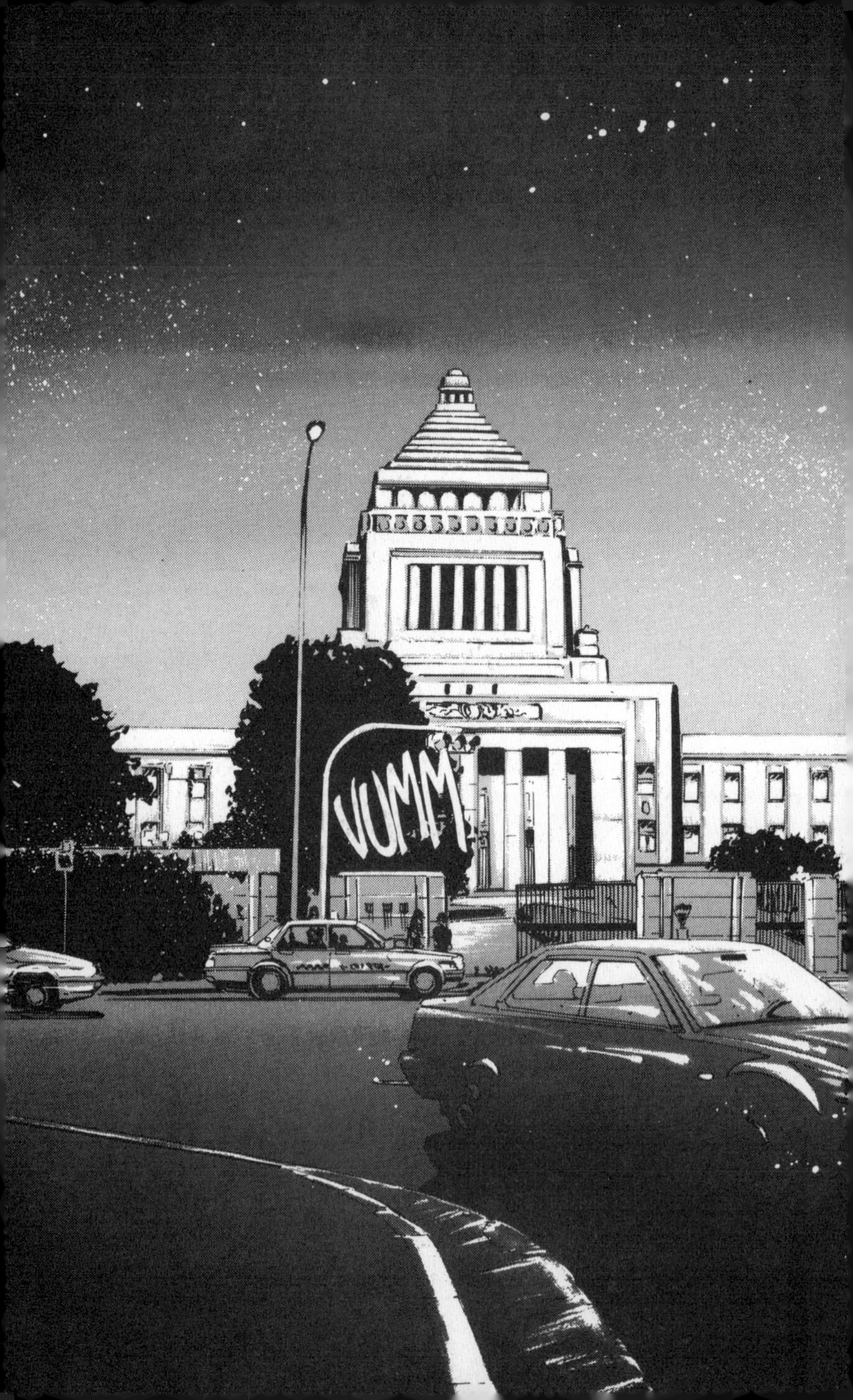
VUMM

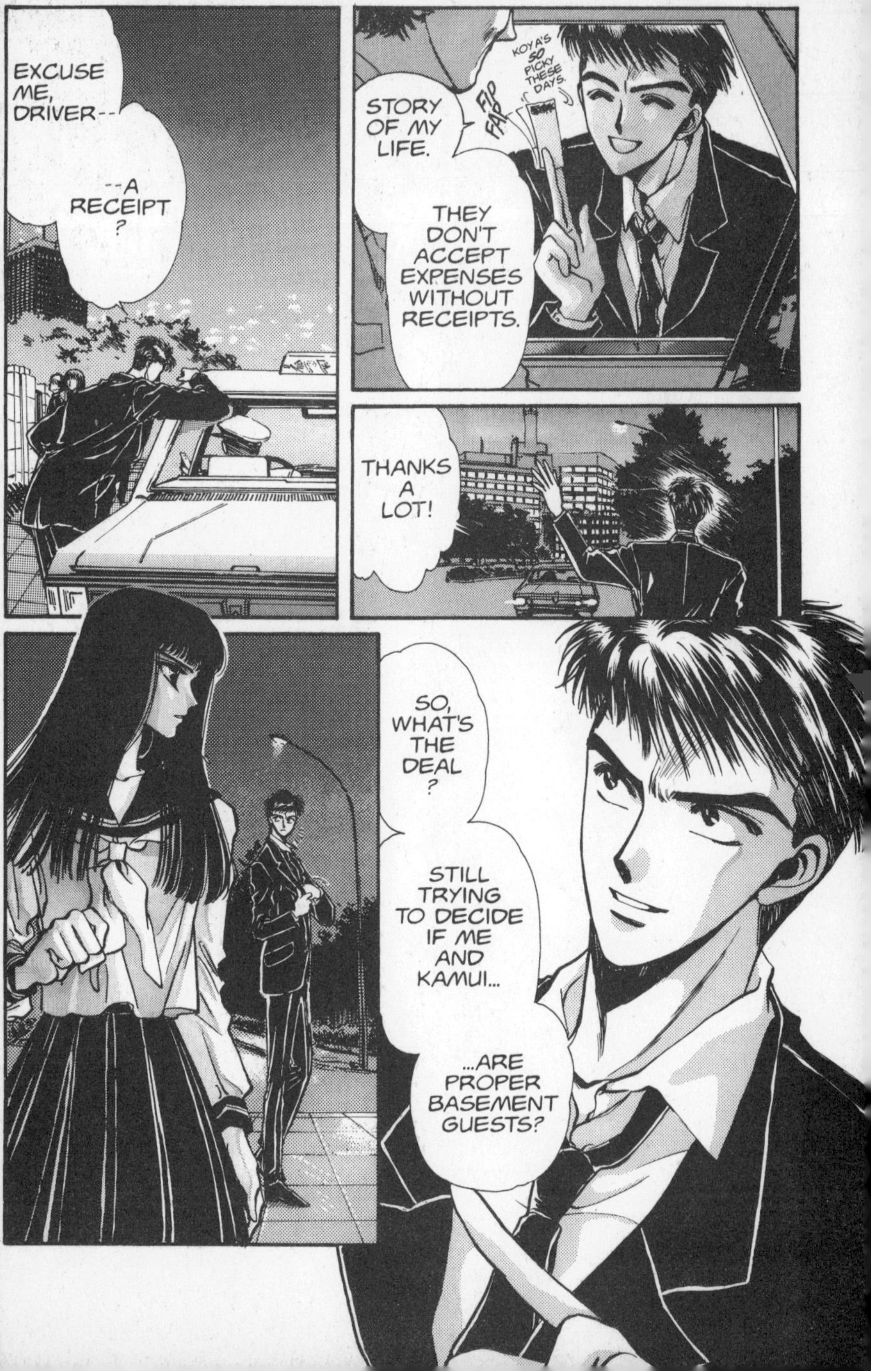
EXCUSE ME, DRIVER--
--A RECEIPT?
STORY OF MY LIFE.
FIP FAP
KOYA'S SO PICKY THESE DAYS.
THEY DON'T ACCEPT EXPENSES WITHOUT RECEIPTS.
THANKS A LOT!
SO, WHAT'S THE DEAL?
STILL TRYING TO DECIDE IF ME AND KAMUI...
...ARE PROPER BASEMENT GUESTS?

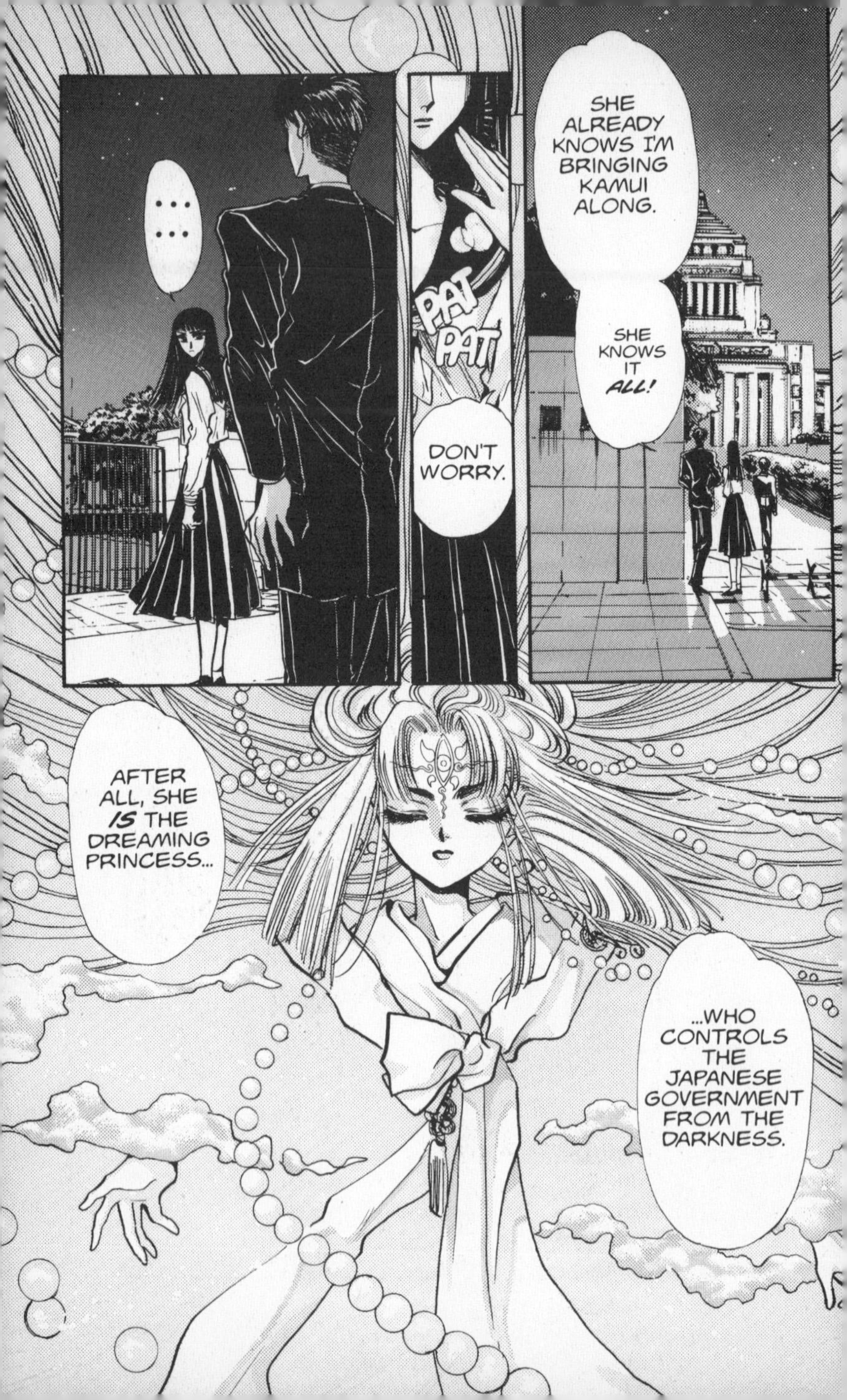

......
PAT PAT
DON'T WORRY.
SHE ALREADY KNOWS I'M BRINGING KAMUI ALONG.
SHE KNOWS IT ALL!
AFTER ALL, SHE IS THE DREAMING PRINCESS...
...WHO CONTROLS THE JAPANESE GOVERNMENT FROM THE DARKNESS.

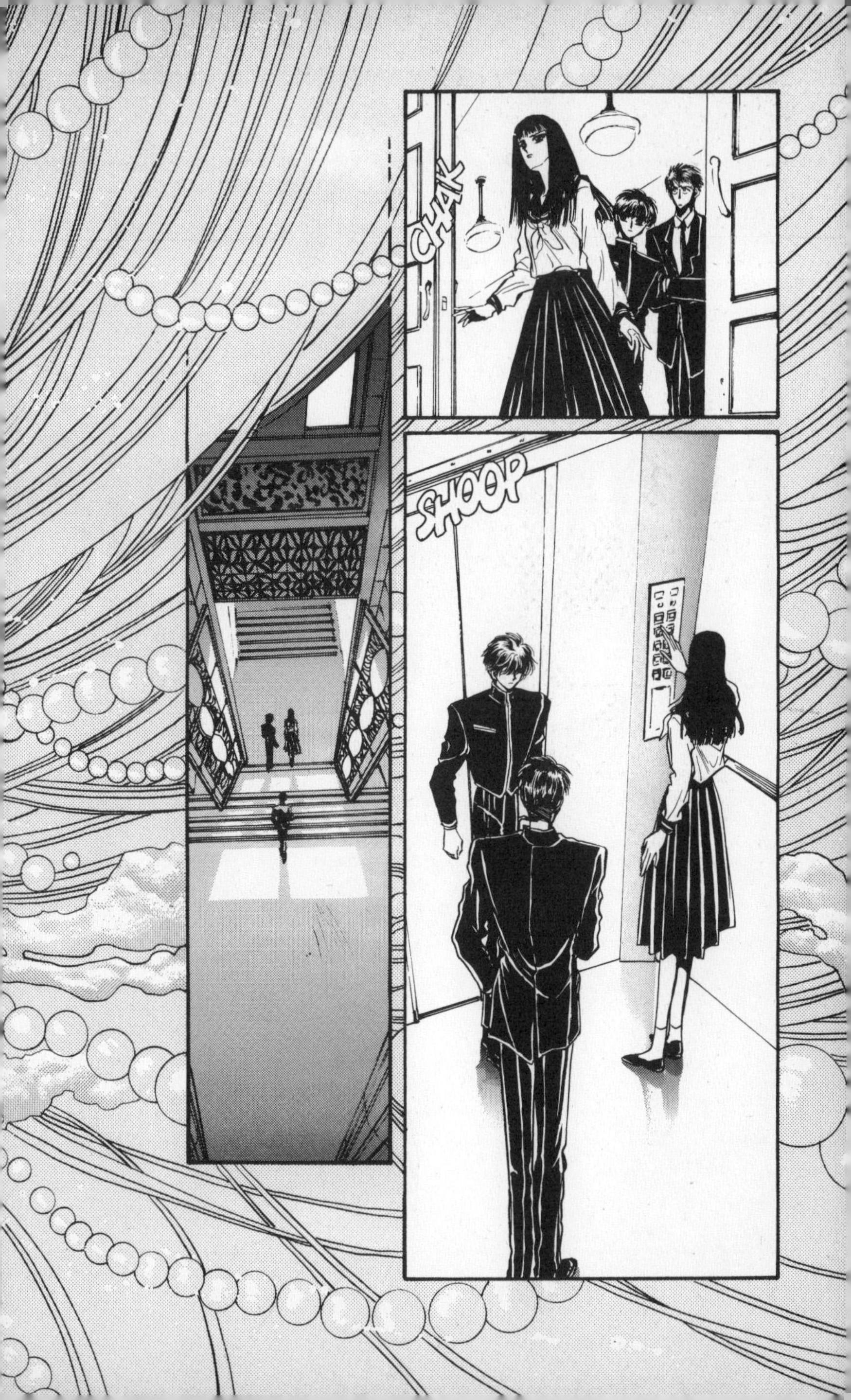
CHAK
SHOOP

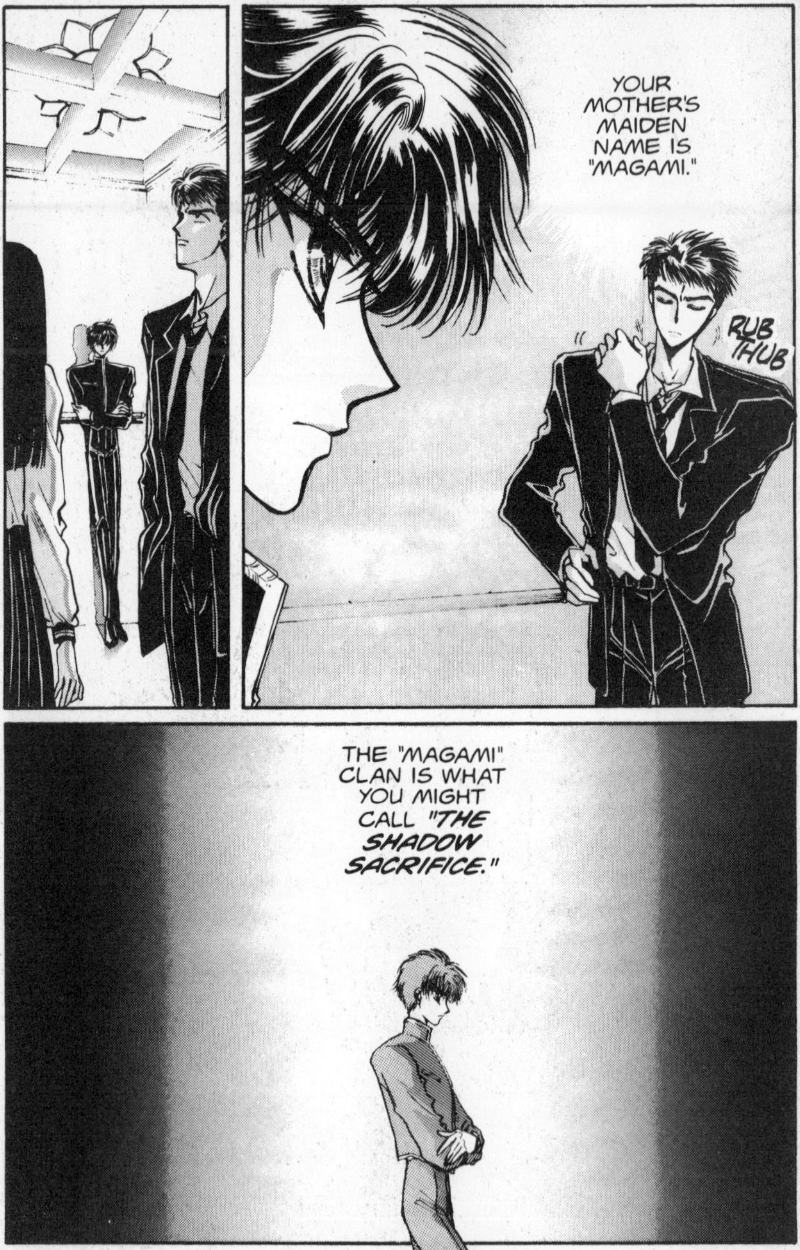
YOUR MOTHER'S MAIDEN NAME IS "MAGAMI."
RUB THUB
THE "MAGAMI" CLAN IS WHAT YOU MIGHT CALL "THE SHADOW SACRIFICE."

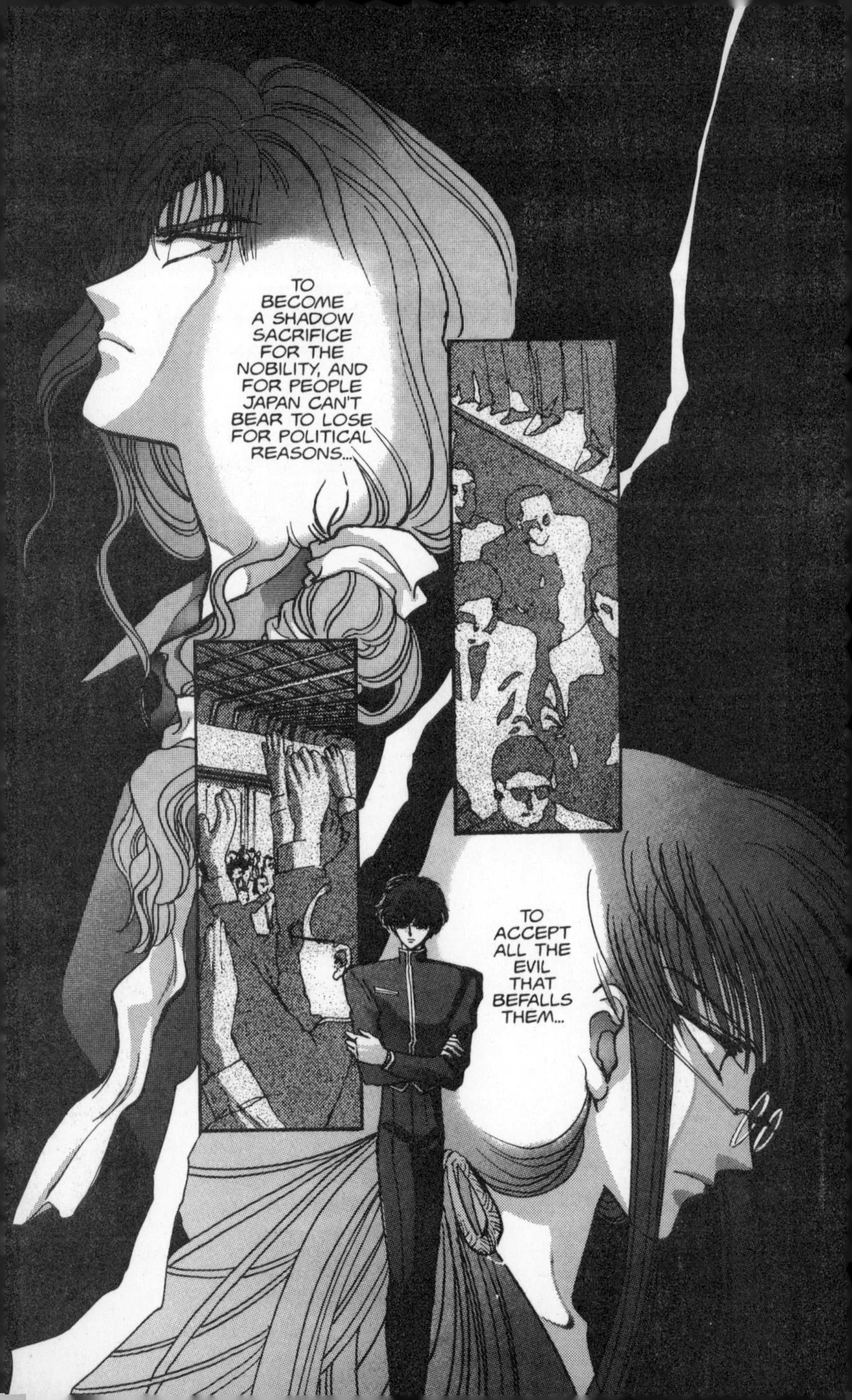
TO BECOME A SHADOW SACRIFICE FOR THE NOBILITY, AND FOR PEOPLE JAPAN CAN'T BEAR TO LOSE FOR POLITICAL REASONS...
TO ACCEPT ALL THE EVIL THAT BEFALLS THEM...

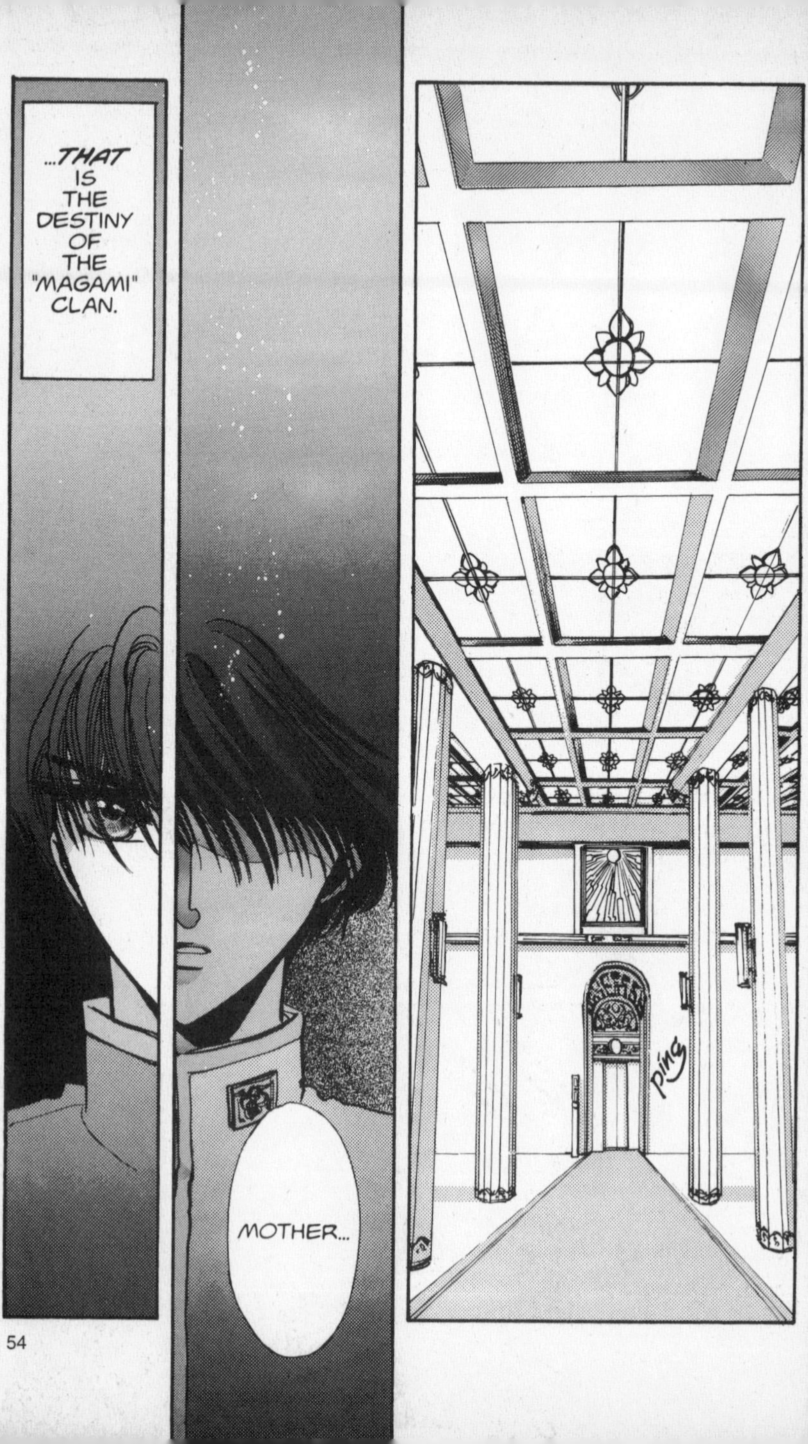
...THAT IS THE DESTINY OF THE "MAGAMI" CLAN.
MOTHER...
ping

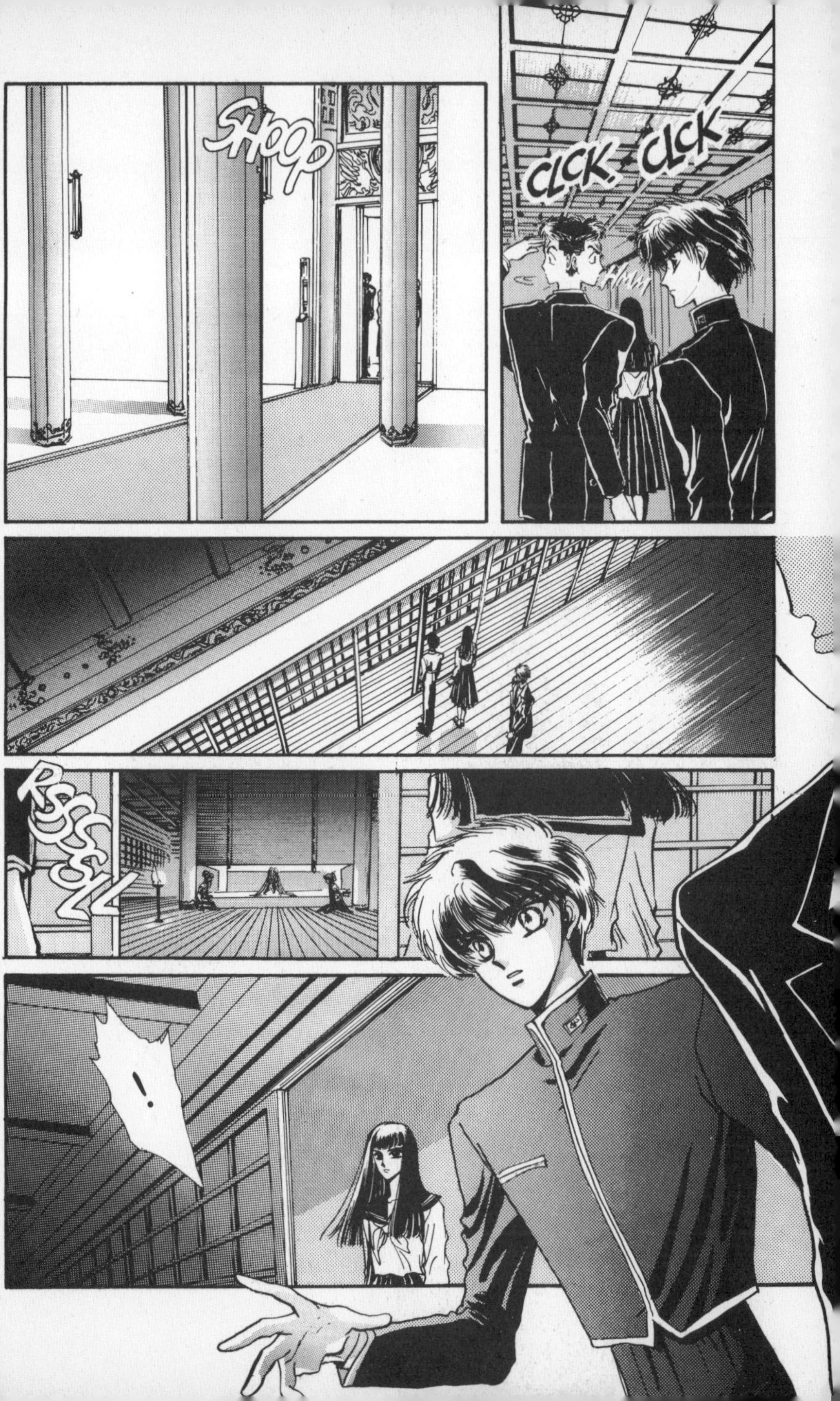
SHOOP
CLICK CLICK
RSSSSH
!

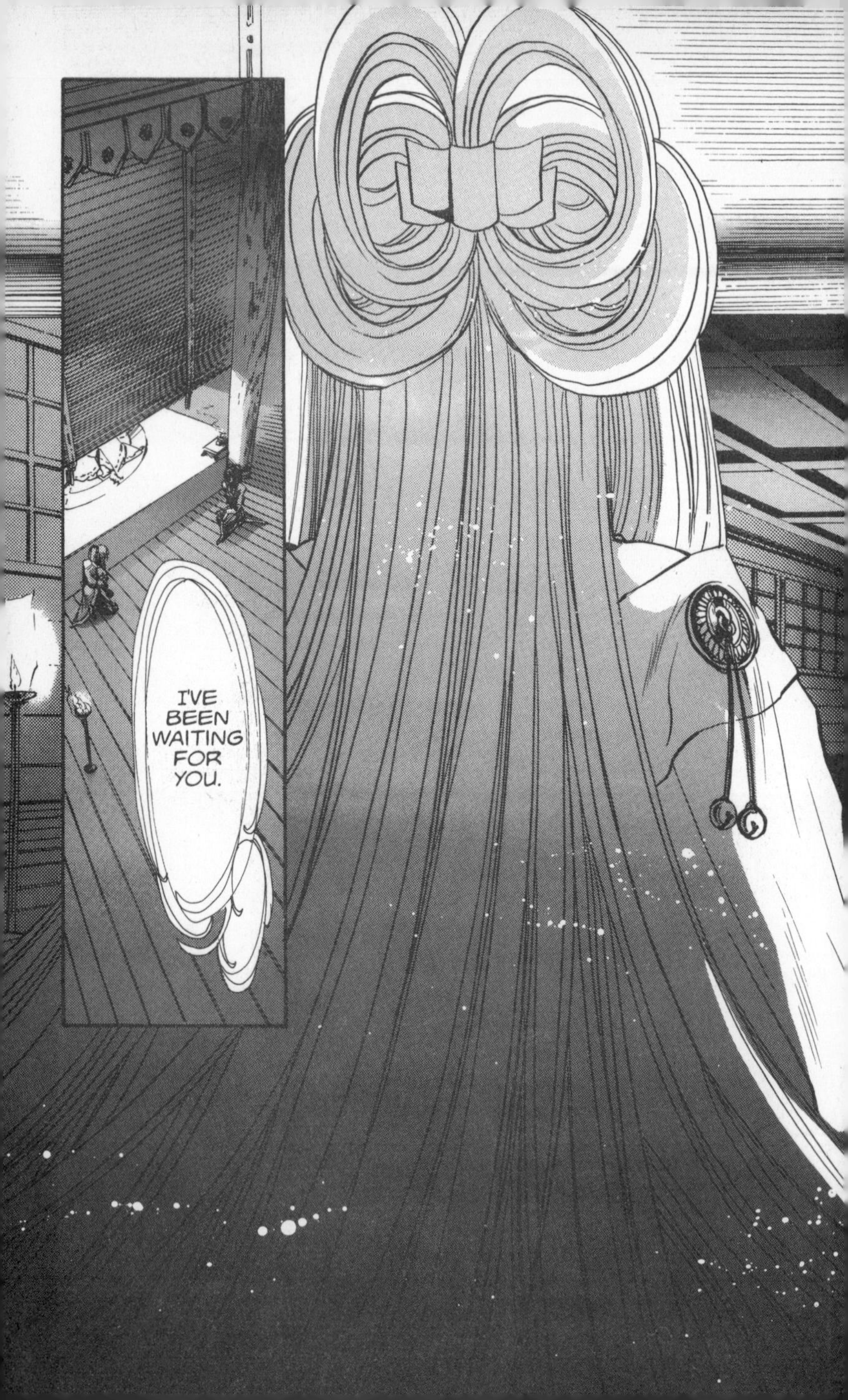
I'VE BEEN WAITING FOR YOU.

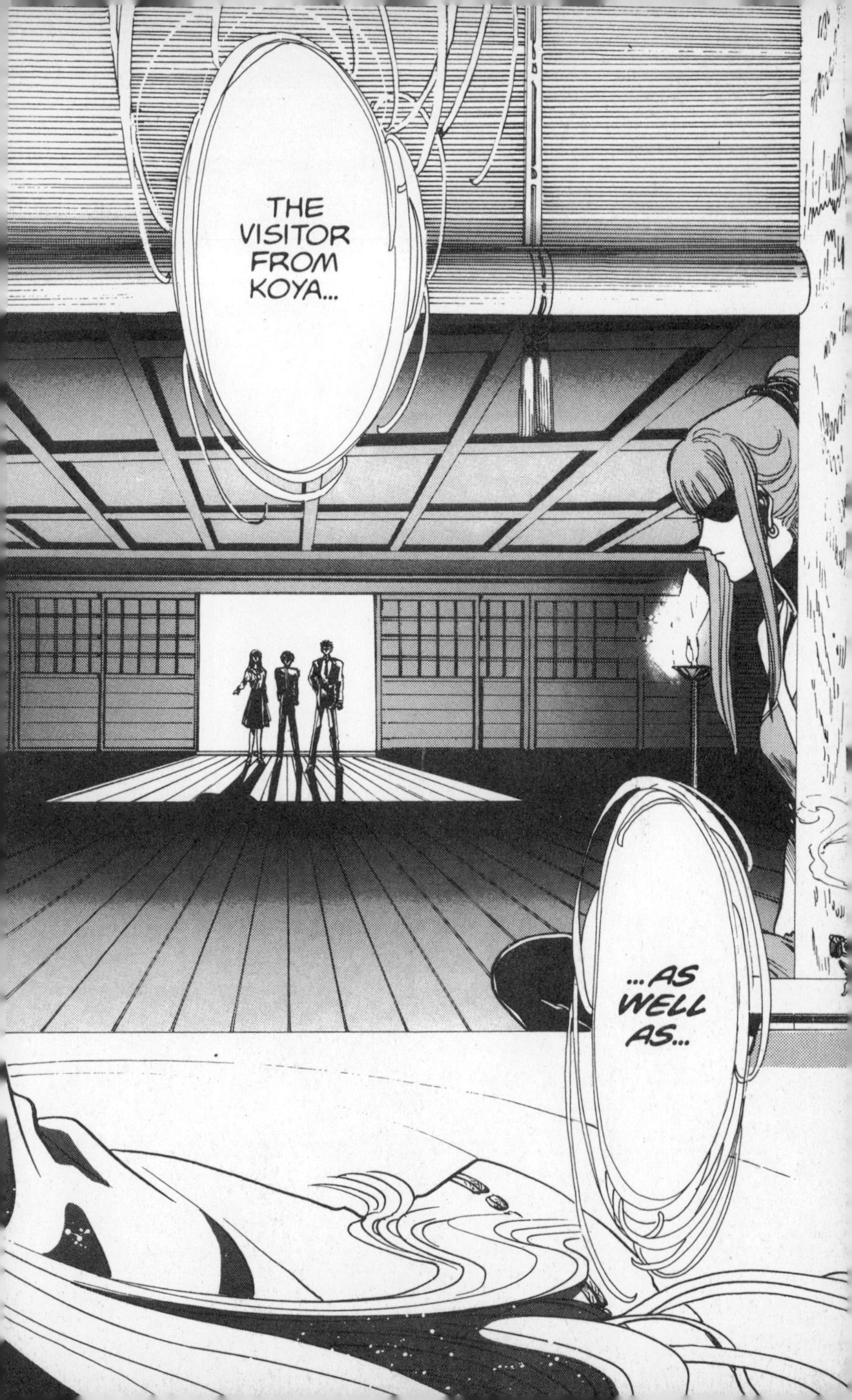
THE VISITOR FROM KOYA...
...AS WELL AS...

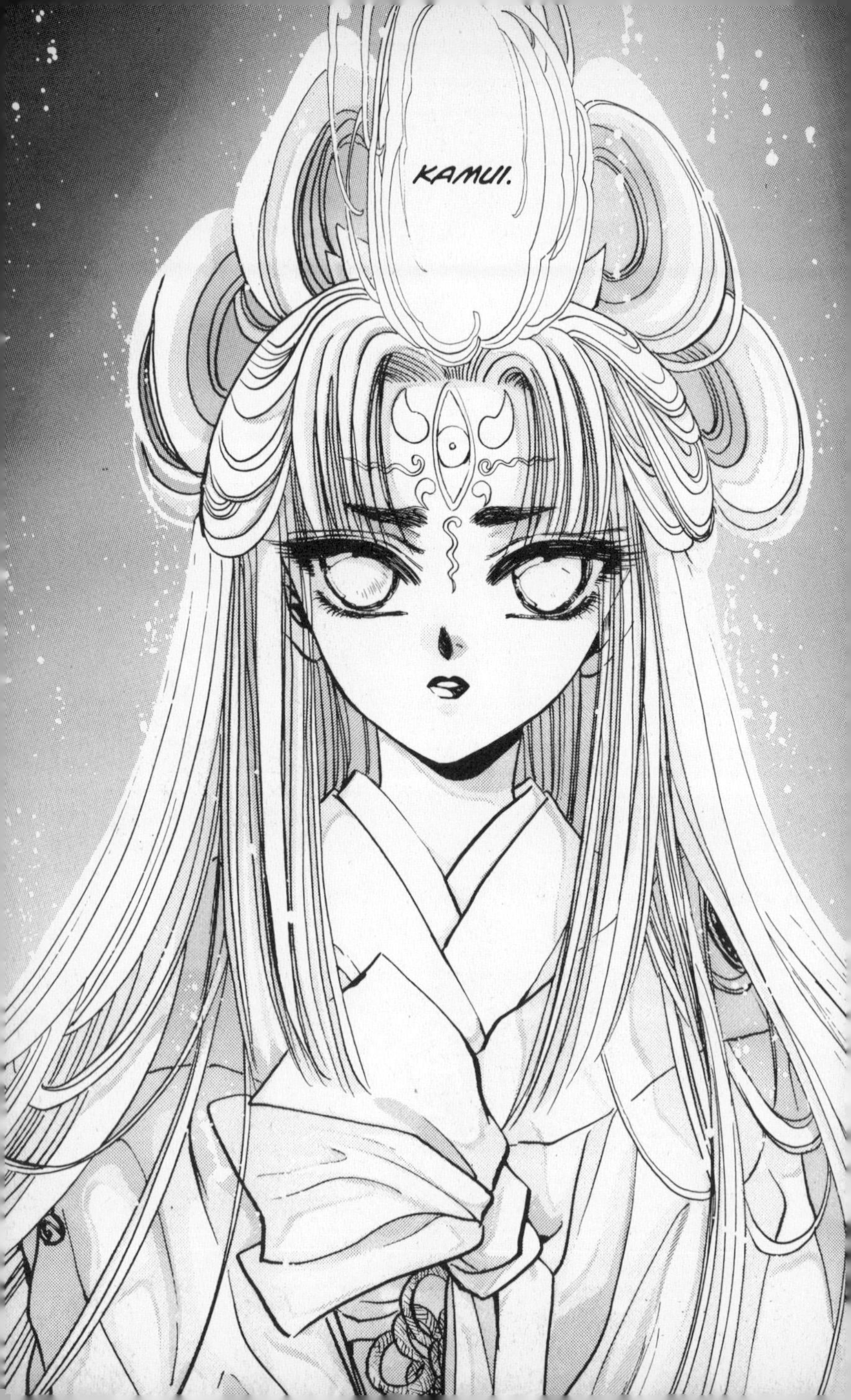
KAMUI.

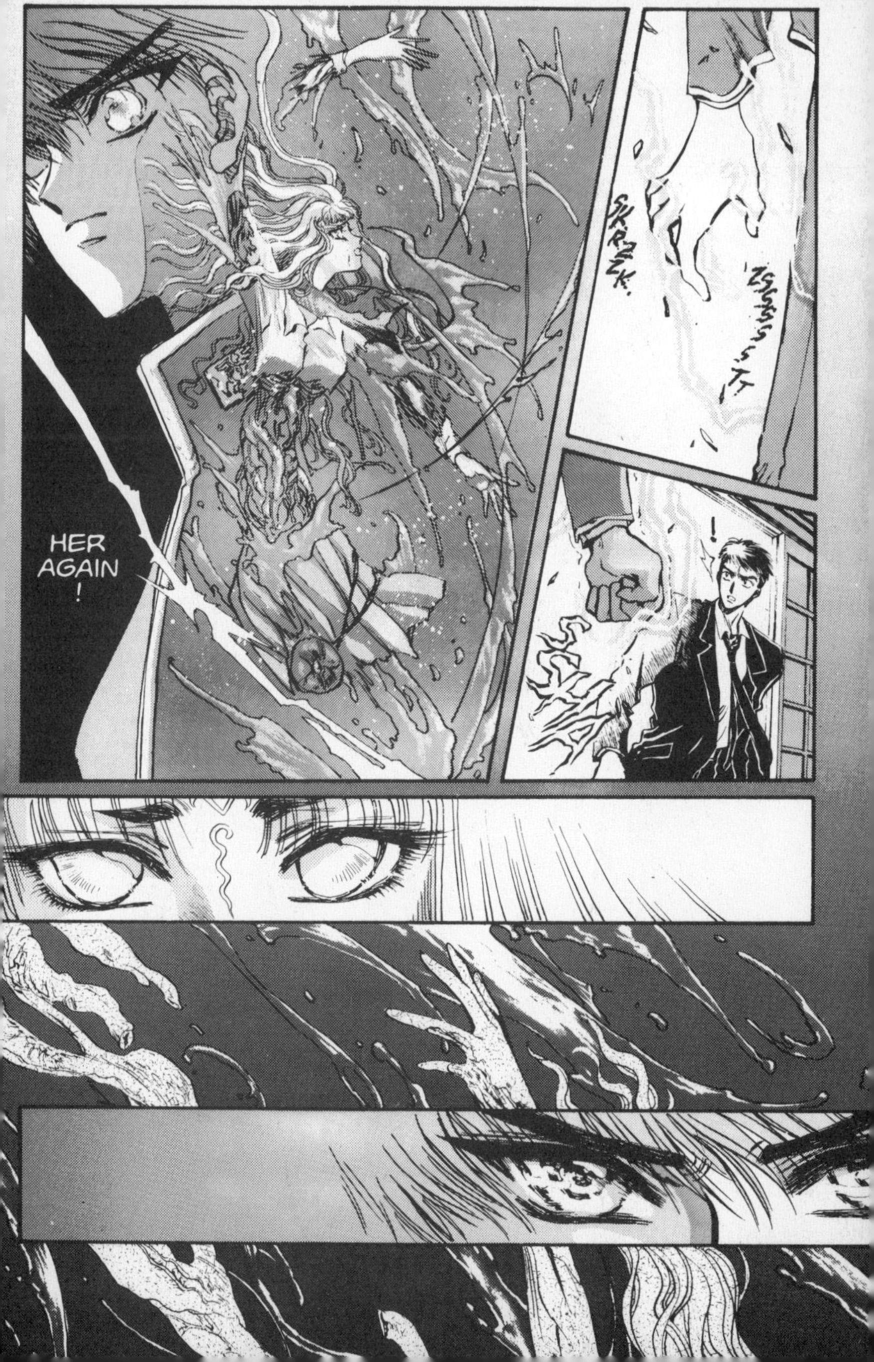
HER AGAIN !
SKRZZK!
ZSSSSSSTT!
!

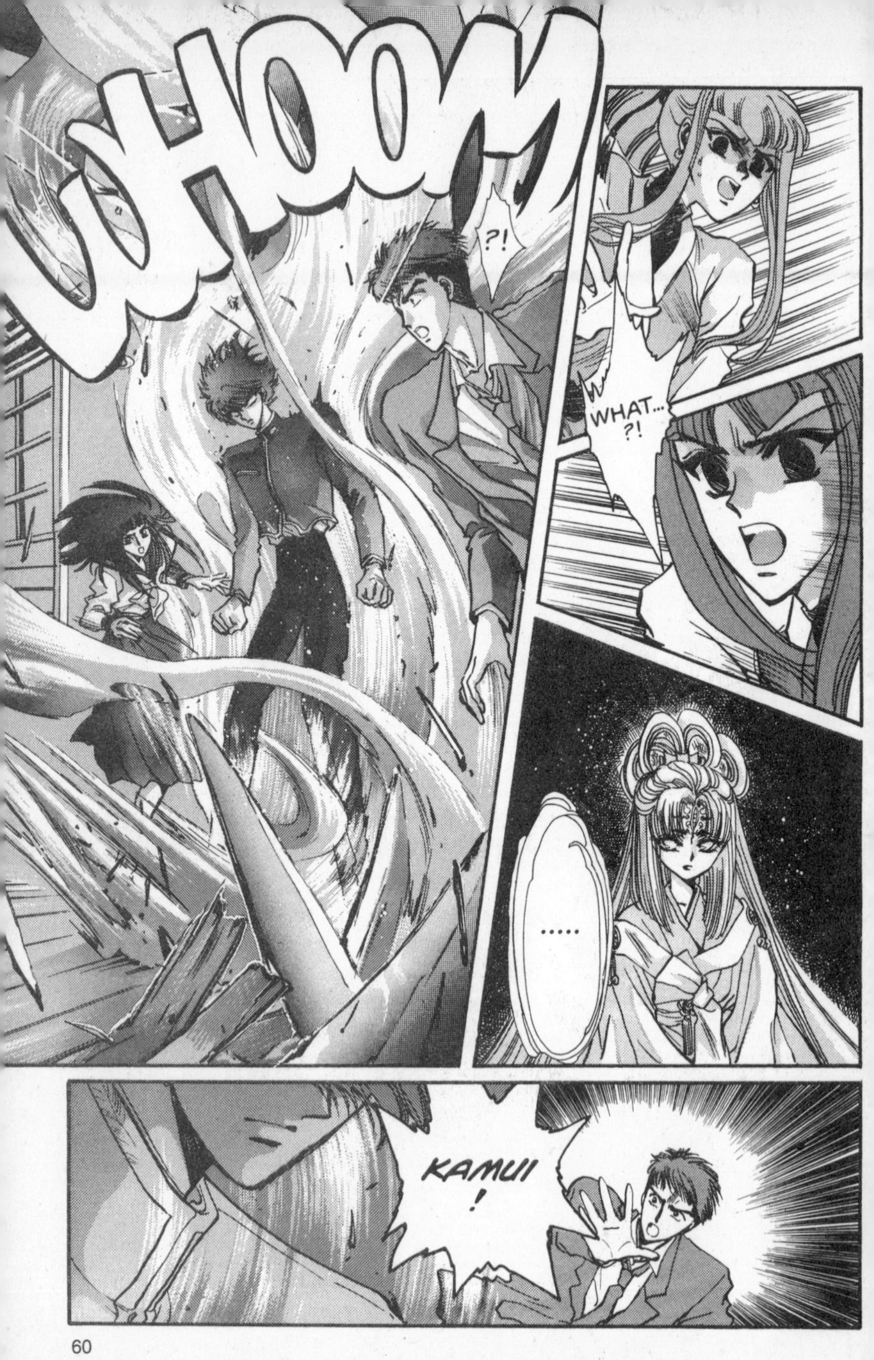
WHOOM
?!
WHAT... ?!
.....
KAMUI !

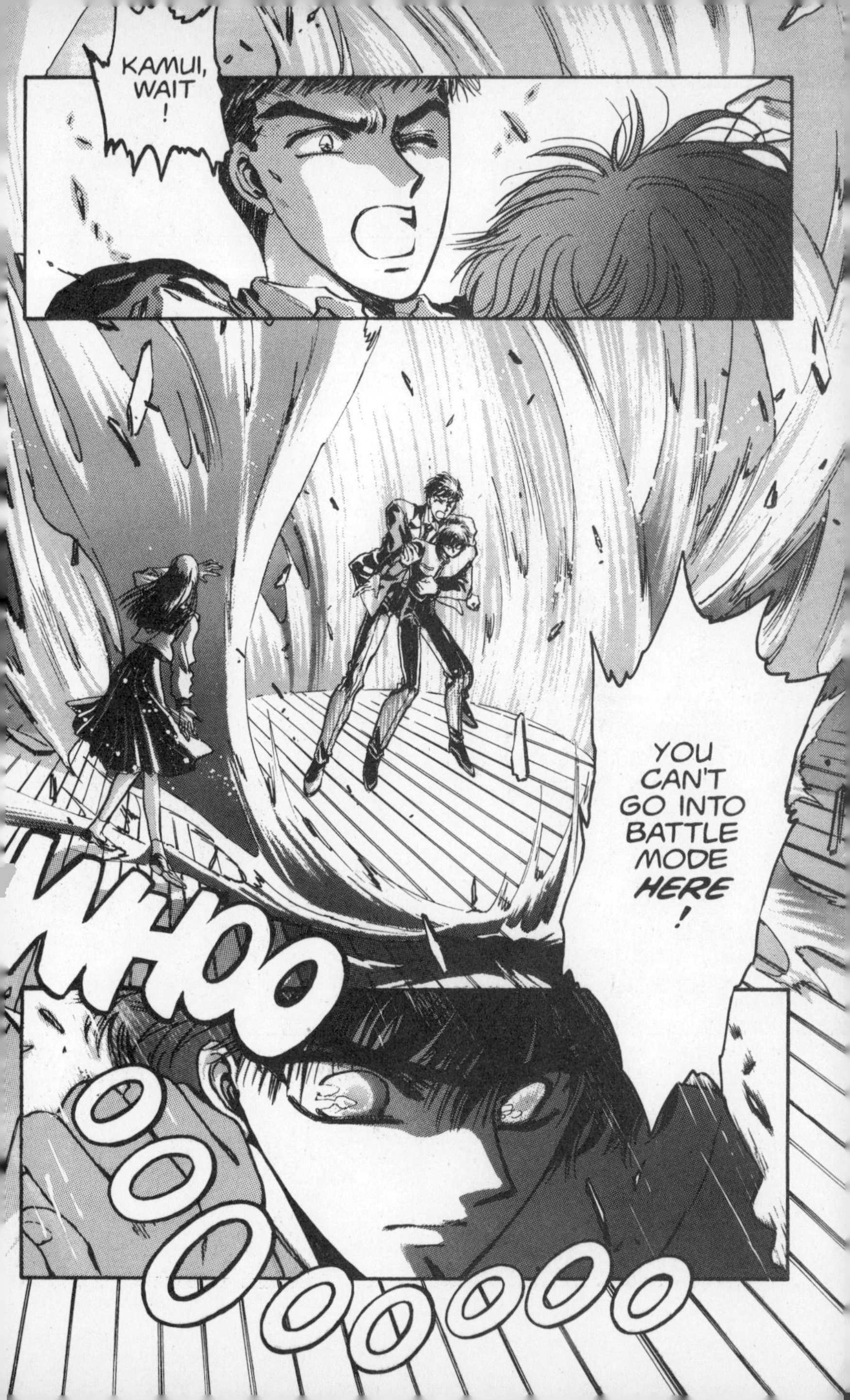
KAMUI, WAIT!
YOU CAN'T GO INTO BATTLE MODE HERE!
WHOOOOOOOOOOOOOO

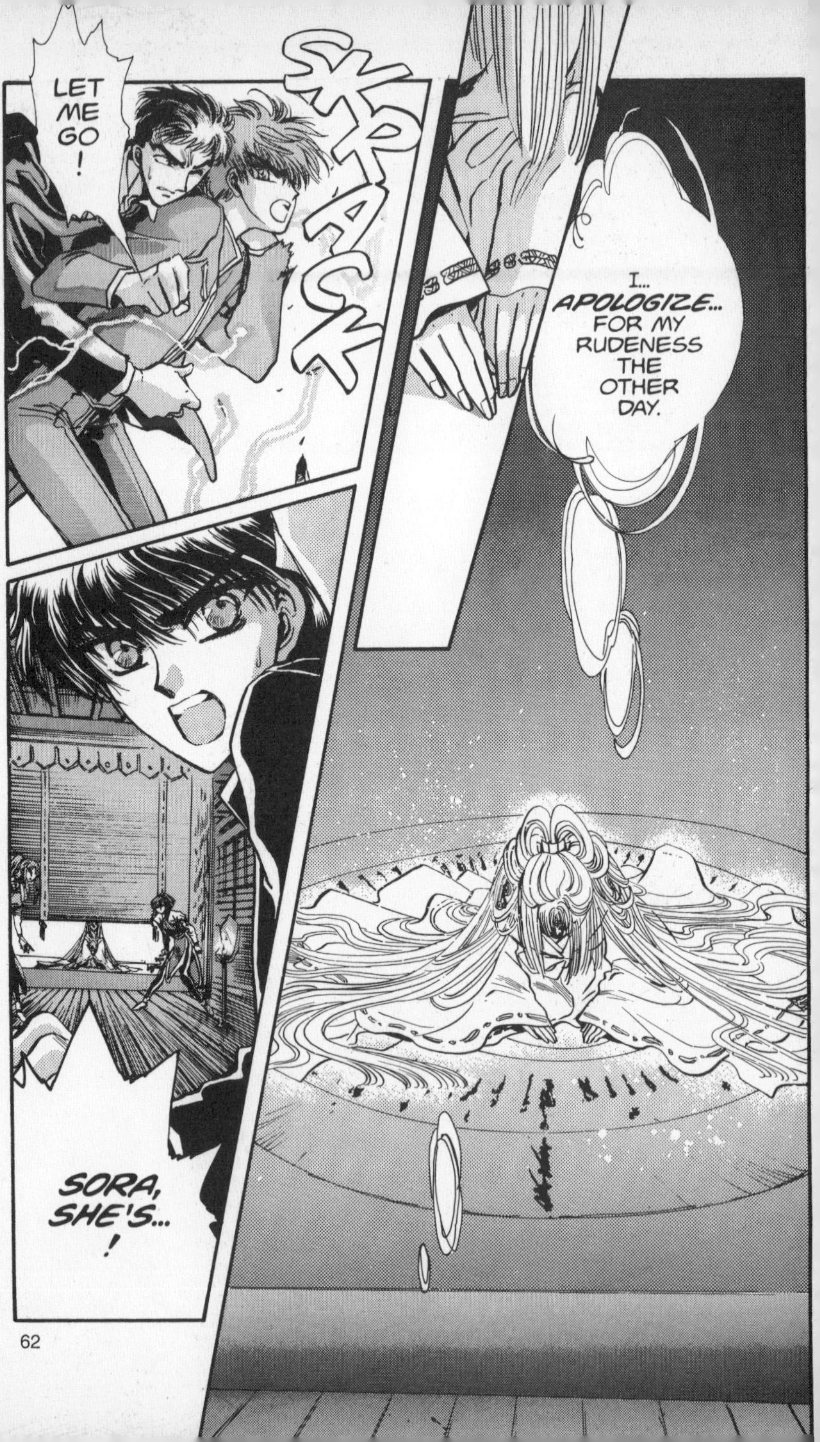
LET ME GO!
SKRACK
SORA, SHE'S... !
I... *APOLOGIZE...* FOR MY RUDENESS THE OTHER DAY.

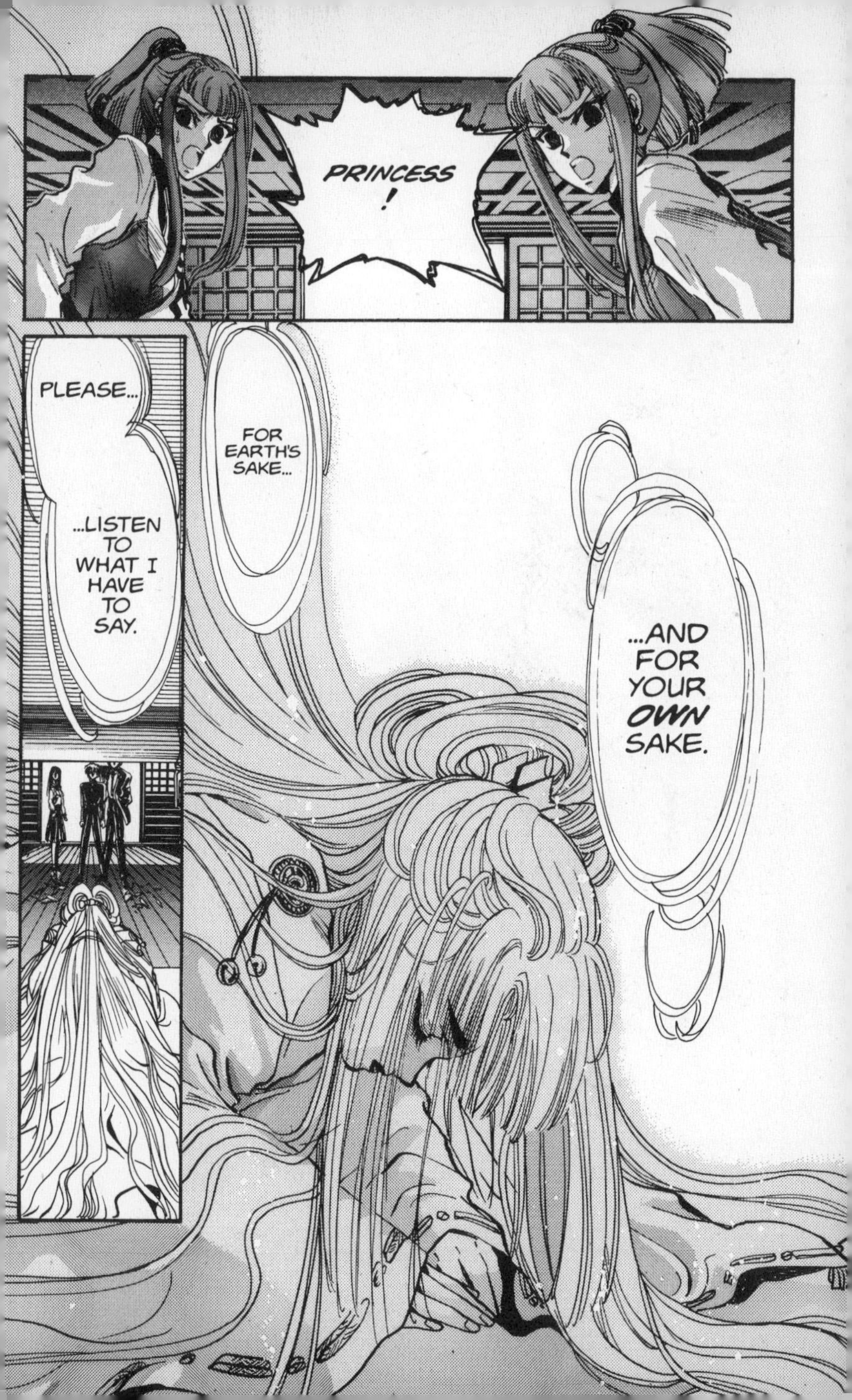
PRINCESS!
PLEASE...
...LISTEN TO WHAT I HAVE TO SAY.
FOR EARTH'S SAKE...
...AND FOR YOUR OWN SAKE.

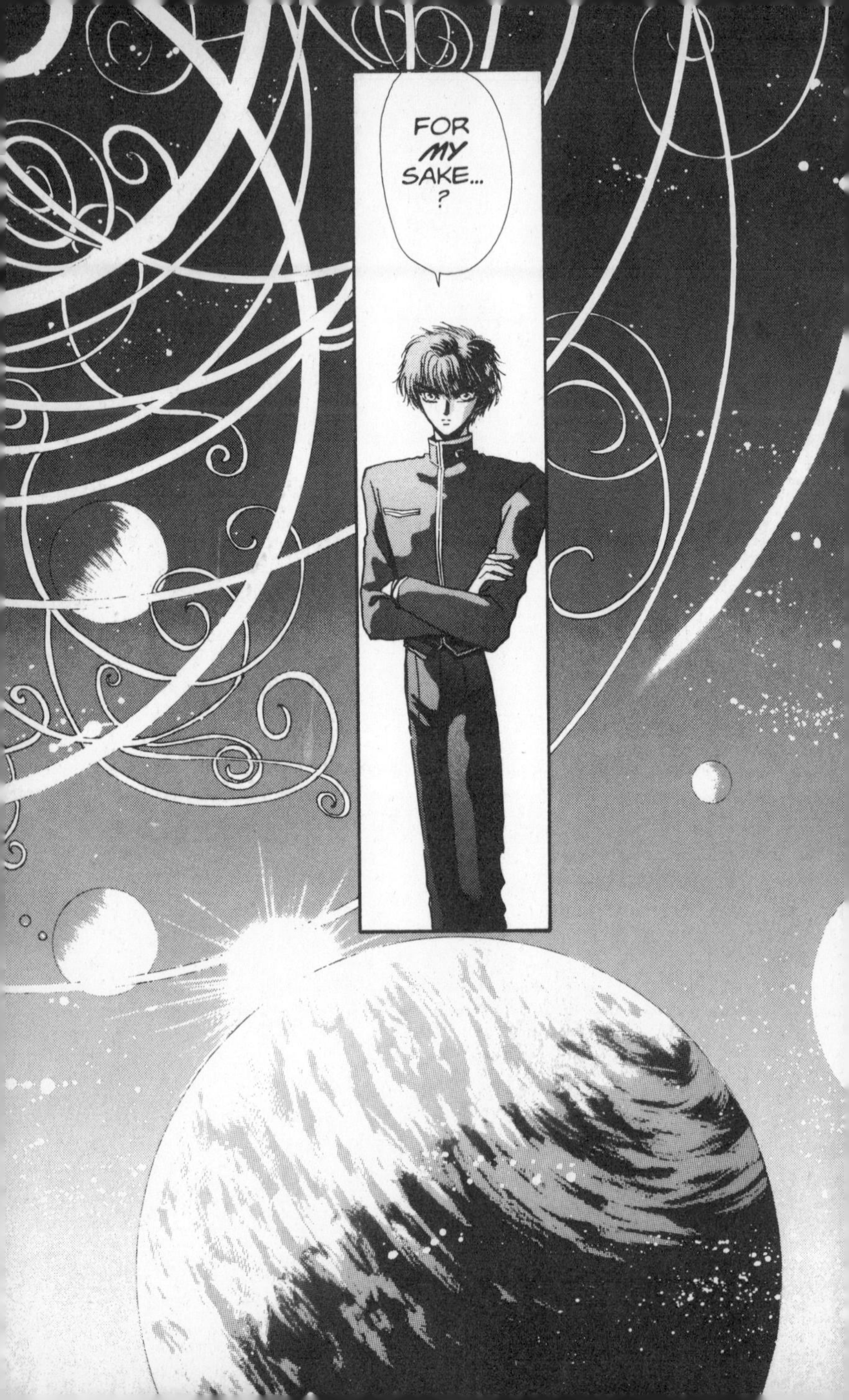
FOR MY SAKE... ?

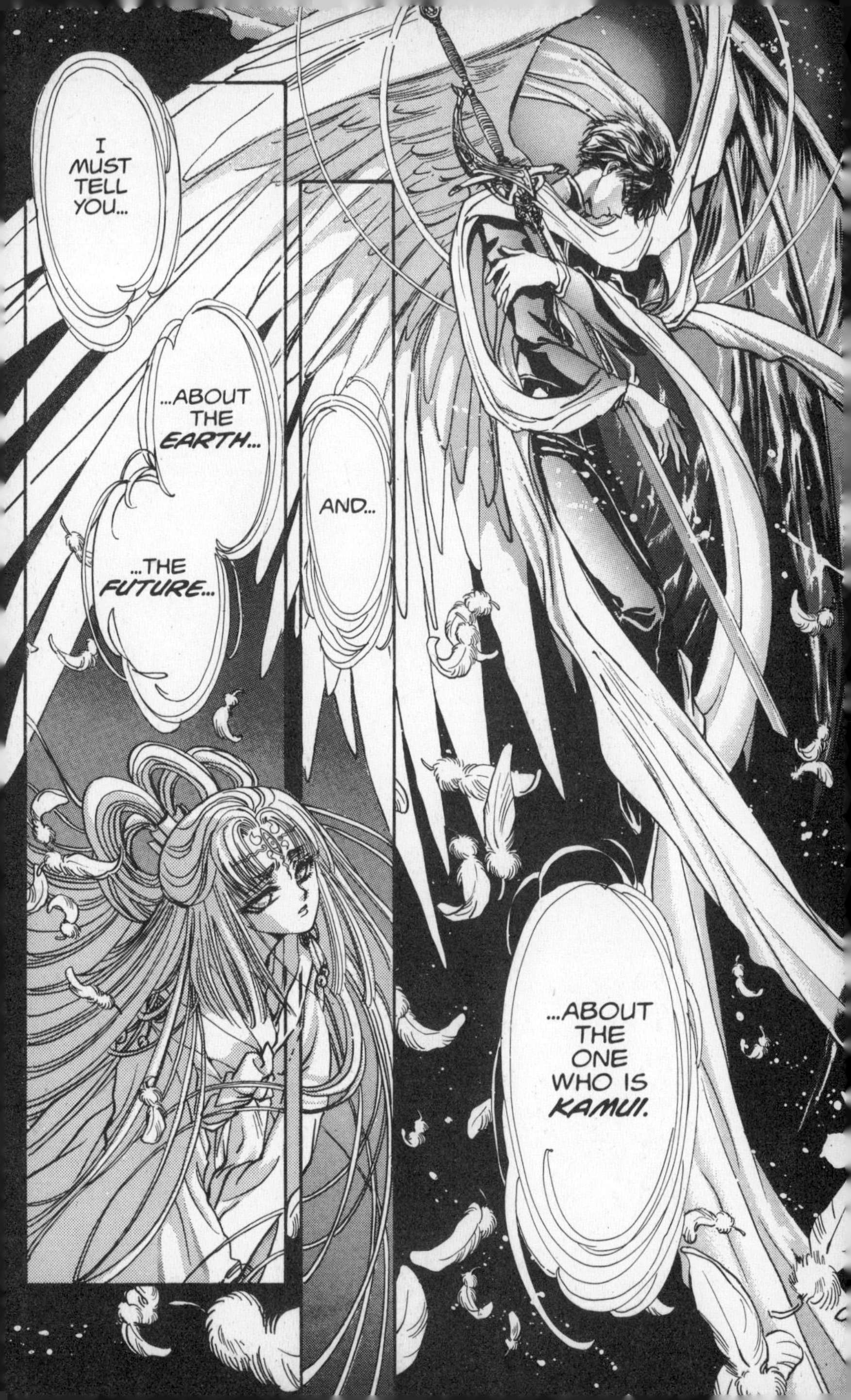
I MUST TELL YOU...
...ABOUT THE *EARTH*...
...THE *FUTURE*...
AND...
...ABOUT THE ONE WHO IS *KAMUI*.

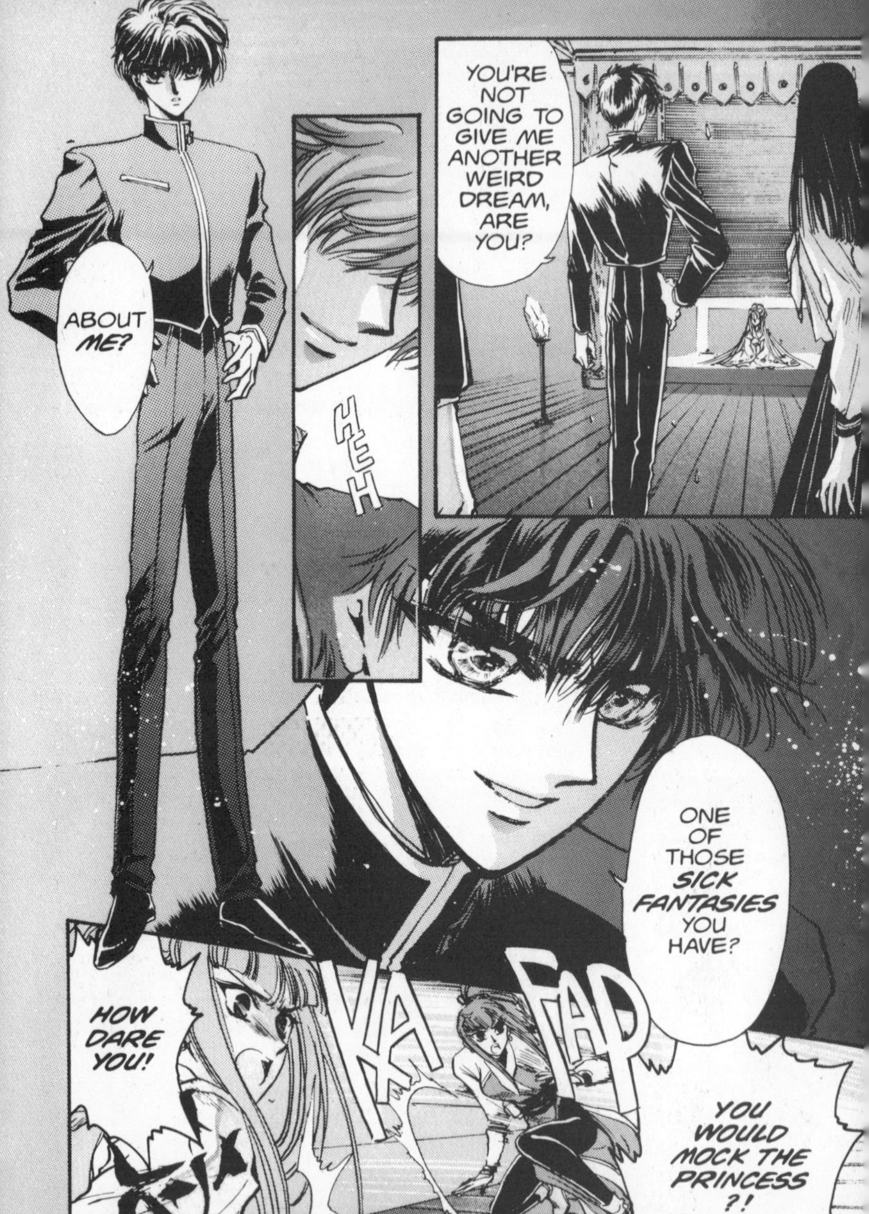
ABOUT ME?
HEH
YOU'RE NOT GOING TO GIVE ME ANOTHER WEIRD DREAM, ARE YOU?
ONE OF THOSE SICK FANTASIES YOU HAVE?
HOW DARE YOU!
KA FAP
YOU WOULD MOCK THE PRINCESS?!

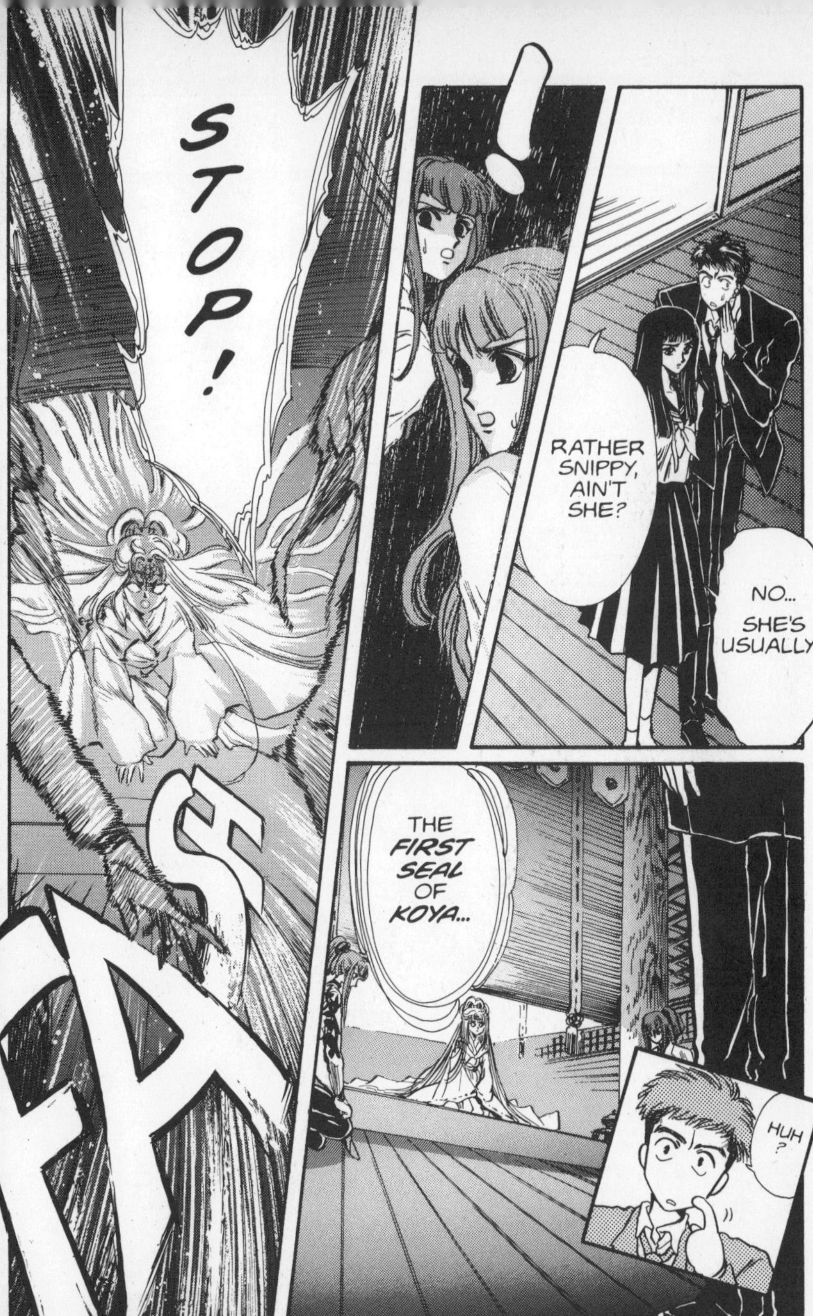
RATHER SNIPPY, AIN'T SHE?
NO... SHE'S USUALLY...
!
THE *FIRST SEAL* OF *KOYA*...
HUH?
STOP!

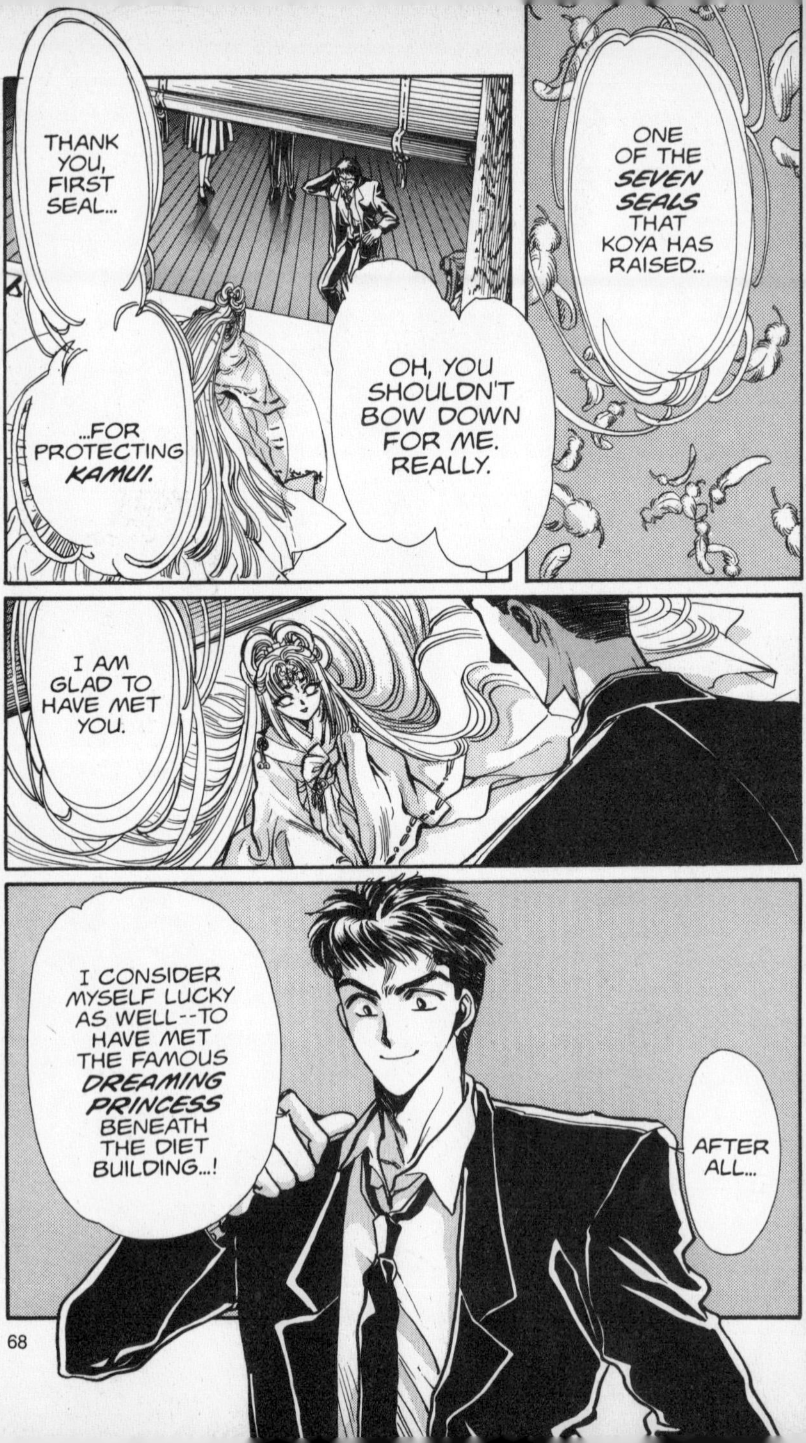
THANK YOU, FIRST SEAL...
...FOR PROTECTING *KAMUI.*
OH, YOU SHOULDN'T BOW DOWN FOR ME. REALLY.
ONE OF THE *SEVEN SEALS* THAT KOYA HAS RAISED...
I AM GLAD TO HAVE MET YOU.
I CONSIDER MYSELF LUCKY AS WELL--TO HAVE MET THE FAMOUS *DREAMING PRINCESS* BENEATH THE DIET BUILDING...!
AFTER ALL...

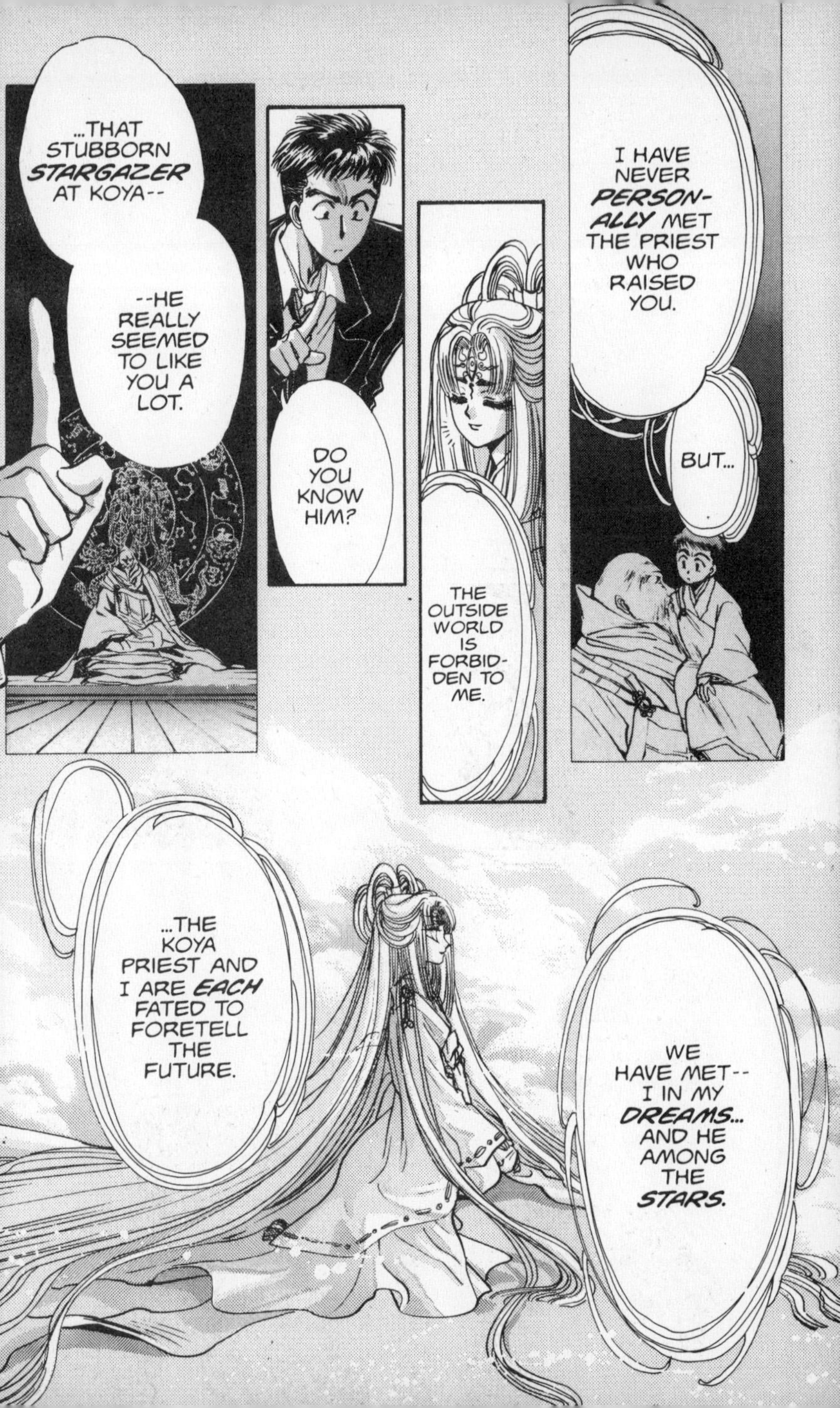
...THAT STUBBORN STARGAZER AT KOYA--
--HE REALLY SEEMED TO LIKE YOU A LOT.
DO YOU KNOW HIM?
THE OUTSIDE WORLD IS FORBIDDEN TO ME.
I HAVE NEVER PERSONALLY MET THE PRIEST WHO RAISED YOU.
BUT...
...THE KOYA PRIEST AND I ARE EACH FATED TO FORETELL THE FUTURE.
WE HAVE MET-- I IN MY DREAMS... AND HE AMONG THE STARS.

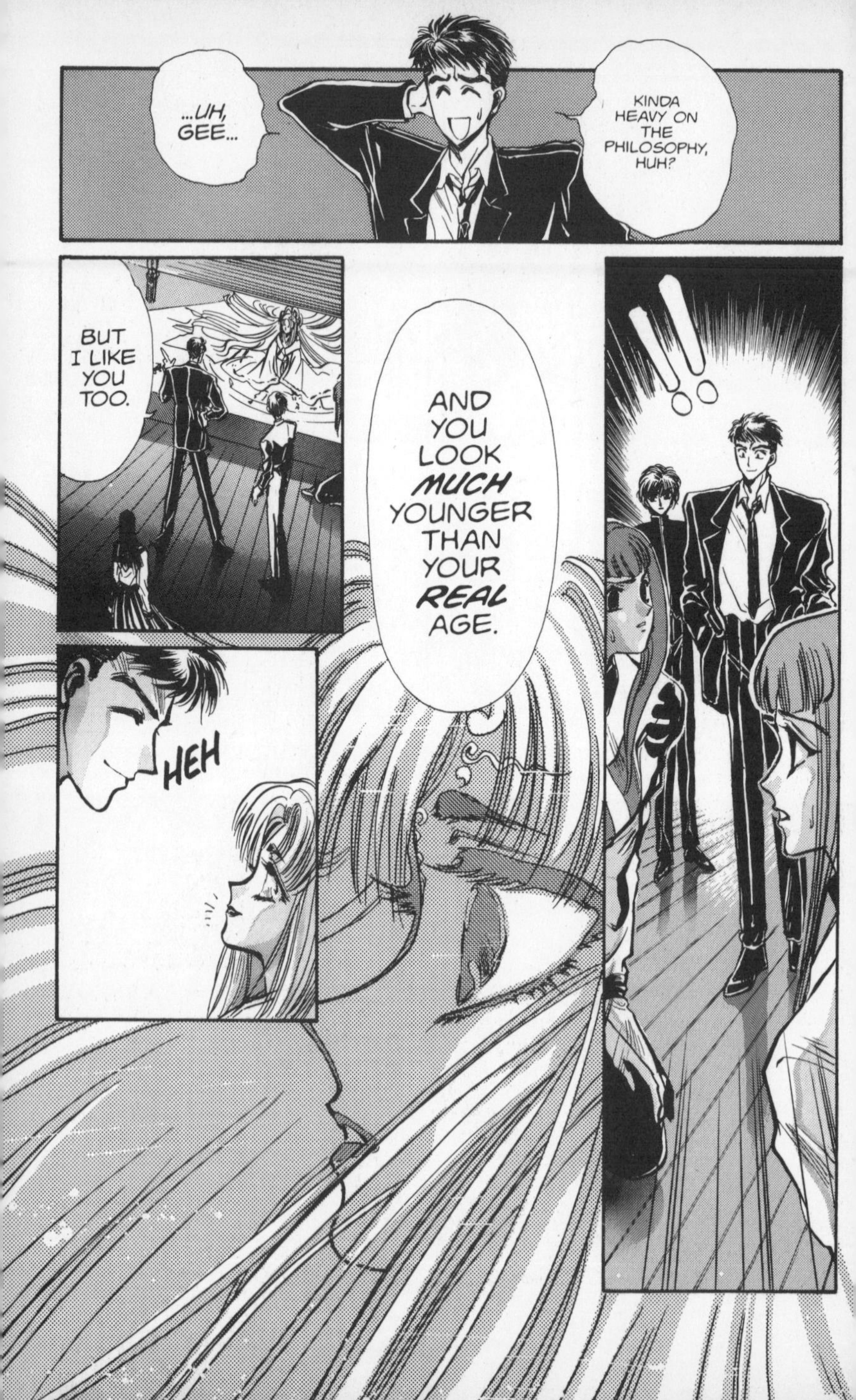
...UH, GEE...
KINDA HEAVY ON THE PHILOSOPHY, HUH?
BUT I LIKE YOU TOO.
HEH
AND YOU LOOK *MUCH* YOUNGER THAN YOUR *REAL* AGE.
!!

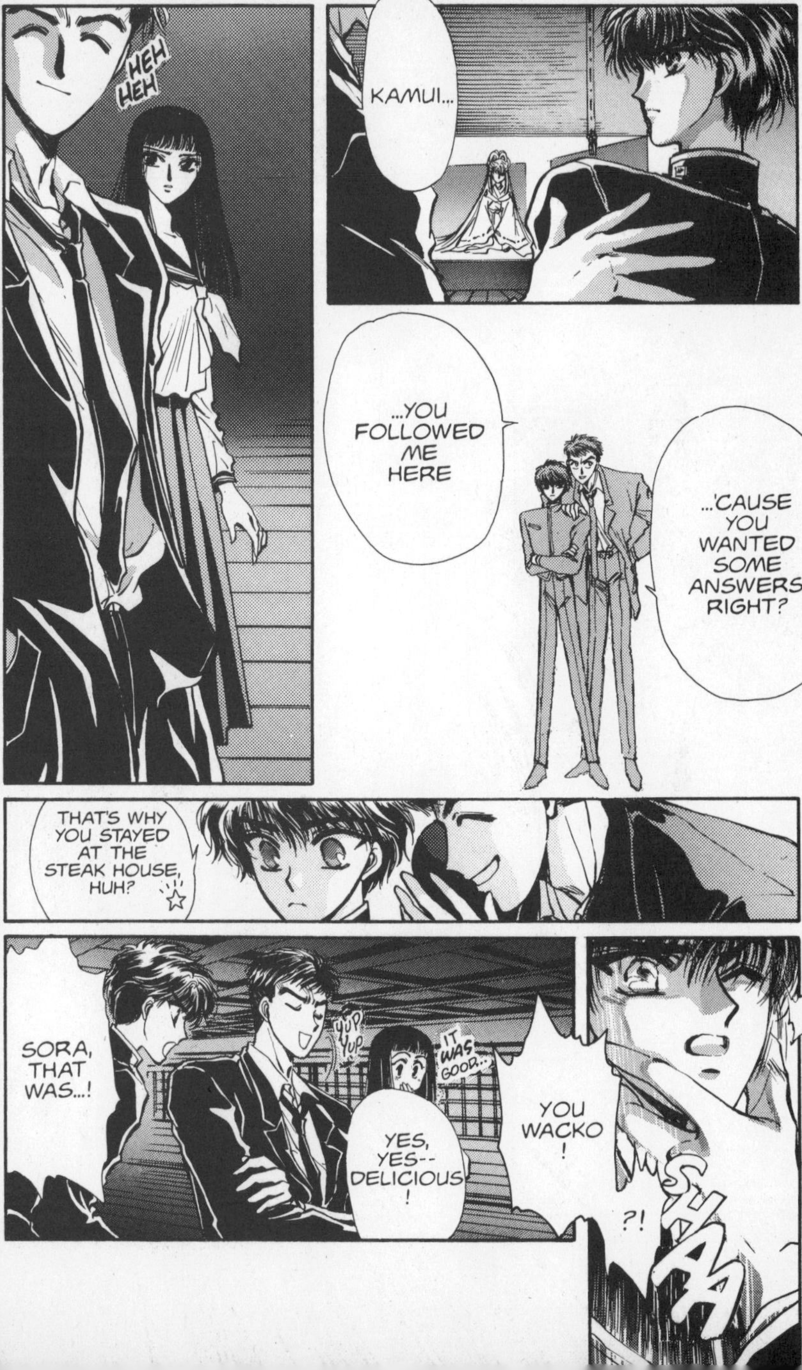
HEH HEH
KAMUI...
...YOU FOLLOWED ME HERE
...'CAUSE YOU WANTED SOME ANSWERS, RIGHT?
THAT'S WHY YOU STAYED AT THE STEAK HOUSE, HUH?
SORA, THAT WAS...!
YUP YUP
IT WAS GOOD...
YES, YES-- DELICIOUS!
YOU WACKO!
?!

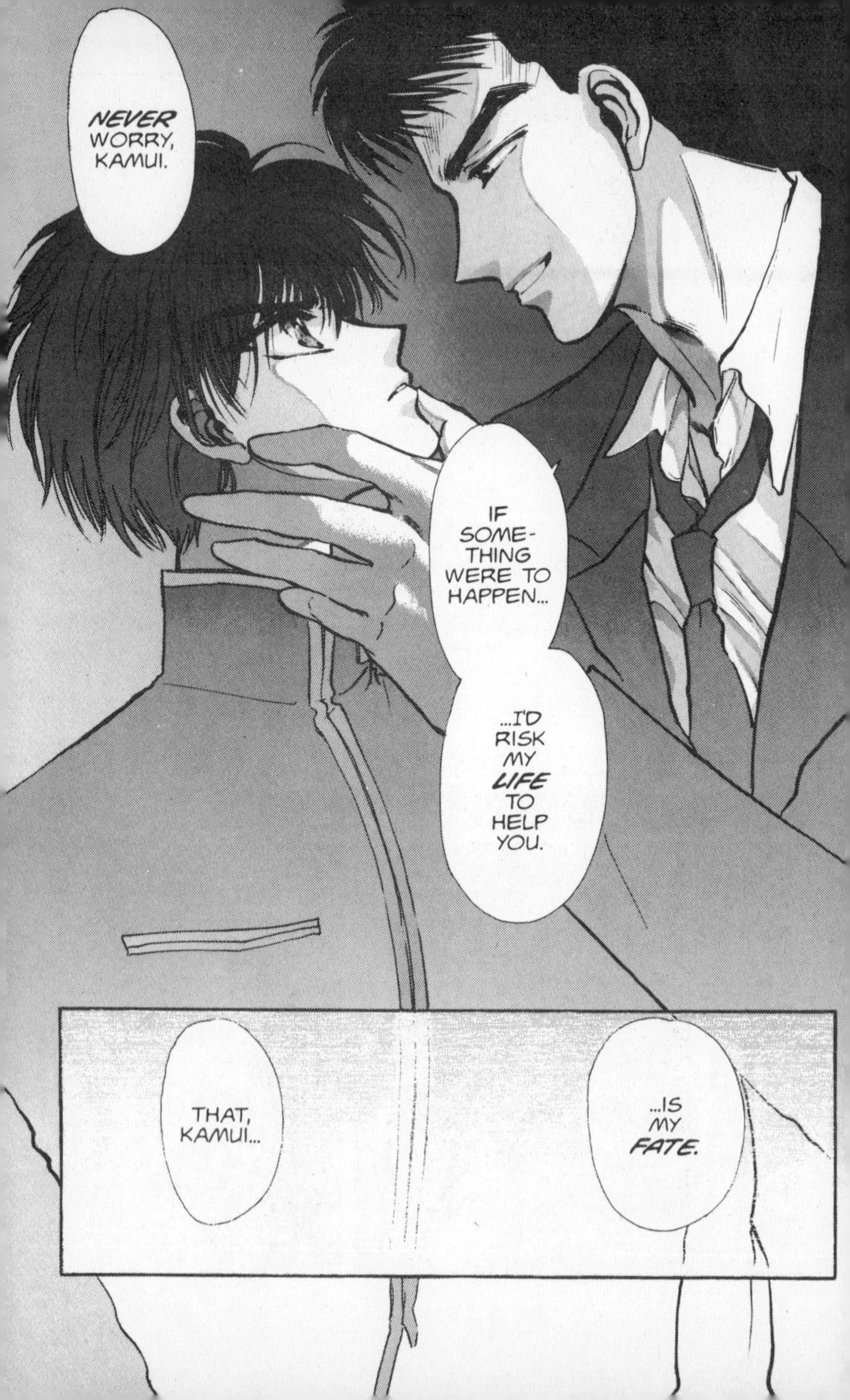
NEVER WORRY, KAMUI.
IF SOME-THING WERE TO HAPPEN...
...I'D RISK MY LIFE TO HELP YOU.
THAT, KAMUI...
...IS MY FATE.

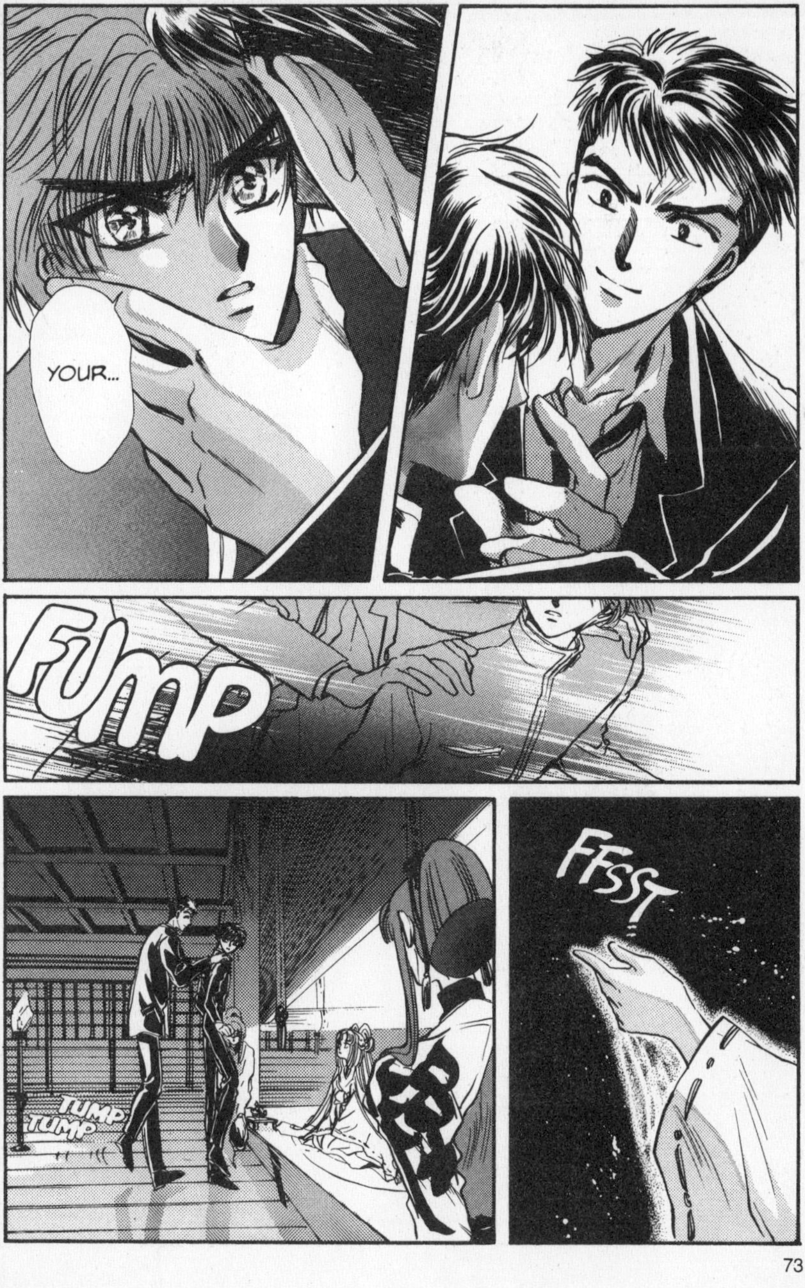
YOUR...
FUMP
TUMP
TUMP
FFSST

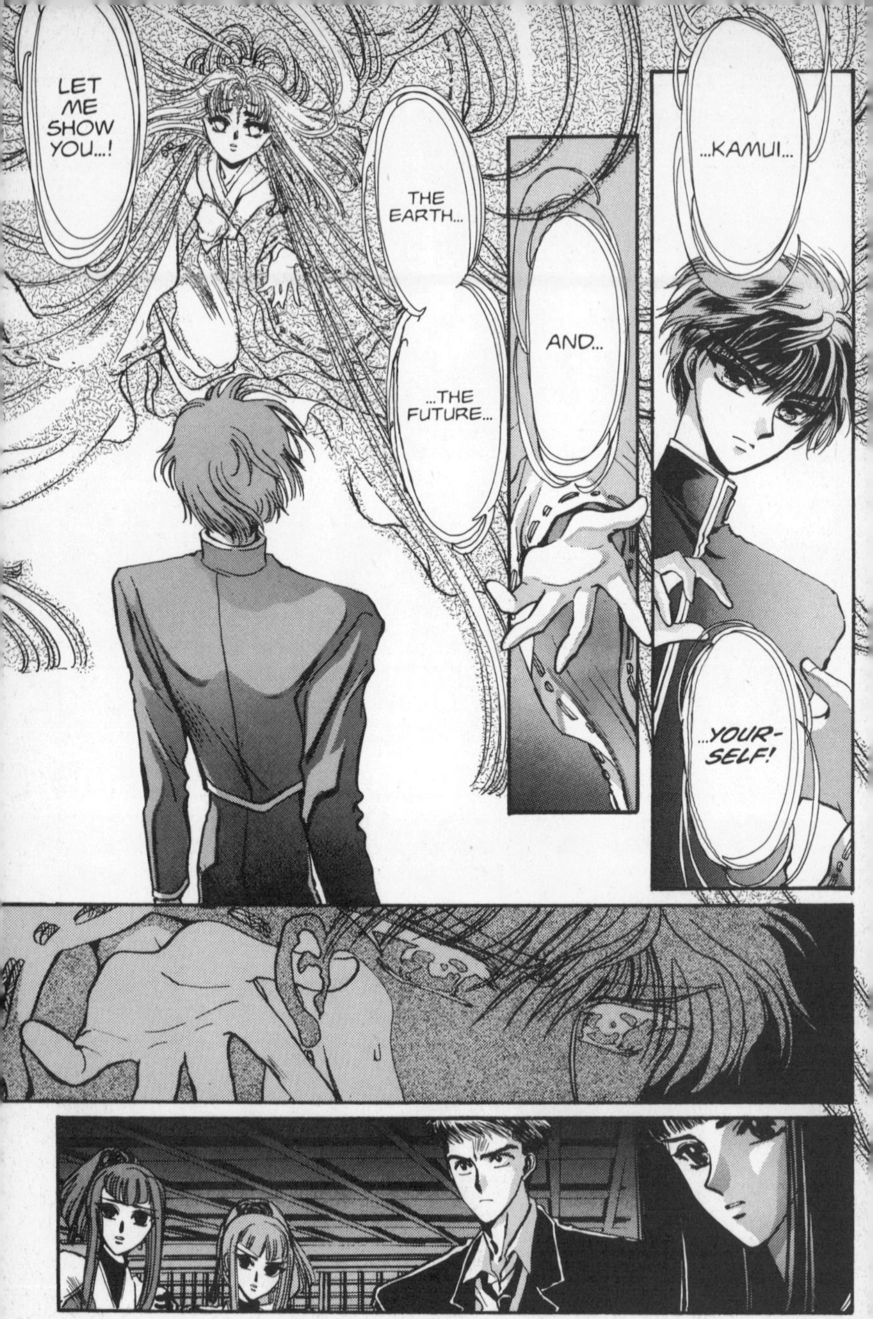
LET ME SHOW YOU...!
THE EARTH...
...THE FUTURE...
AND...
...KAMUI...
...YOUR-SELF!

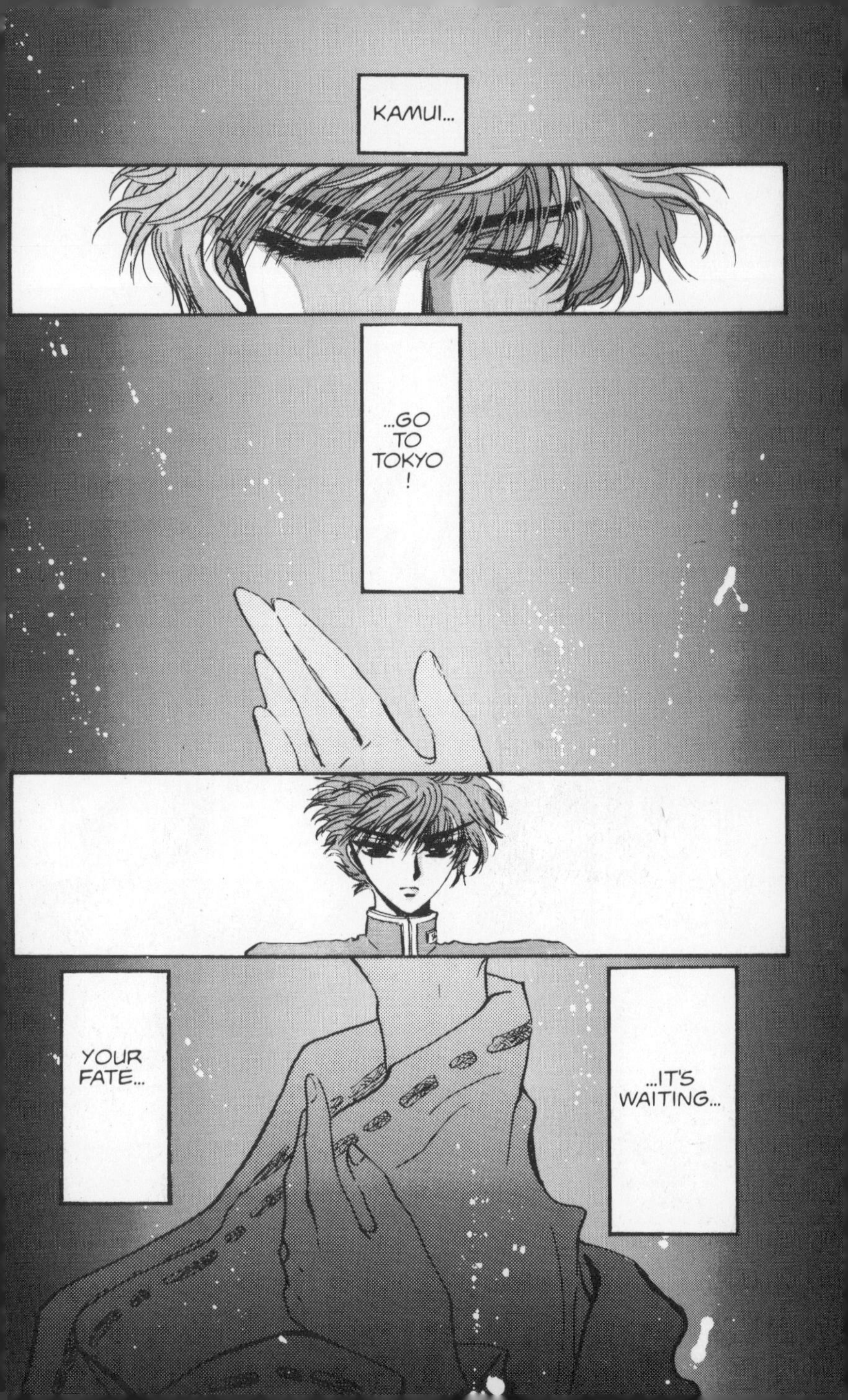
KAMUI...
...GO TO TOKYO!
YOUR FATE...
...IT'S WAITING...

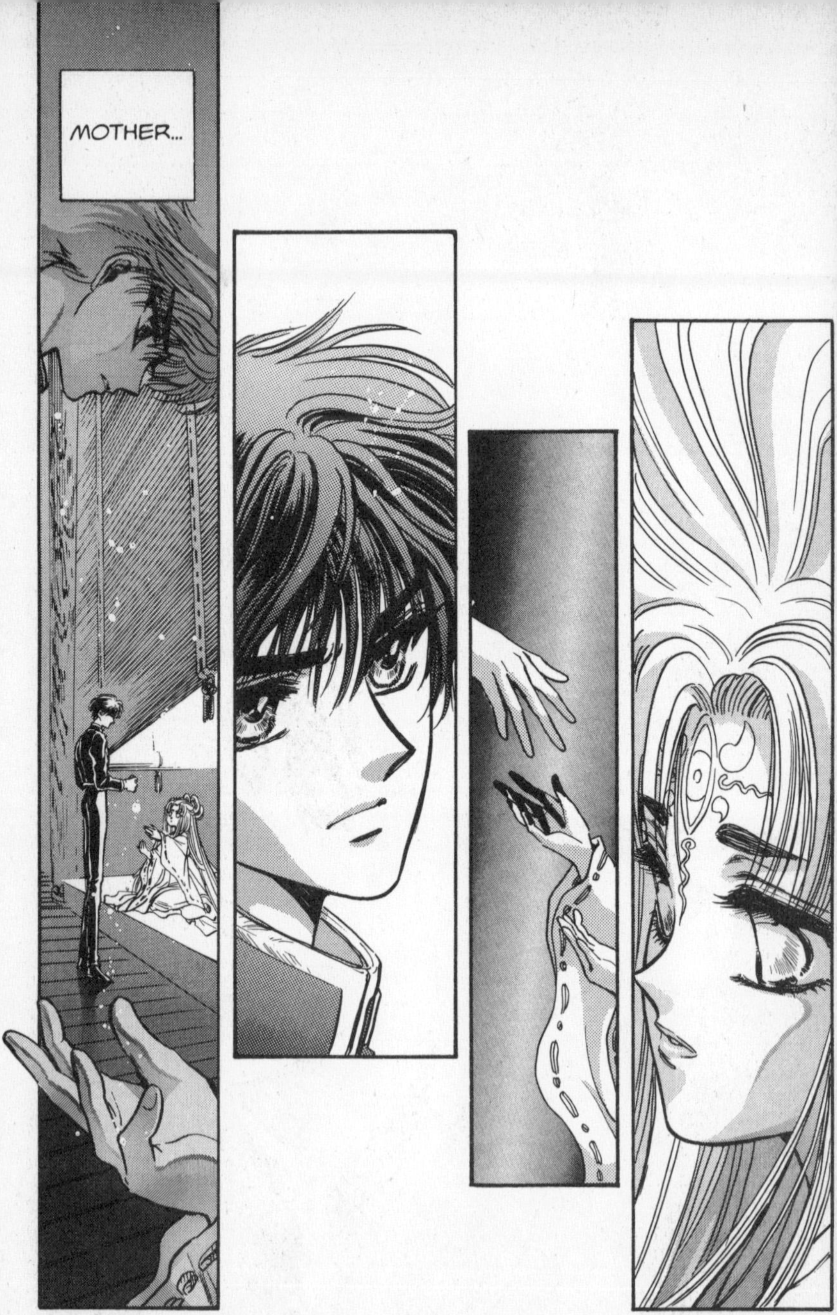
MOTHER...

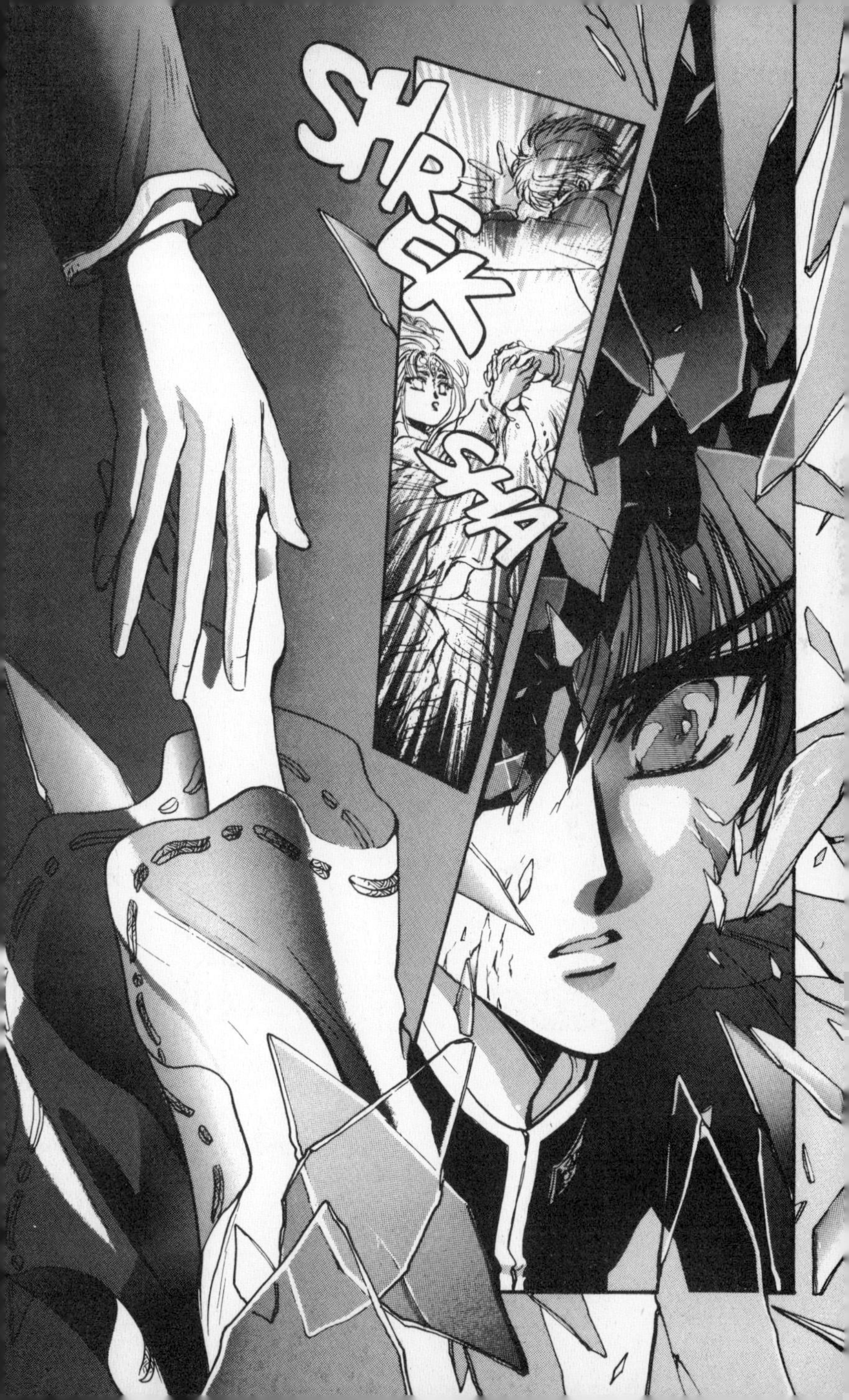
SHREK
SHA

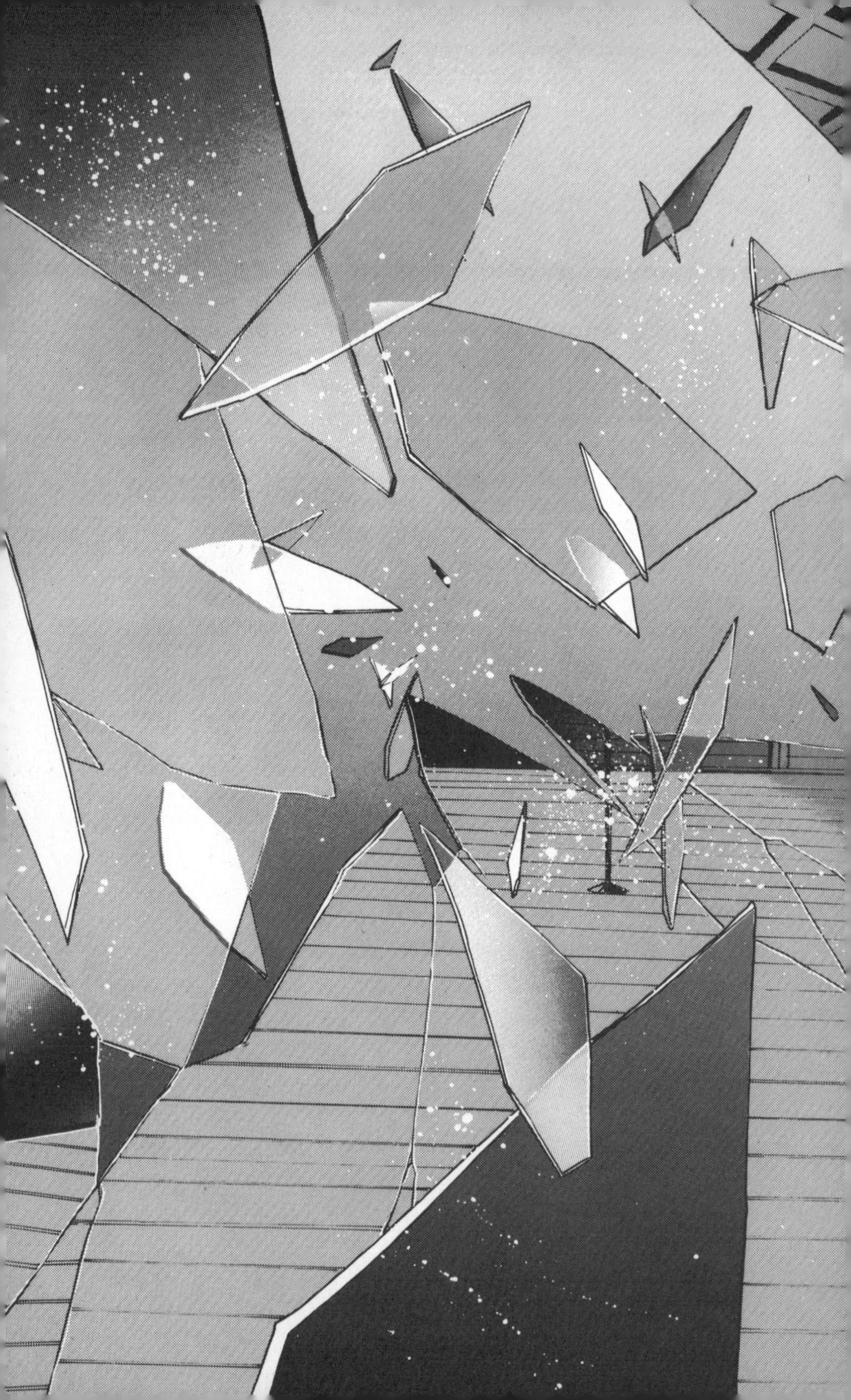

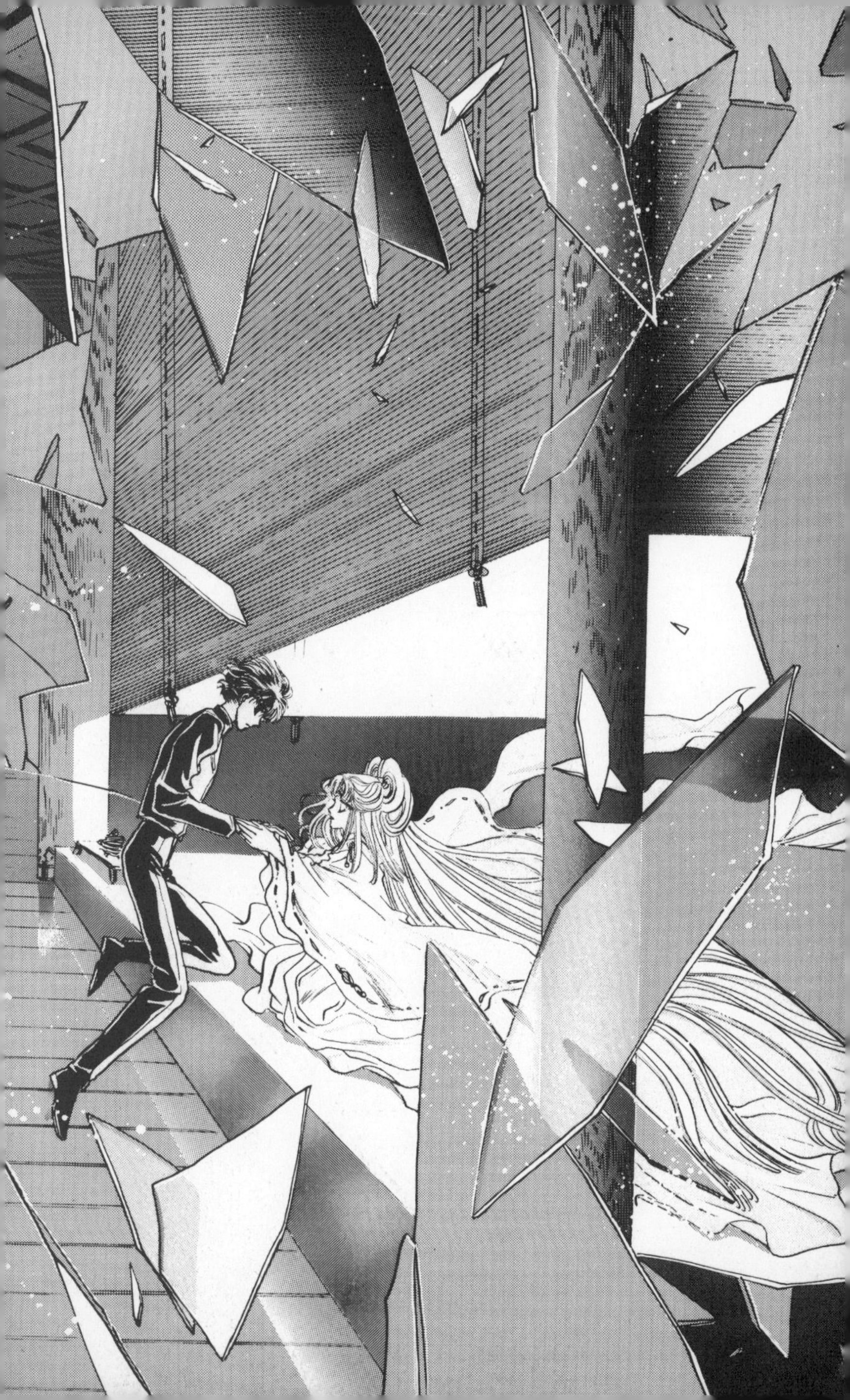

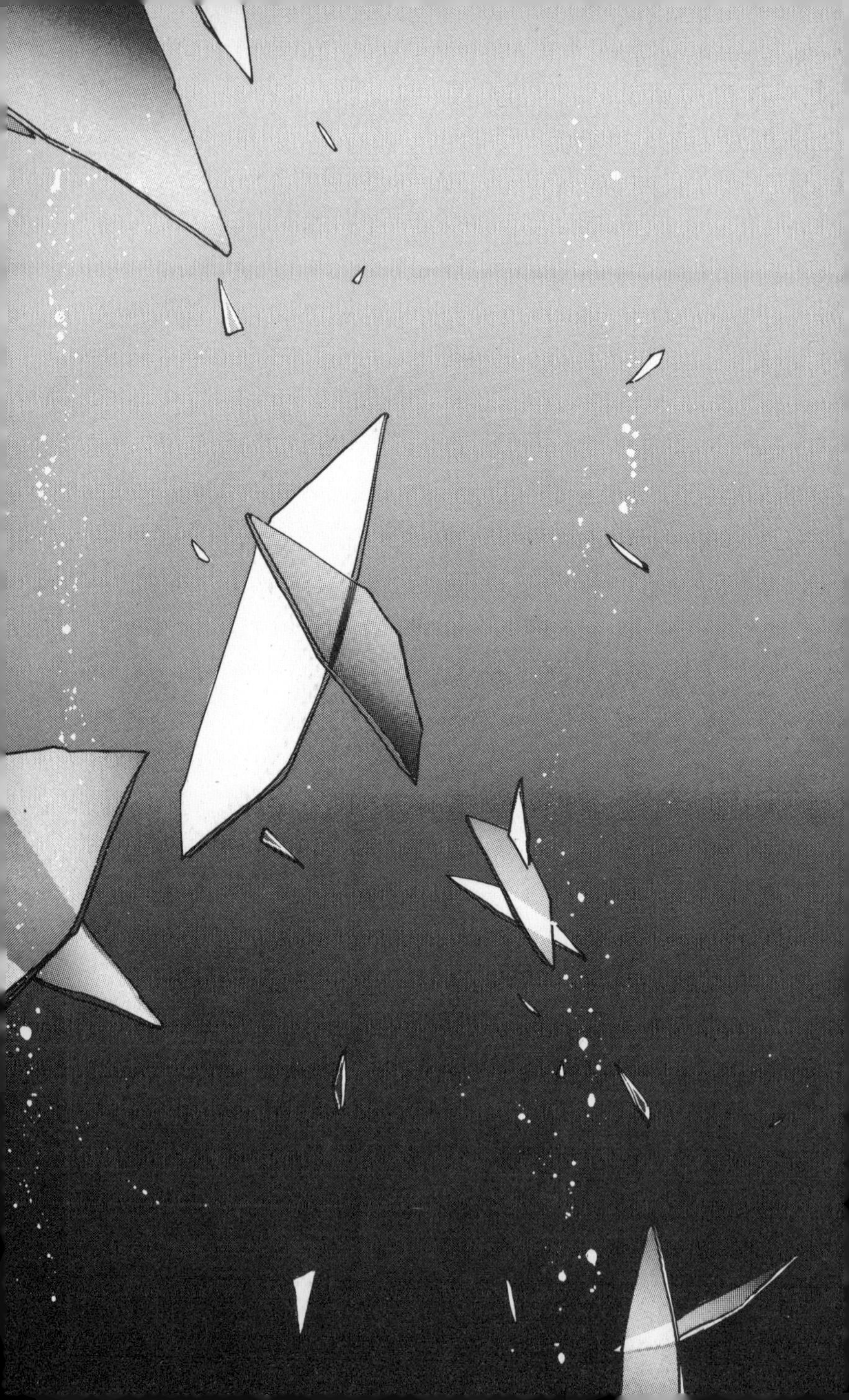

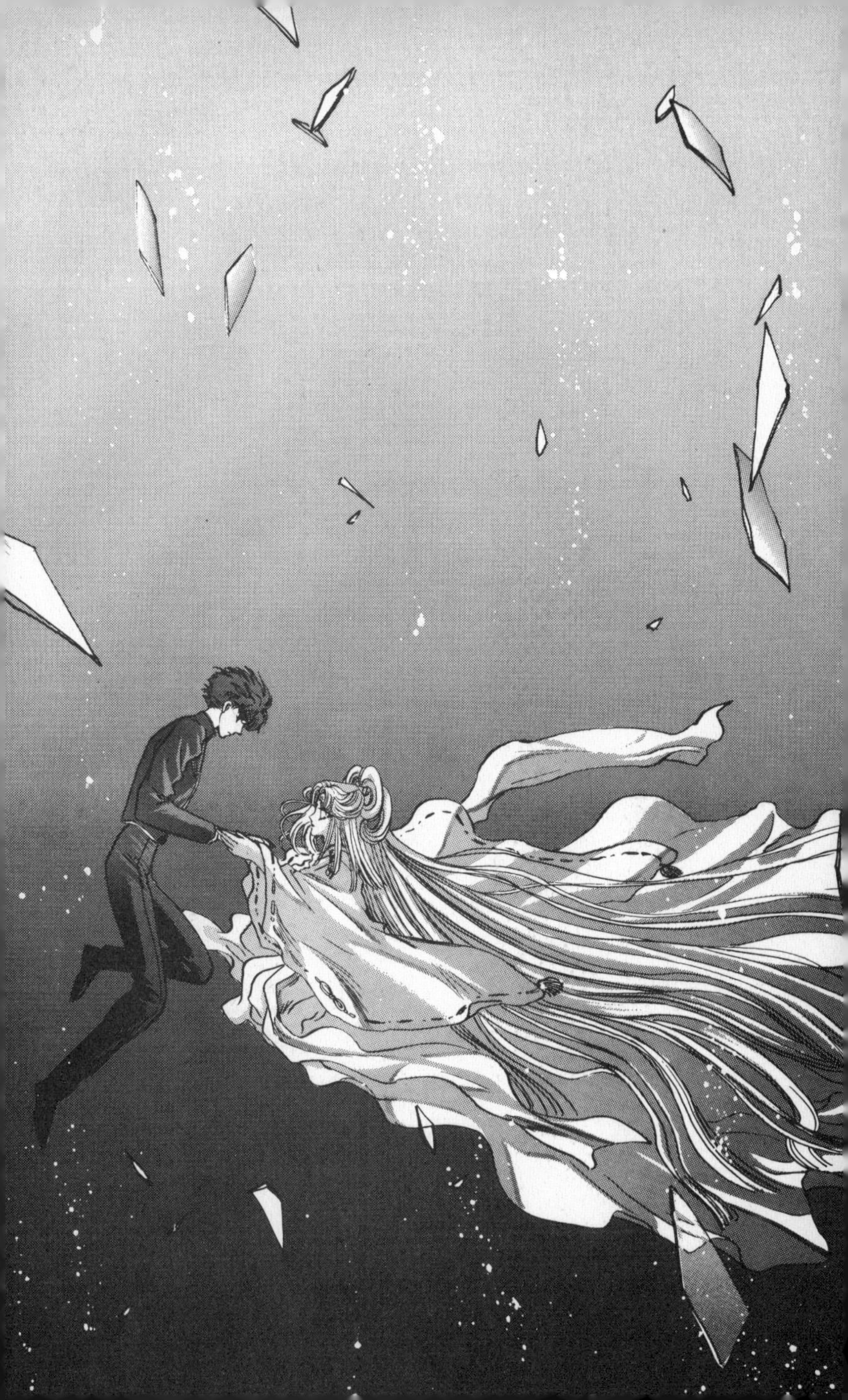

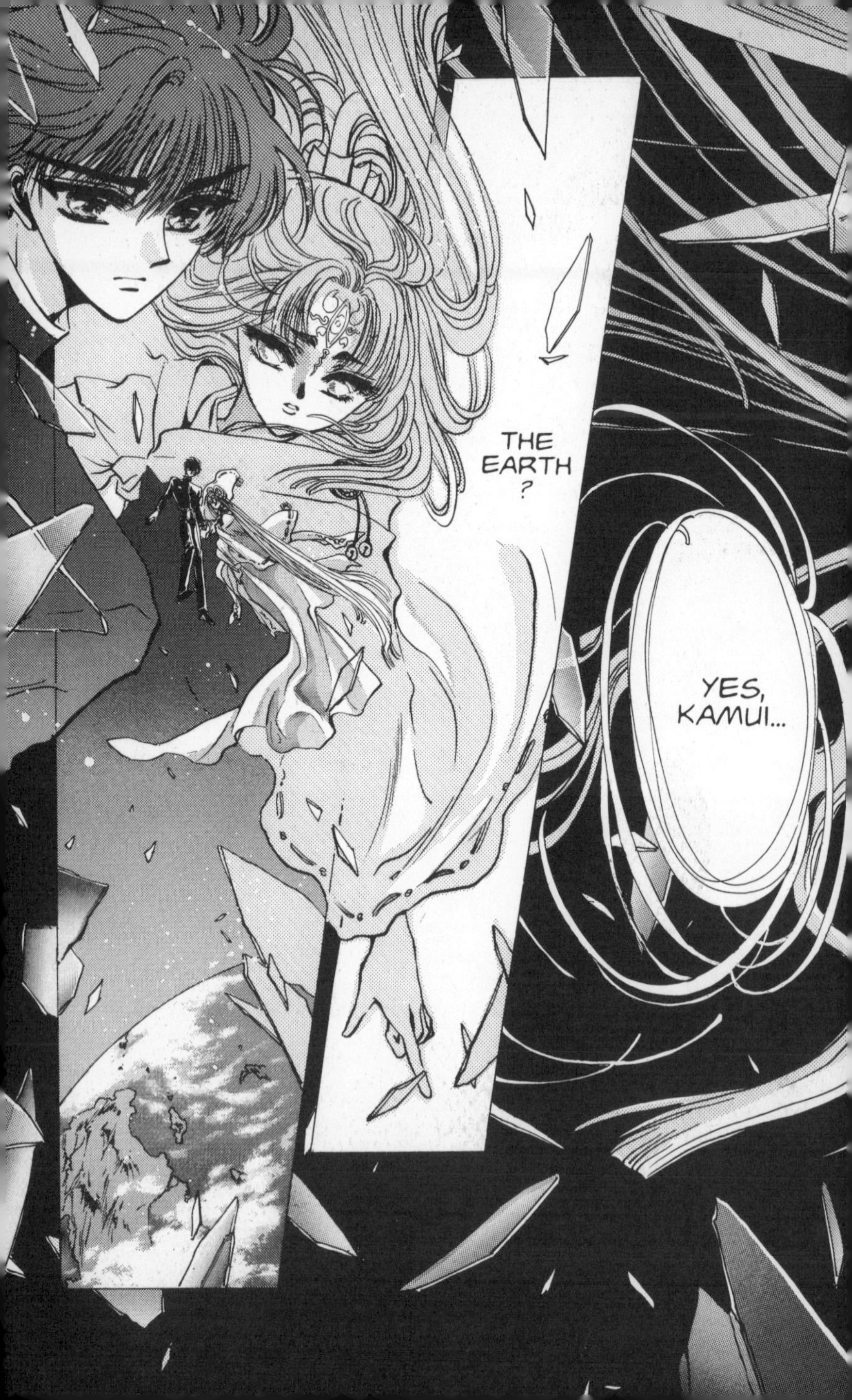
THE EARTH ?
YES, KAMUI...

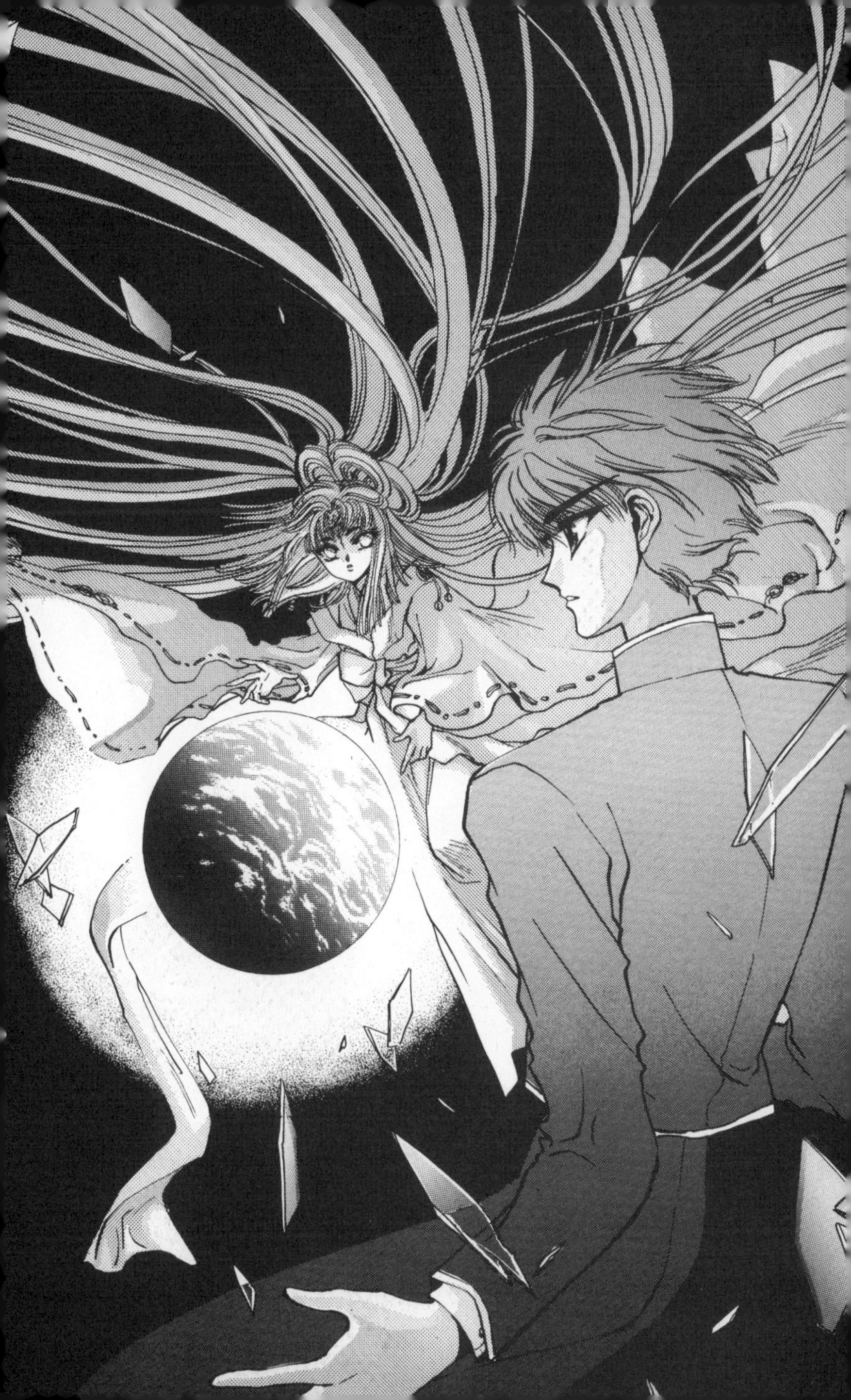

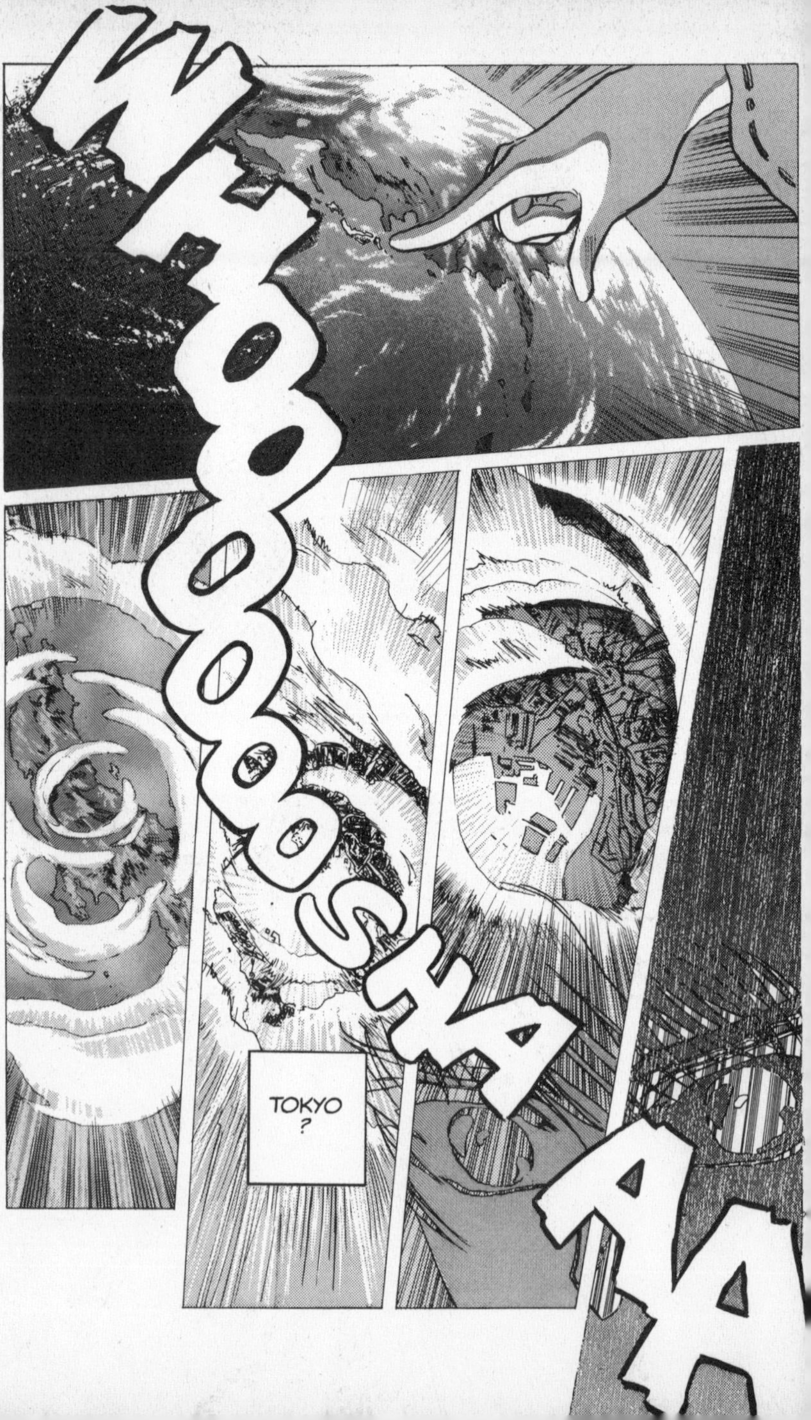
WHOOOOOOSHAAA
TOKYO ?

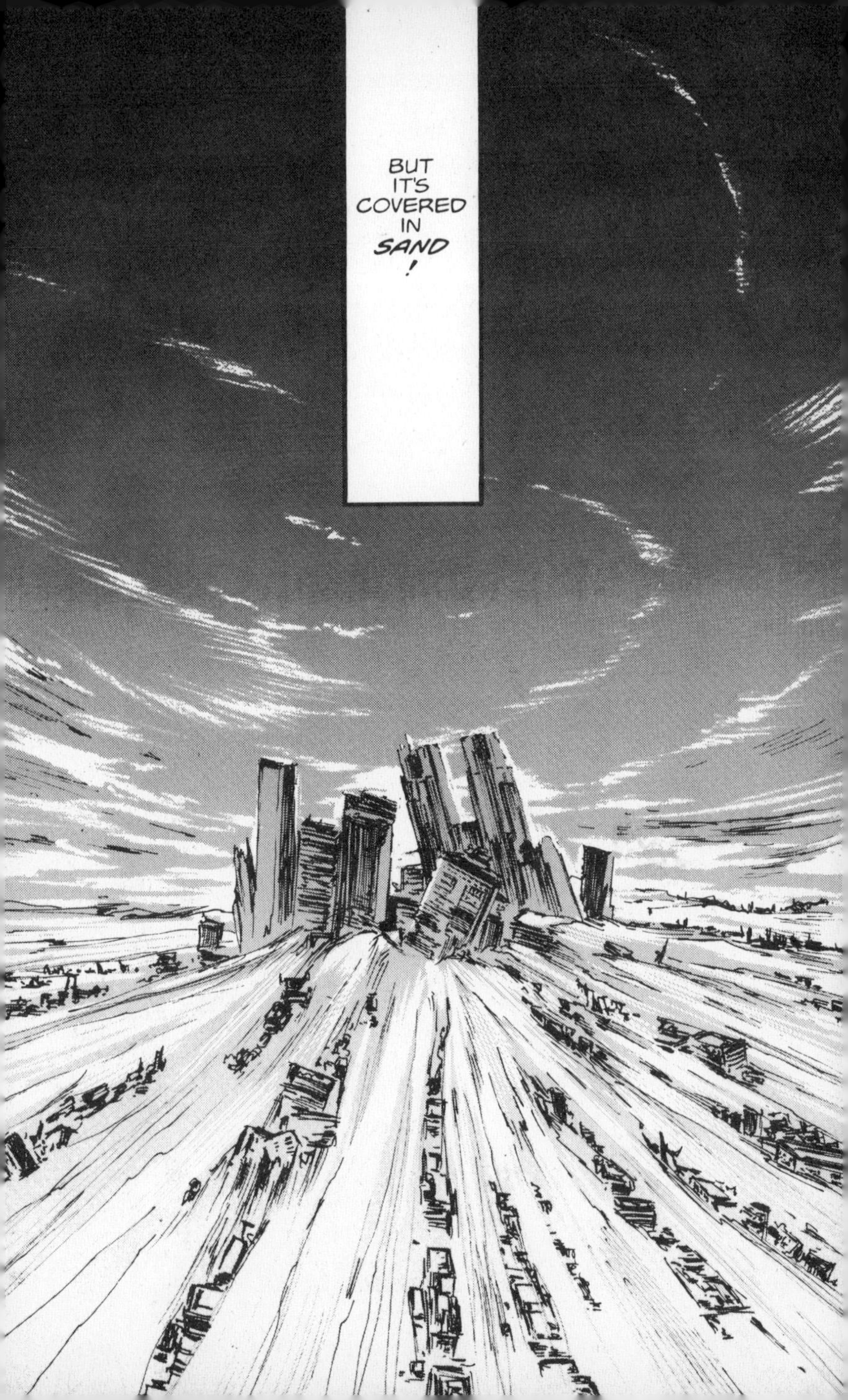
BUT IT'S COVERED IN SAND !

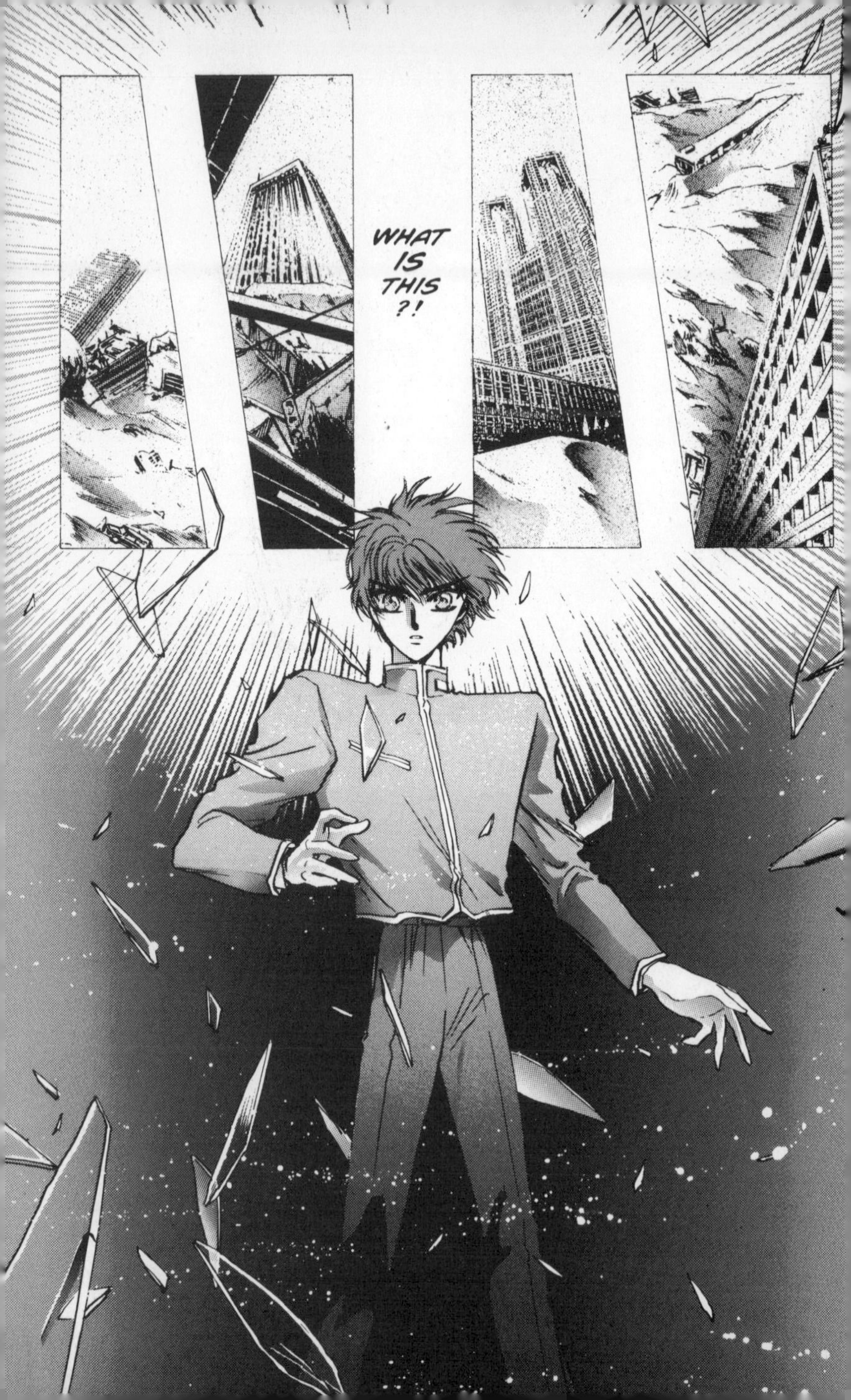
WHAT IS THIS ?!

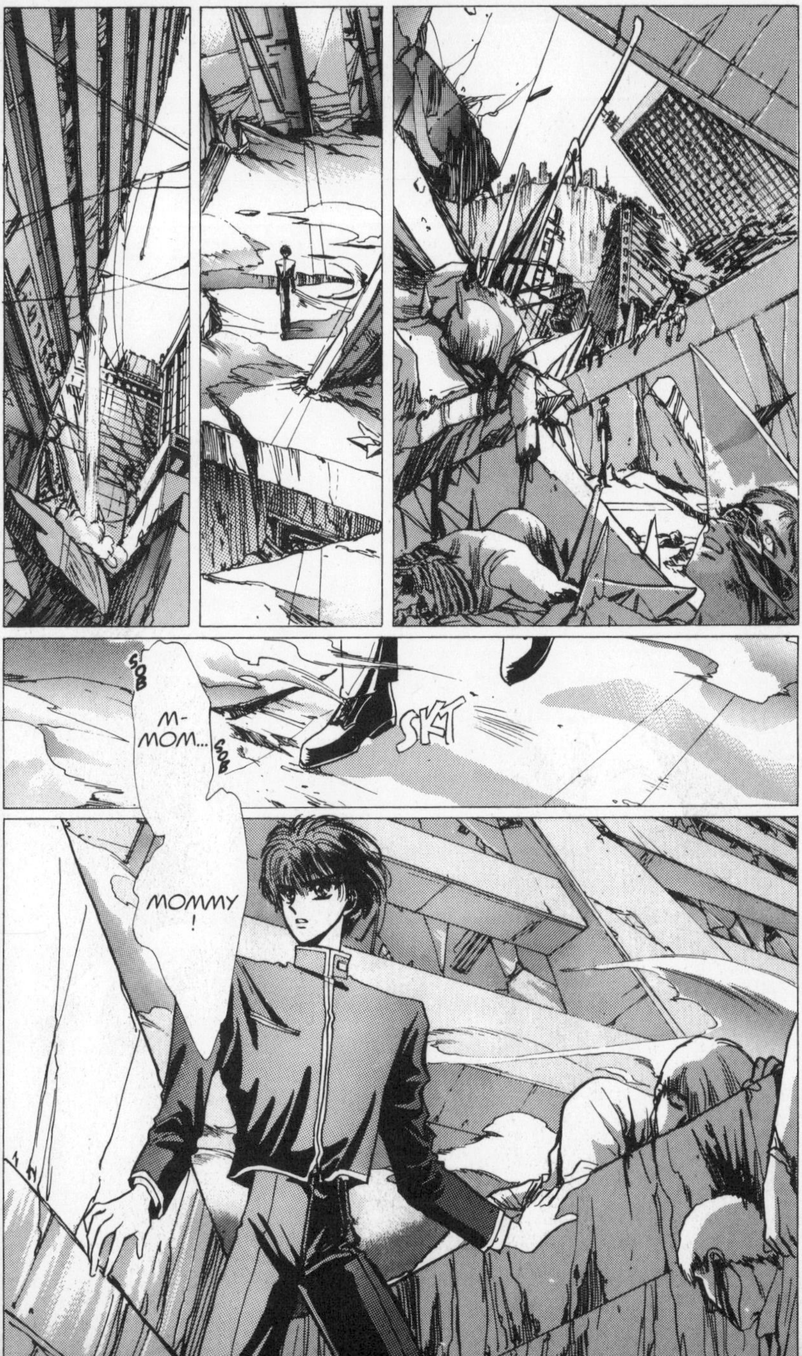
SOB
M-MOM...
SOB
SKT
MOMMY!

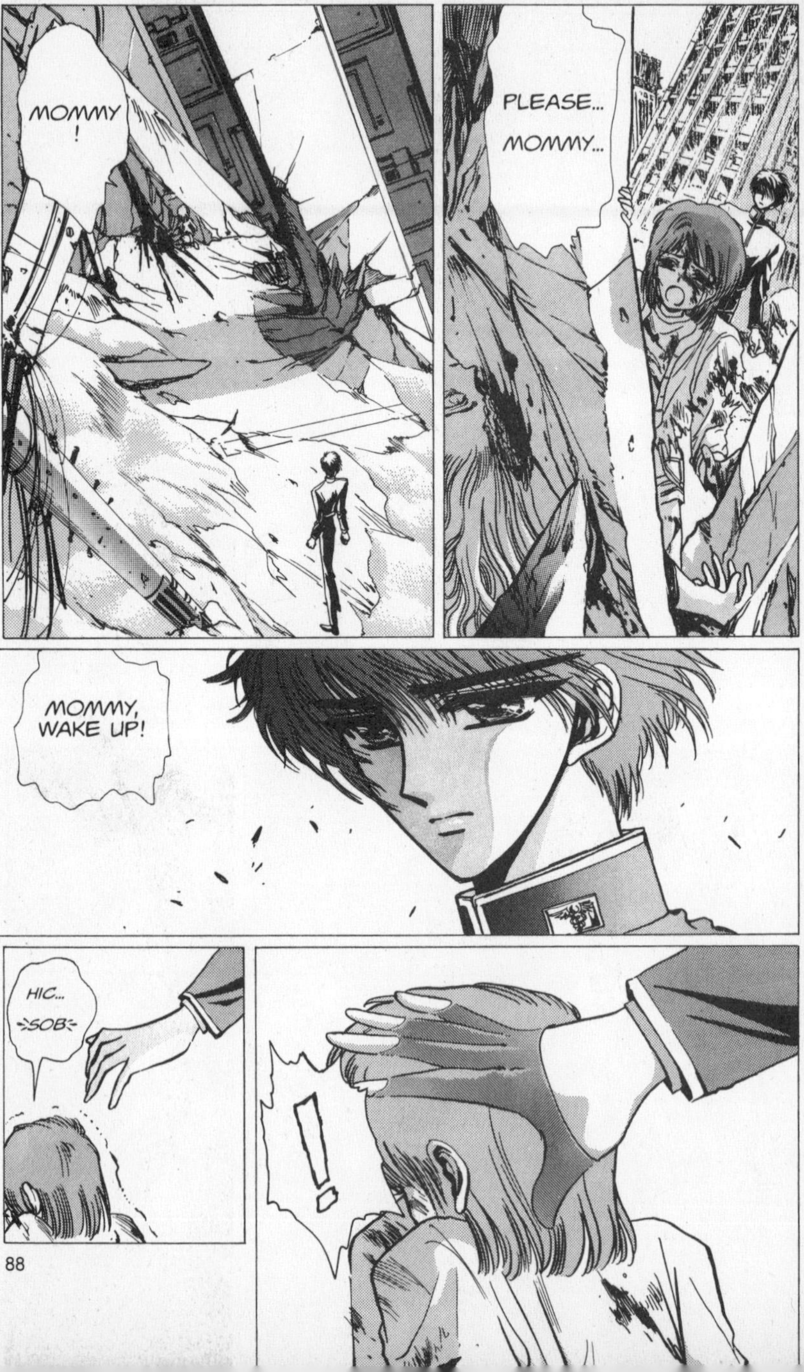
MOMMY!
PLEASE... MOMMY...
MOMMY, WAKE UP!
HIC... SOB
!

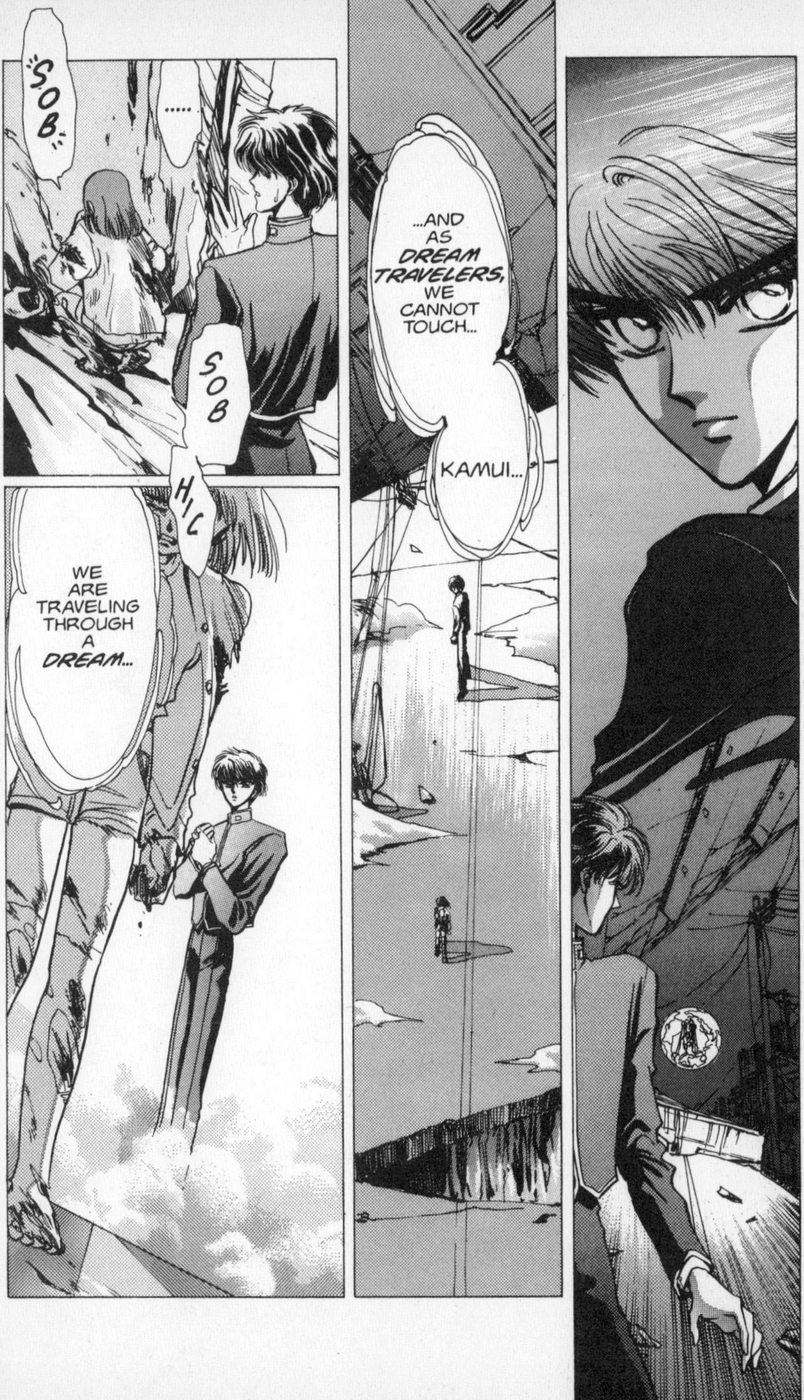

SOB
......
SOB
HIC
WE ARE TRAVELING THROUGH A *DREAM*...
...AND AS *DREAM TRAVELERS,* WE CANNOT TOUCH...
KAMUI...

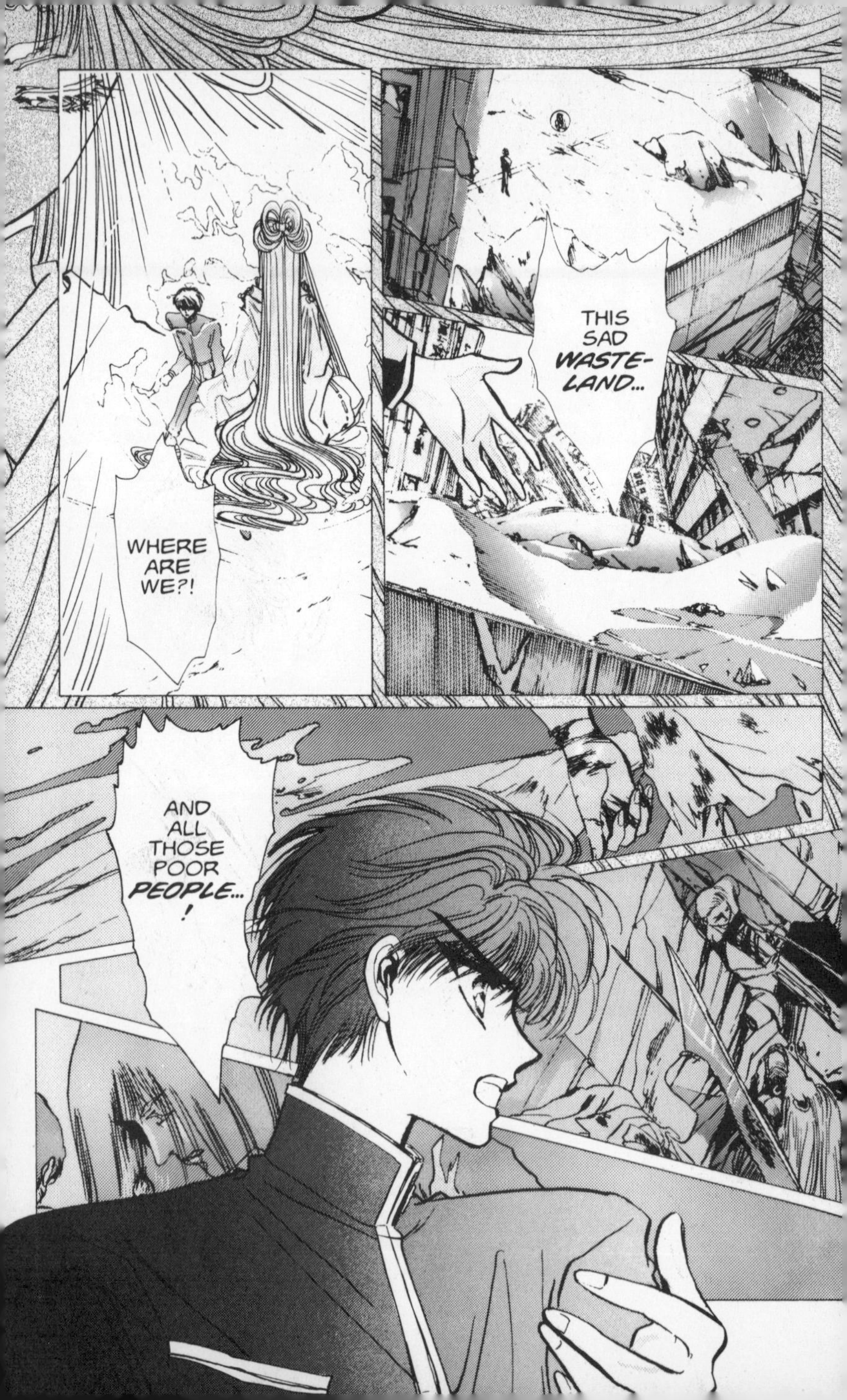
WHERE ARE WE?!
THIS SAD WASTE-LAND...
AND ALL THOSE POOR PEOPLE... !

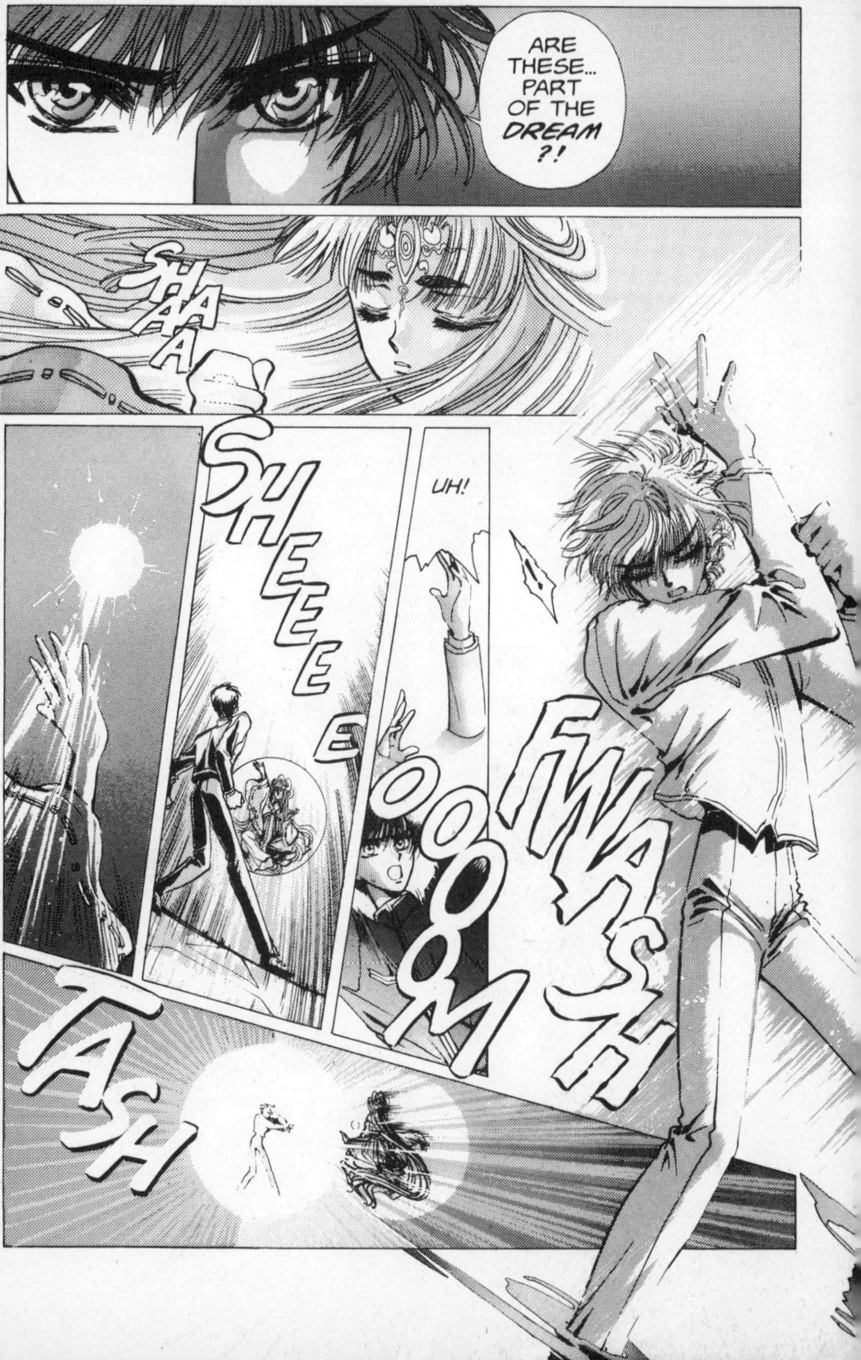
ARE THESE... PART OF THE DREAM ?!
SHAAAA
SHEEEEE
UH!
!
OOOOM
FWASH
TASH

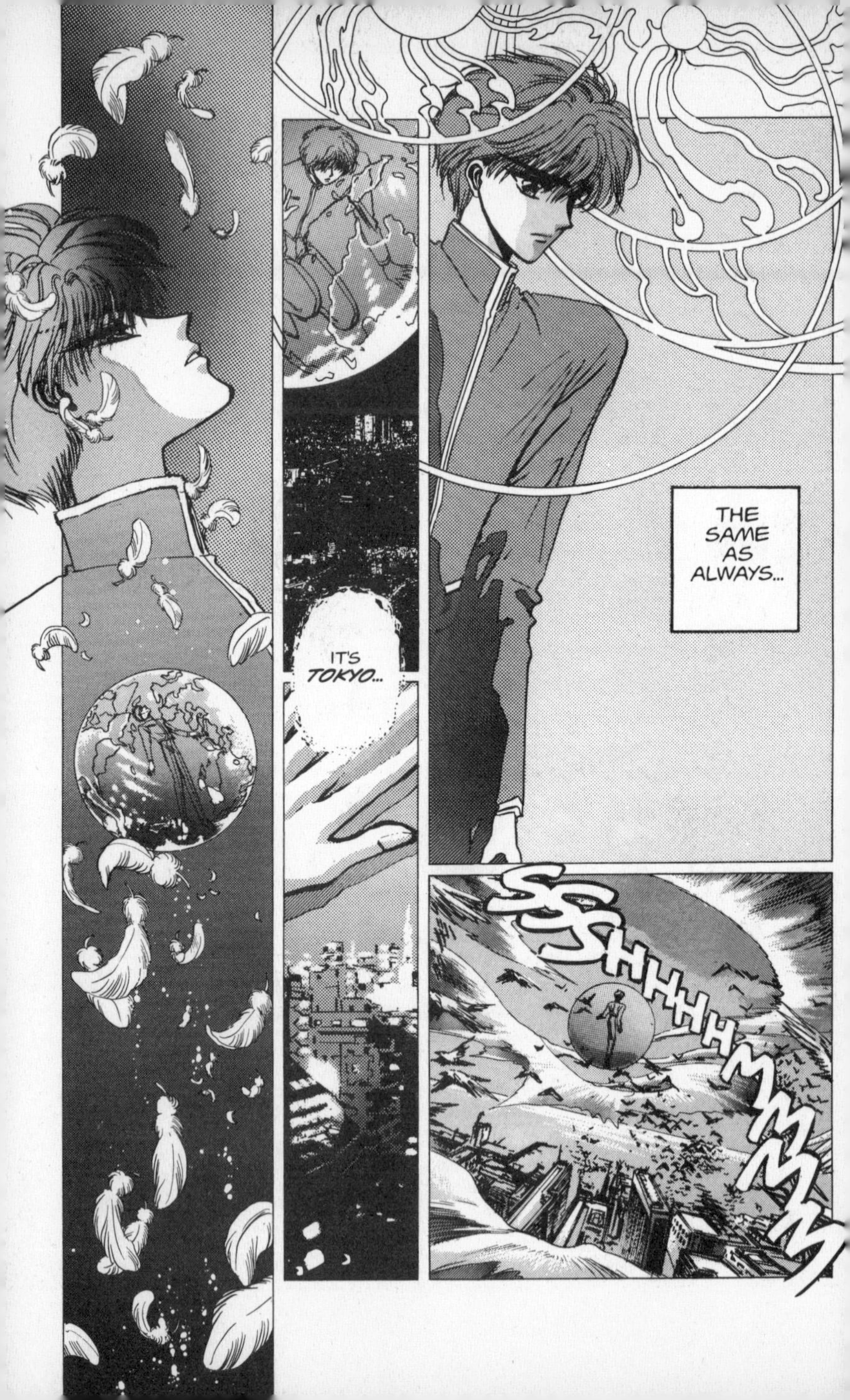
IT'S *TOKYO...*
THE SAME AS ALWAYS...
SSSHHHHHMMMMM

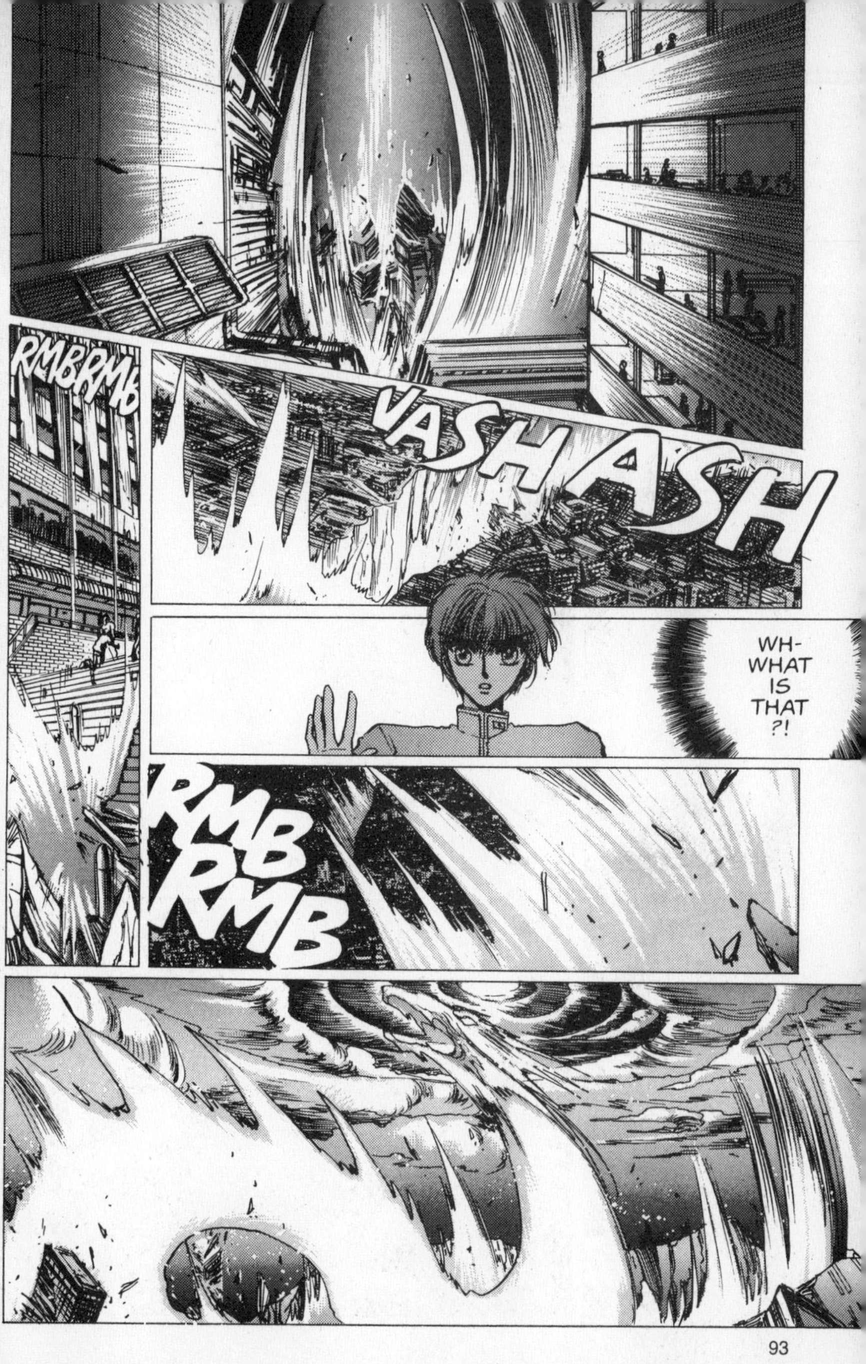
RMBRMB
VASHASH
WH- WHAT IS THAT ?!
RMB RMB RMB

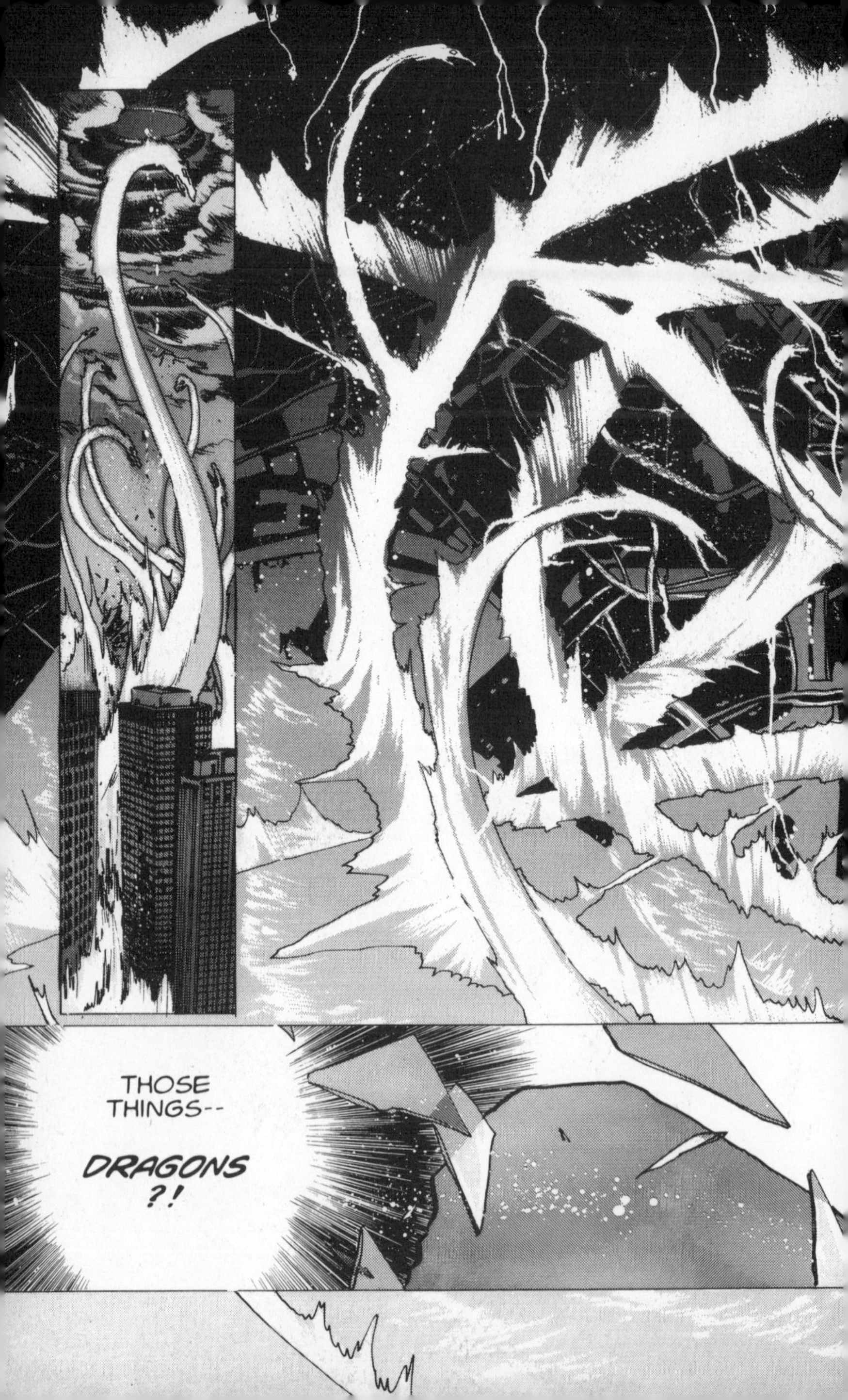
THOSE THINGS--
DRAGONS ?!

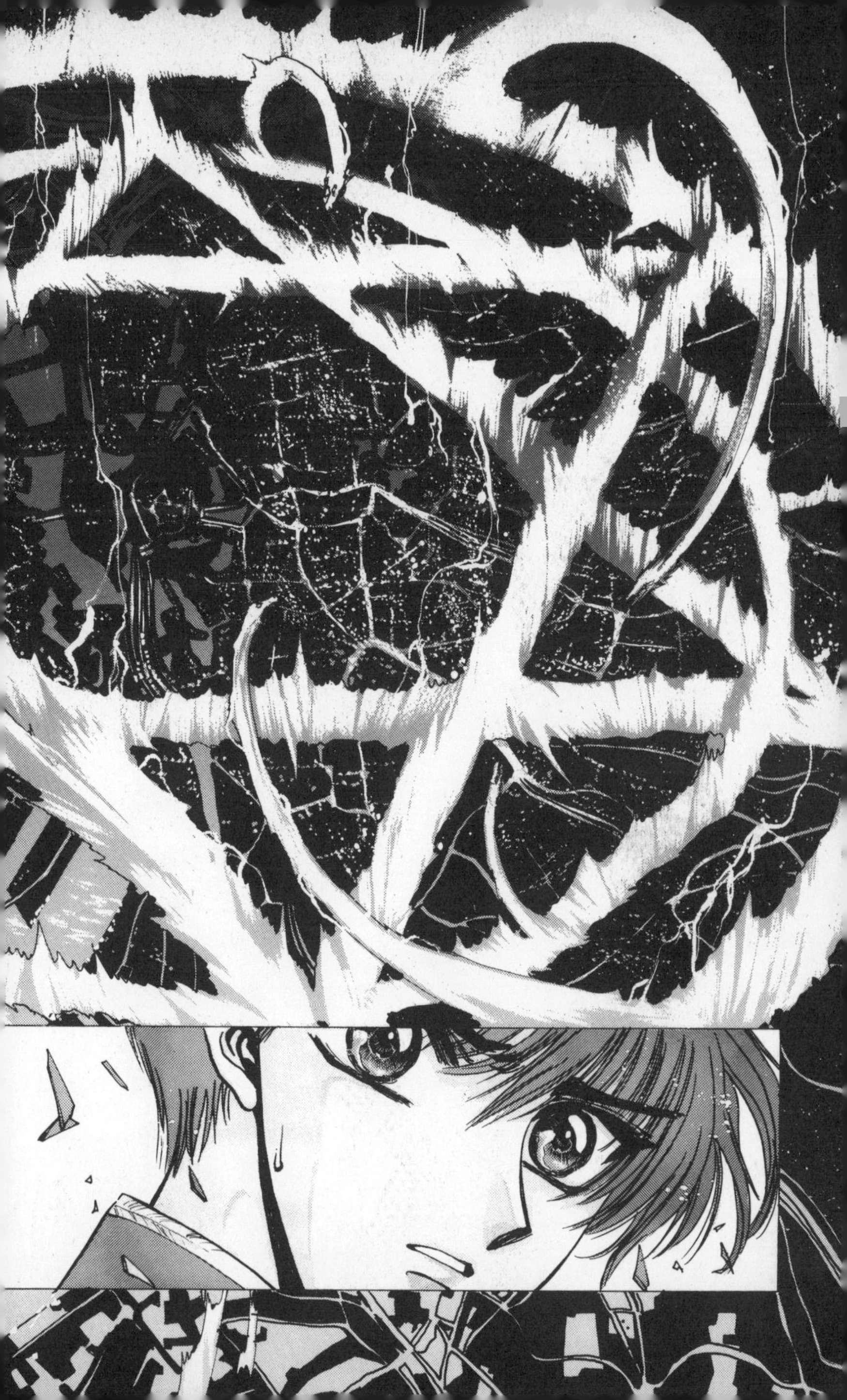

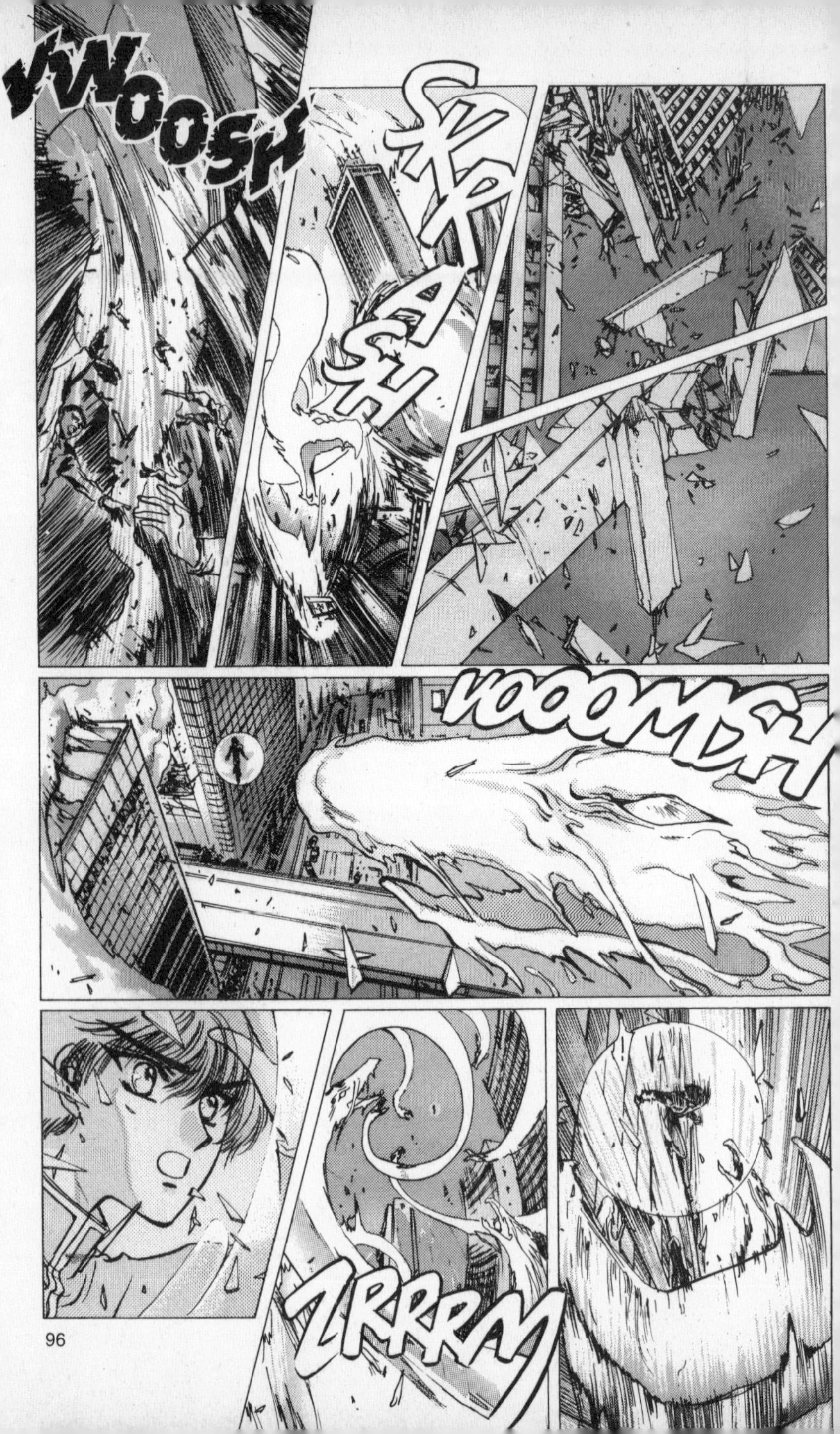
VWOOSH
SPLASH
VOOOMSH
ZRRRM

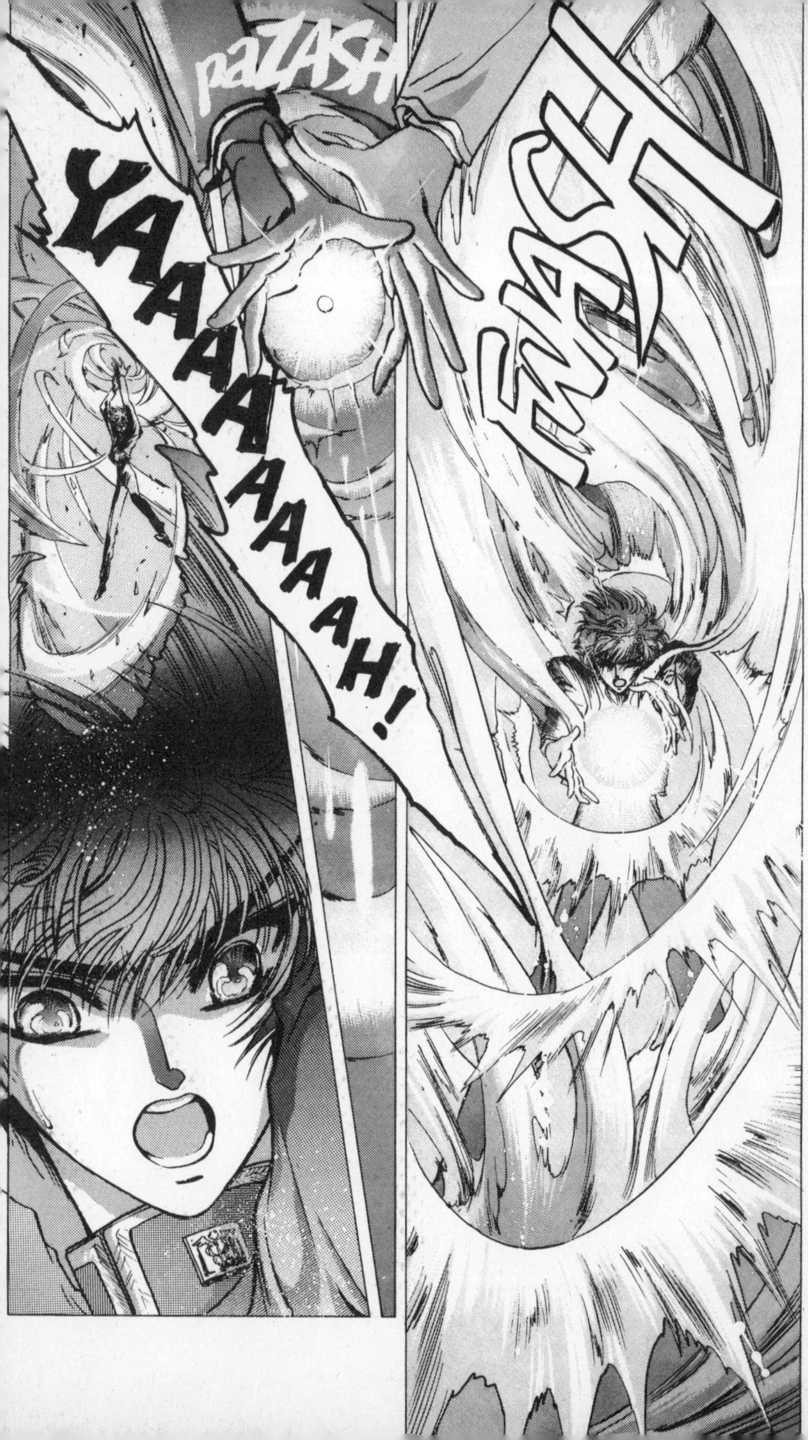
FWASH!
paZASH
YAAAAAAAAAH!

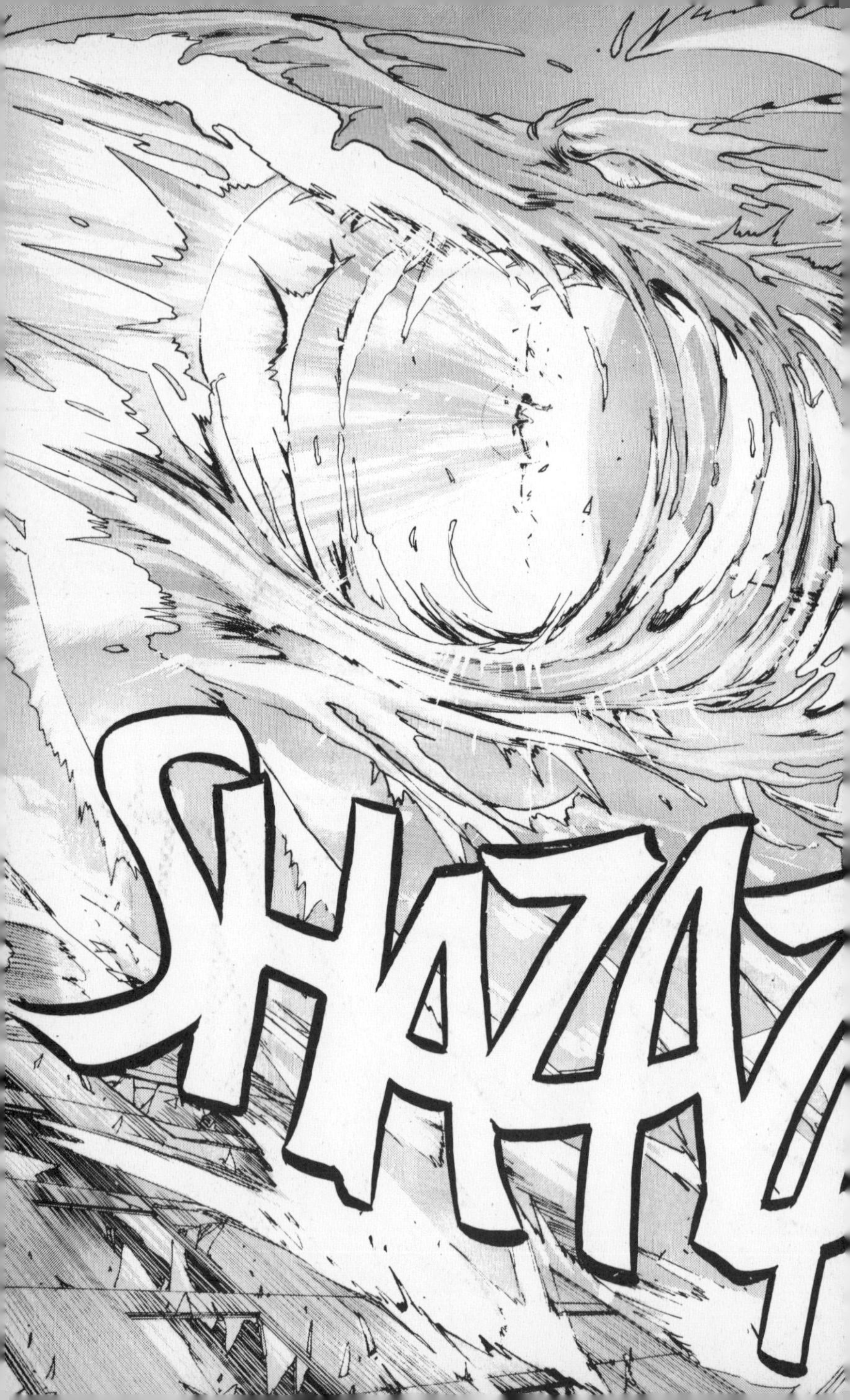
SHAZA

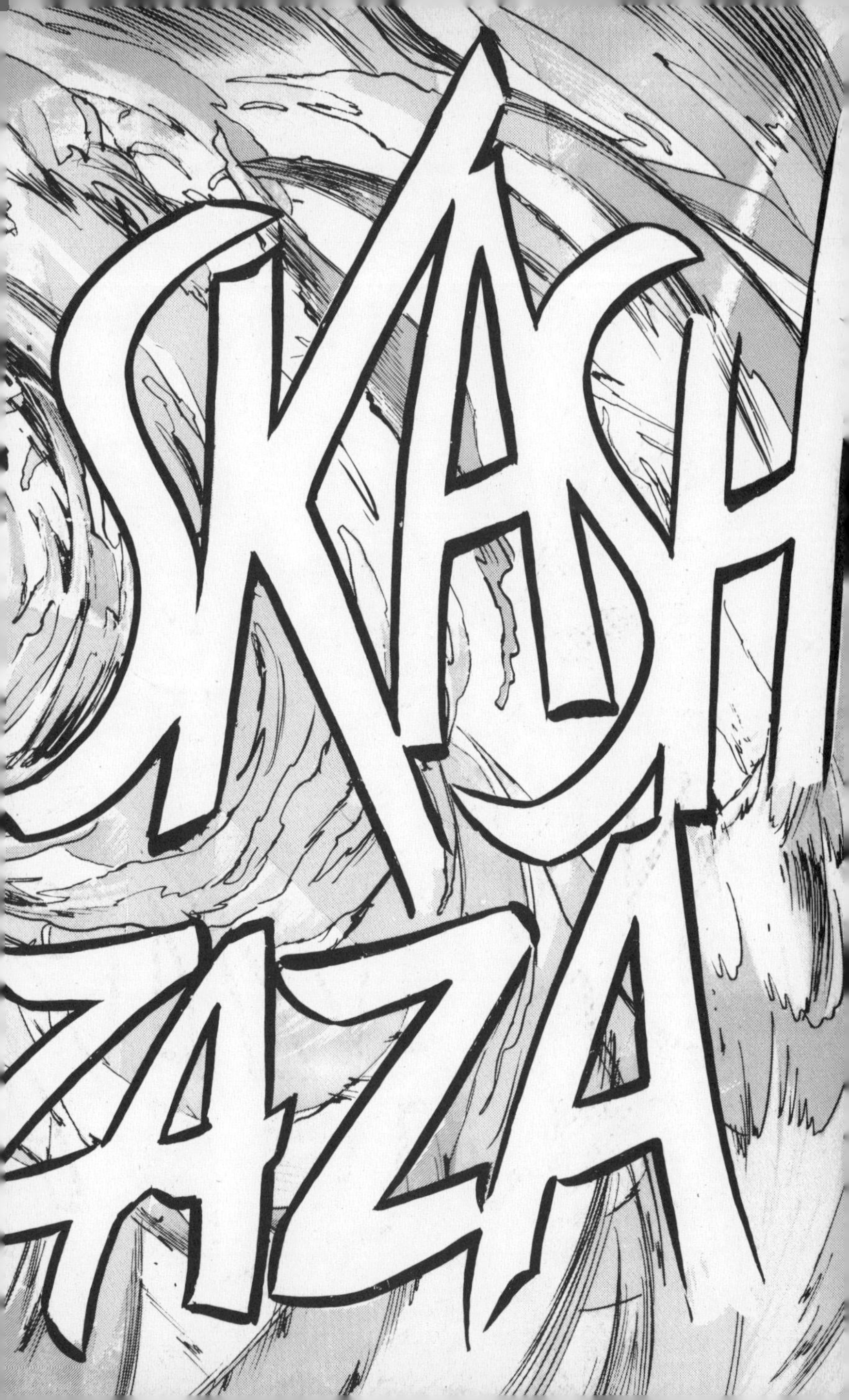
SKASH

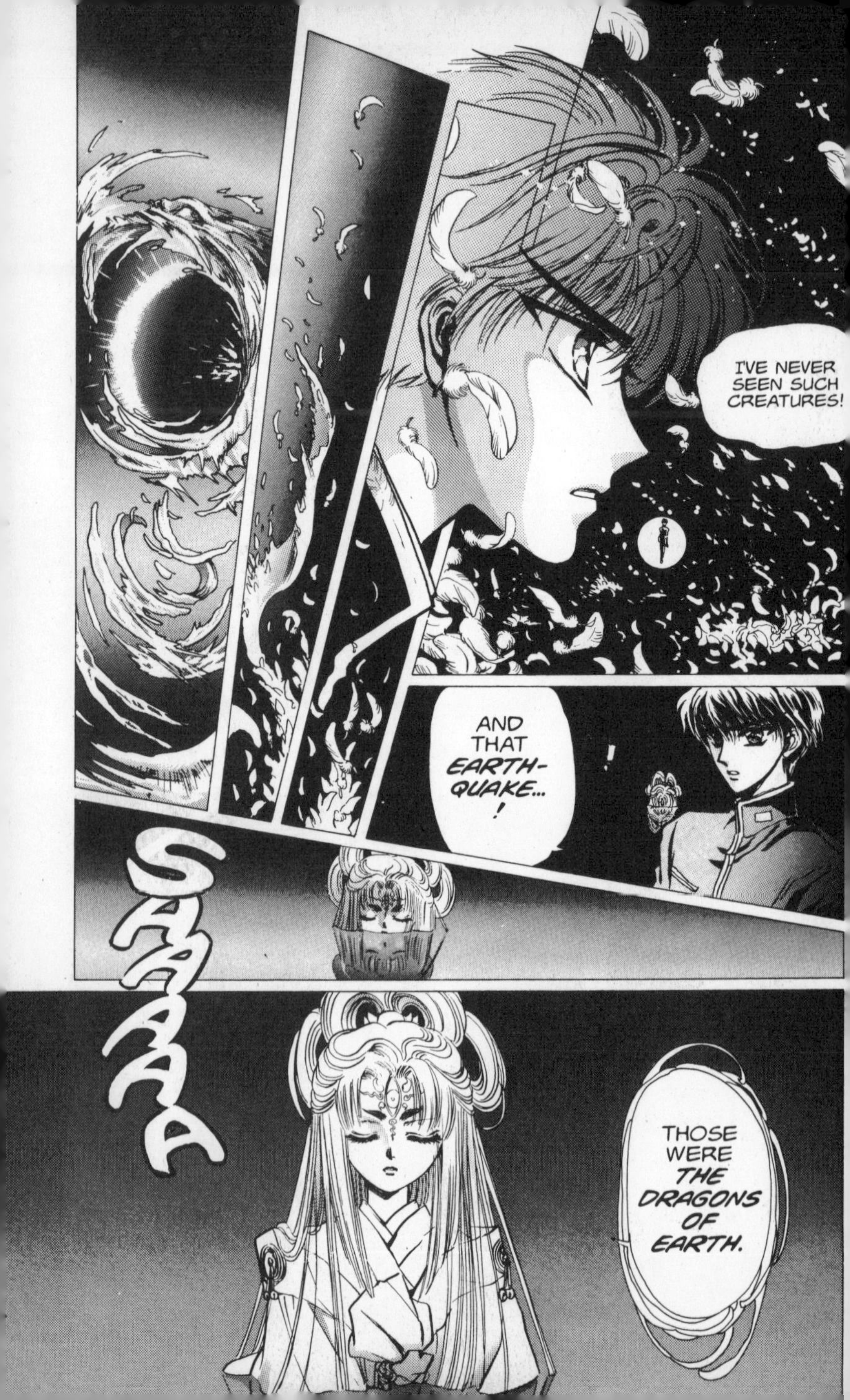
I'VE NEVER SEEN SUCH CREATURES!
AND THAT EARTH-QUAKE...!
SHAAAA
THOSE WERE THE DRAGONS OF EARTH.

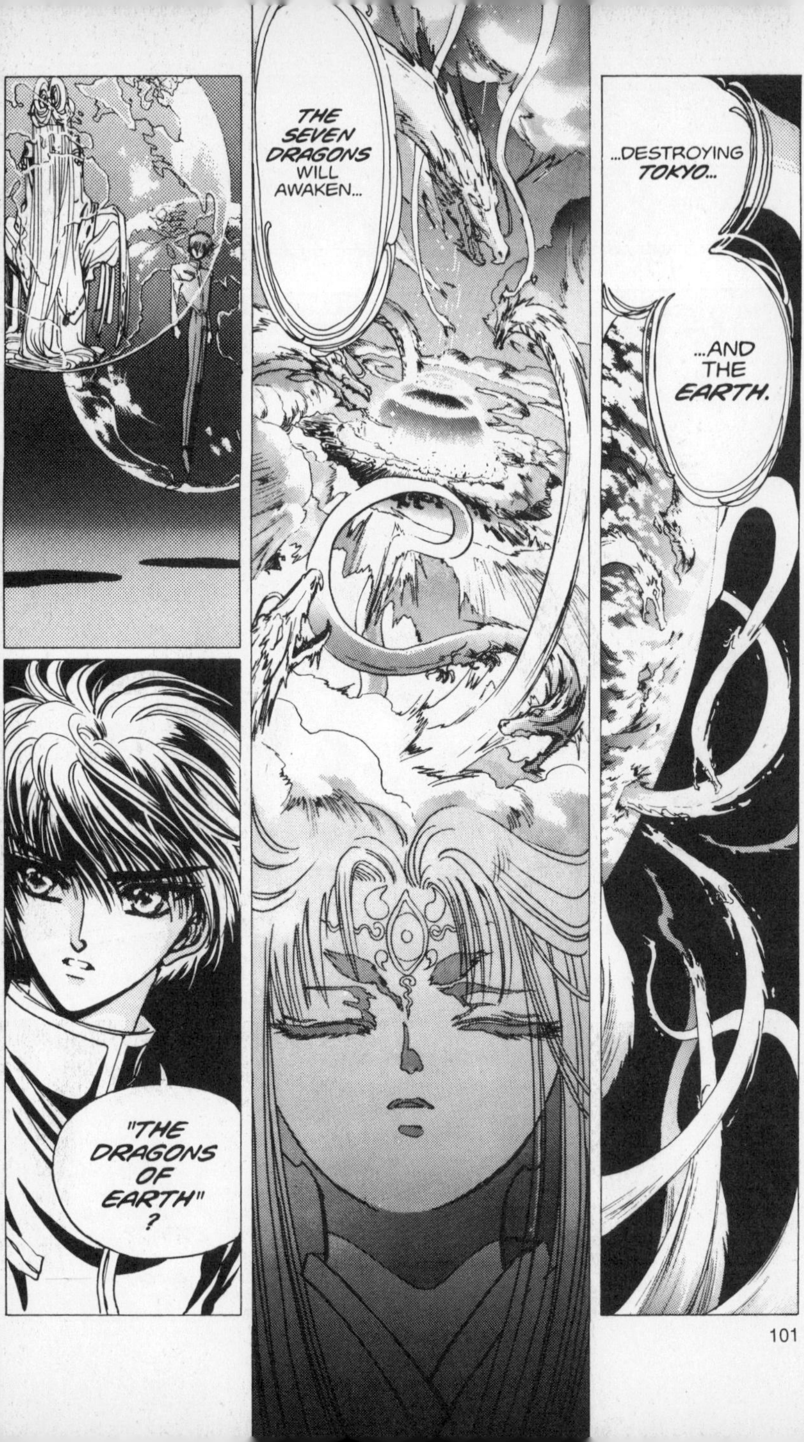
"THE DRAGONS OF EARTH" ?
THE SEVEN DRAGONS WILL AWAKEN...
...DESTROYING TOKYO...
...AND THE EARTH.

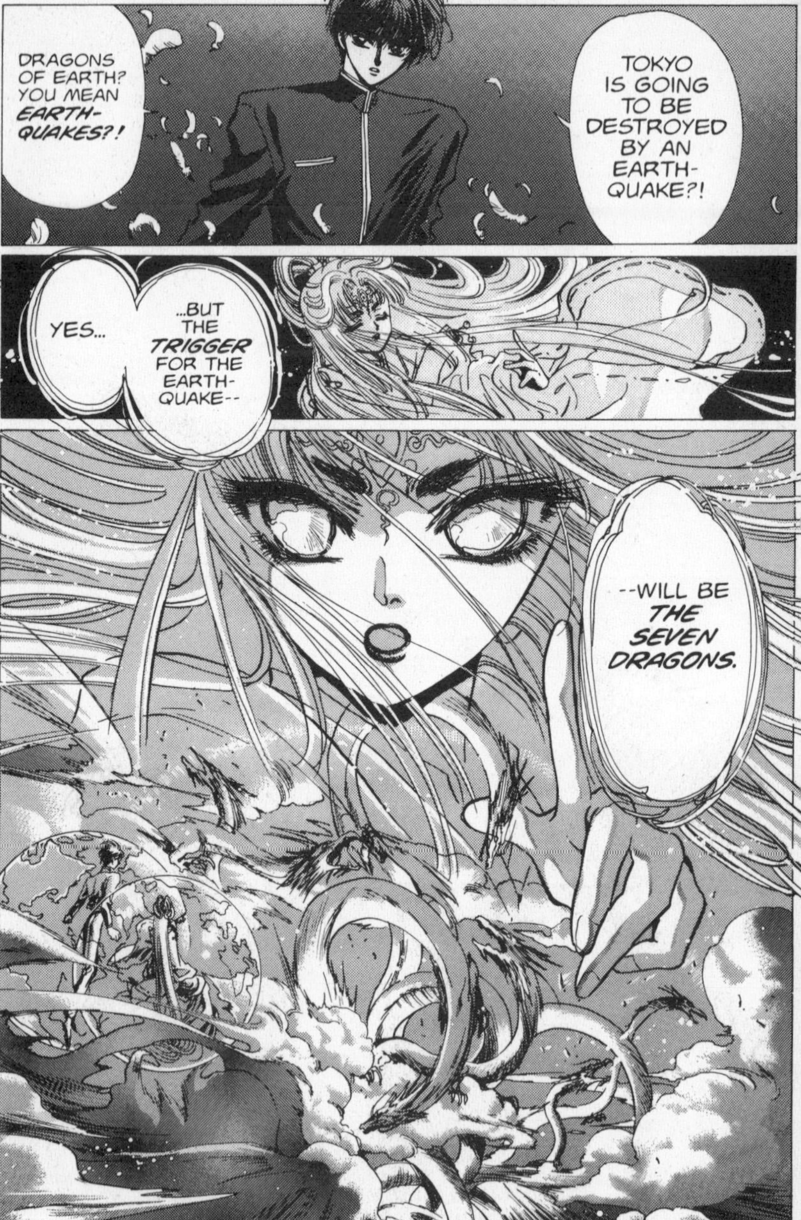
DRAGONS OF EARTH? YOU MEAN *EARTH-QUAKES?!*
TOKYO IS GOING TO BE DESTROYED BY AN EARTH-QUAKE?!
YES...
...BUT THE *TRIGGER* FOR THE EARTH-QUAKE--
--WILL BE *THE SEVEN DRAGONS.*

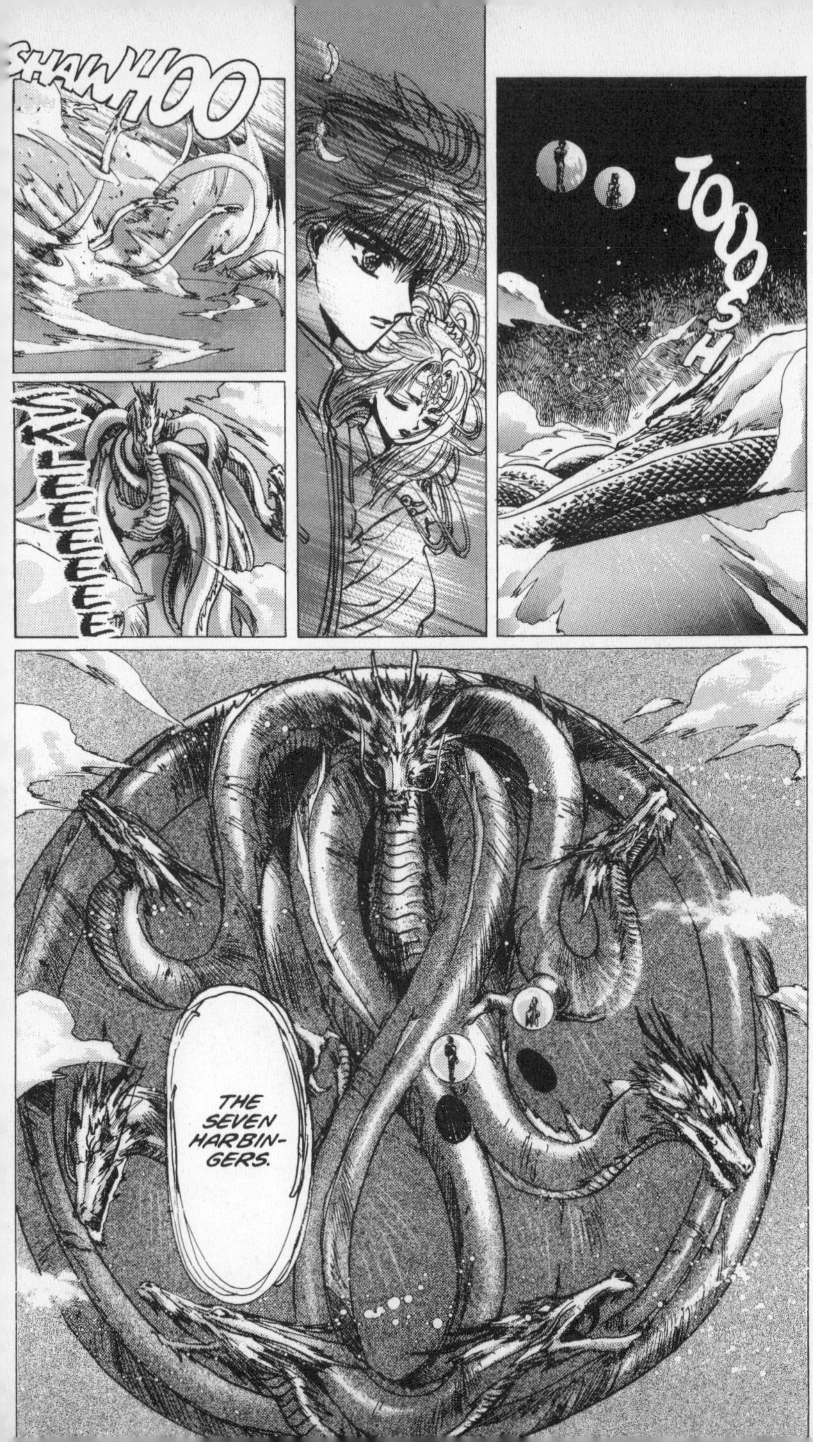
SHAWHOO
SKLEEEEEEE
TOOOOSH
THE SEVEN HARBIN-GERS.

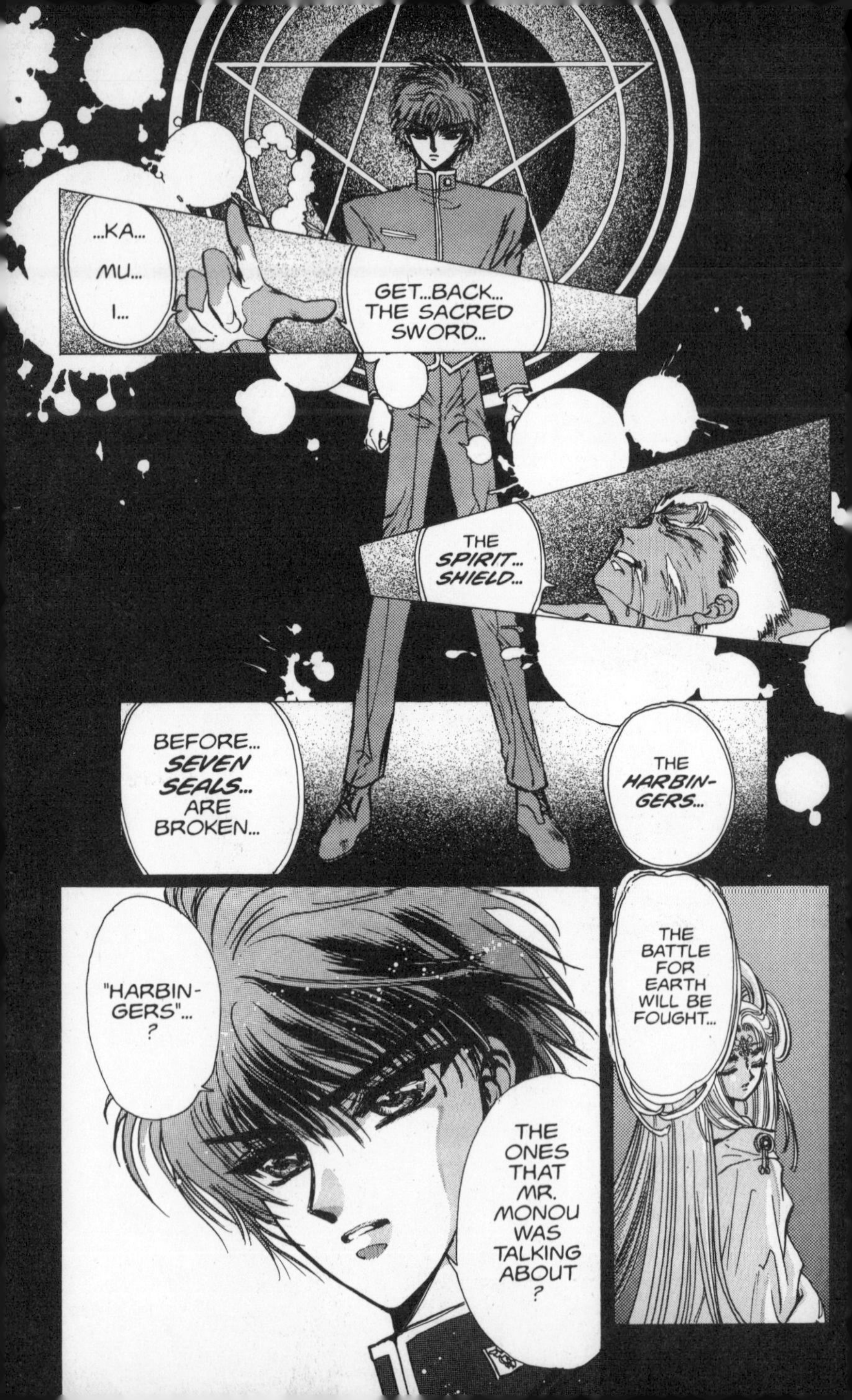
...KA... MU... I...
GET...BACK... THE SACRED SWORD...
THE SPIRIT... SHIELD...
BEFORE... SEVEN SEALS... ARE BROKEN...
THE HARBINGERS...
"HARBINGERS"... ?
THE ONES THAT MR. MONOU WAS TALKING ABOUT ?
THE BATTLE FOR EARTH WILL BE FOUGHT...

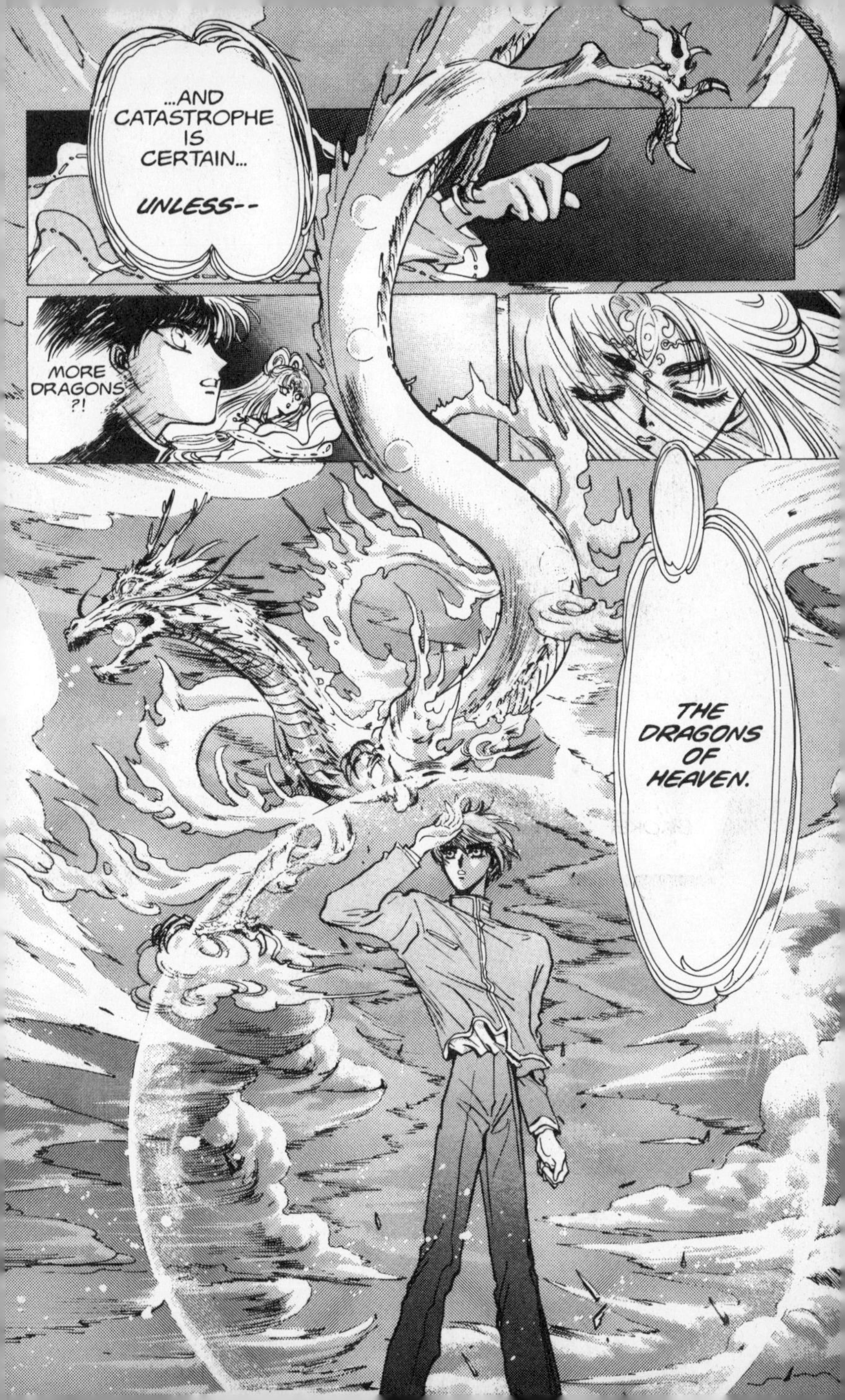
...AND CATASTROPHE IS CERTAIN...
UNLESS--
MORE DRAGONS?!
THE DRAGONS OF HEAVEN.

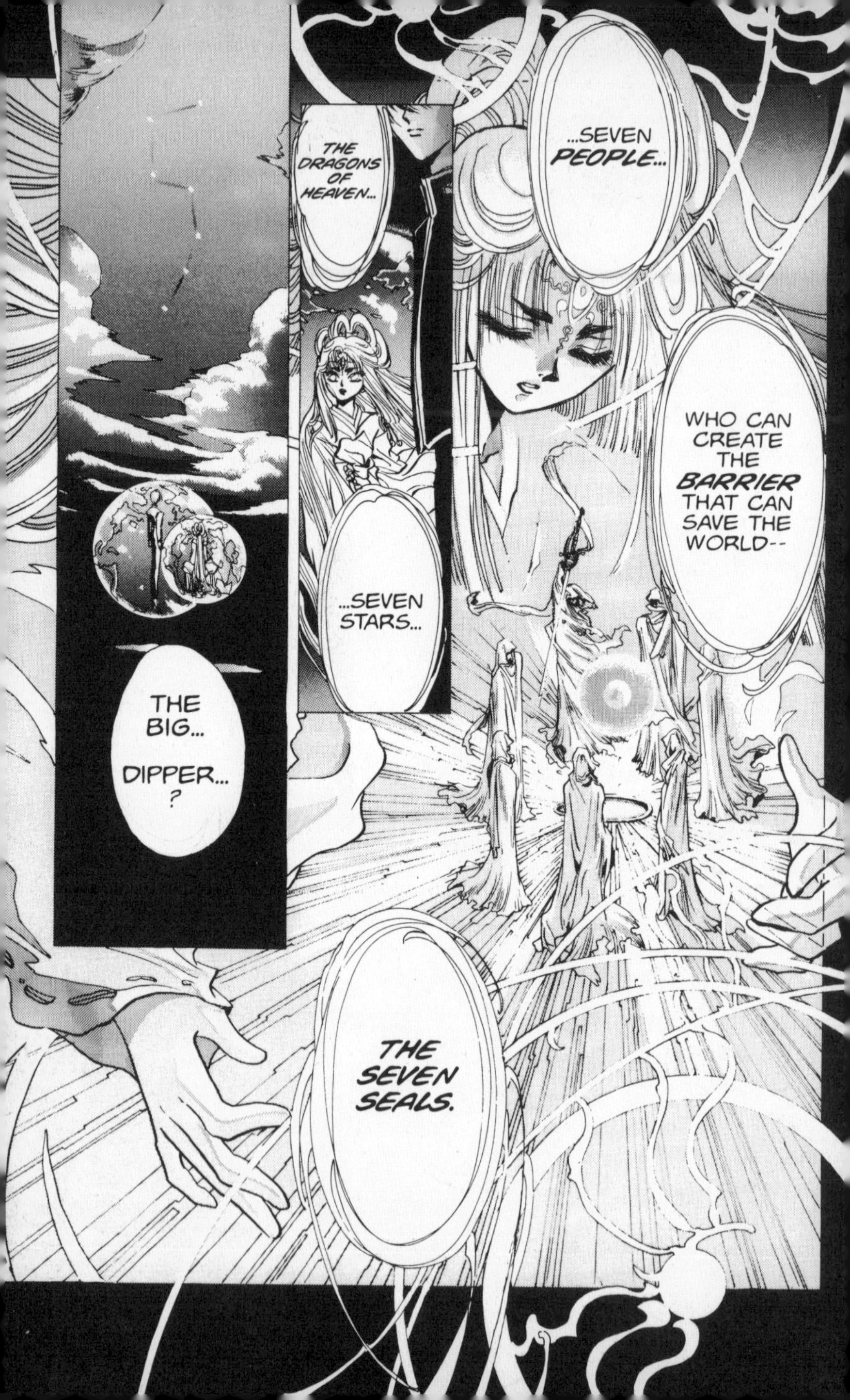
THE BIG... DIPPER...?
THE DRAGONS OF HEAVEN...
...SEVEN STARS...
...SEVEN PEOPLE...
WHO CAN CREATE THE BARRIER THAT CAN SAVE THE WORLD--
THE SEVEN SEALS.

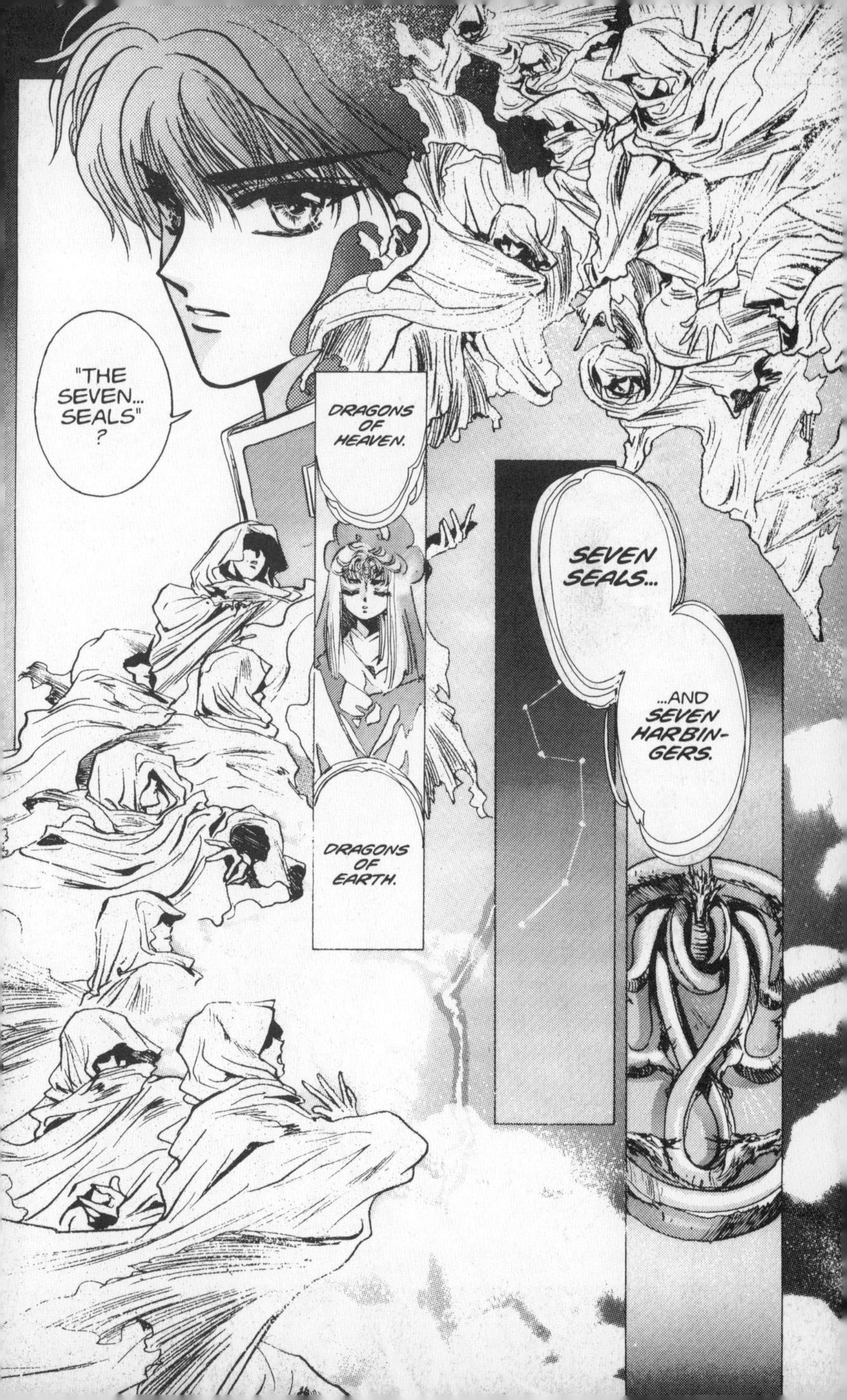
"THE SEVEN... SEALS"?
DRAGONS OF HEAVEN.
DRAGONS OF EARTH.
SEVEN SEALS...
...AND SEVEN HARBIN-GERS.

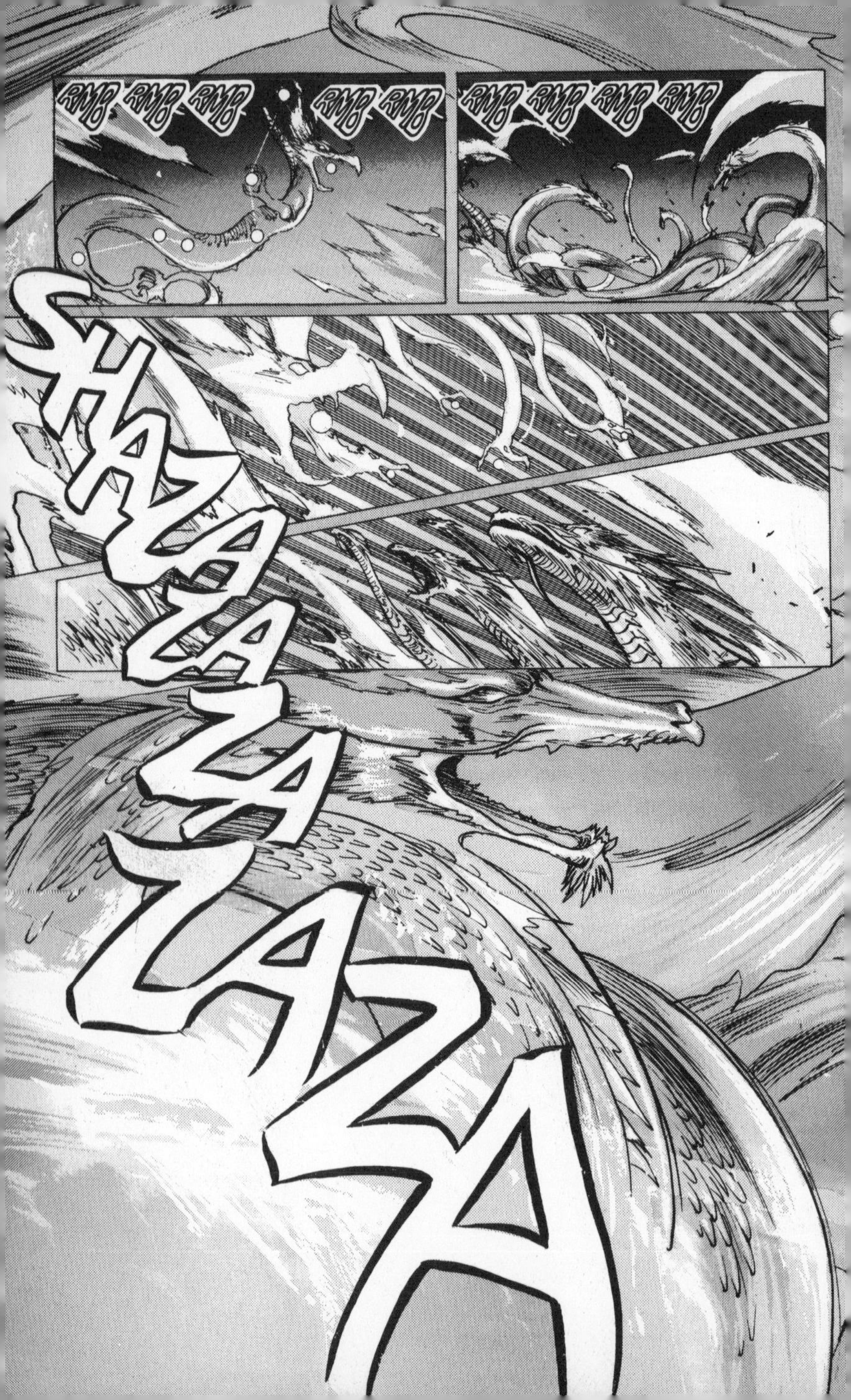
RMB RMB RMB
RMB RMB
RMB RMB RMB RMB
SHAZAZALAZA

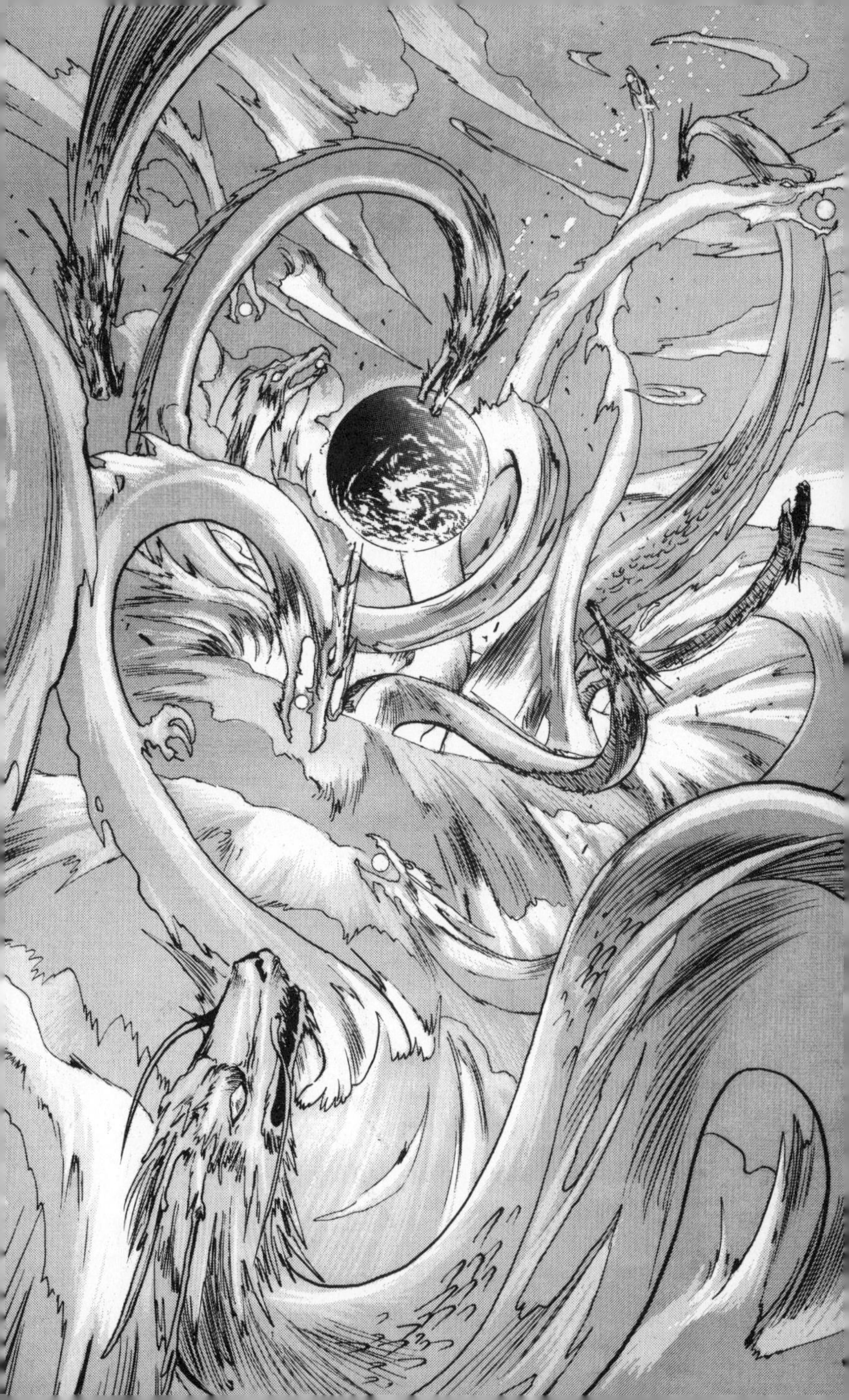

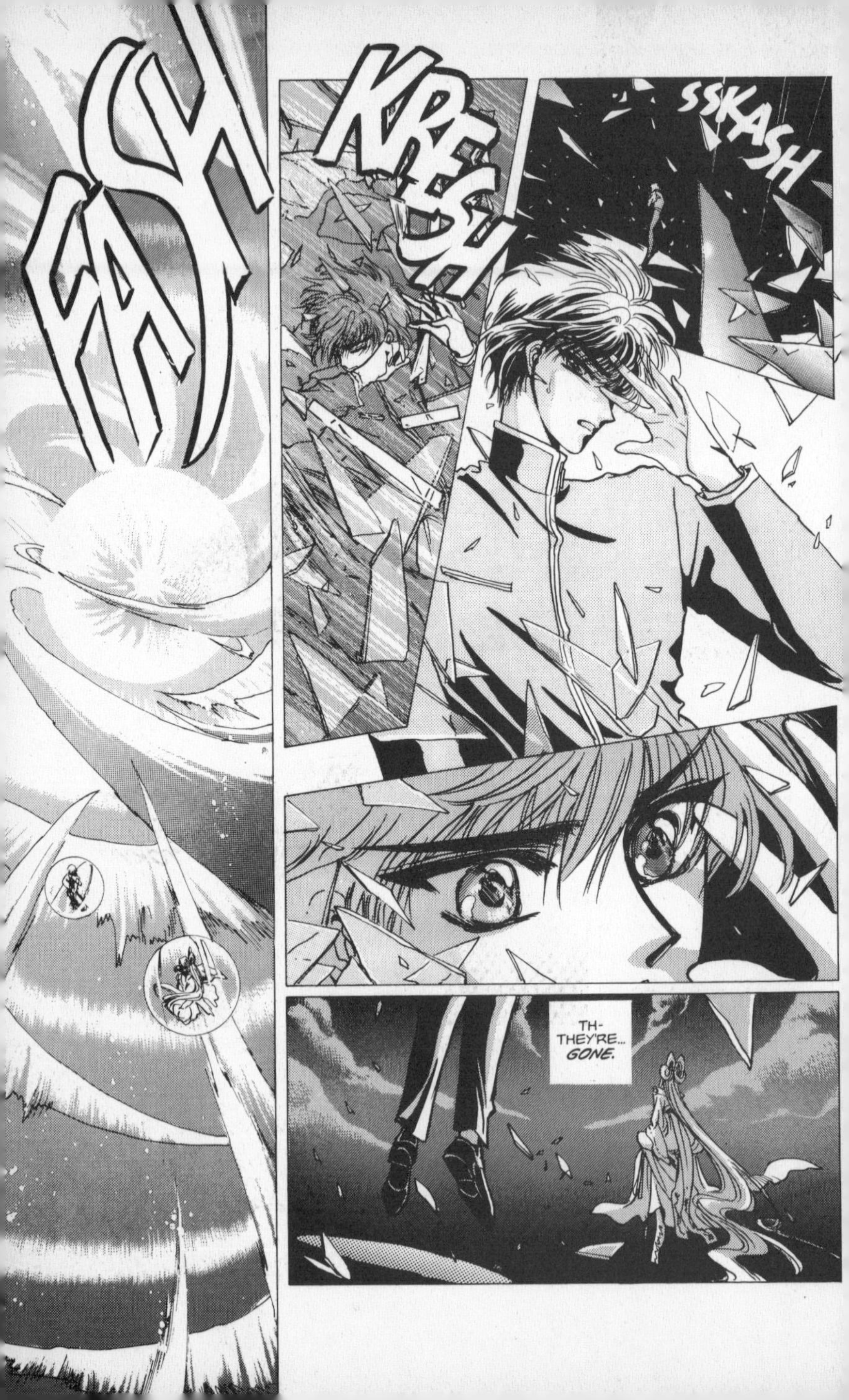
FASH
KRESH
SSKASH
TH-THEY'RE... GONE.

KAMUI...

THE RECENT EARTHQUAKES...

...EACH OVER FIVE ON THE RICHTER SCALE...

...ARE MERELY THE *SIGNS.*

BUT *WHY?*

IF THE *DRAGONS OF EARTH* DEFEAT THE *DRAGONS OF HEAVEN...*

...THE EARTH WILL PERISH!

I DON'T UNDERSTAND HOW THE WHOLE *EARTH* WILL PERISH IF *TOKYO* IS DESTROYED BY QUAKES...

TOKYO IS THE *"TIE"* THAT BINDS--

--THE *BARRIERS* THAT PROTECT THE *EARTH.*

111

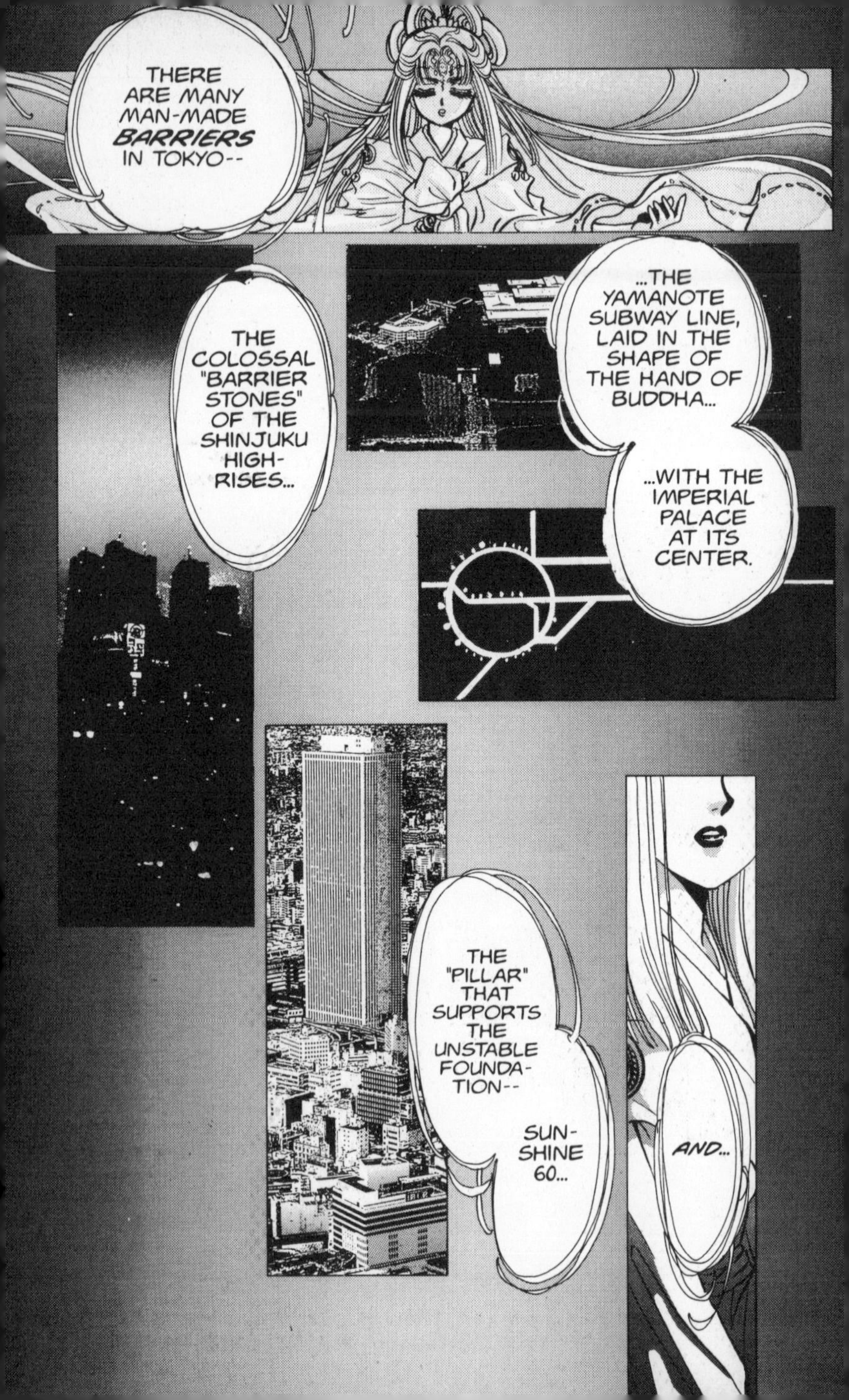
THERE ARE MANY MAN-MADE BARRIERS IN TOKYO--
THE COLOSSAL "BARRIER STONES" OF THE SHINJUKU HIGH-RISES...
...THE YAMANOTE SUBWAY LINE, LAID IN THE SHAPE OF THE HAND OF BUDDHA...
...WITH THE IMPERIAL PALACE AT ITS CENTER.
THE "PILLAR" THAT SUPPORTS THE UNSTABLE FOUNDA-TION--
SUN-SHINE 60...
AND...

THE TOKYO TOWER.

THE TOKYO TOWER?

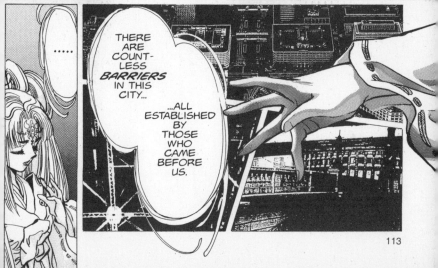

.....

THERE ARE COUNTLESS *BARRIERS* IN THIS CITY...

...ALL ESTABLISHED BY THOSE WHO CAME BEFORE US.

113

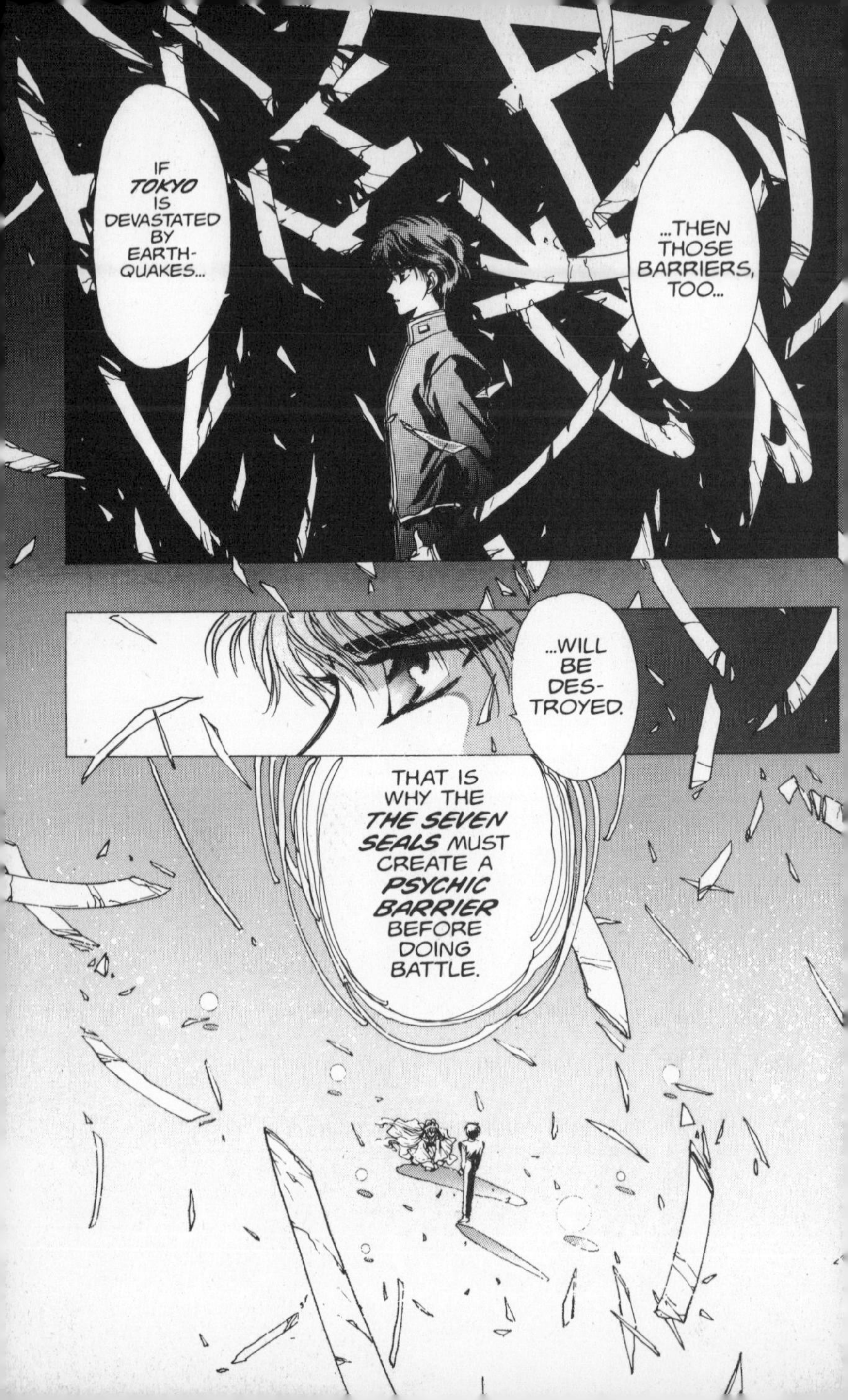
IF *TOKYO* IS DEVASTATED BY EARTH-QUAKES...
...THEN THOSE BARRIERS, TOO...
...WILL BE DES-TROYED.
THAT IS WHY THE *THE SEVEN SEALS* MUST CREATE A *PSYCHIC BARRIER* BEFORE DOING BATTLE.

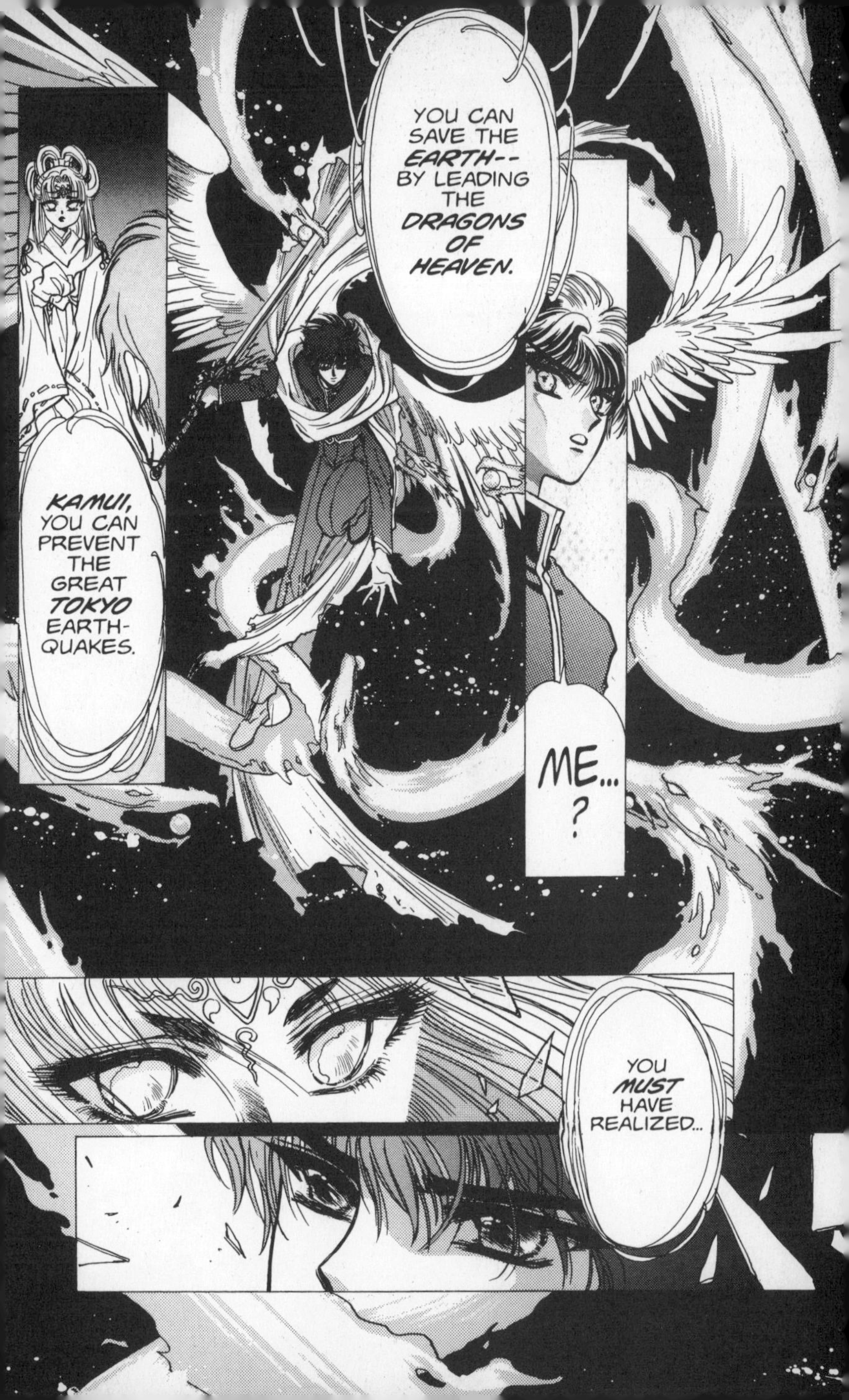
KAMUI, YOU CAN PREVENT THE GREAT TOKYO EARTH-QUAKES.
YOU CAN SAVE THE EARTH-- BY LEADING THE DRAGONS OF HEAVEN.
ME...?
YOU MUST HAVE REALIZED...

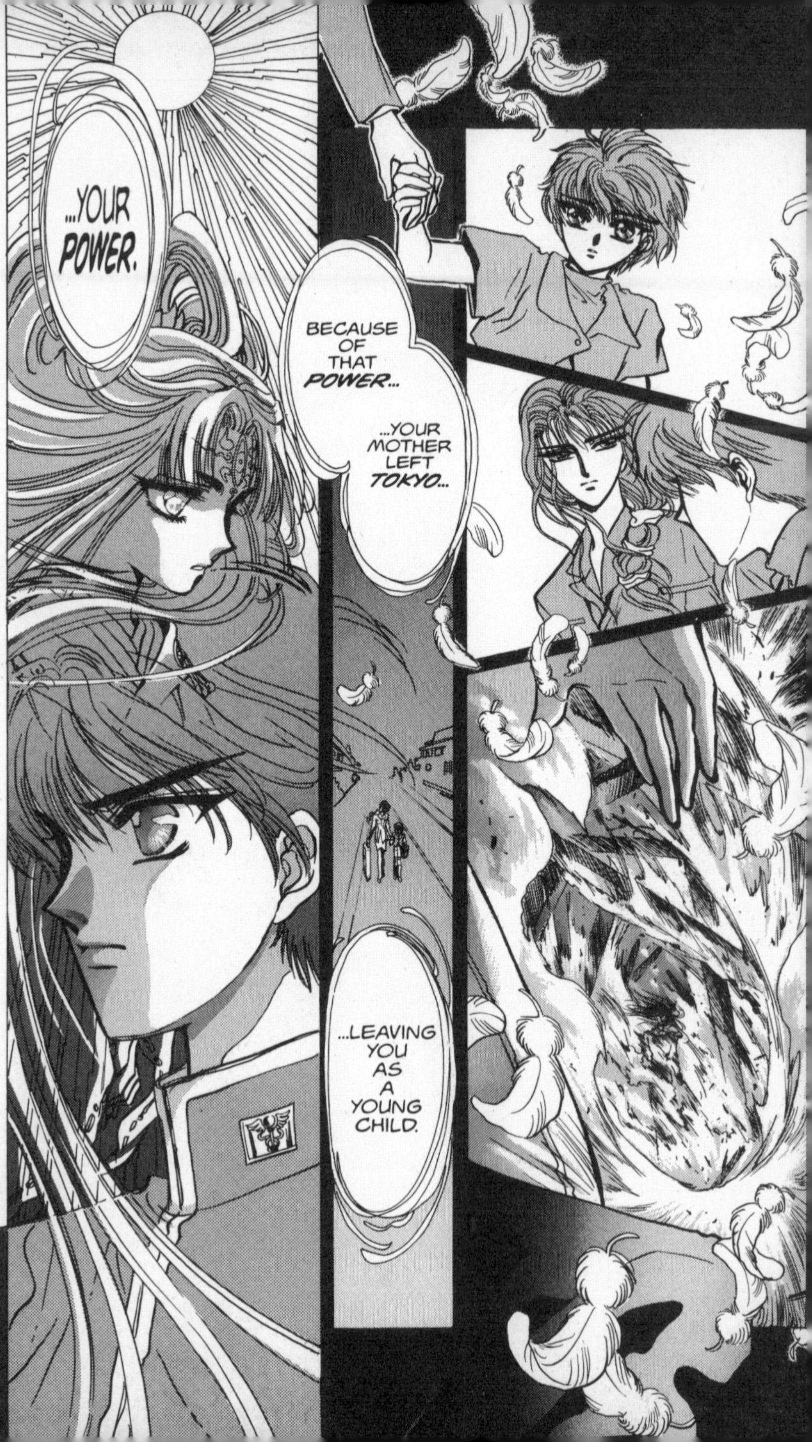

...YOUR POWER.
BECAUSE OF THAT POWER...
...YOUR MOTHER LEFT TOKYO...
...LEAVING YOU AS A YOUNG CHILD.

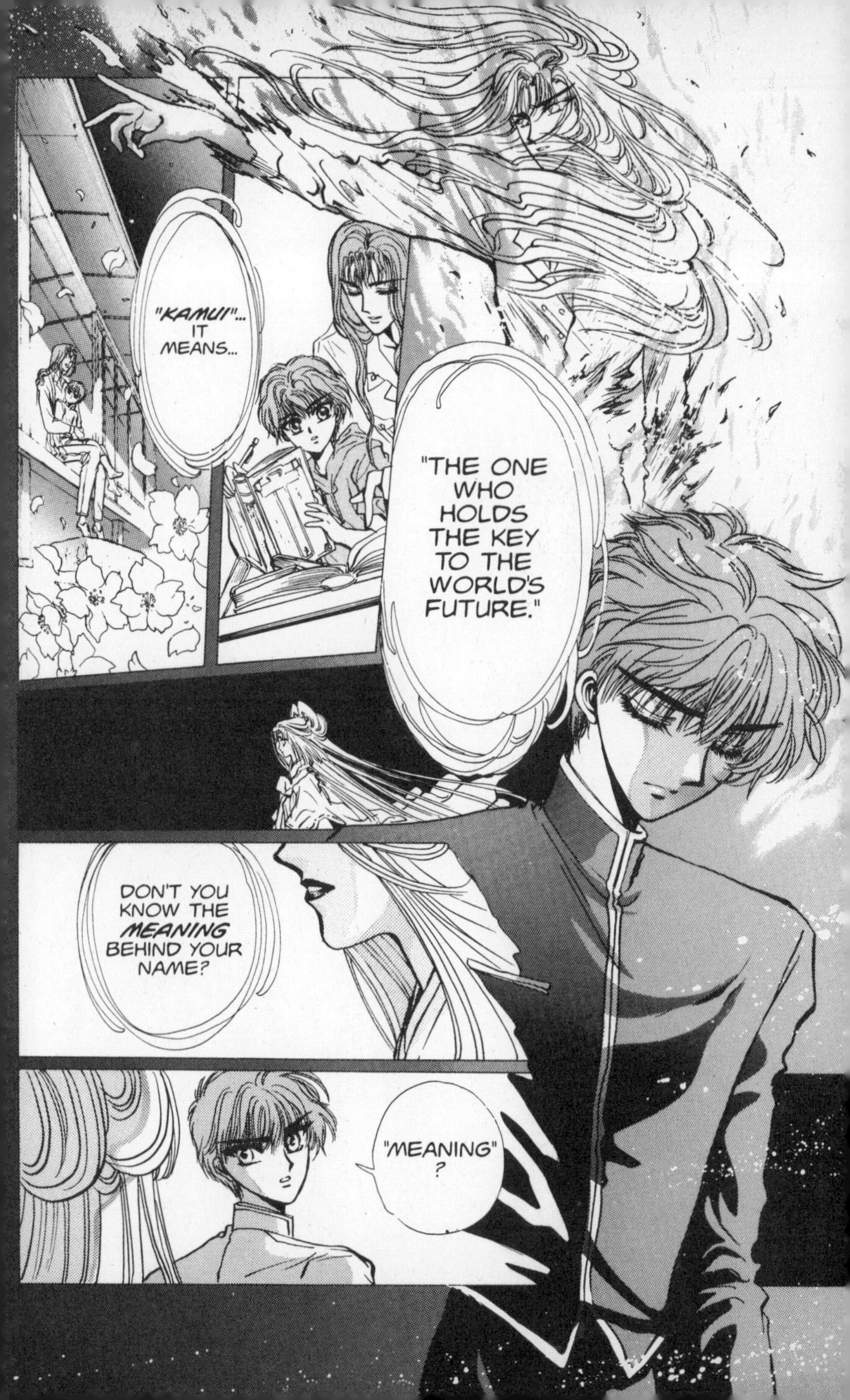
"KAMUI"... IT MEANS...
"THE ONE WHO HOLDS THE KEY TO THE WORLD'S FUTURE."
DON'T YOU KNOW THE MEANING BEHIND YOUR NAME?
"MEANING"?

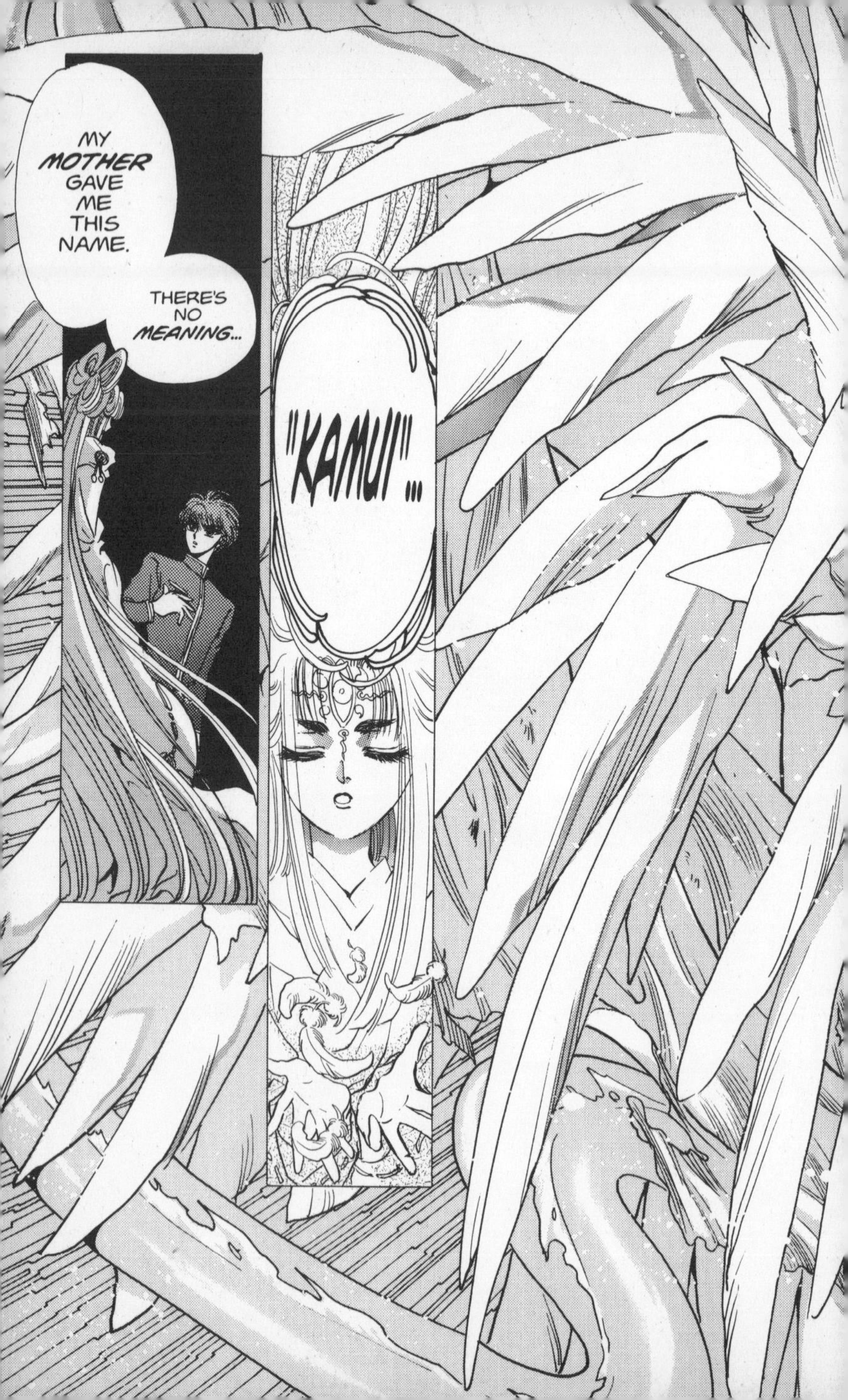
MY MOTHER GAVE ME THIS NAME.
THERE'S NO MEANING...
"KAMUI"...

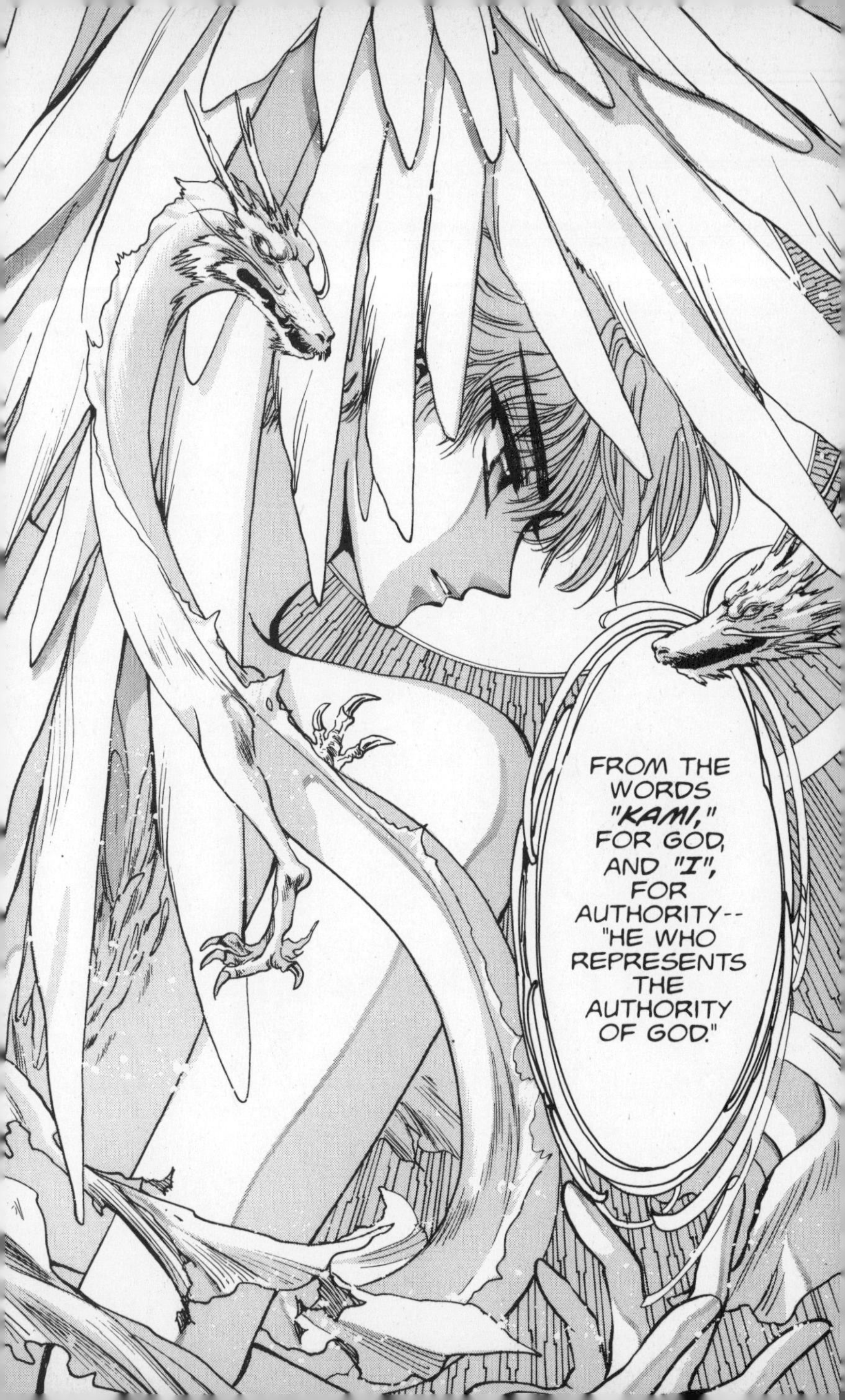
FROM THE WORDS "KAMI," FOR GOD, AND "I", FOR AUTHORITY-- "HE WHO REPRESENTS THE AUTHORITY OF GOD."

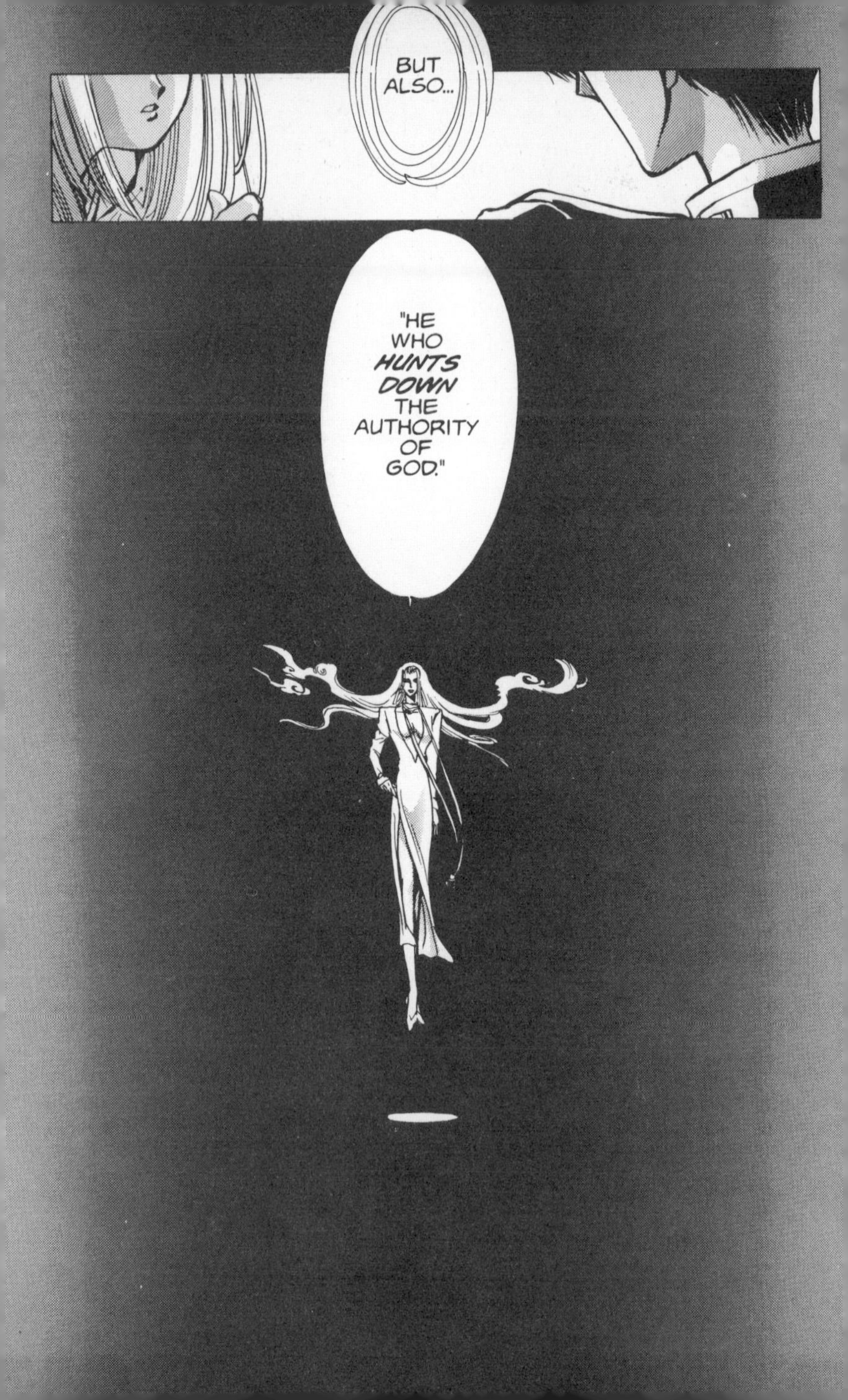
BUT ALSO...
"HE WHO HUNTS DOWN THE AUTHORITY OF GOD."

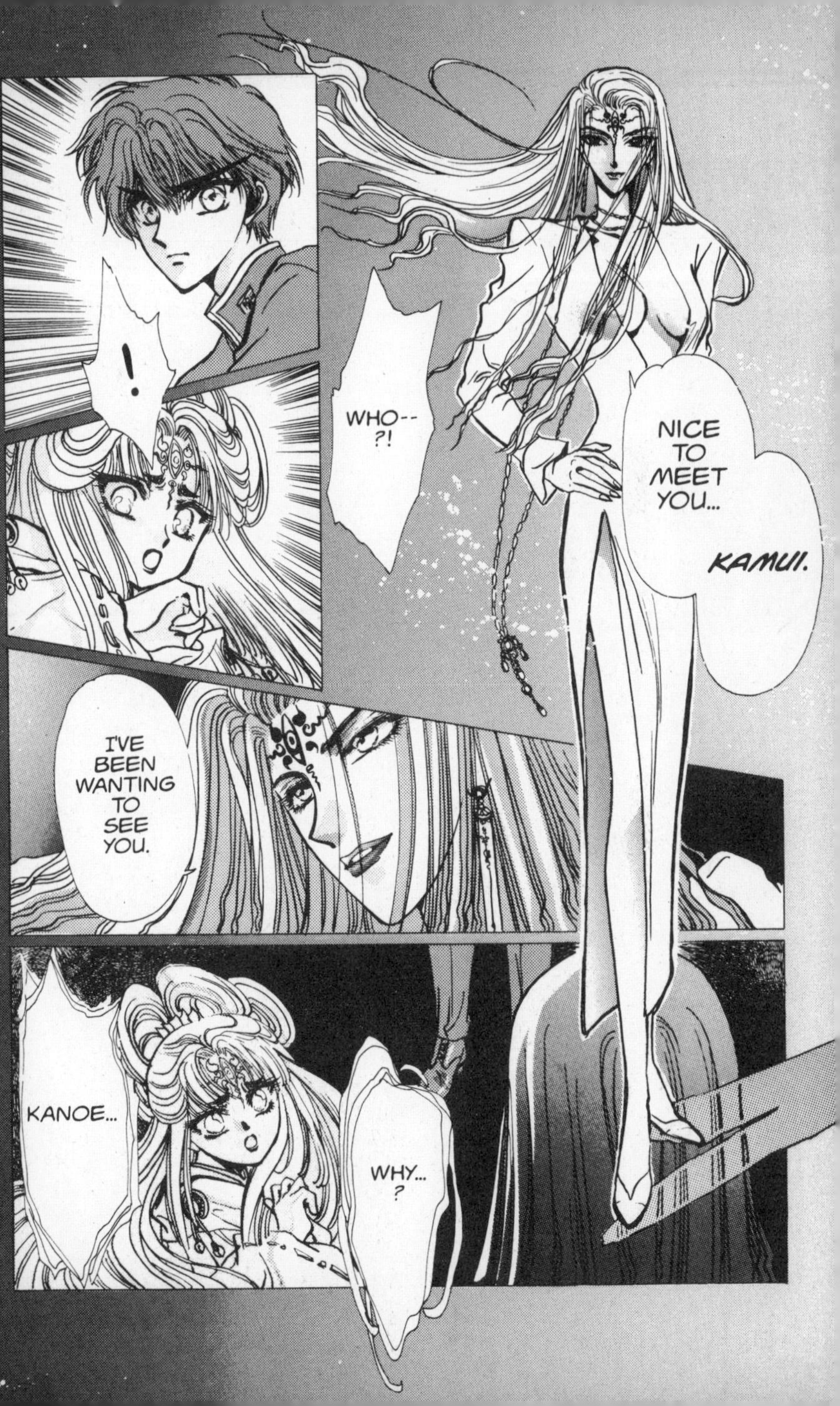
!
I'VE BEEN WANTING TO SEE YOU.
KANOE...
WHY... ?
WHO-- ?!
NICE TO MEET YOU...
KAMUI.

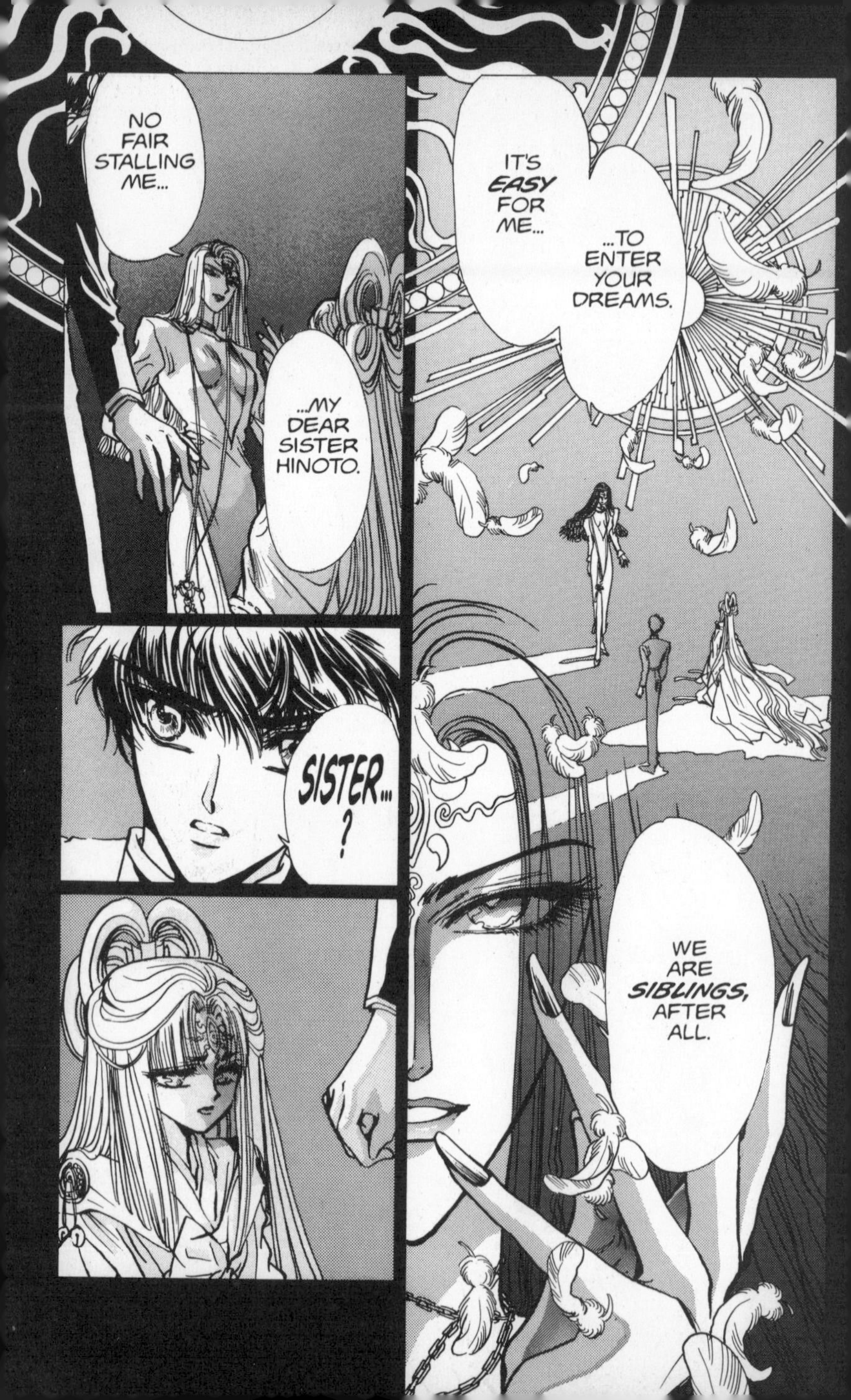
NO FAIR STALLING ME...
...MY DEAR SISTER HINOTO.
SISTER... ?
IT'S *EASY* FOR ME...
...TO ENTER YOUR DREAMS.
WE ARE *SIBLINGS*, AFTER ALL.

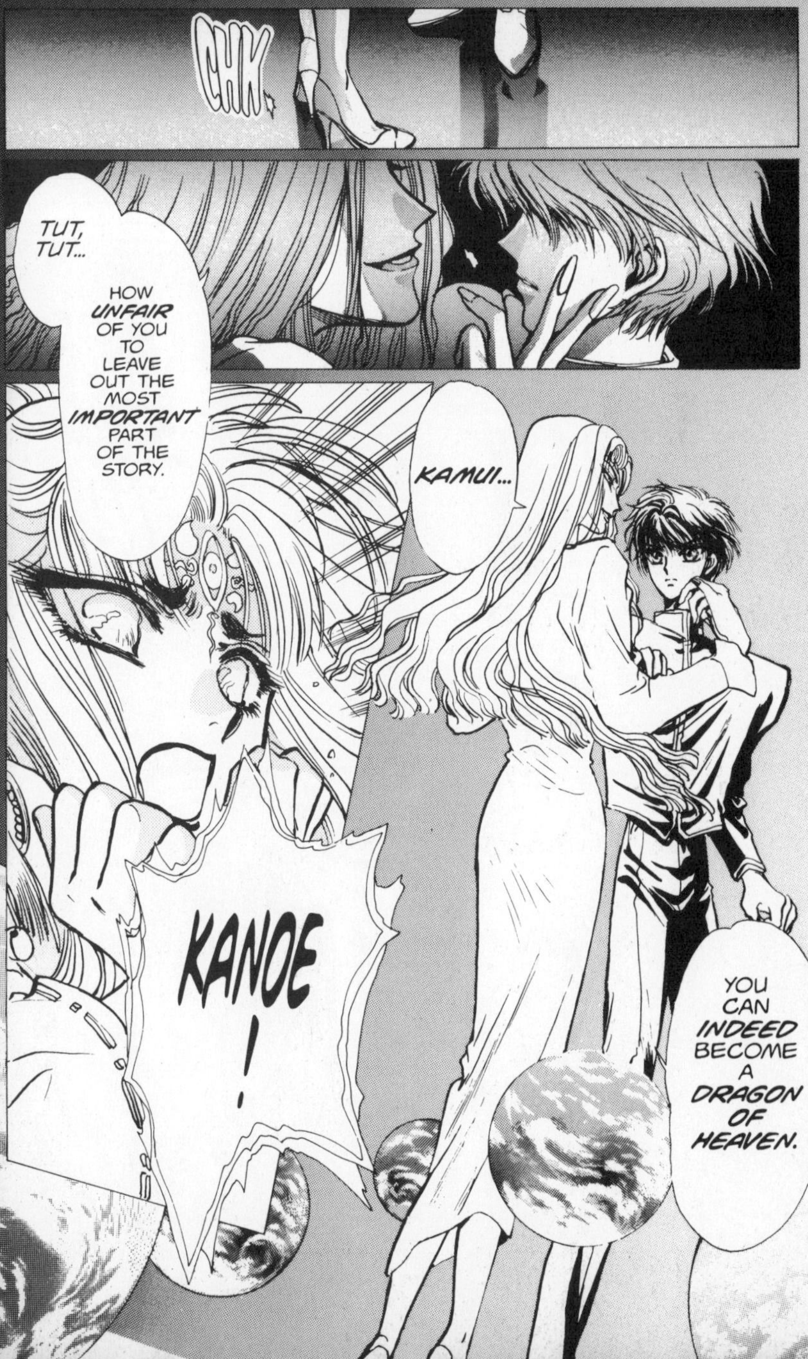
CHK
TUT, TUT...
HOW UNFAIR OF YOU TO LEAVE OUT THE MOST IMPORTANT PART OF THE STORY.
KAMUI...
YOU CAN INDEED BECOME A DRAGON OF HEAVEN.
KANOE!

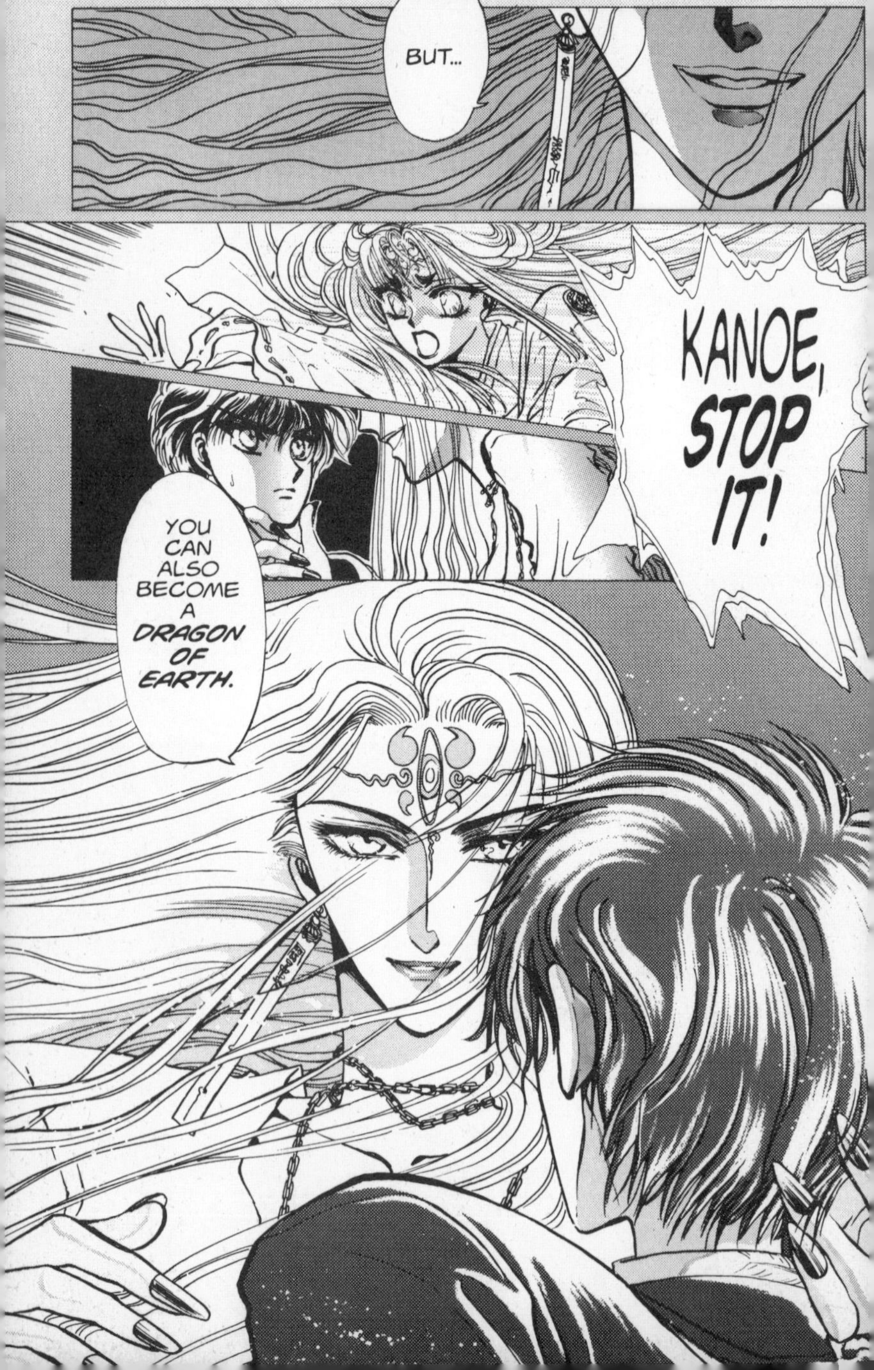
BUT...
KANOE, STOP IT!
YOU CAN ALSO BECOME A DRAGON OF EARTH.

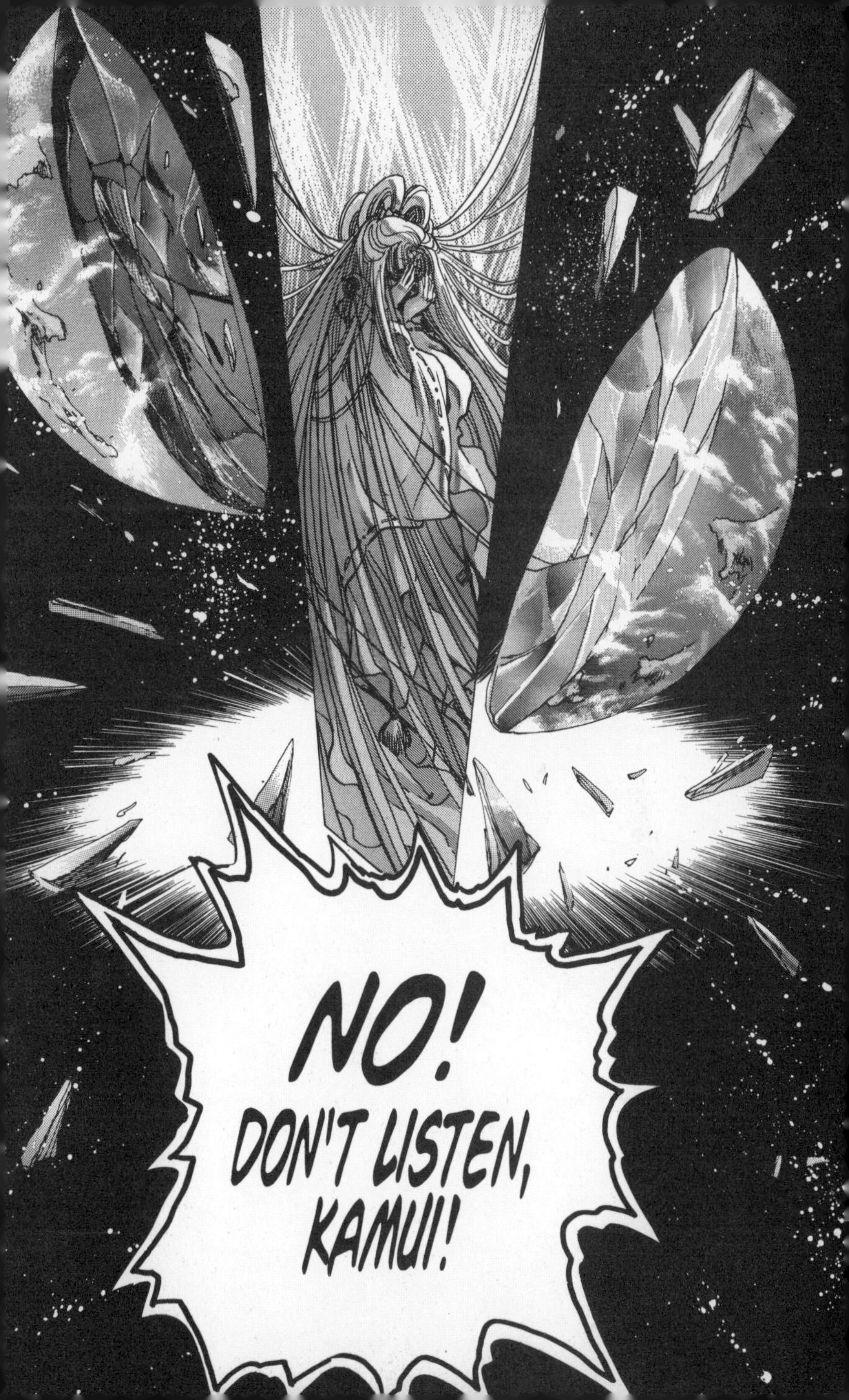
NO!
DON'T LISTEN, KAMUI!

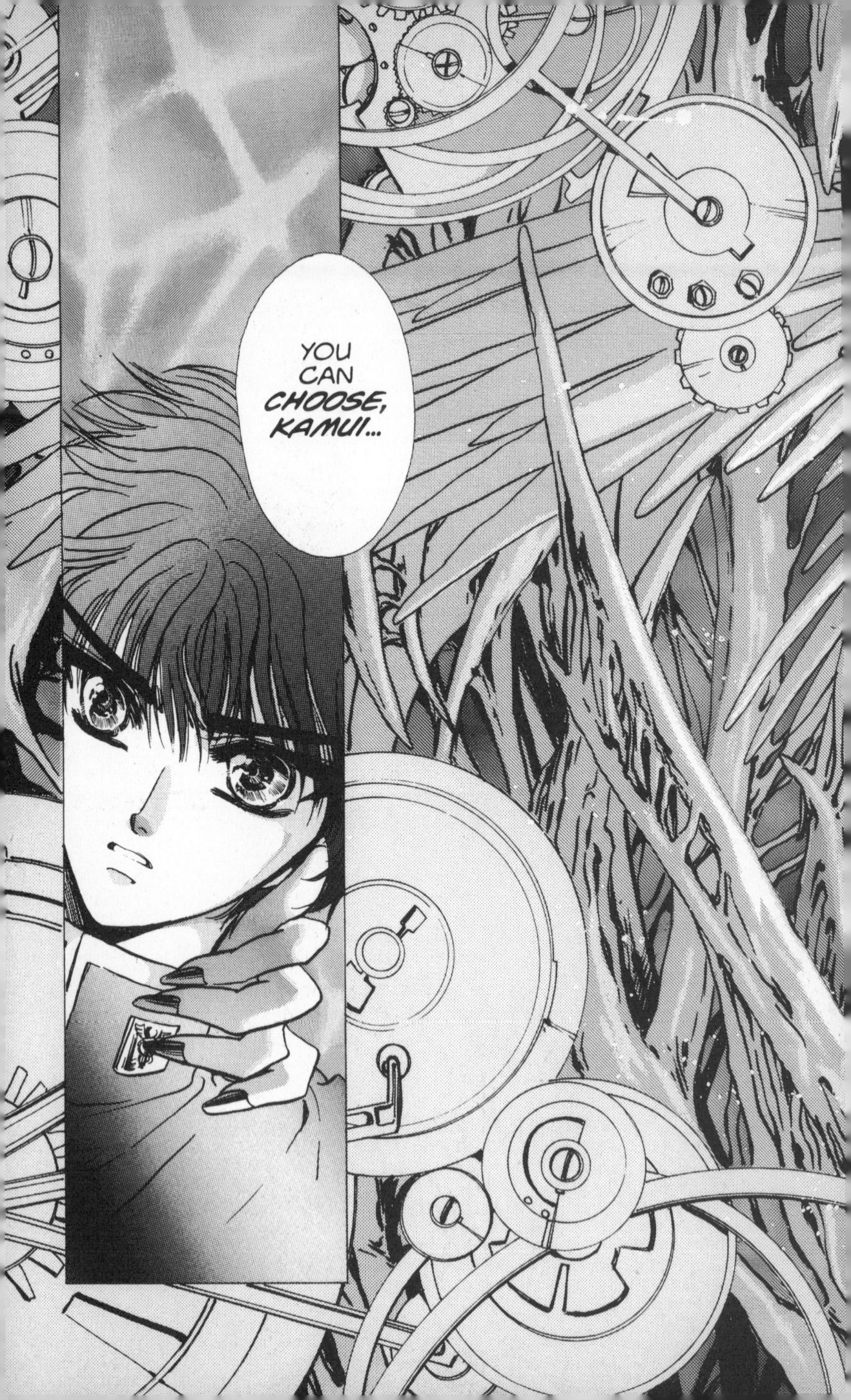
YOU CAN CHOOSE, KAMUI...

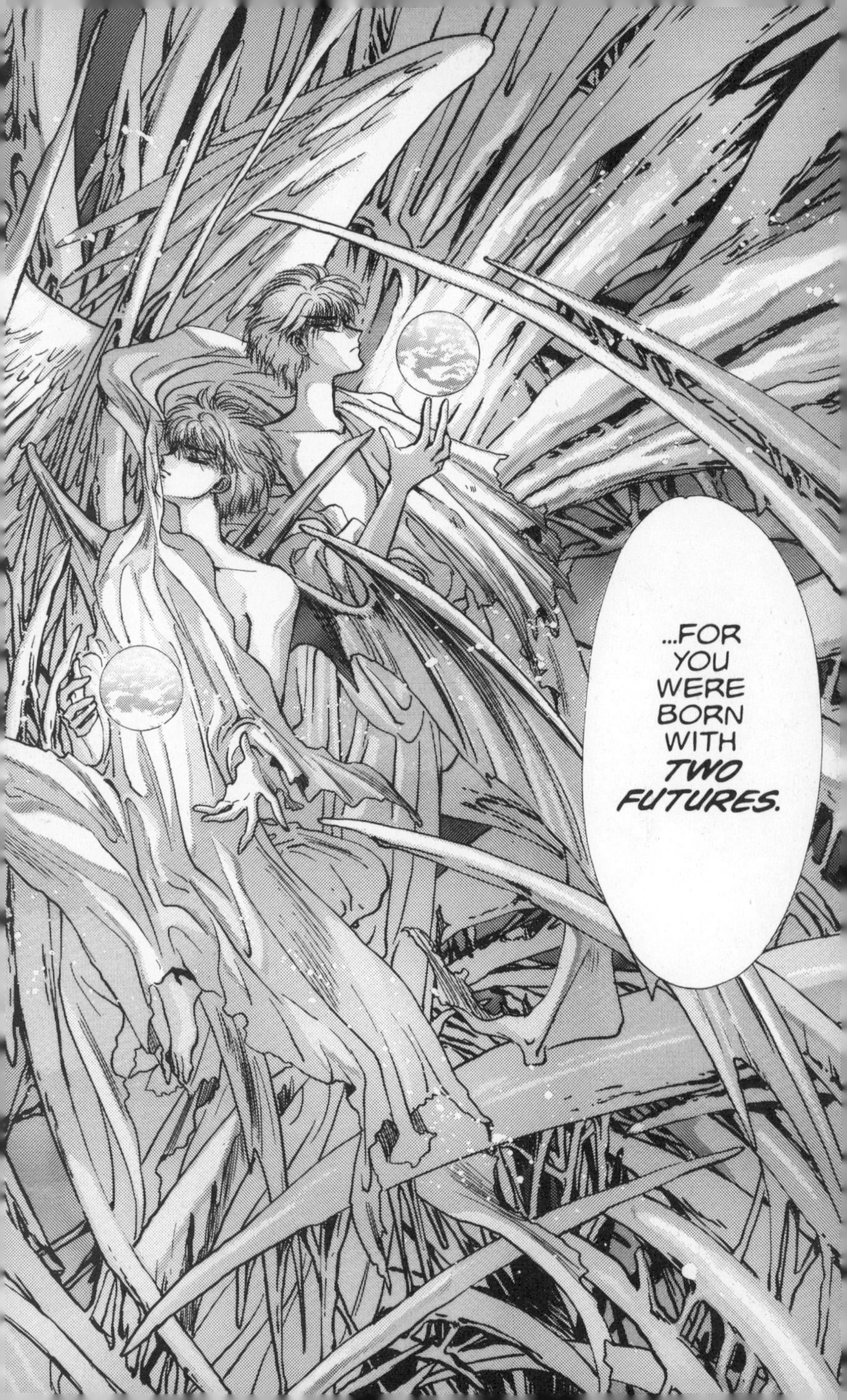
...FOR YOU WERE BORN WITH *TWO FUTURES.*

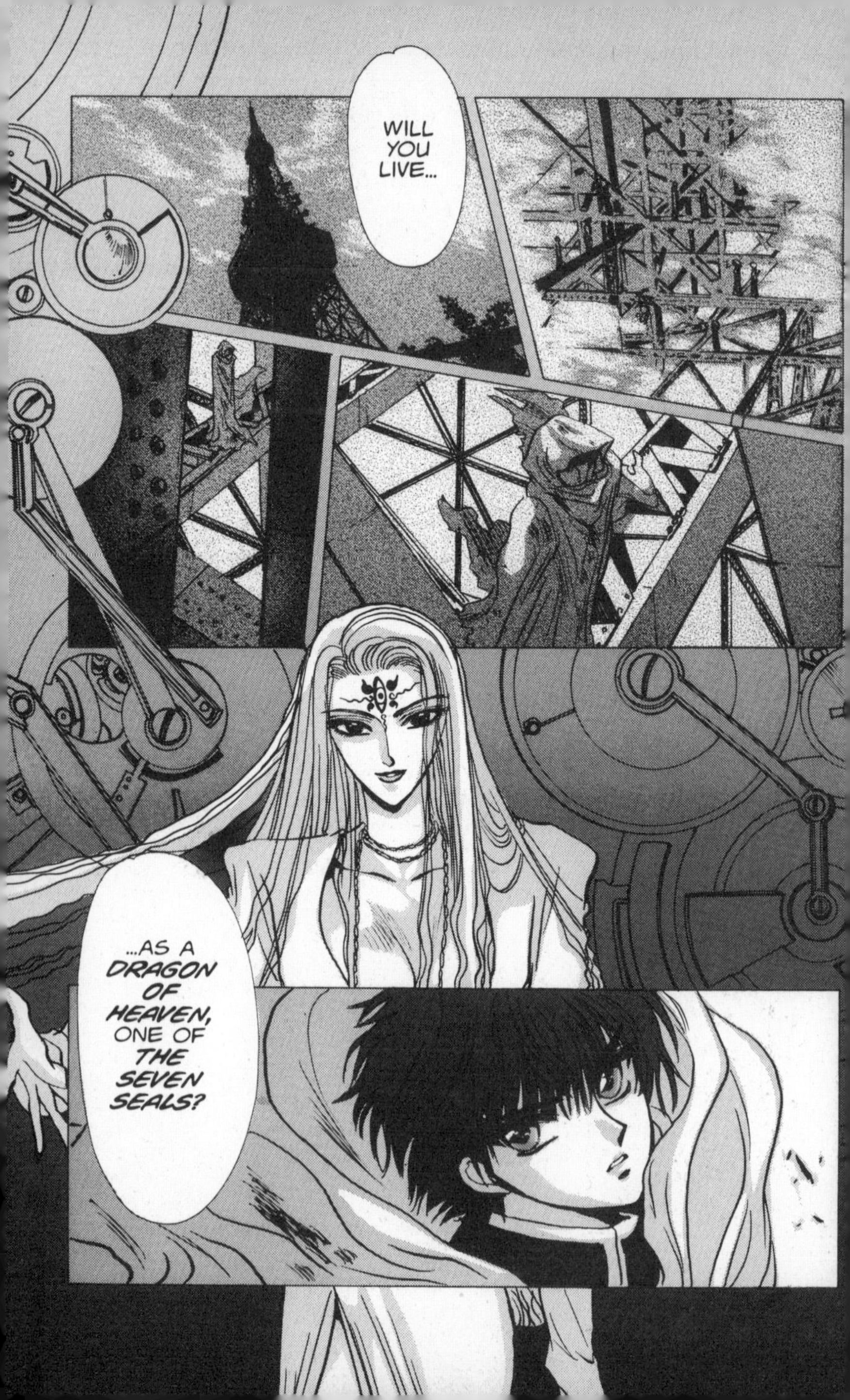
WILL YOU LIVE...
...AS A DRAGON OF HEAVEN, ONE OF THE SEVEN SEALS?

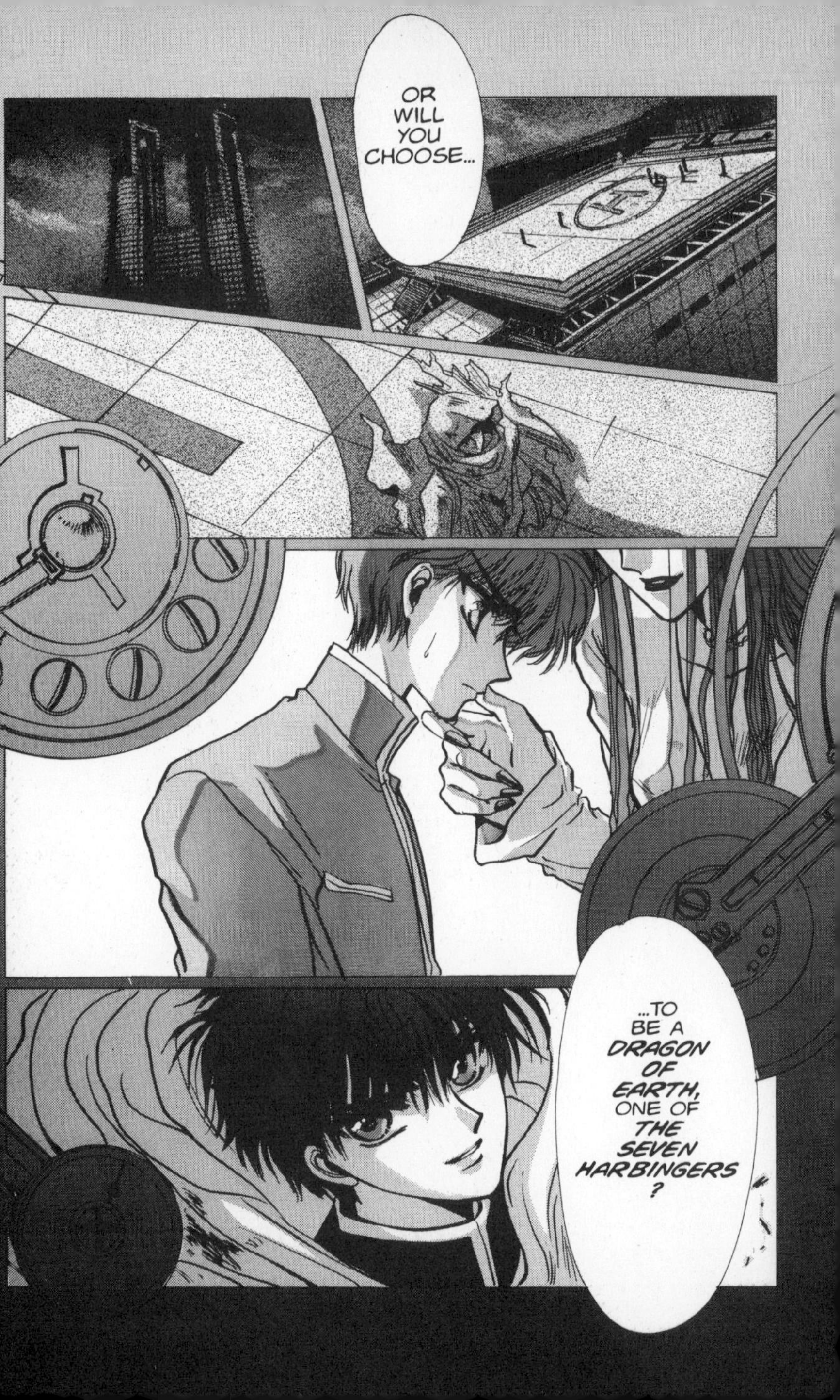
OR WILL YOU CHOOSE...
...TO BE A DRAGON OF EARTH, ONE OF THE SEVEN HARBINGERS?

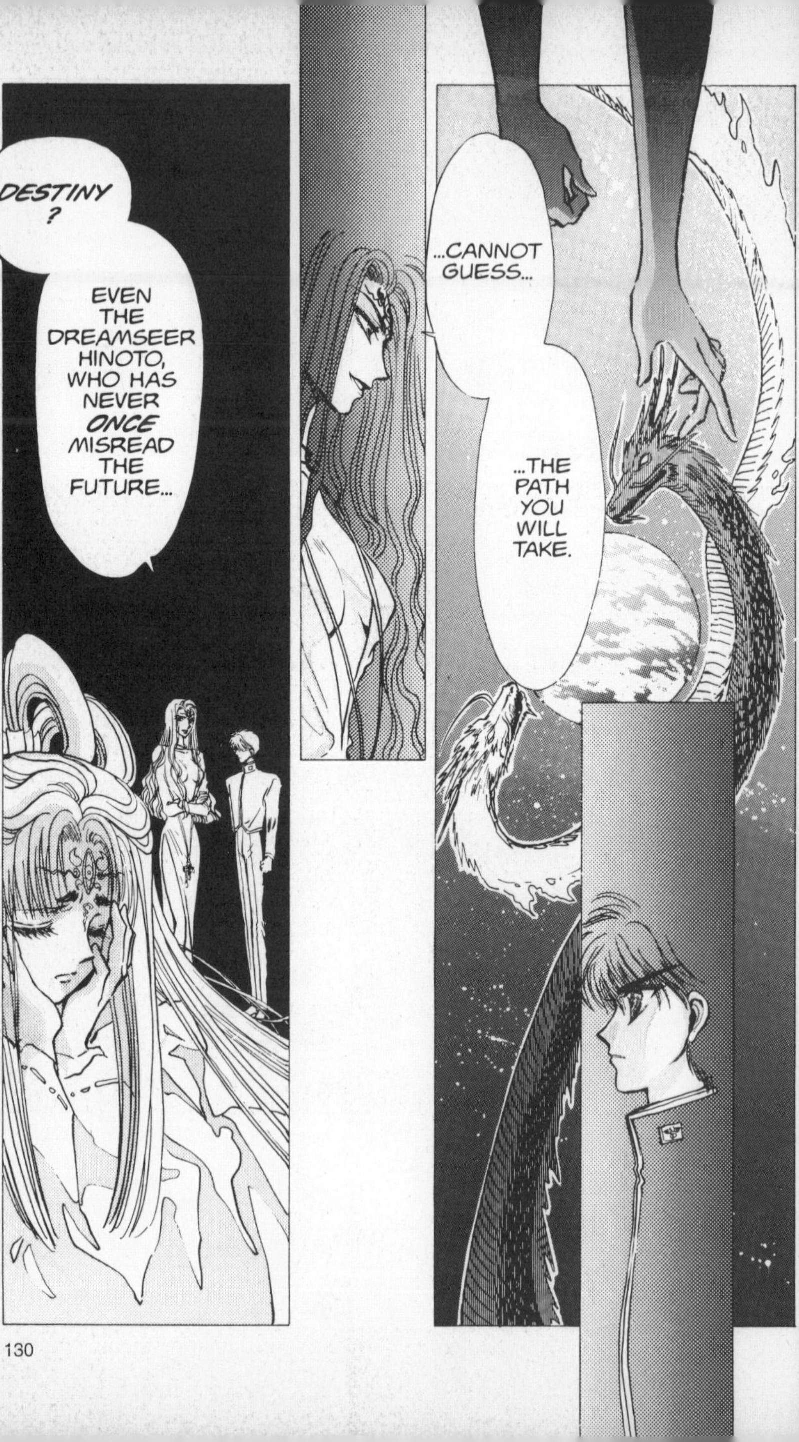
DESTINY?
EVEN THE DREAMSEER HINOTO, WHO HAS NEVER *ONCE* MISREAD THE FUTURE...
...CANNOT GUESS...
...THE PATH YOU WILL TAKE.

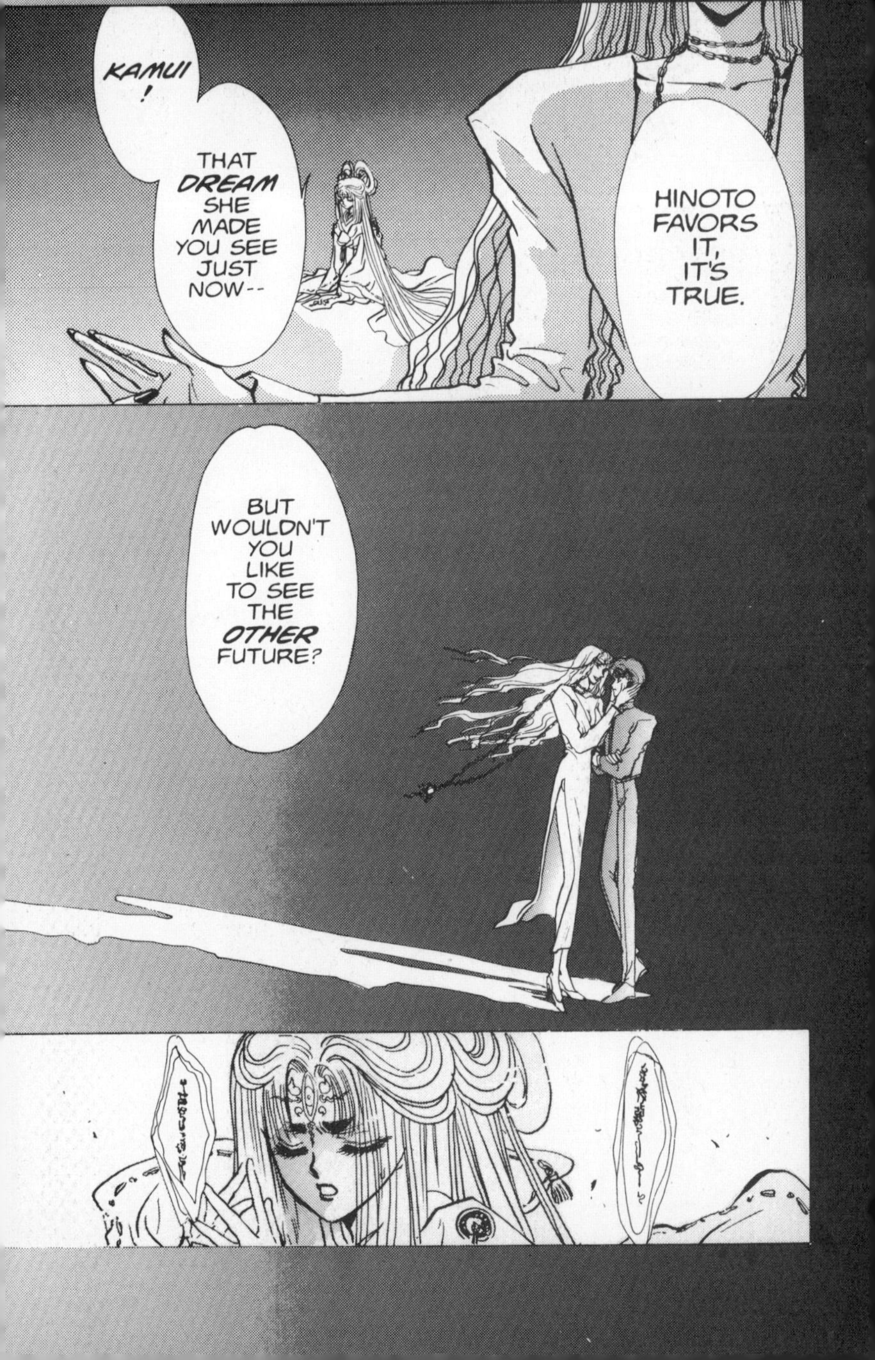
KAMUI!
THAT DREAM SHE MADE YOU SEE JUST NOW--
HINOTO FAVORS IT, IT'S TRUE.
BUT WOULDN'T YOU LIKE TO SEE THE OTHER FUTURE?

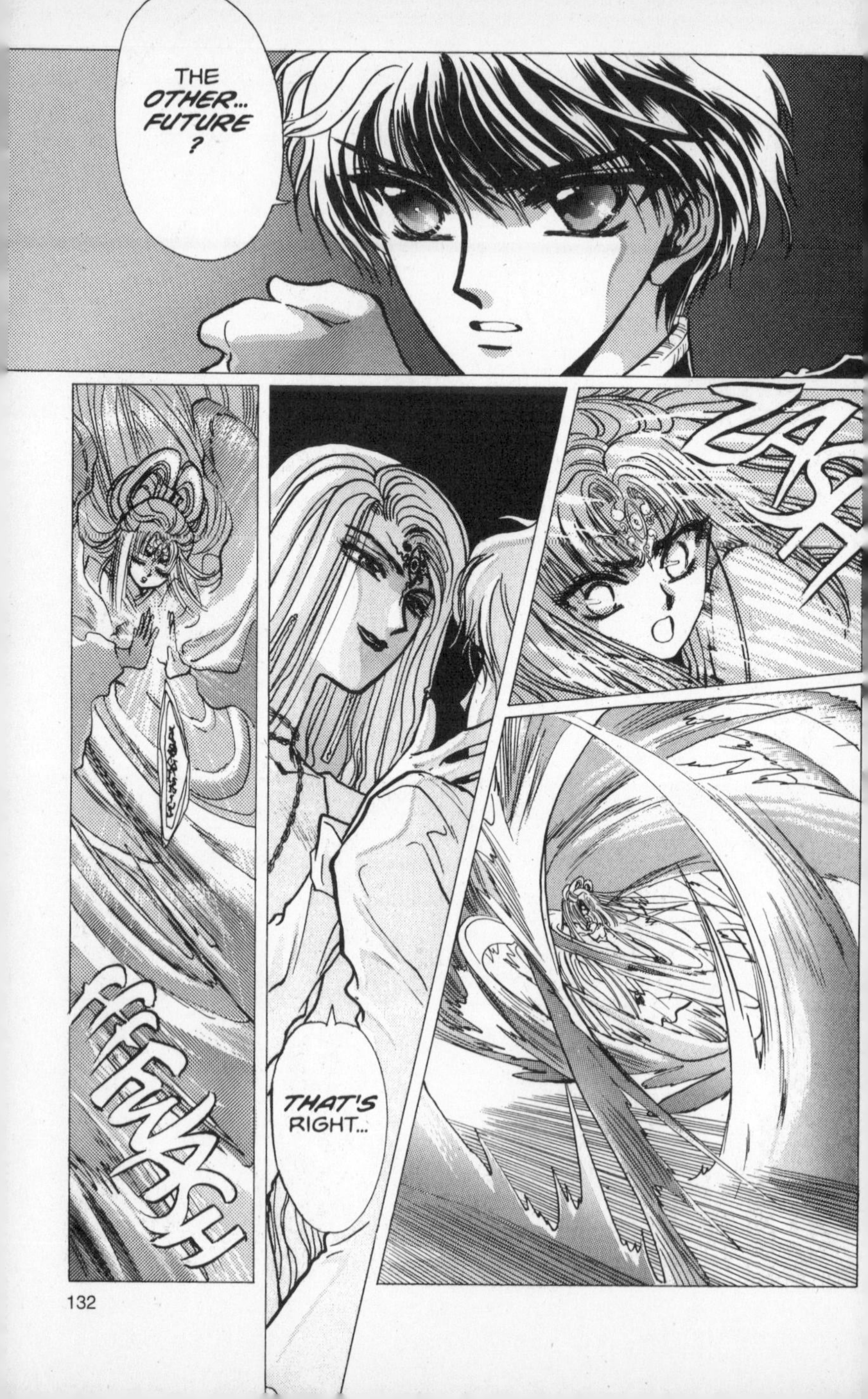
THE OTHER... FUTURE ?
FFFWASH
THAT'S RIGHT...
ZASH

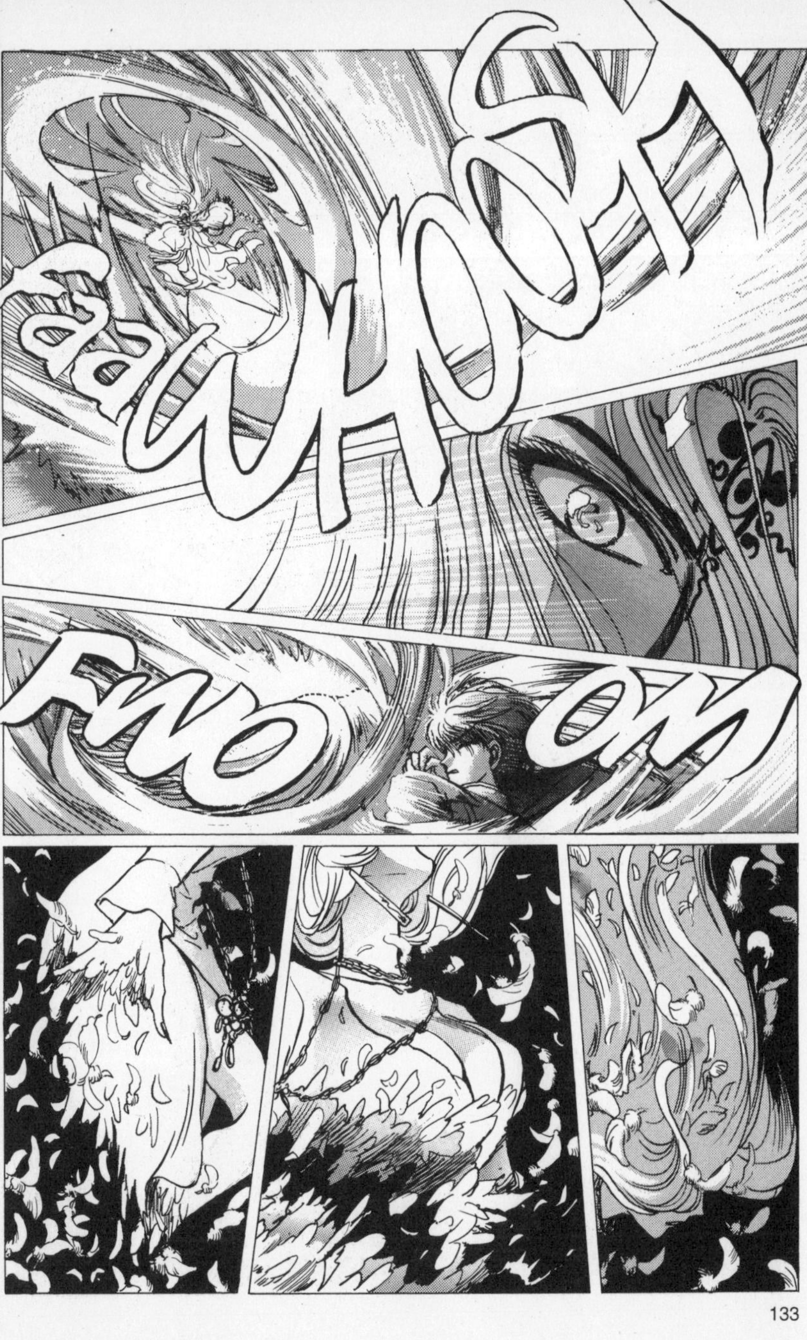
FWOOSH
FWOOM

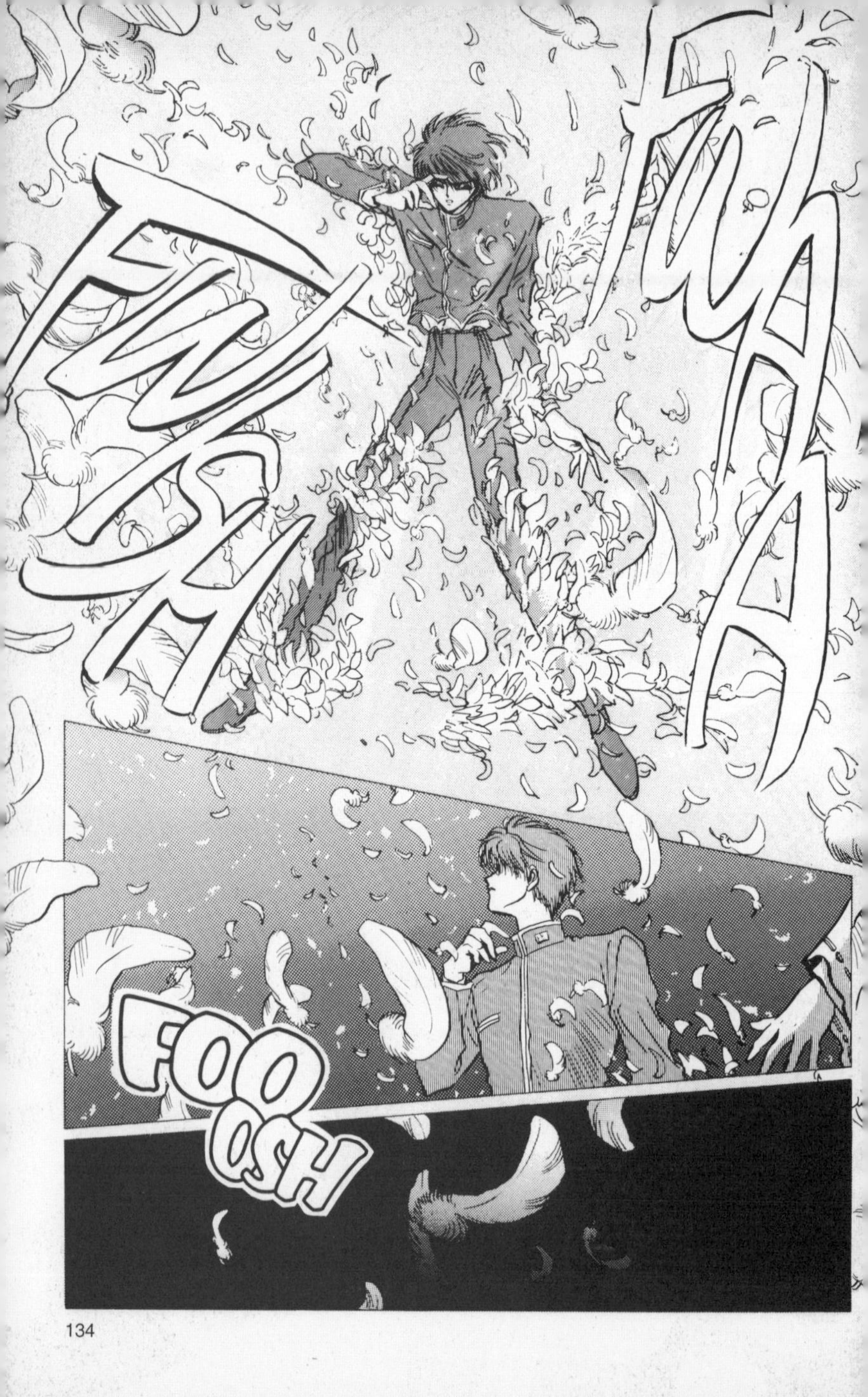
FWSH
FOO
OSH

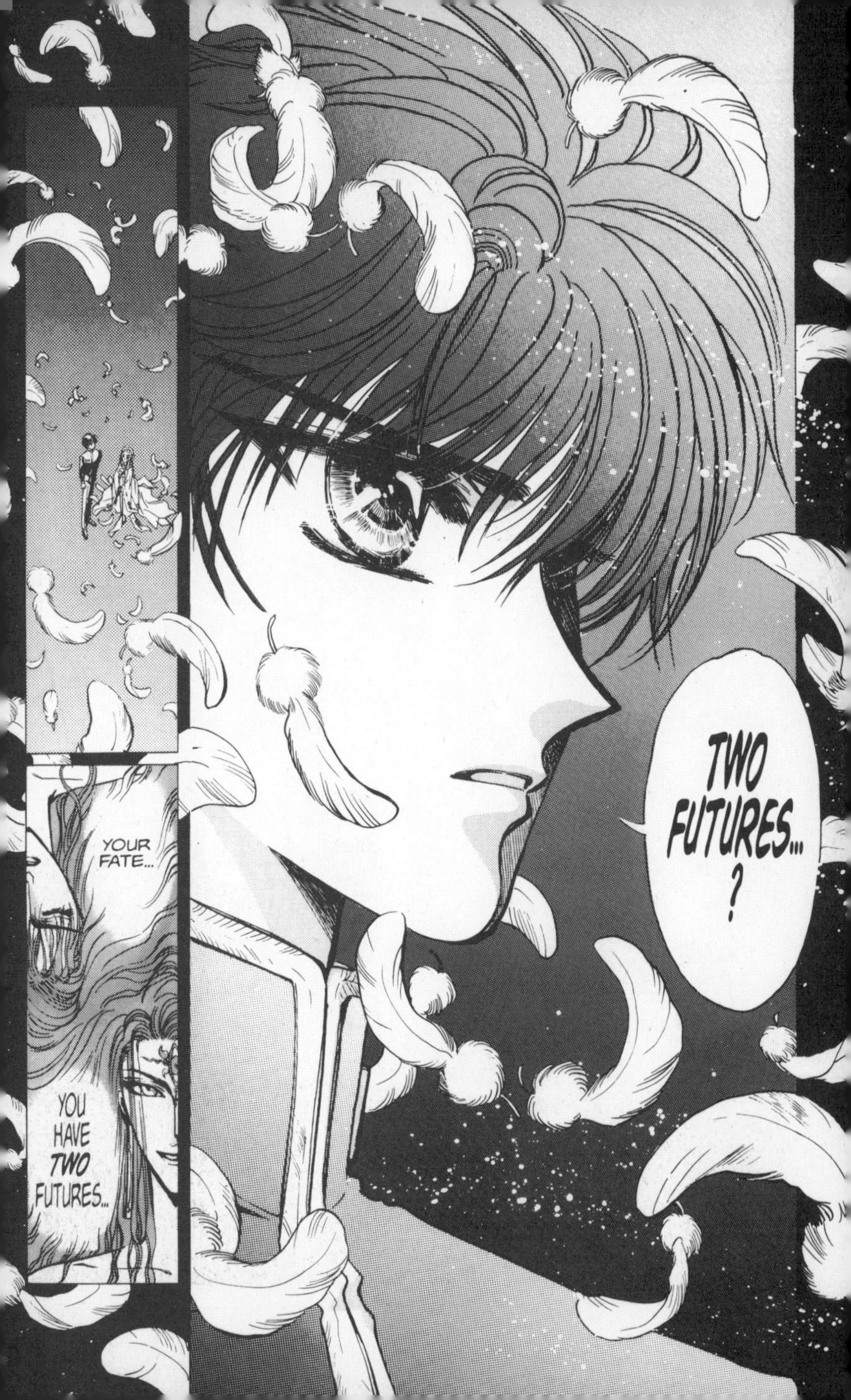
YOUR FATE...
YOU HAVE *TWO* FUTURES...
TWO FUTURES... ?

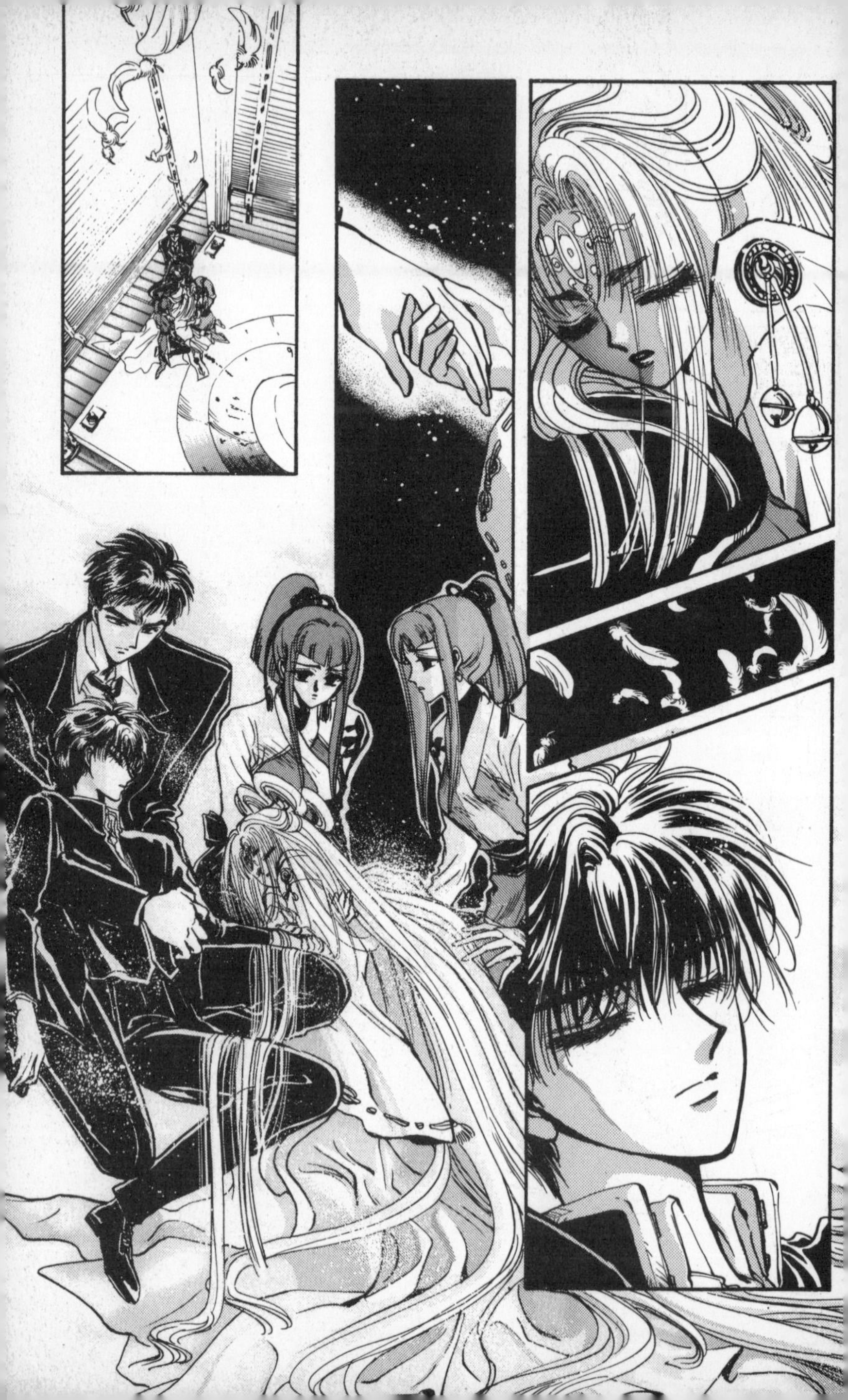

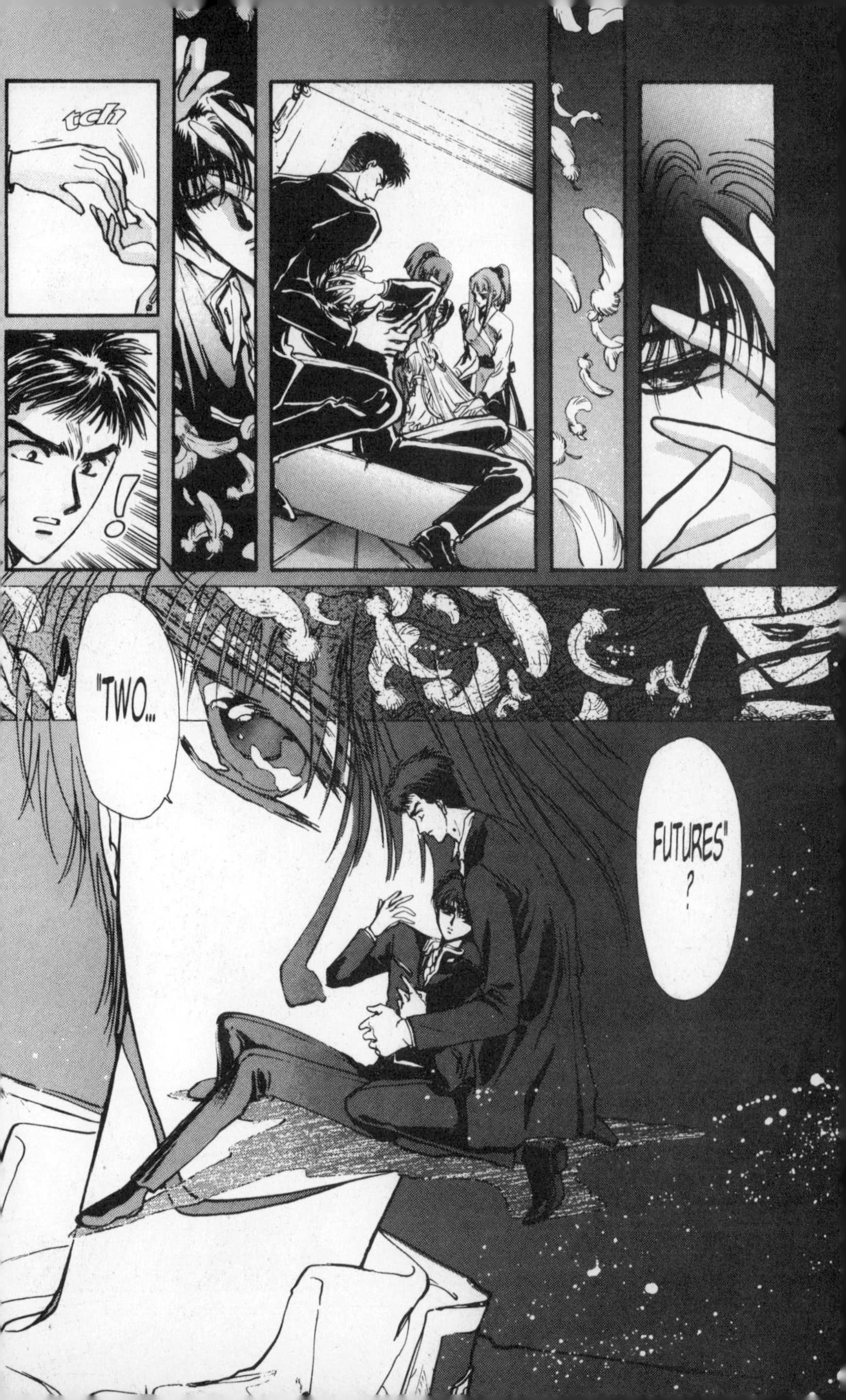
tch
!
"TWO...
FUTURES"
?

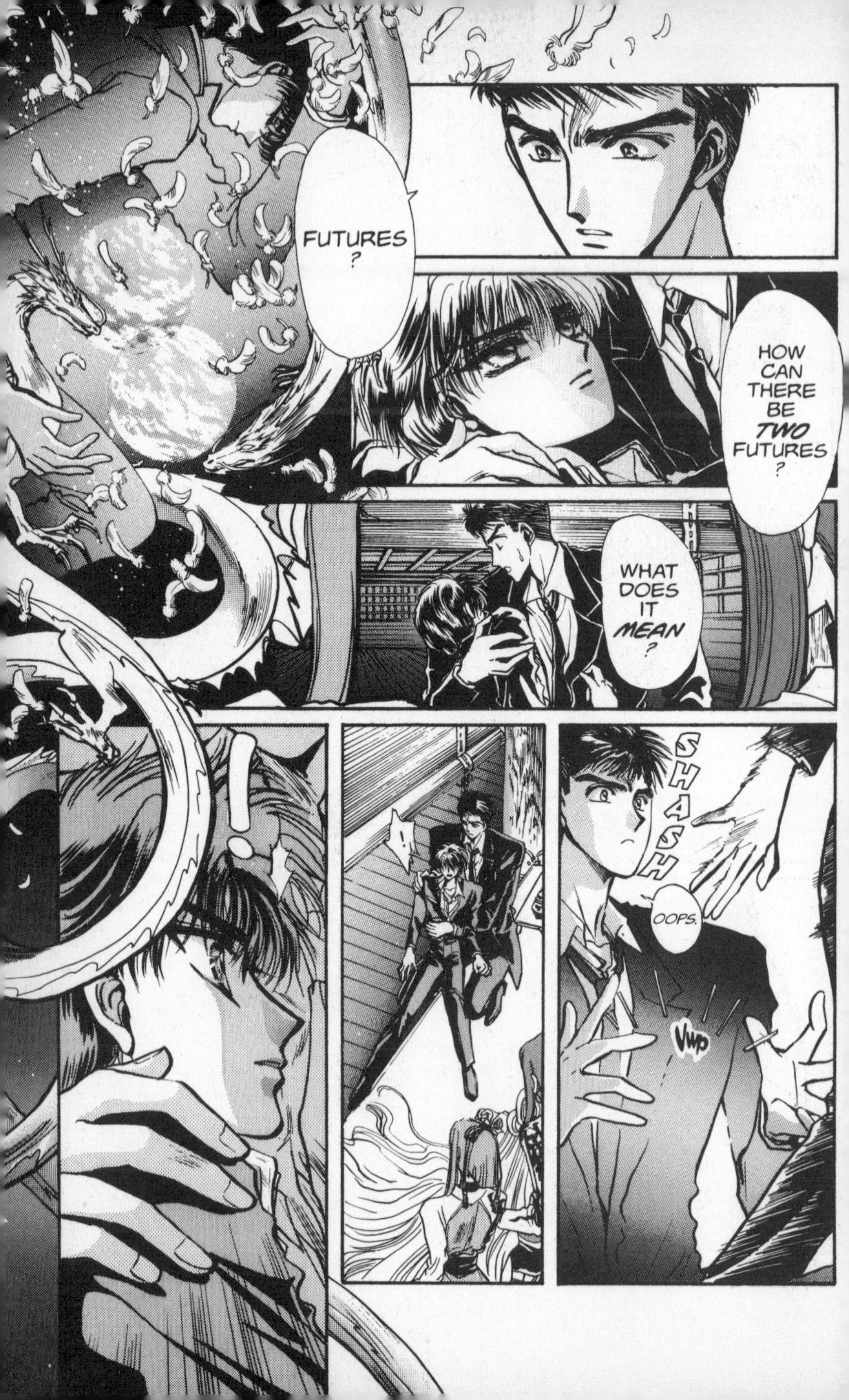
FUTURES?
HOW CAN THERE BE TWO FUTURES?
WHAT DOES IT MEAN?
!
!
SHASH
OOPS.
VWP

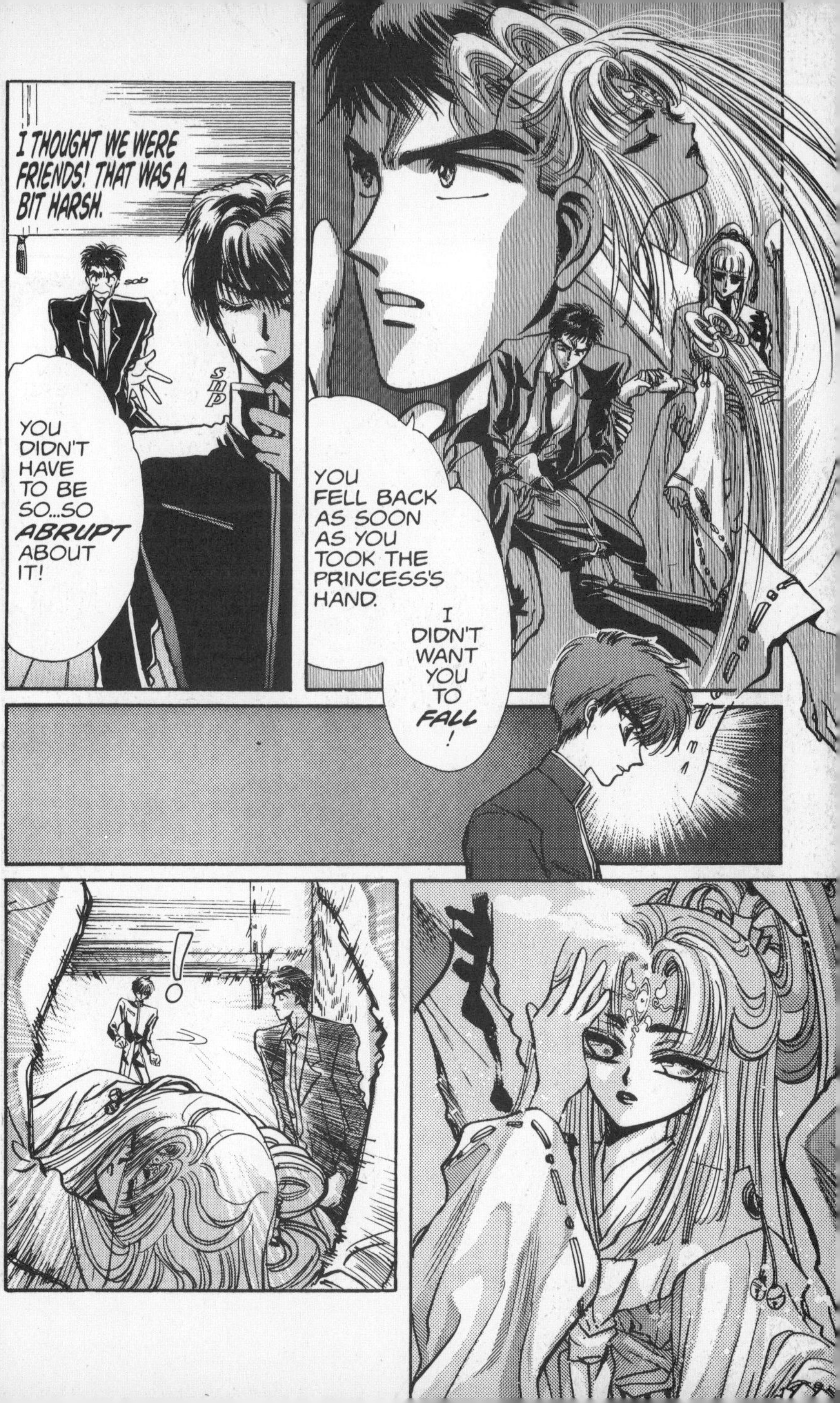
I THOUGHT WE WERE FRIENDS! THAT WAS A BIT HARSH.
sob
snp
YOU DIDN'T HAVE TO BE SO...SO ABRUPT ABOUT IT!
YOU FELL BACK AS SOON AS YOU TOOK THE PRINCESS'S HAND.
I DIDN'T WANT YOU TO FALL!
!

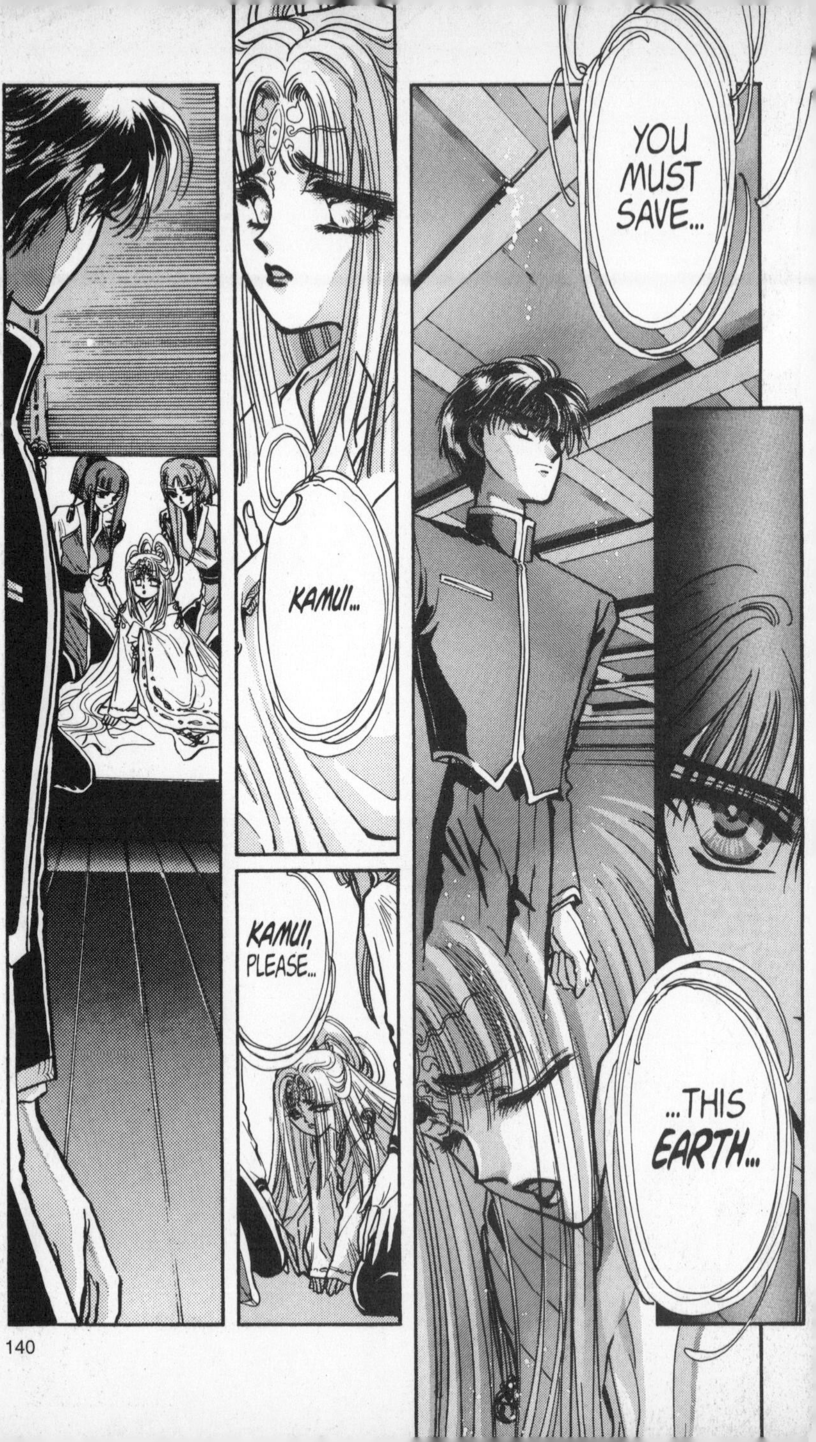
KAMUI...
KAMUI, PLEASE...
YOU MUST SAVE...
...THIS EARTH...

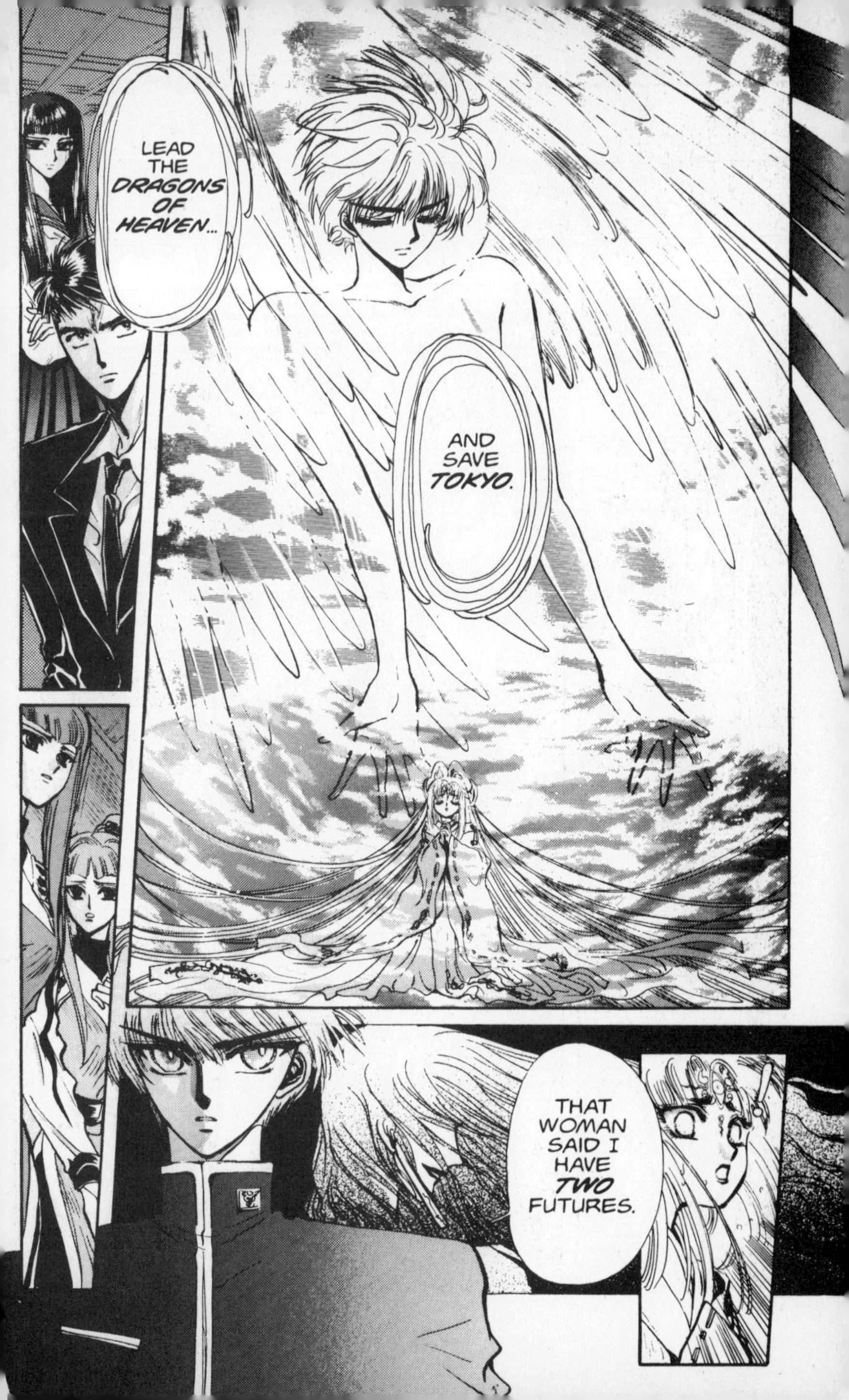
LEAD THE *DRAGONS OF HEAVEN...*
AND SAVE *TOKYO.*
THAT WOMAN SAID I HAVE ***TWO*** FUTURES.

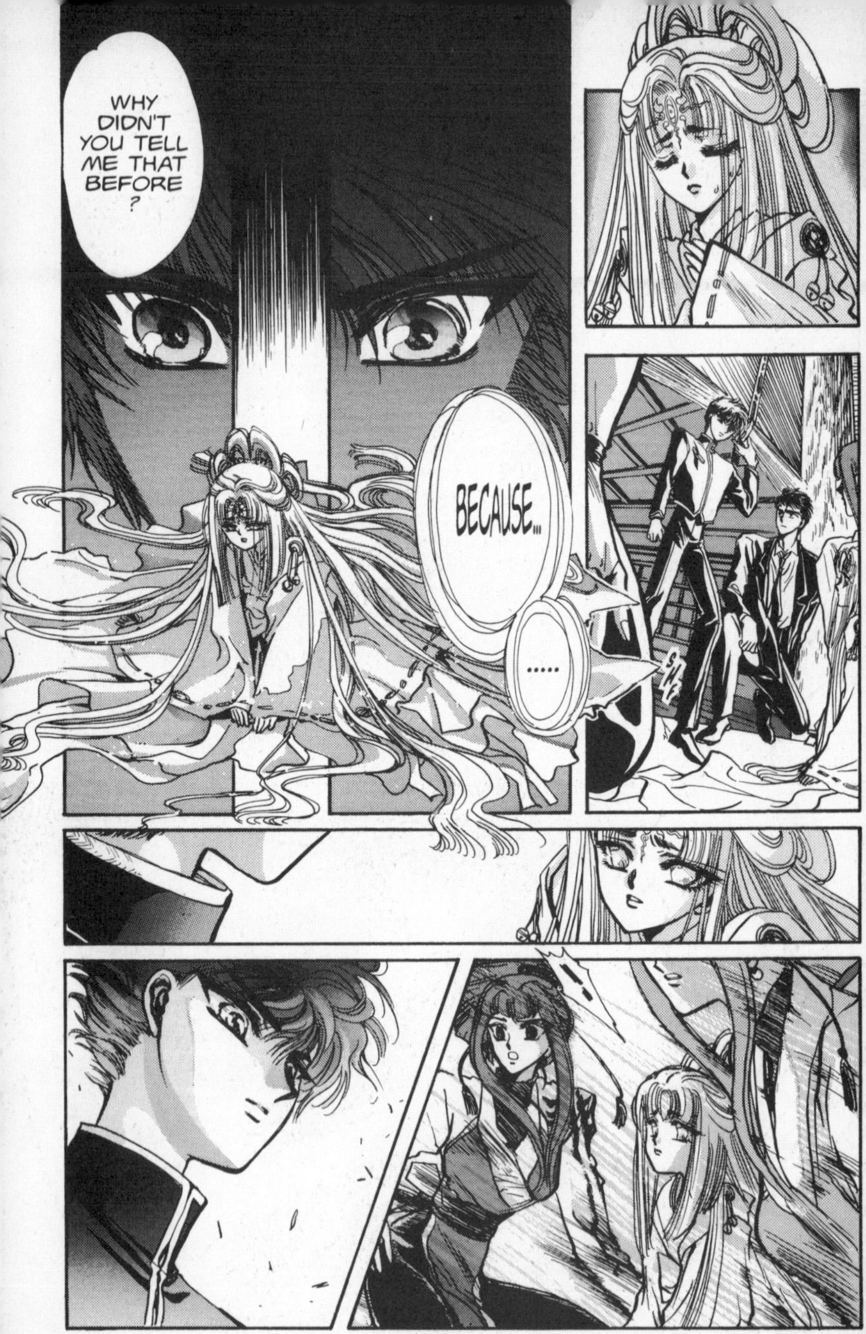
WHY DIDN'T YOU TELL ME THAT BEFORE ?
BECAUSE...
.....

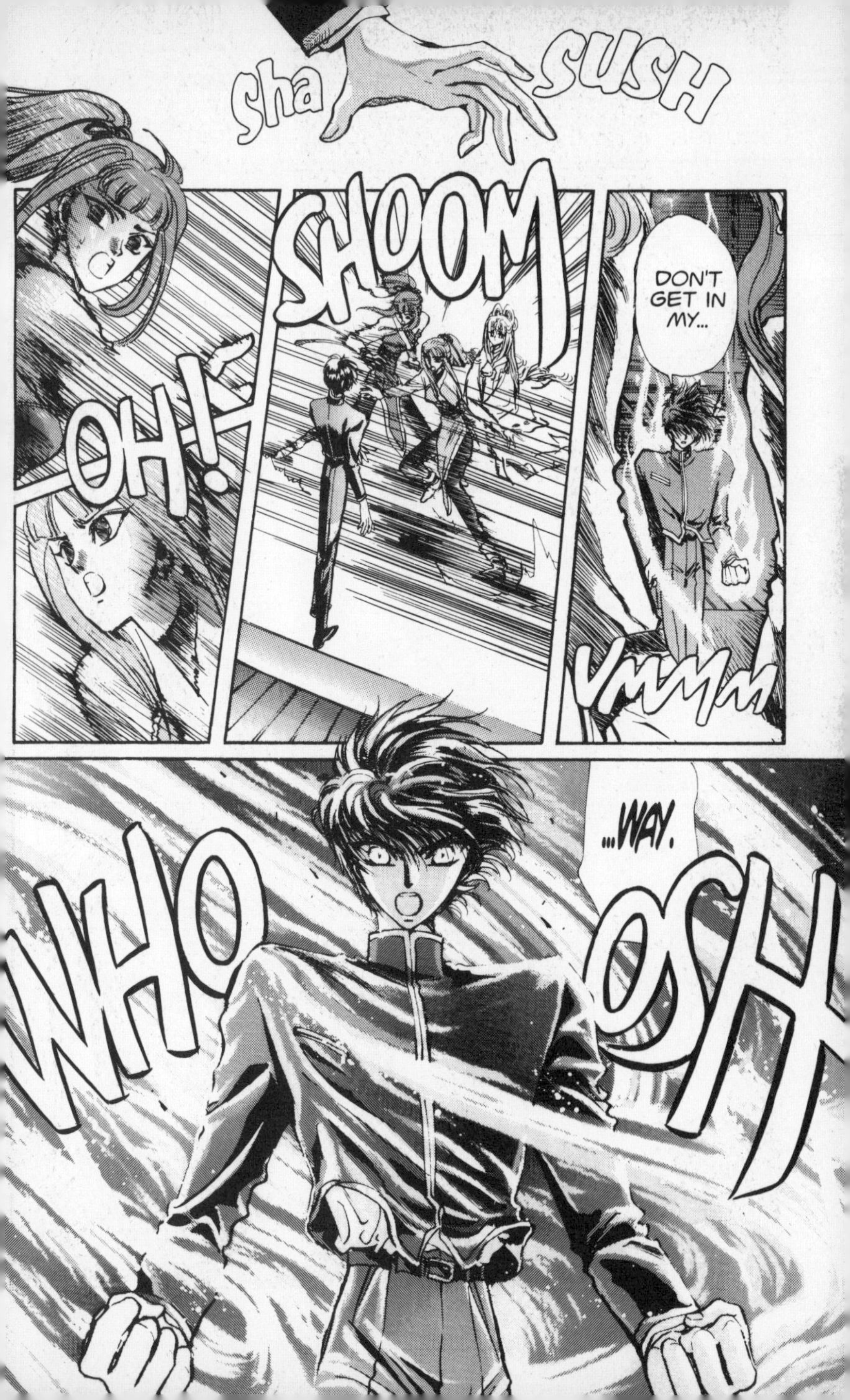
Sha
SUSH
OH!
SHOOM
DON'T GET IN MY...
VMMMM
WHO
...WAY.
OSH

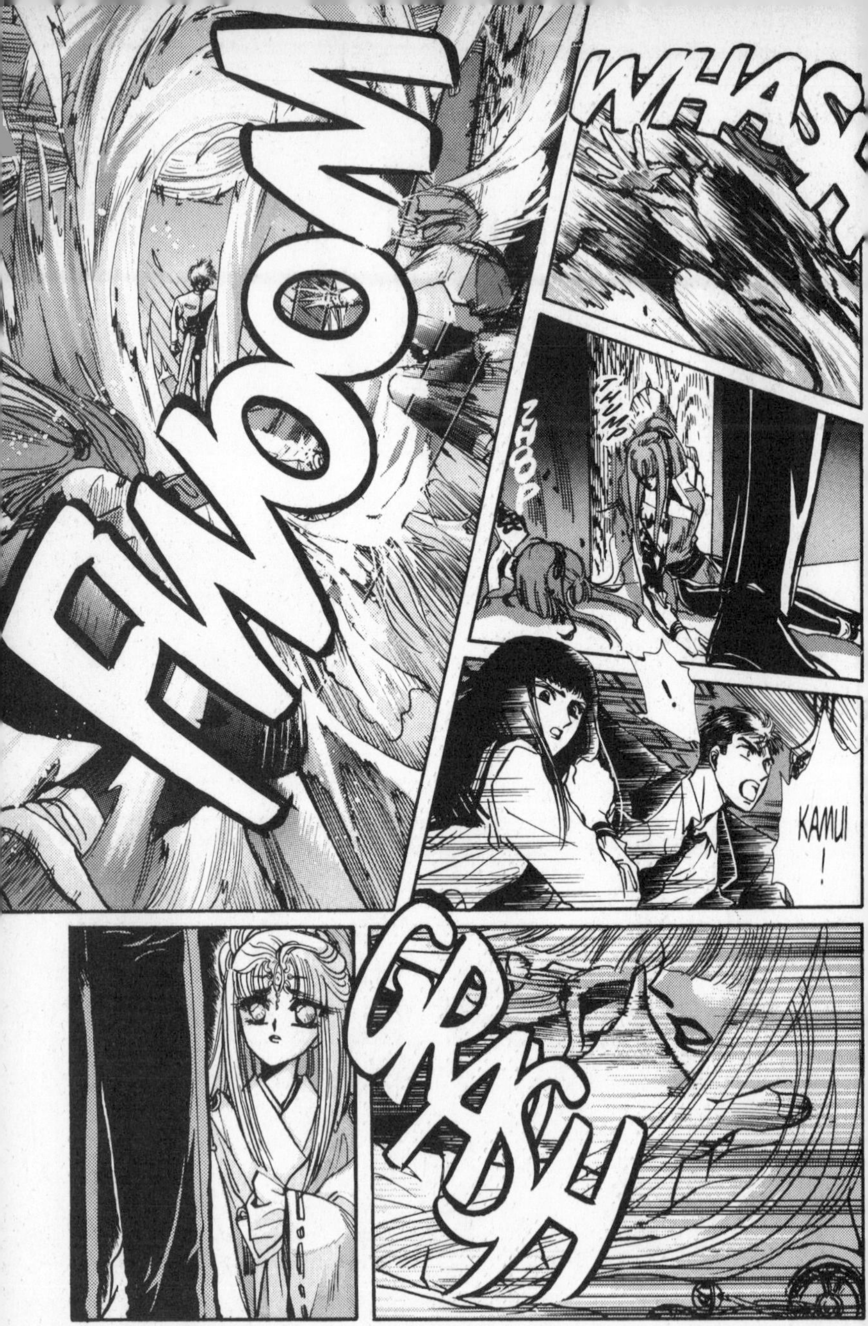
WHOOM
WHASH...
THUMP
WHOOP
!
KAMUI!
CRASH

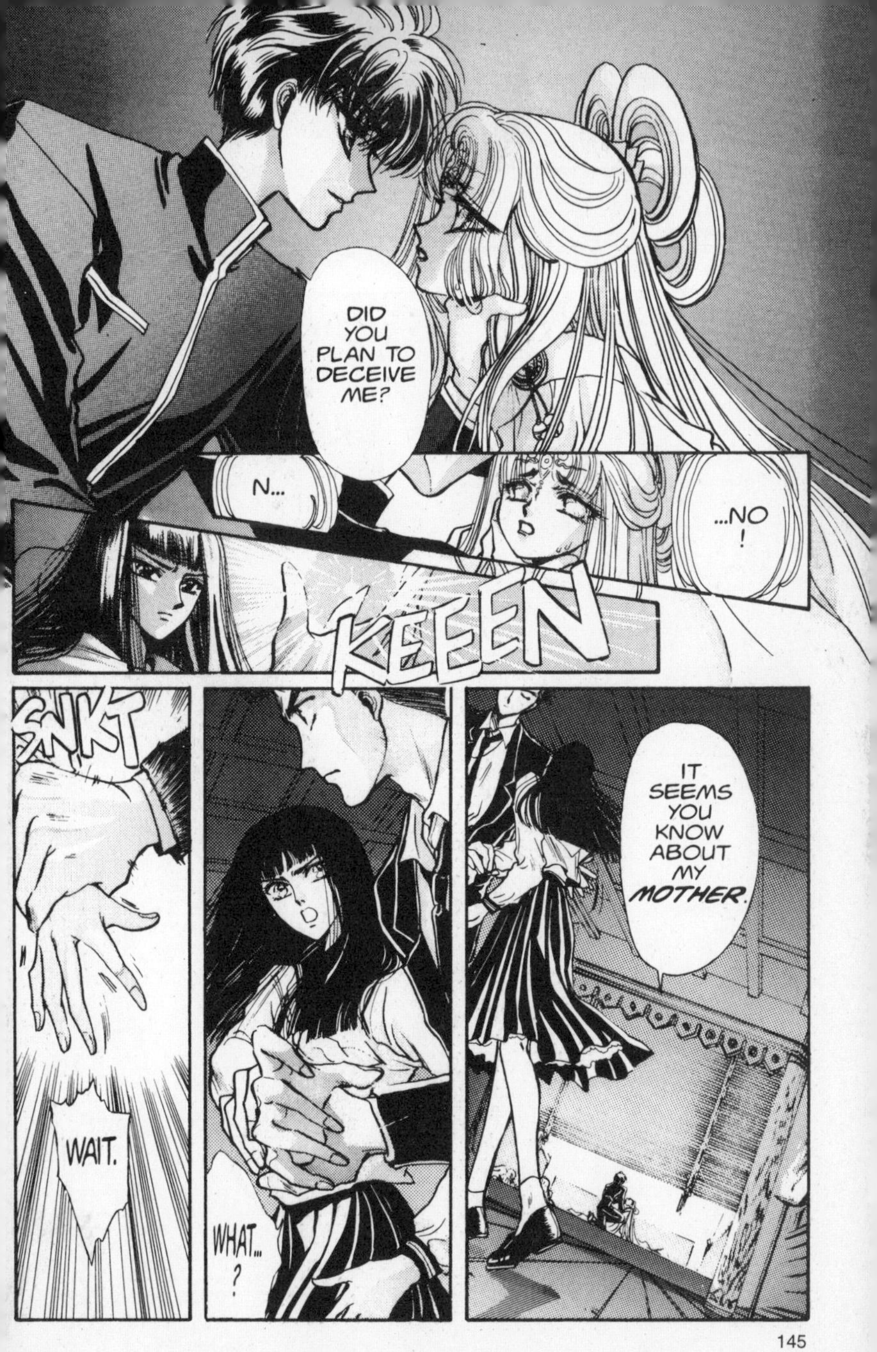
DID YOU PLAN TO DECEIVE ME?
N...
...NO !
KEEEN
SNKT
WAIT.
WHAT... ?
IT SEEMS YOU KNOW ABOUT MY MOTHER.

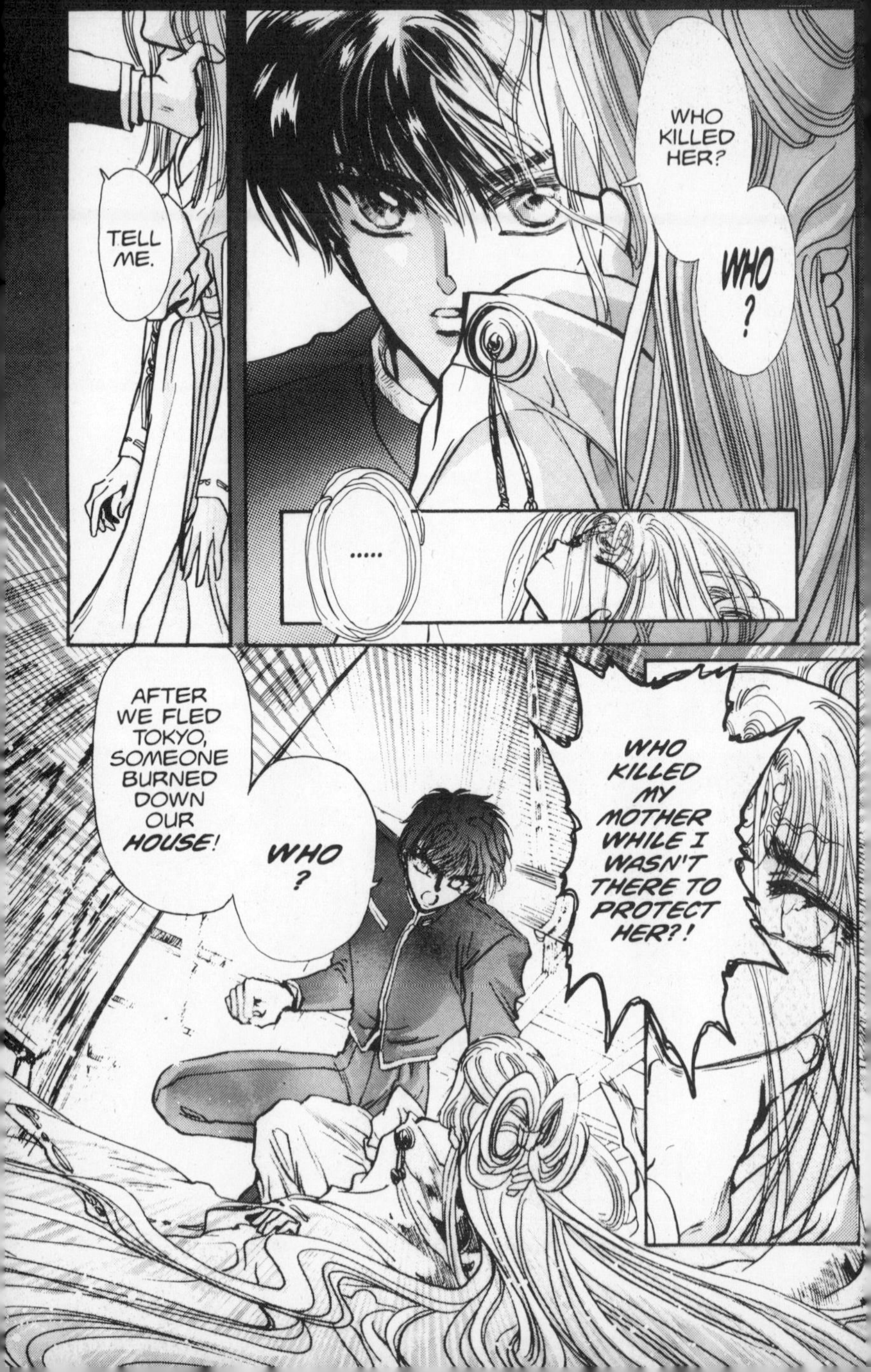
TELL ME.
WHO KILLED HER?
WHO ?
.....
AFTER WE FLED TOKYO, SOMEONE BURNED DOWN OUR HOUSE!
WHO ?
WHO KILLED MY MOTHER WHILE I WASN'T THERE TO PROTECT HER?!

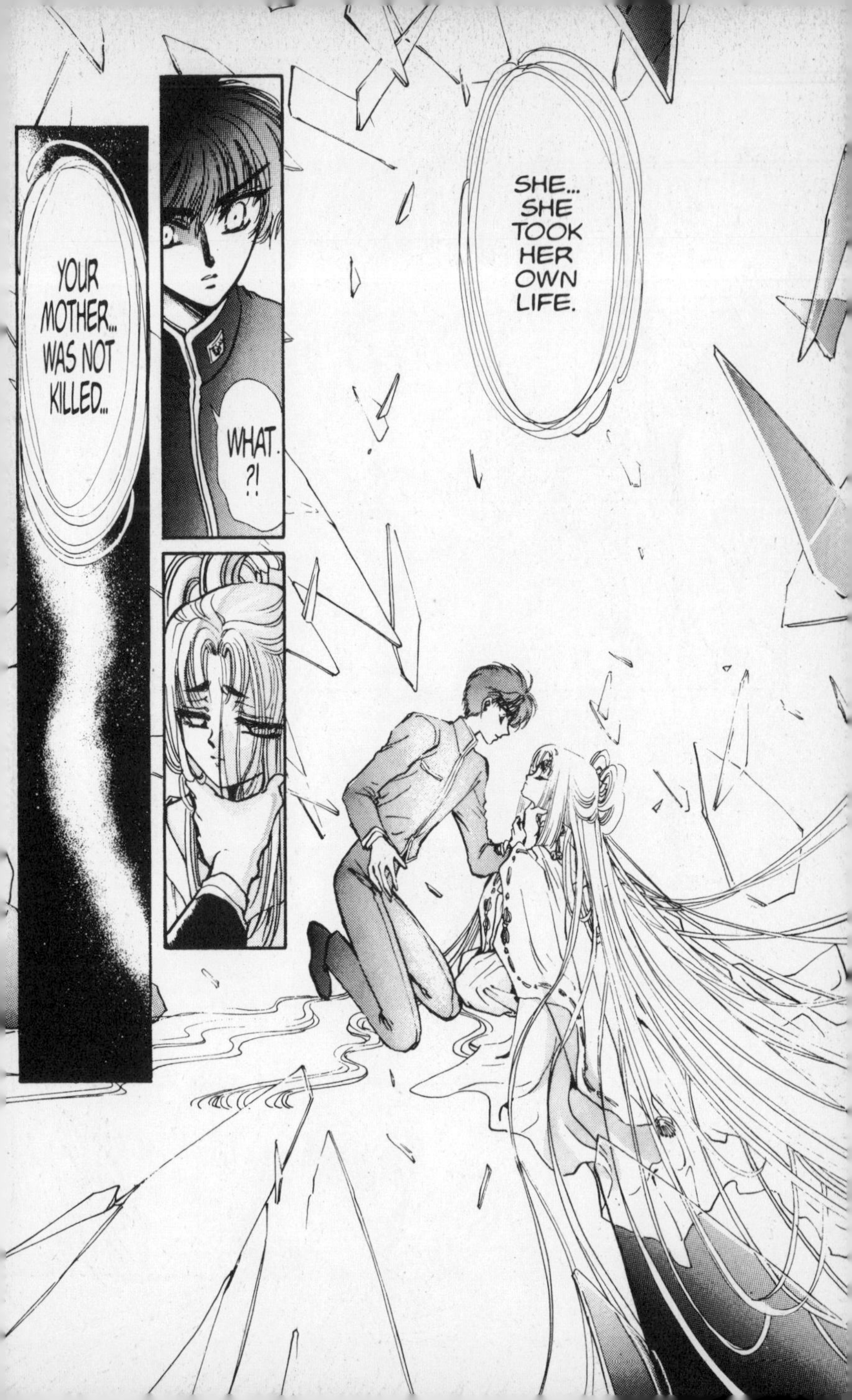
YOUR MOTHER... WAS NOT KILLED...
WHAT?!
SHE... SHE TOOK HER OWN LIFE.

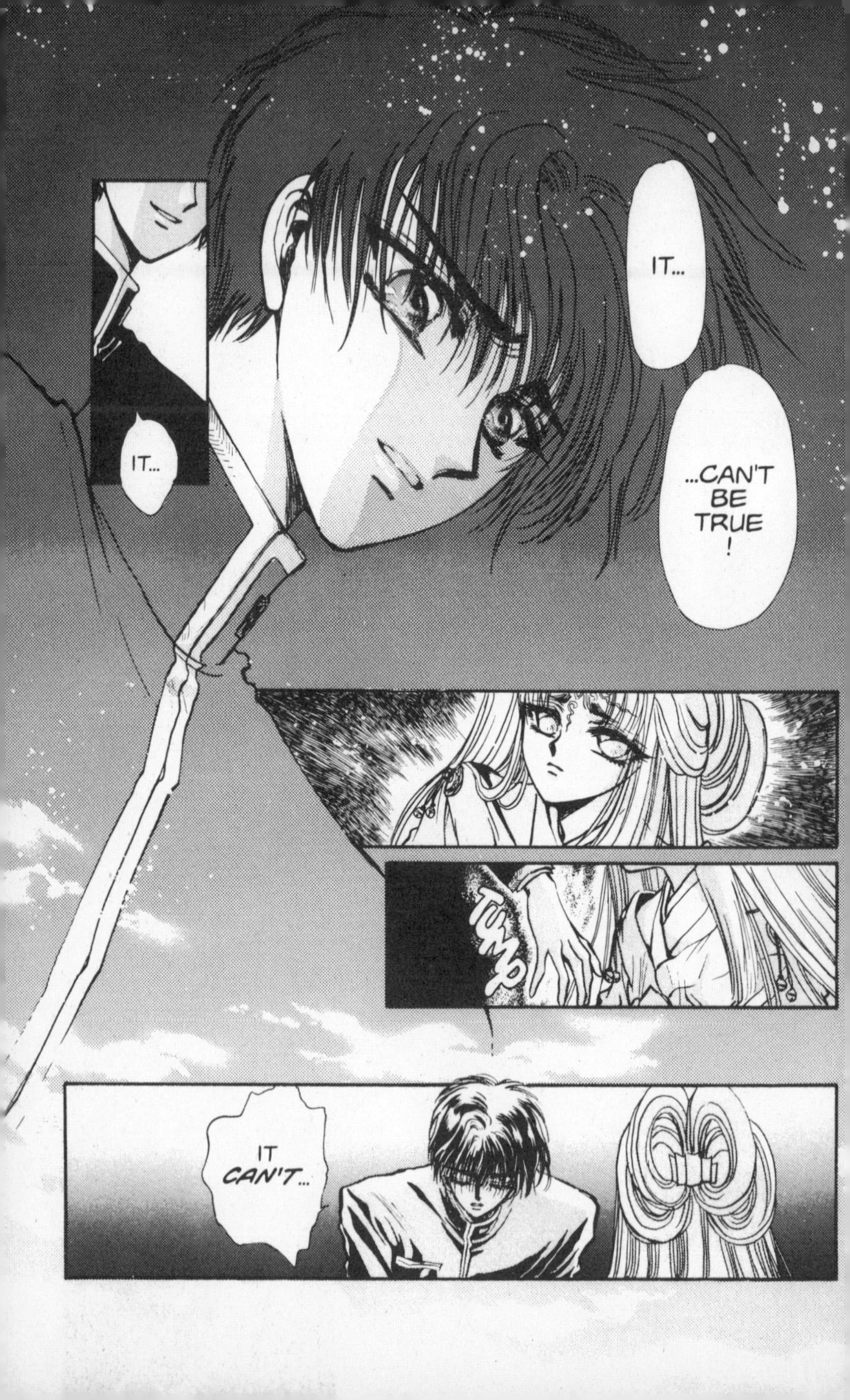
IT...
IT...
...CAN'T BE TRUE!
TUMP
IT CAN'T...

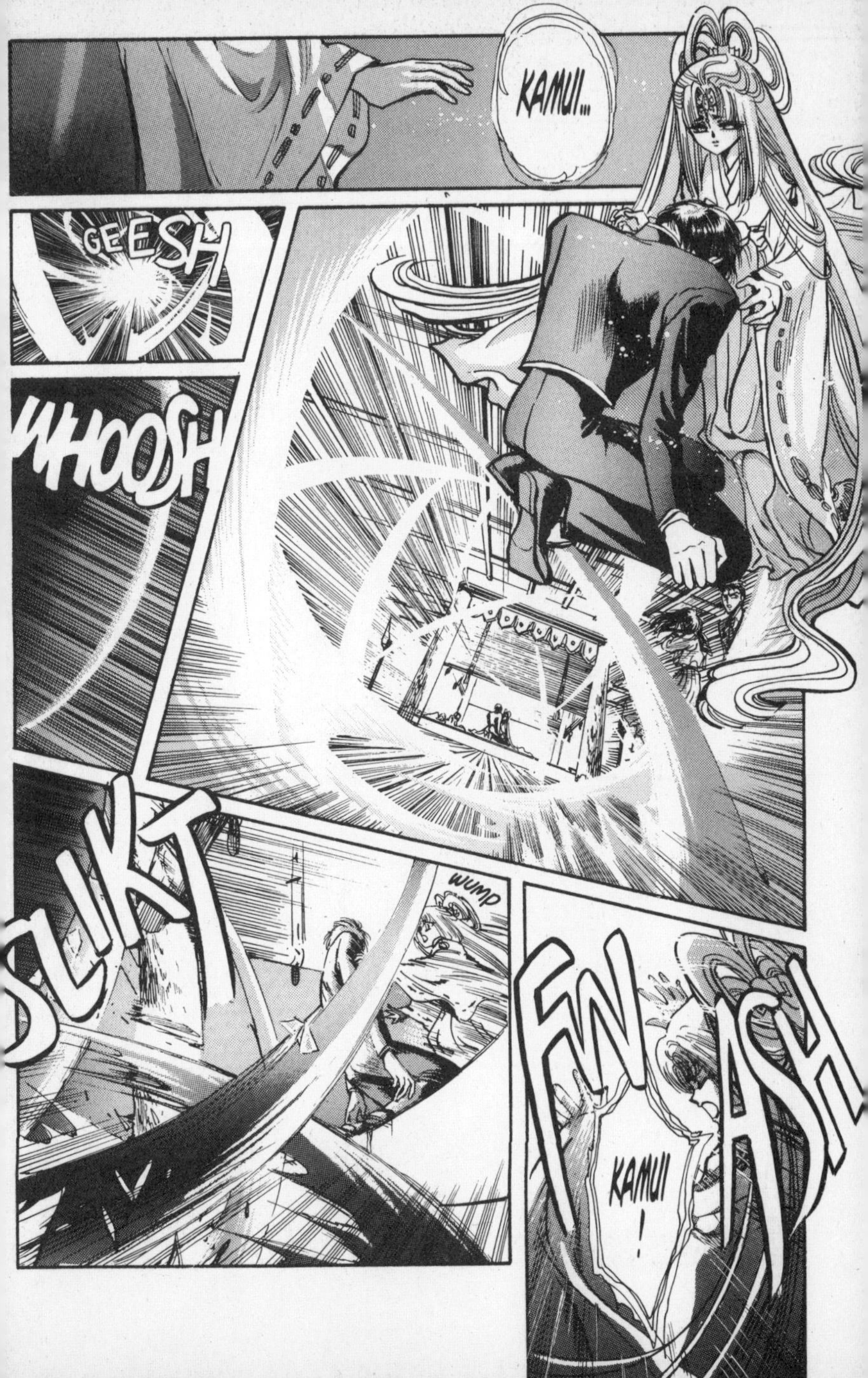
KAMUI...
GEESH
WHOOSH
SLIKT
wump
FWASH
KAMUI
!

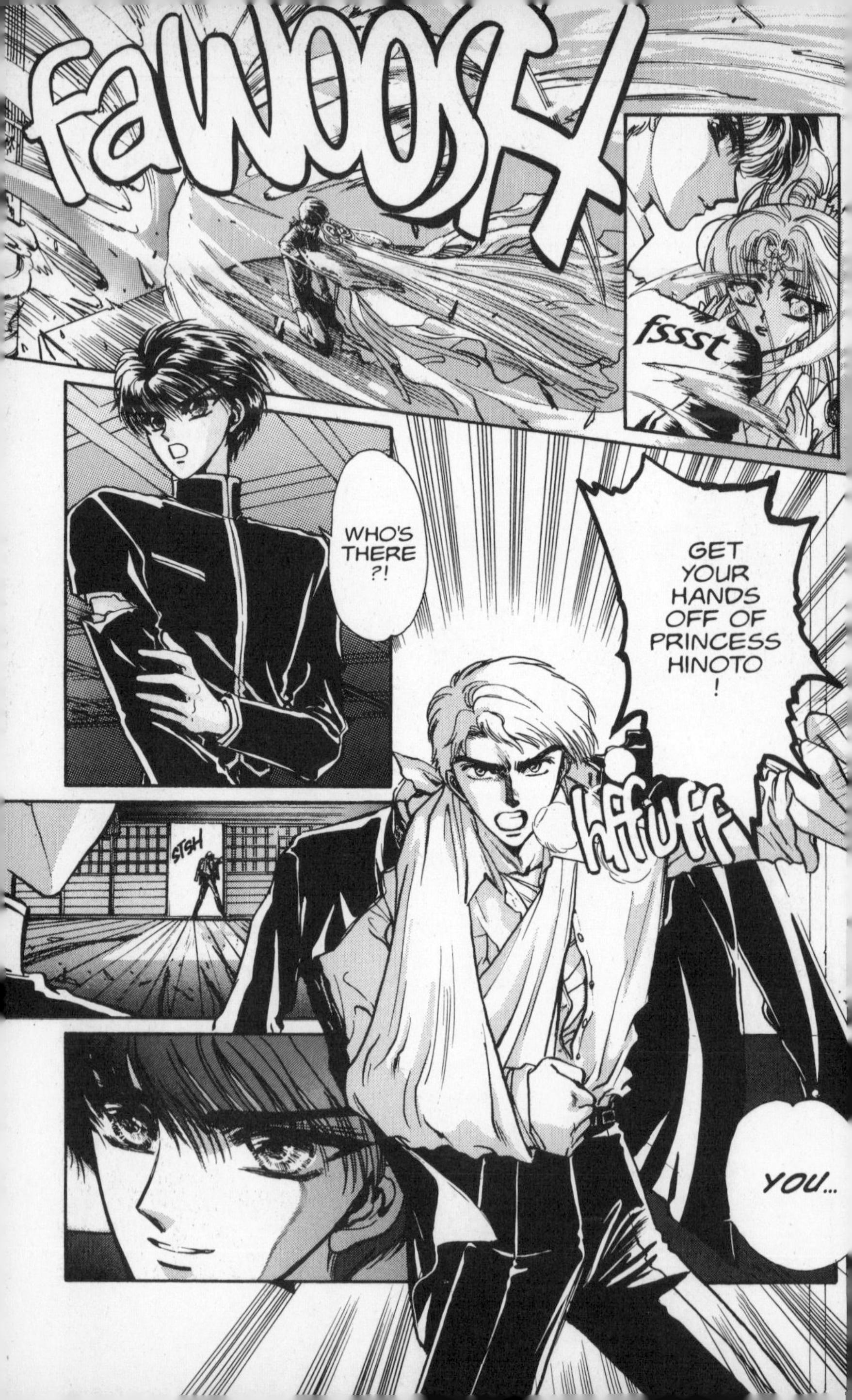
fawoosh
fssst
WHO'S THERE ?!
GET YOUR HANDS OFF OF PRINCESS HINOTO !
hfuff
STSH
YOU...

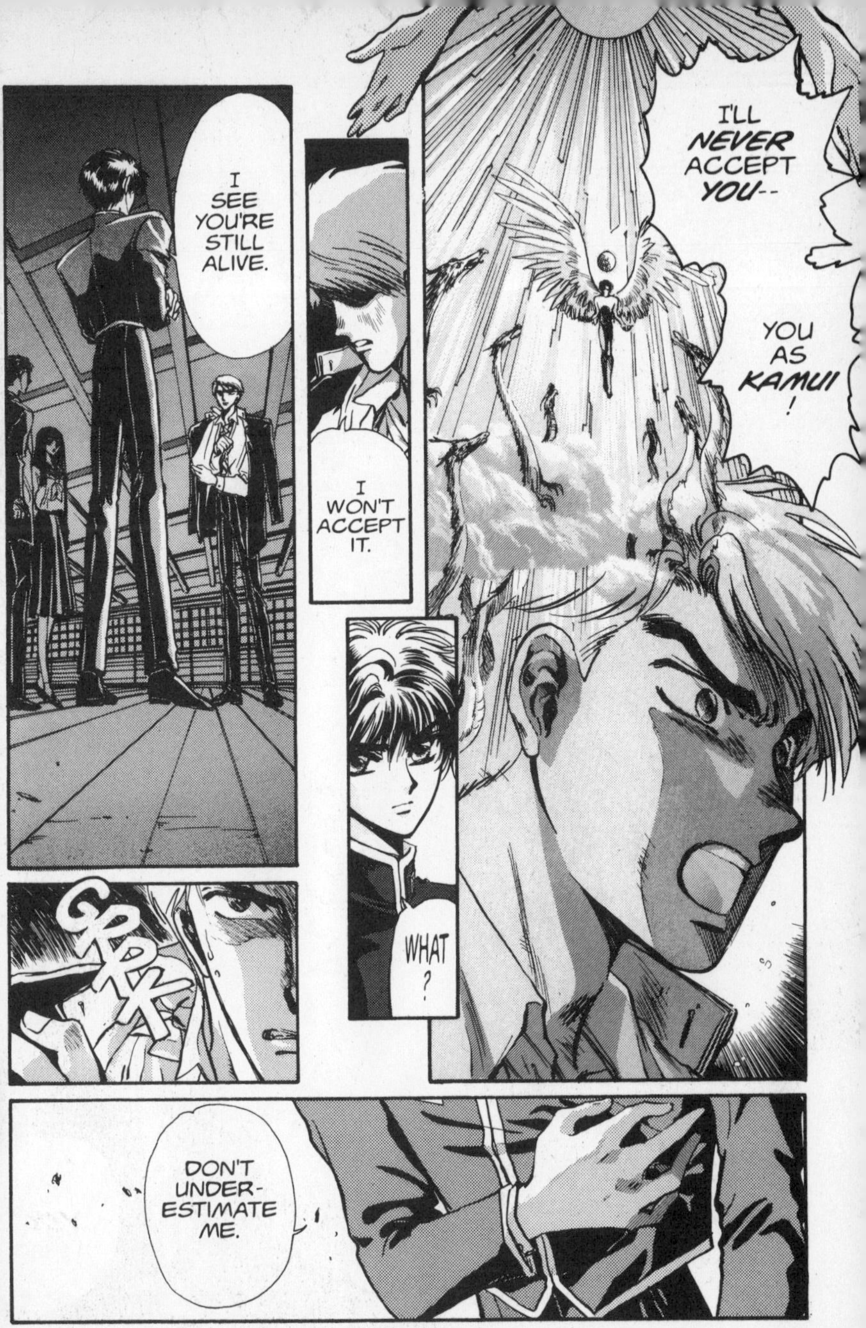
I SEE YOU'RE STILL ALIVE.
I WON'T ACCEPT IT.
WHAT ?
I'LL NEVER ACCEPT YOU--
YOU AS KAMUI !
GRRK
DON'T UNDER-ESTIMATE ME.

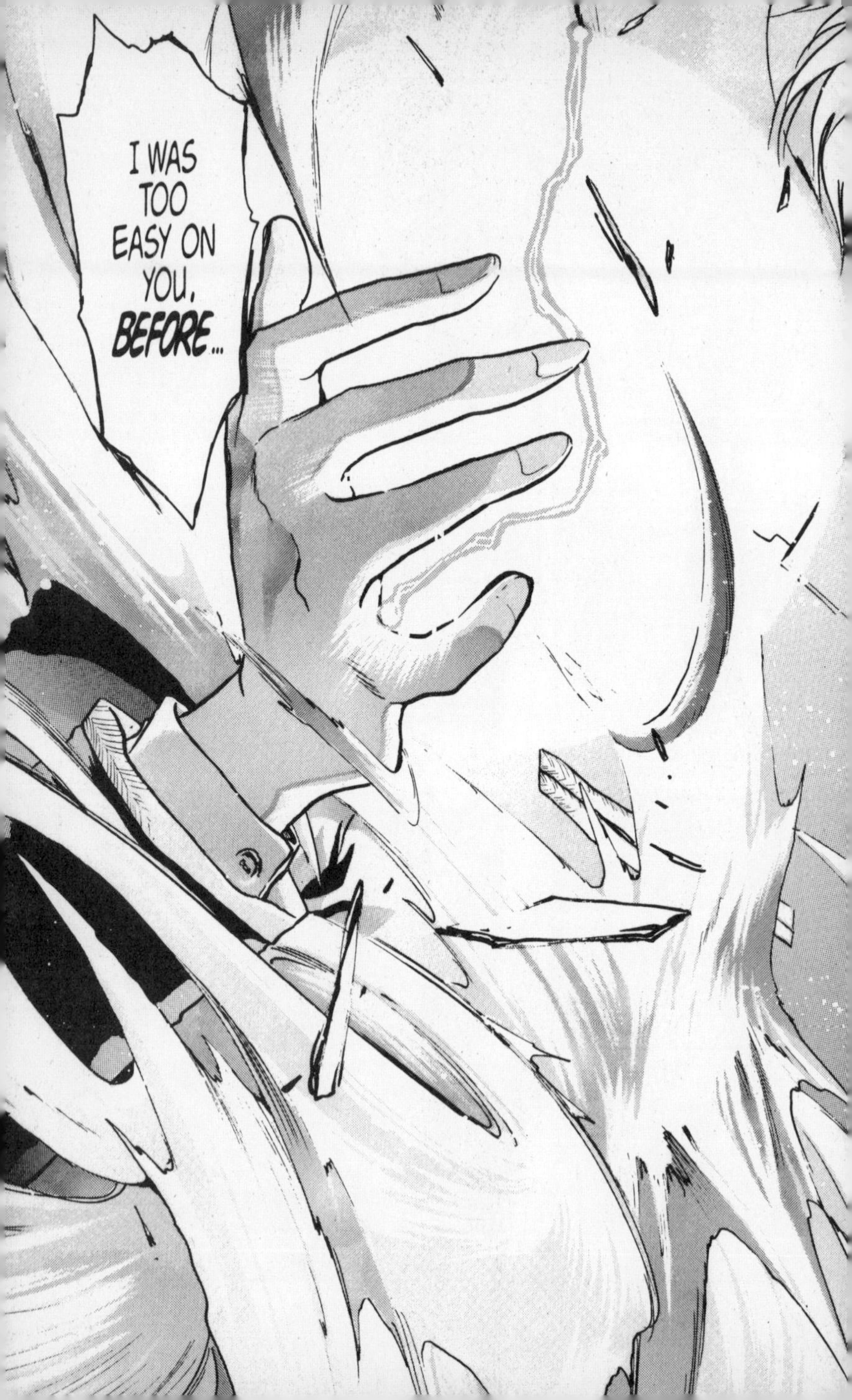
I WAS TOO EASY ON YOU, BEFORE...

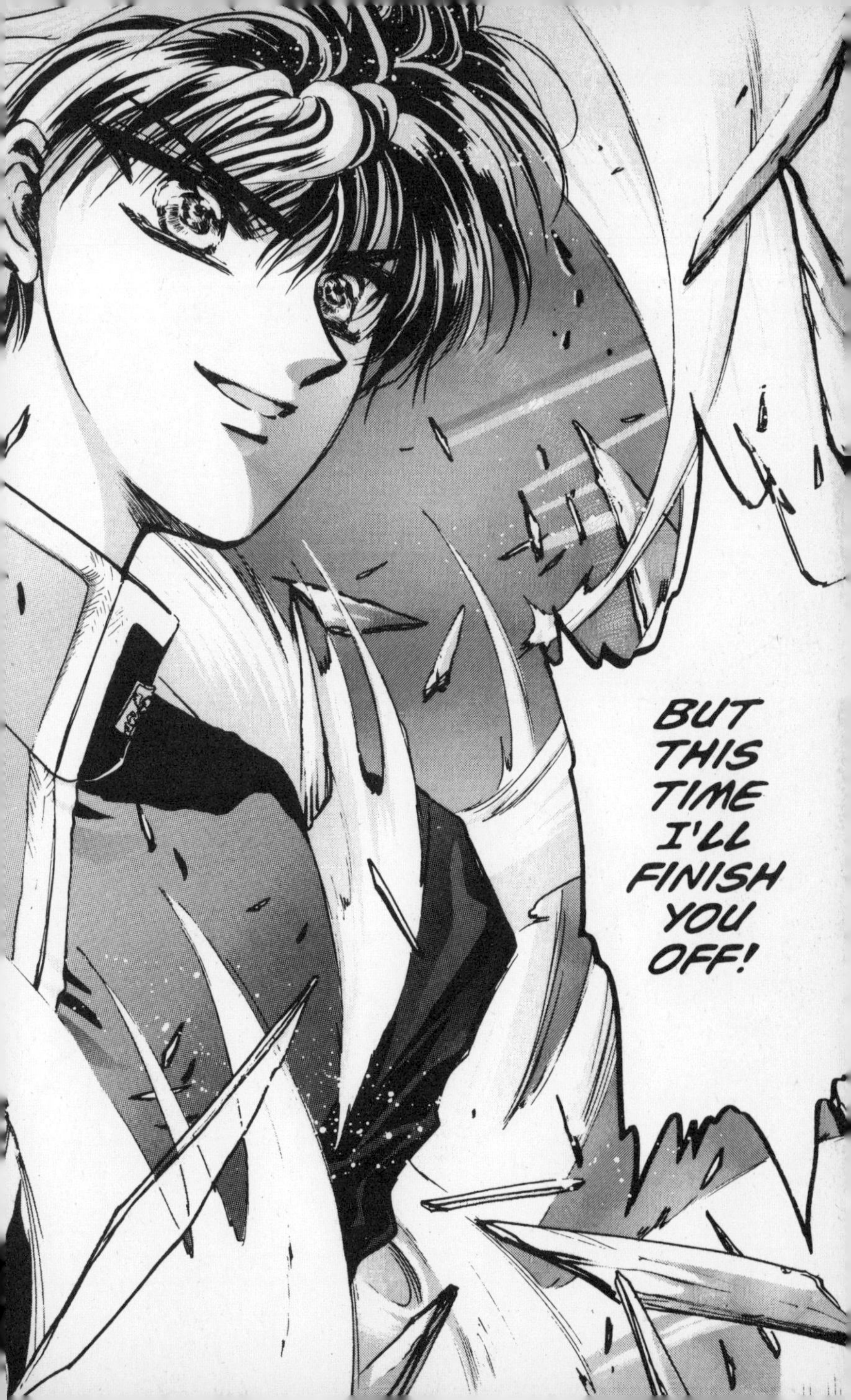
BUT THIS TIME I'LL FINISH YOU OFF!

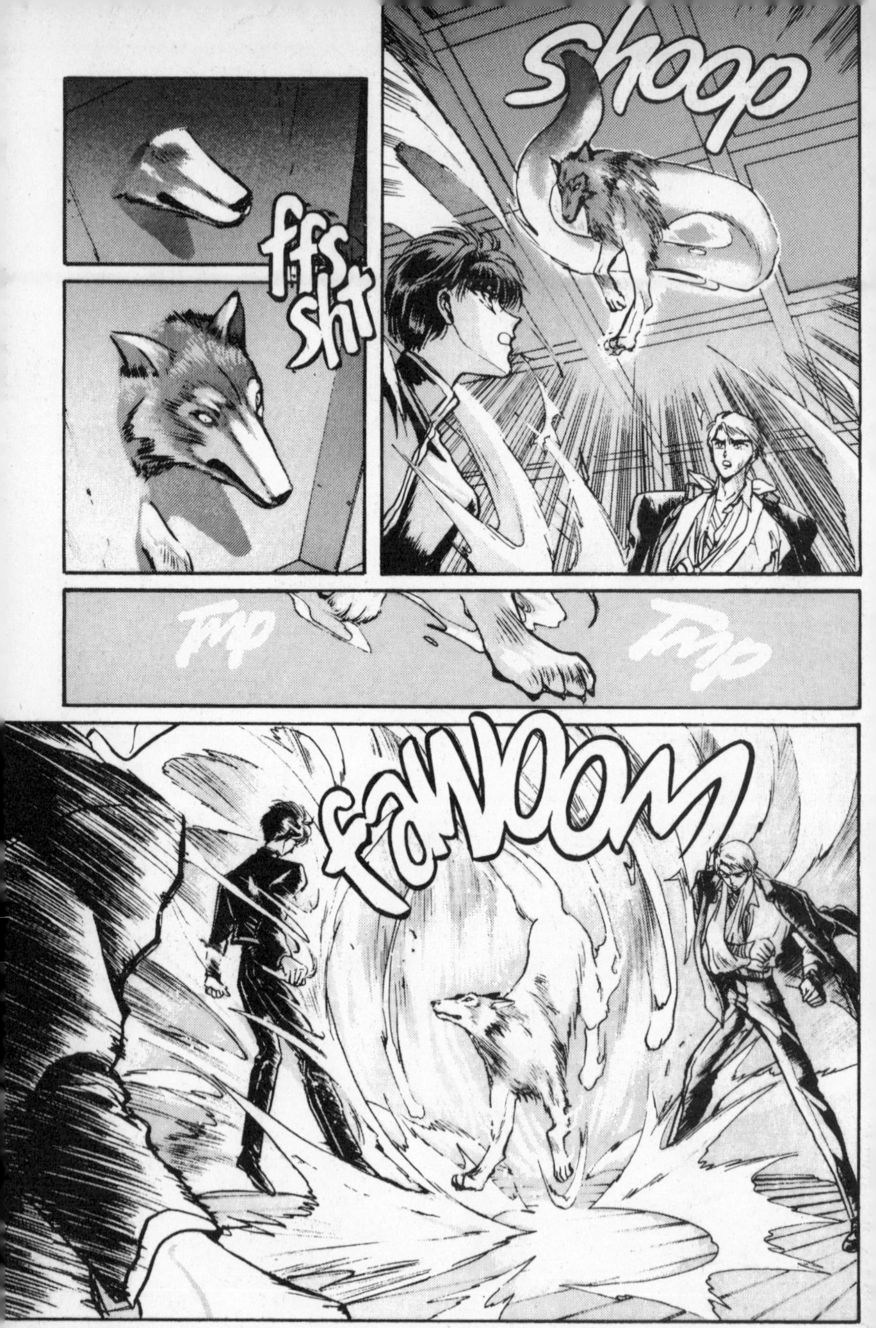
Shoop
ffs sht
Tmp
Tmp
fwoom

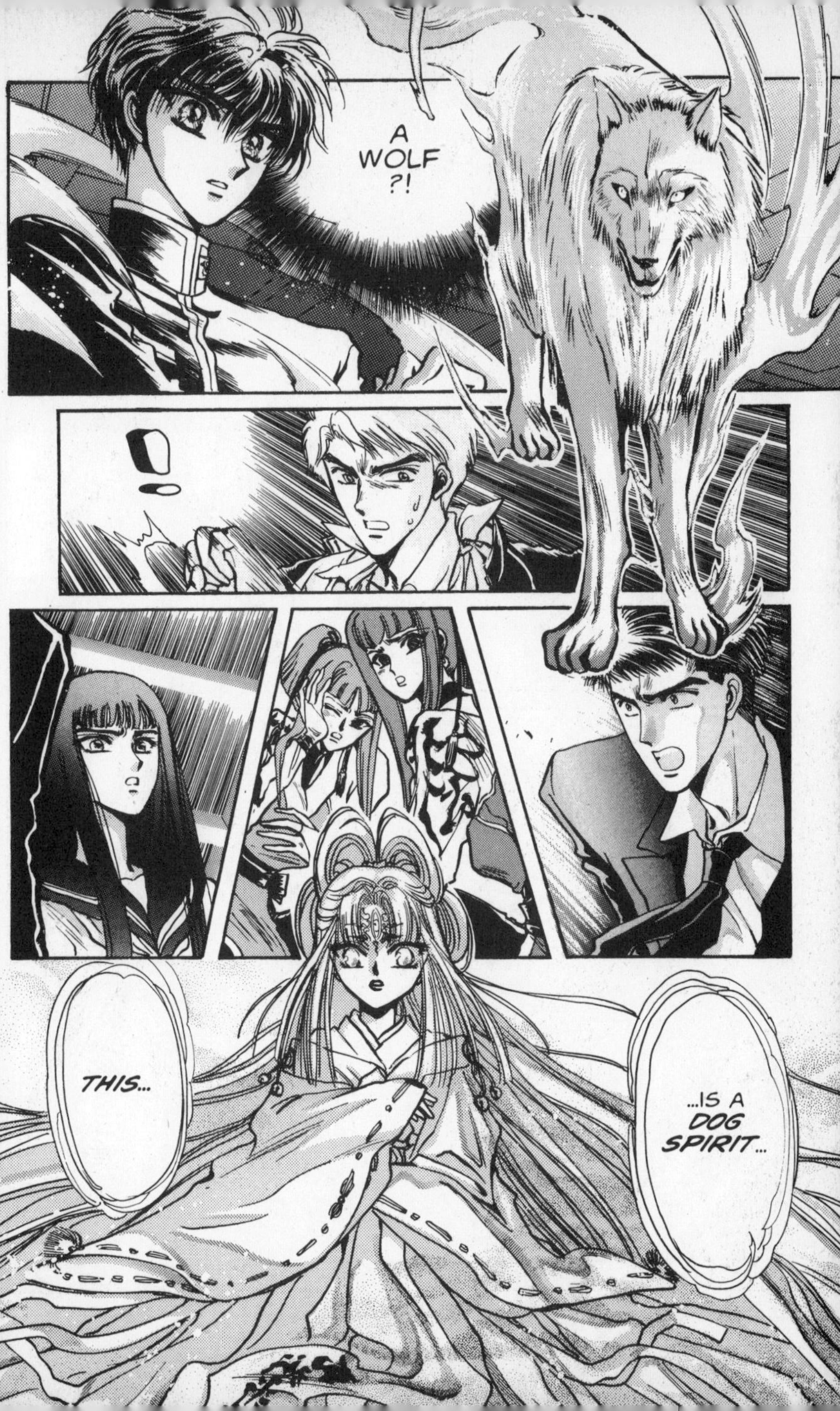
A WOLF ?!
!
THIS...
...IS A DOG SPIRIT...

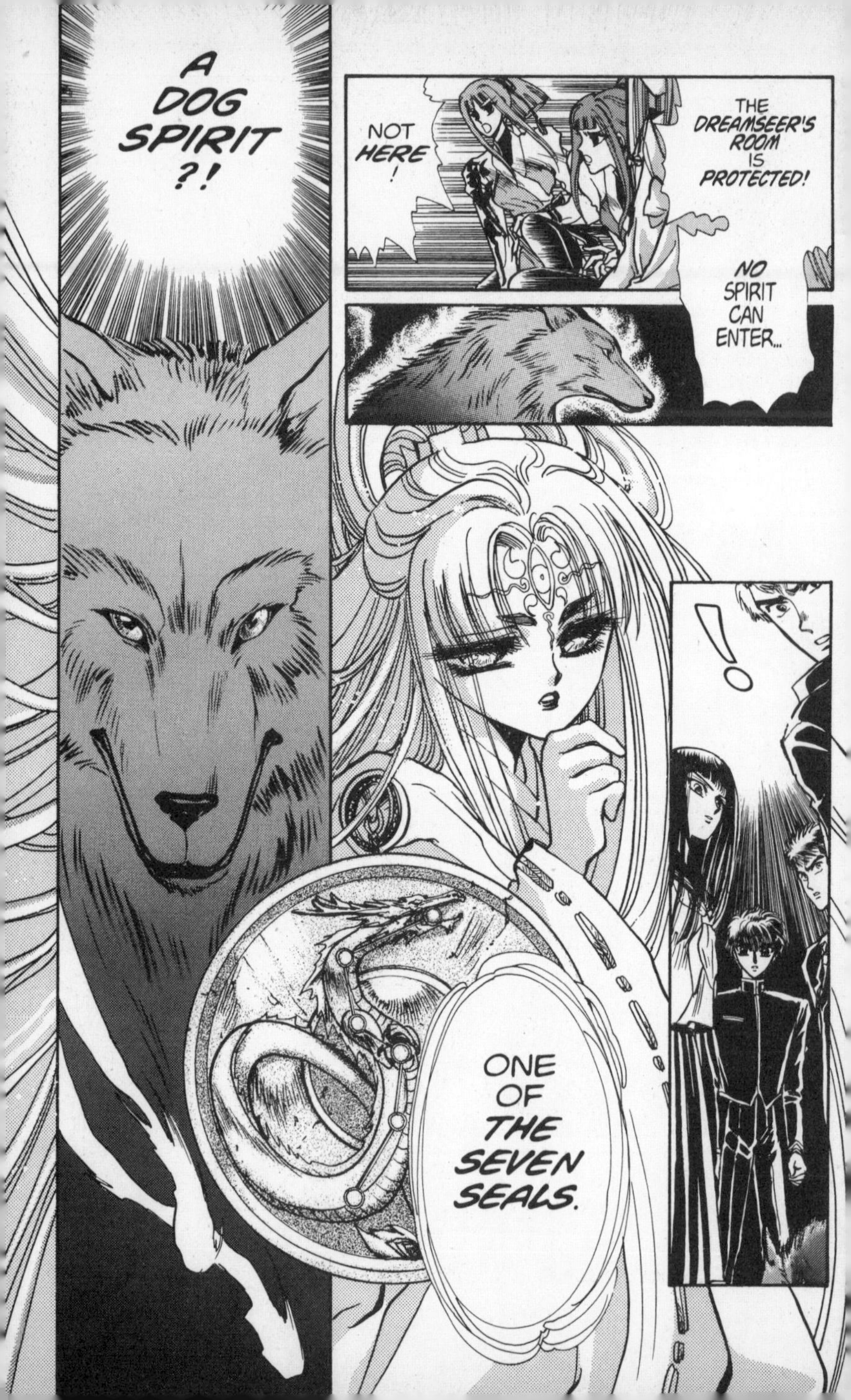
A DOG SPIRIT ?!
NOT HERE !
THE DREAMSEER'S ROOM IS PROTECTED!
NO SPIRIT CAN ENTER...
ONE OF THE SEVEN SEALS.
!

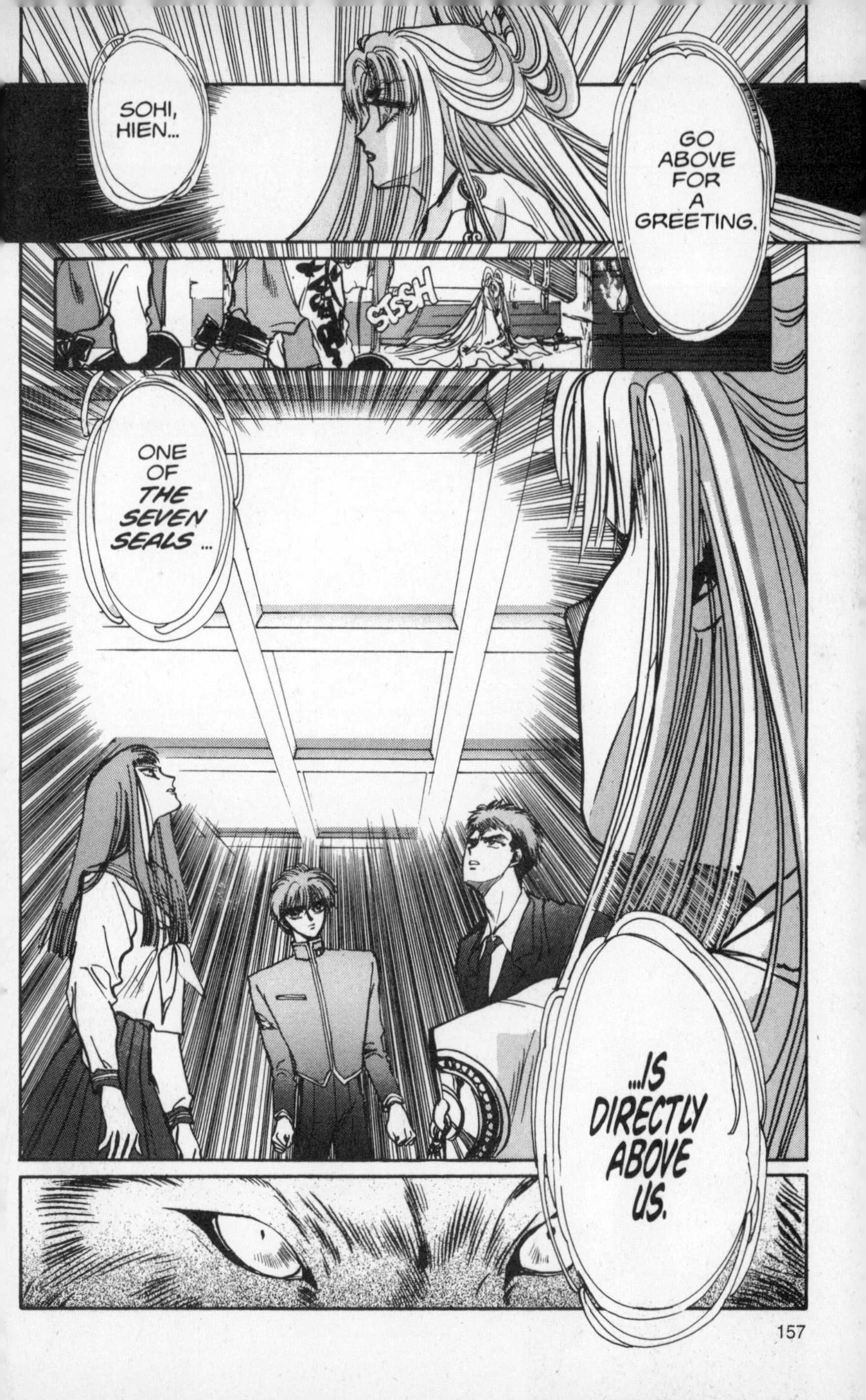
SOHI, HIEN...
GO ABOVE FOR A GREETING.
SHSSH
ONE OF *THE SEVEN SEALS* ...
...IS DIRECTLY ABOVE US.

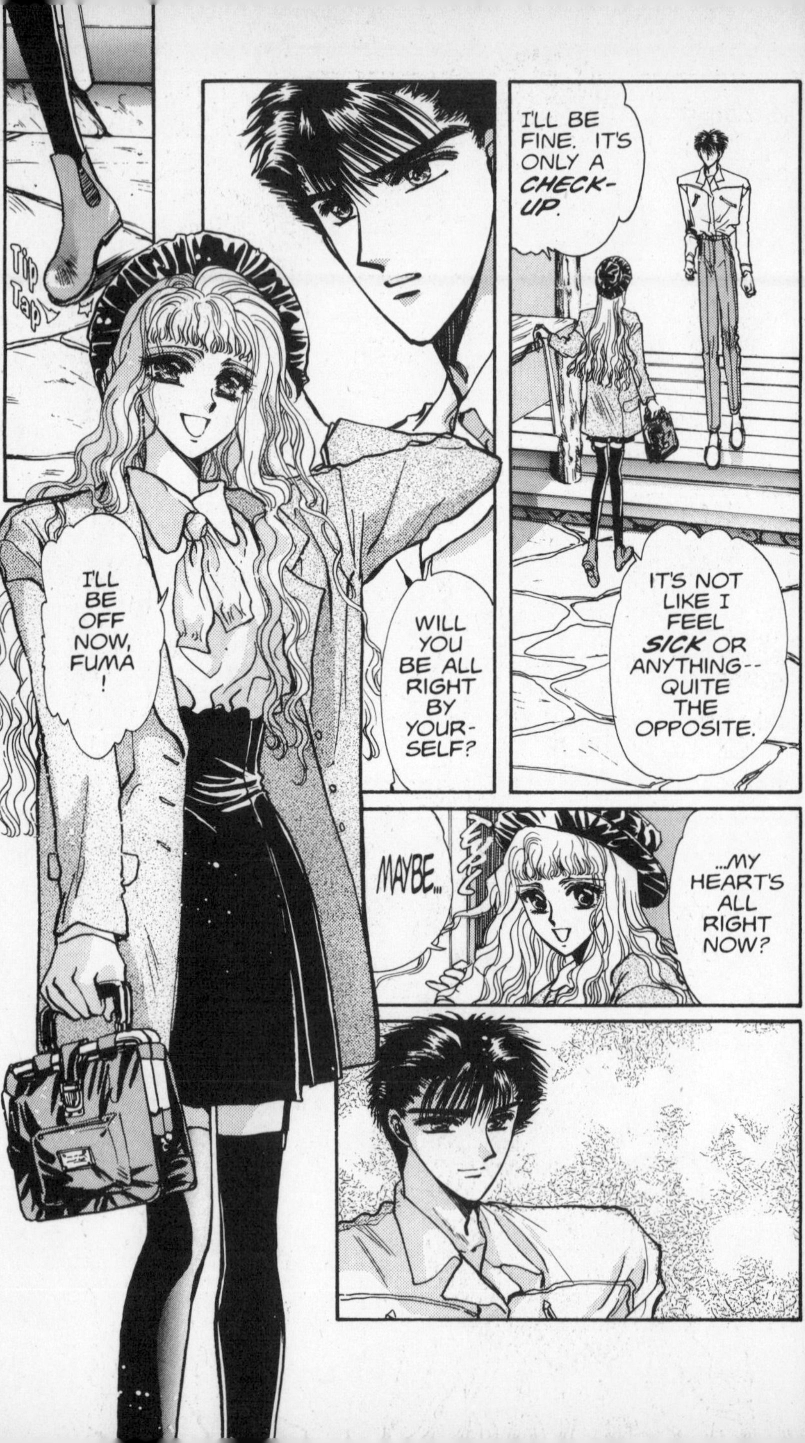
Tip Tap
I'LL BE OFF NOW, FUMA!
WILL YOU BE ALL RIGHT BY YOURSELF?
I'LL BE FINE. IT'S ONLY A CHECK-UP.
IT'S NOT LIKE I FEEL SICK OR ANYTHING--QUITE THE OPPOSITE.
MAYBE...
...MY HEART'S ALL RIGHT NOW?

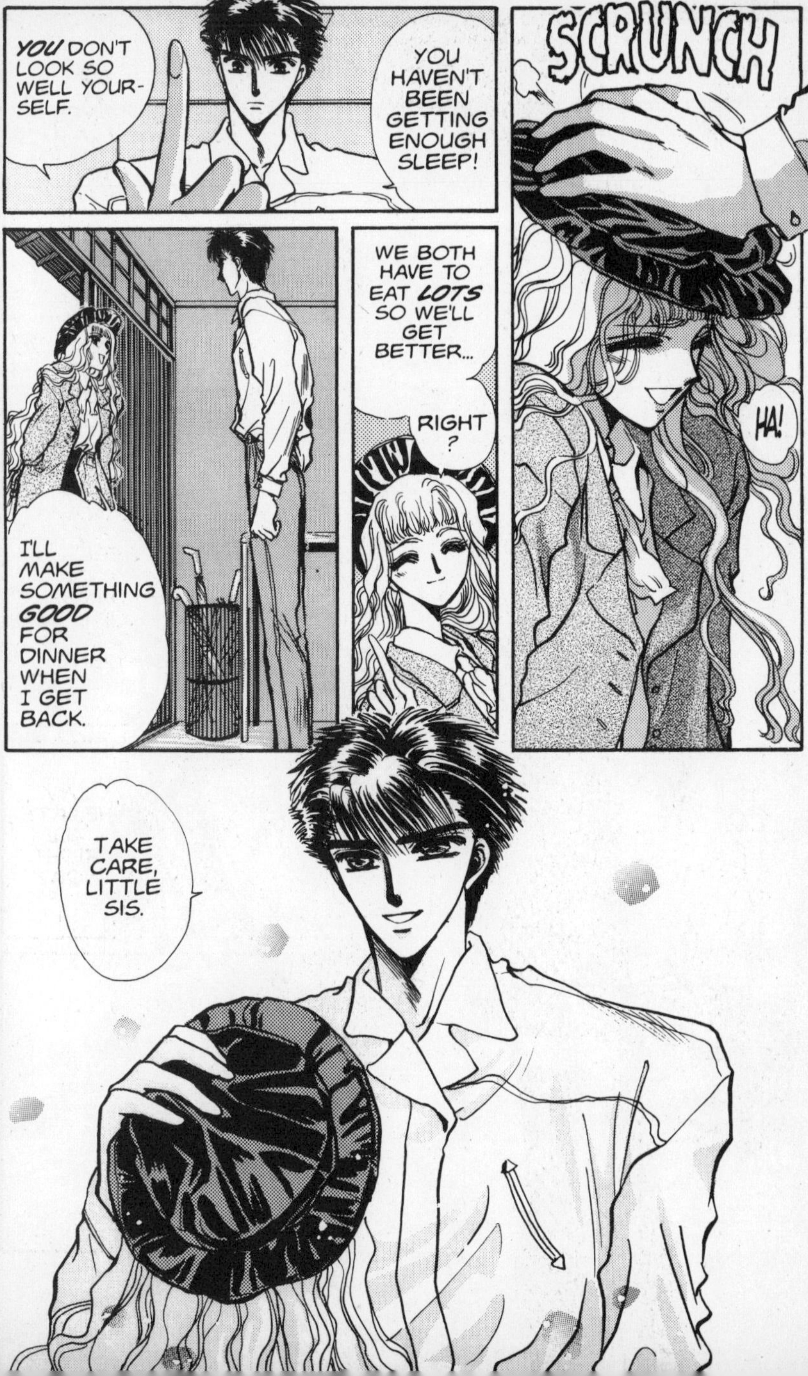
YOU DON'T LOOK SO WELL YOURSELF.
YOU HAVEN'T BEEN GETTING ENOUGH SLEEP!
I'LL MAKE SOMETHING GOOD FOR DINNER WHEN I GET BACK.
WE BOTH HAVE TO EAT LOTS SO WE'LL GET BETTER...
RIGHT?
SCRUNCH
HA!
TAKE CARE, LITTLE SIS.

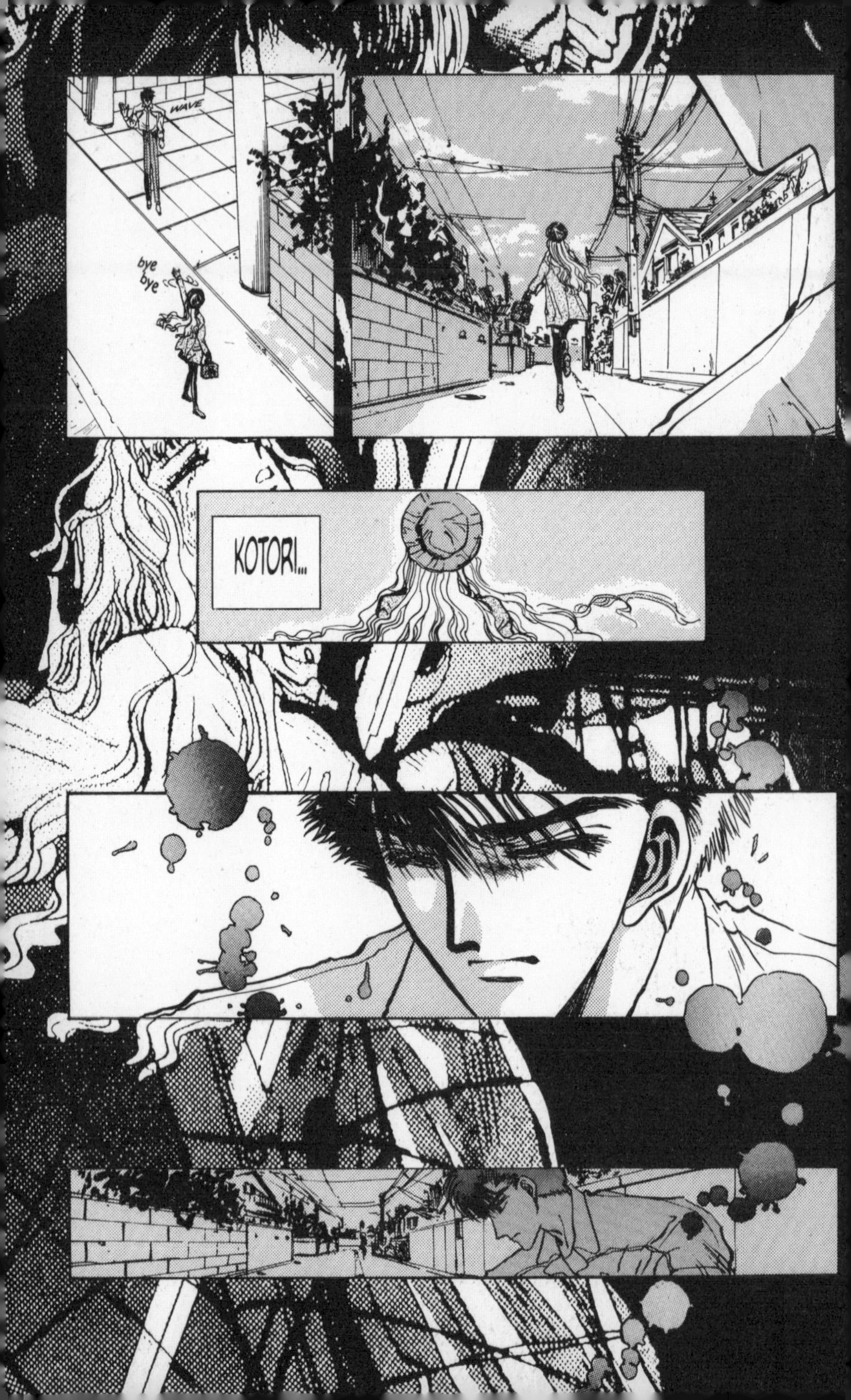
WAVE
bye bye
KOTORI...

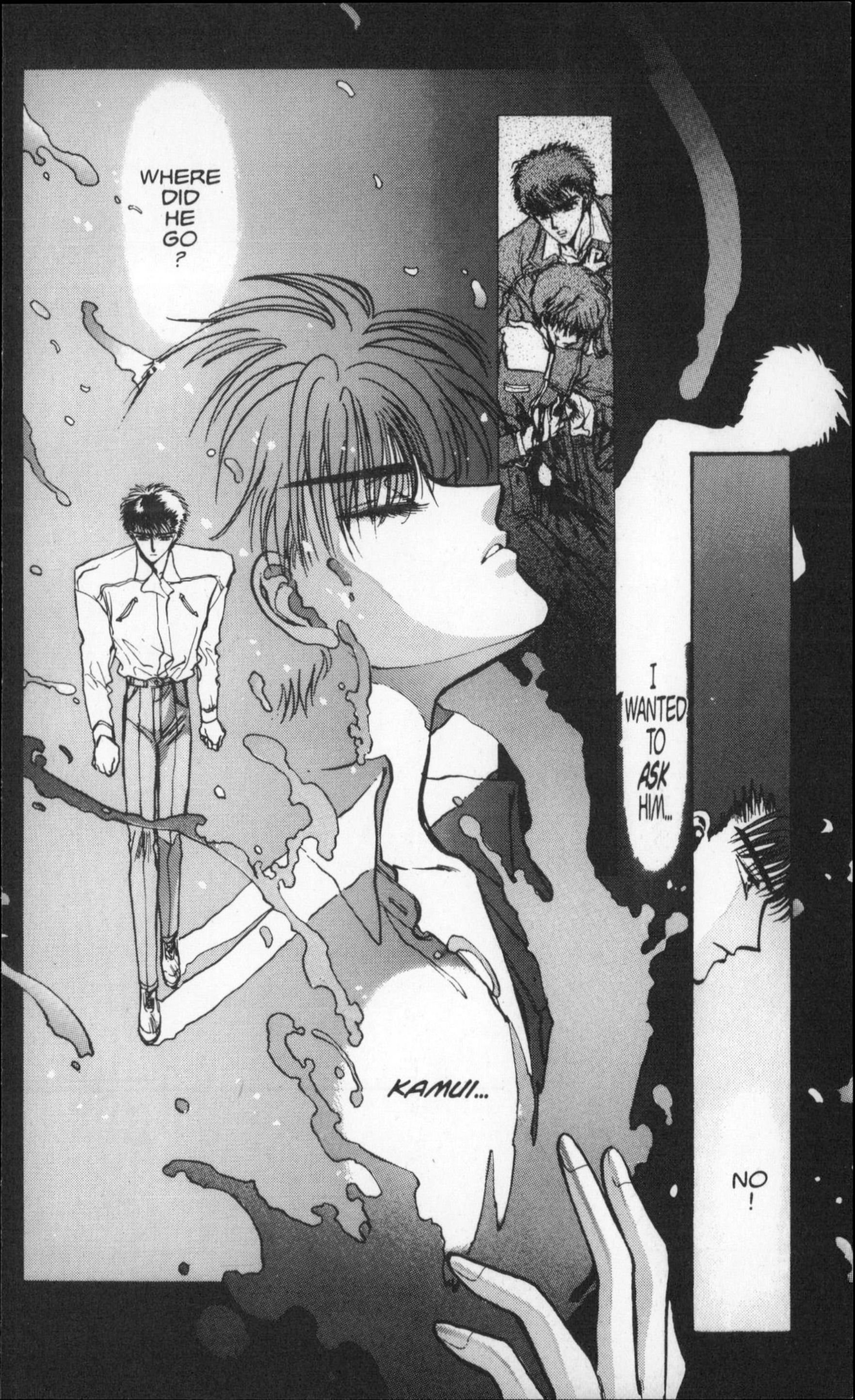
WHERE DID HE GO?
I WANTED TO ASK HIM...
KAMUI...
NO!

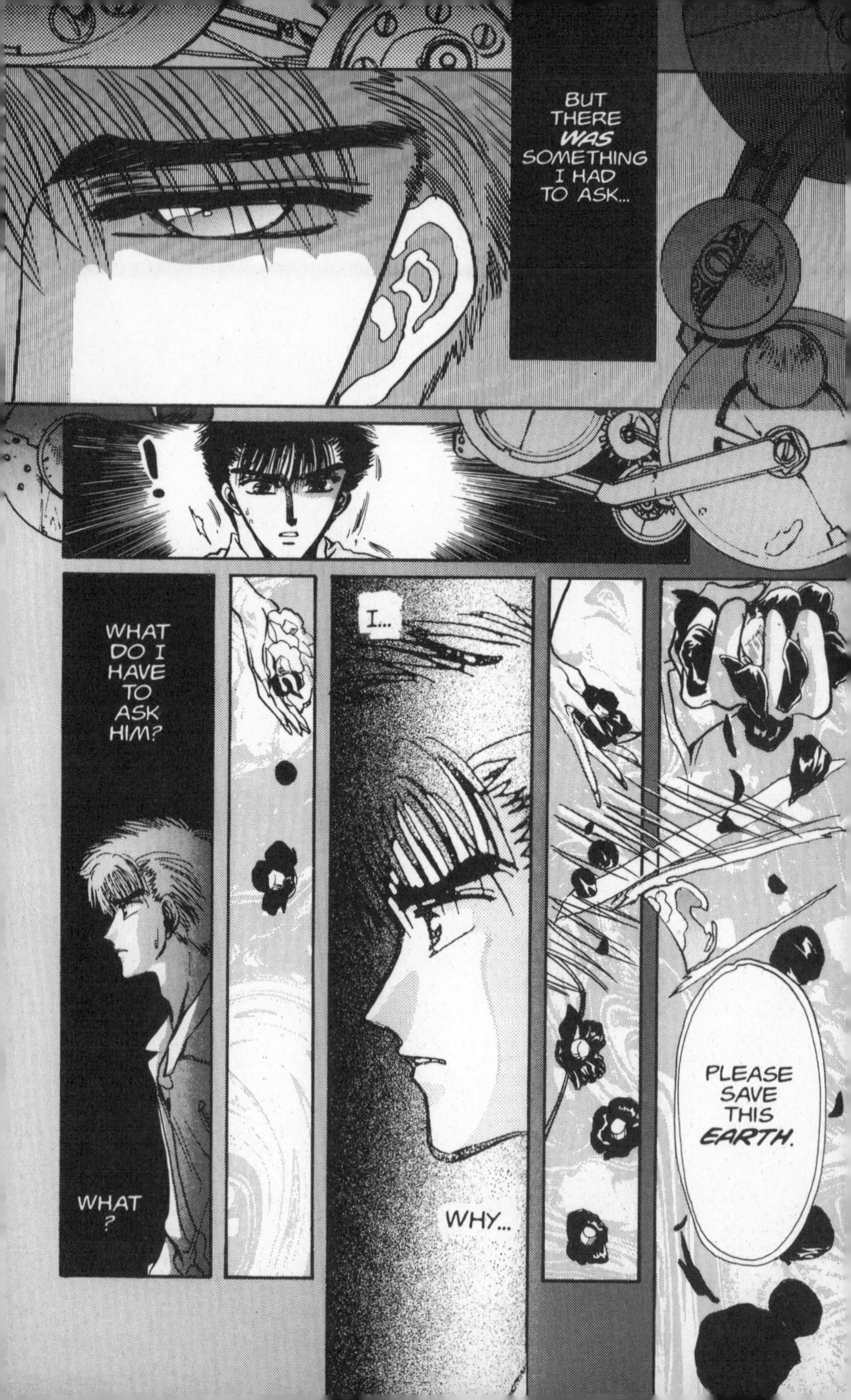
BUT THERE *WAS* SOMETHING I HAD TO ASK...
!
WHAT DO I HAVE TO ASK HIM?
WHAT ?
I...
WHY...
PLEASE SAVE THIS *EARTH*.

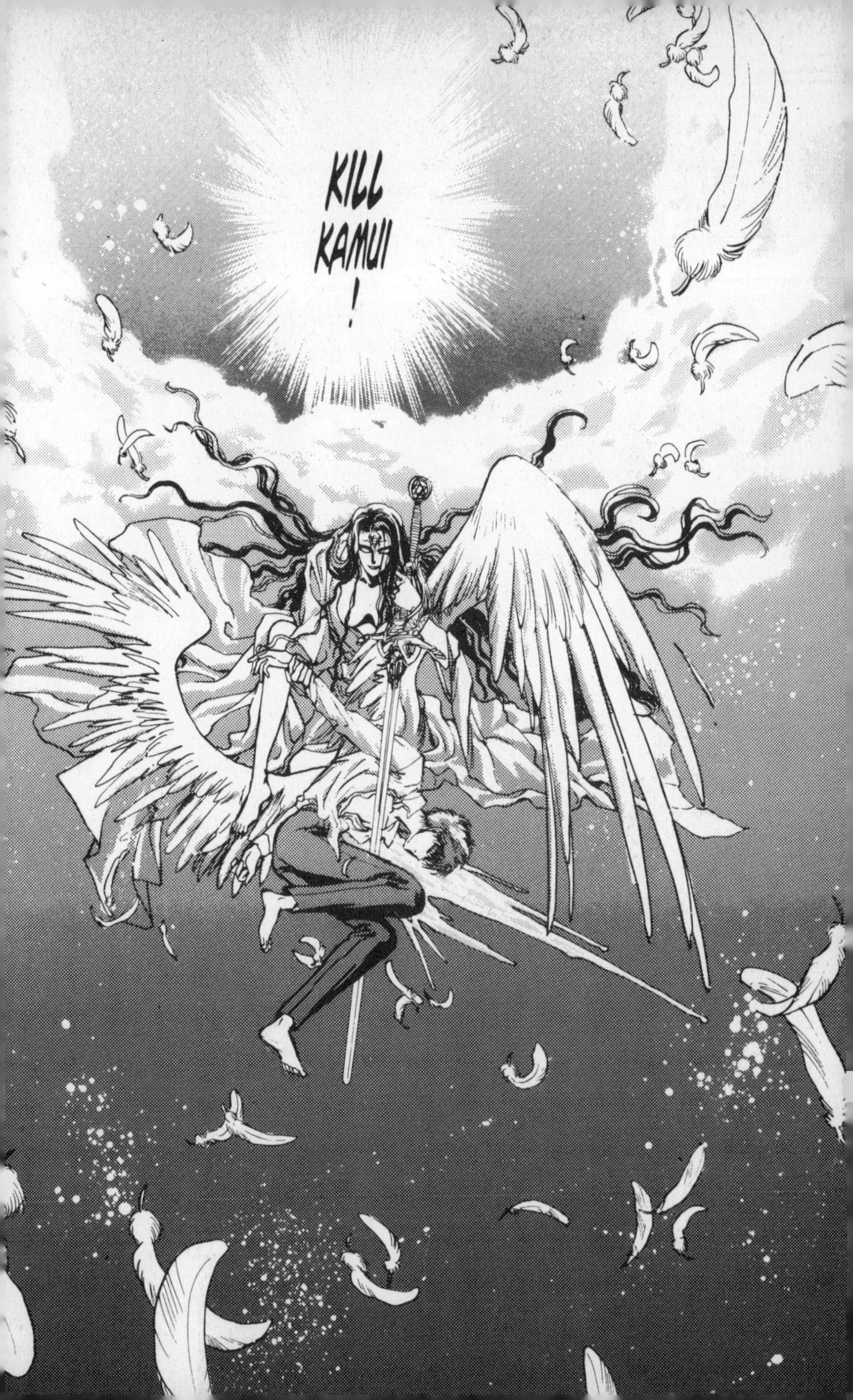
KILL KAMUI !

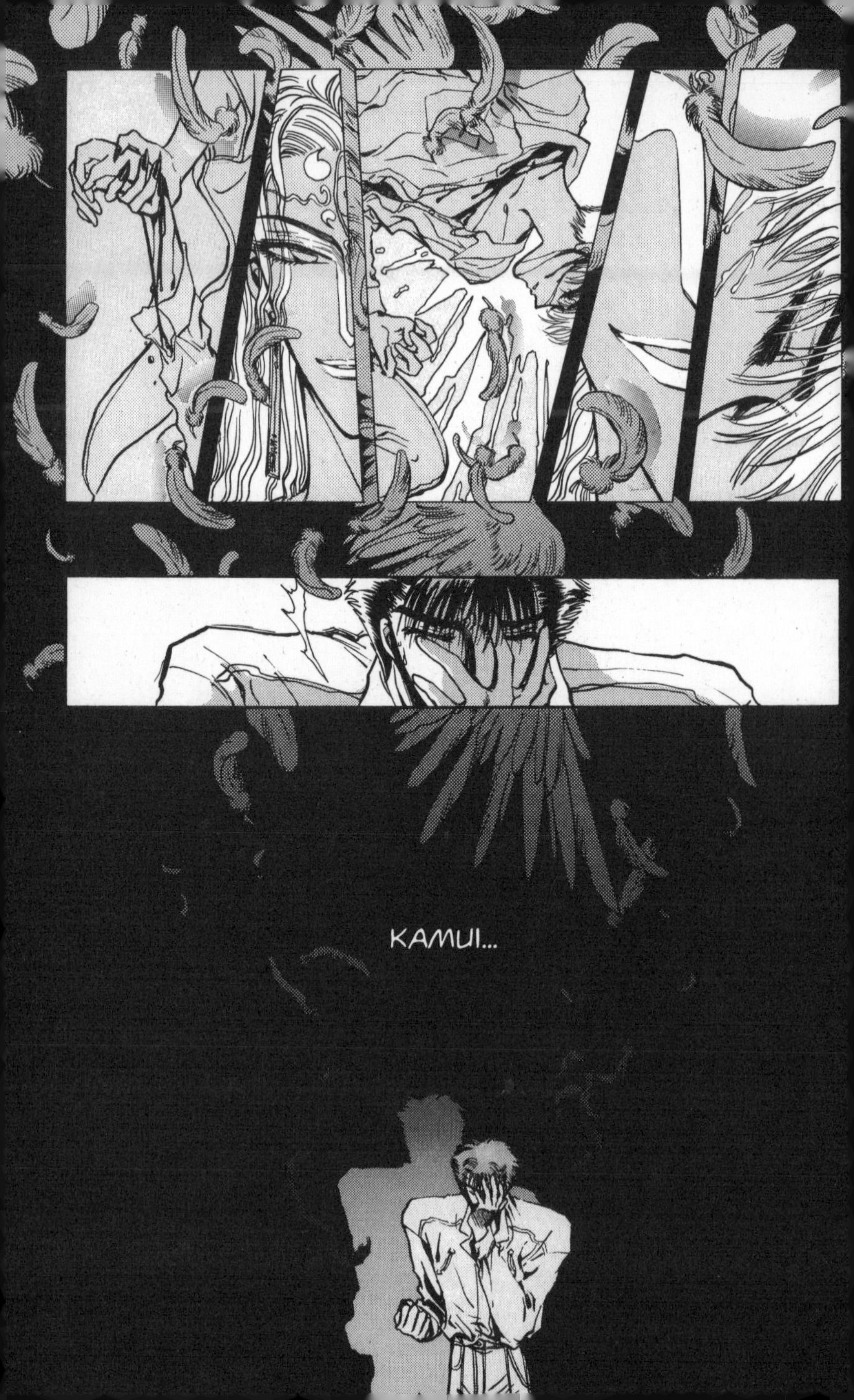
KAMUI...

KAMUI...
?

SUESH

WHERE COULD HE HAVE GONE...?

HE WAS HURT SO *BAD!* IS HE ALL RIGHT...?

RMM RMM RMM RMM

KACHOM

AREA UNDER CONSTRUCTION

THIS PLACE... IT'S *KAMUI'S...*

Sttt

THE OLD HOUSE HE USED TO LIVE IN...

Shiro

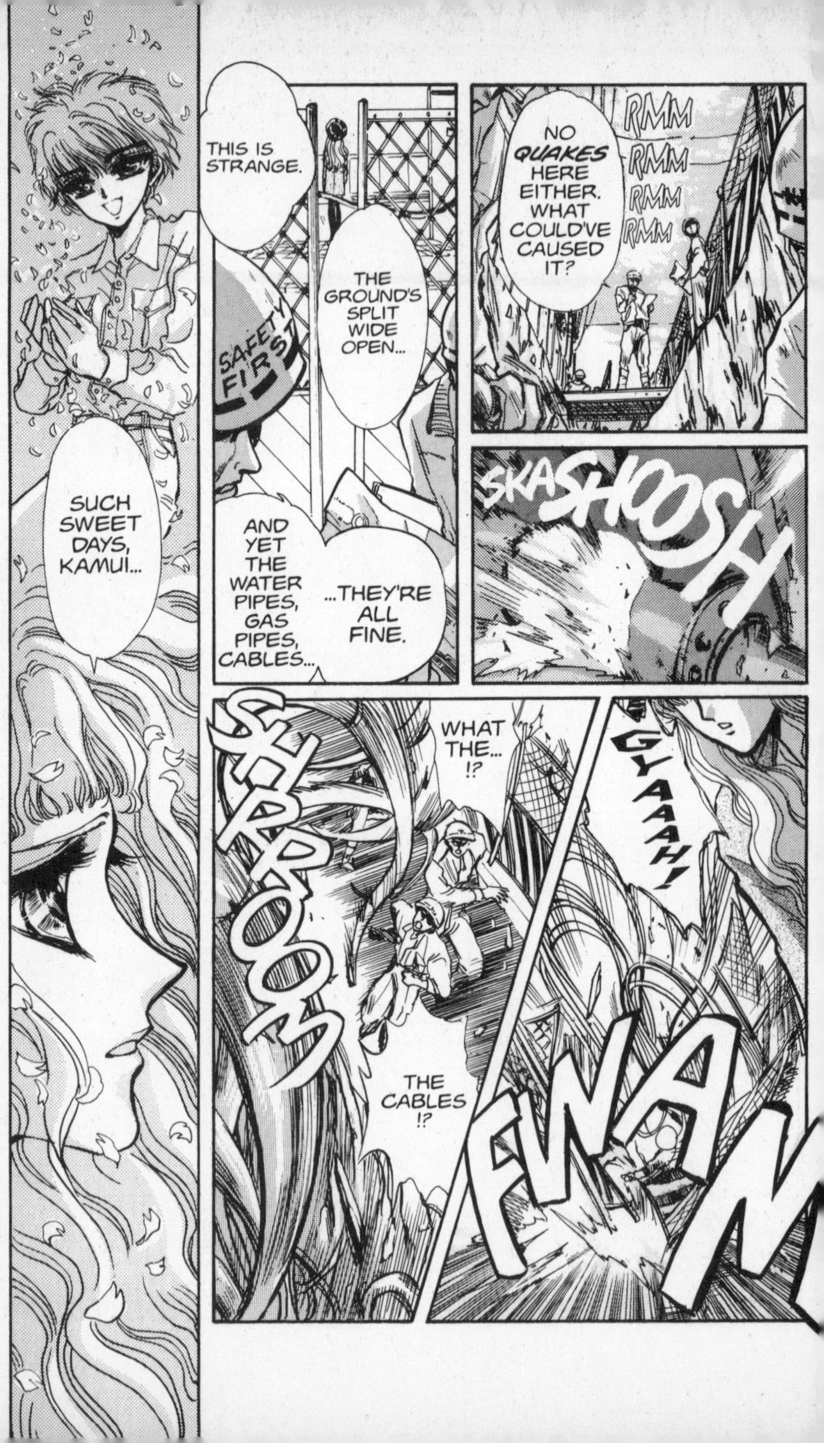
SUCH SWEET DAYS, KAMUI...
THIS IS STRANGE.
THE GROUND'S SPLIT WIDE OPEN...
SAFETY FIRST
AND YET THE WATER PIPES, GAS PIPES, CABLES...
...THEY'RE ALL FINE.
NO QUAKES HERE EITHER. WHAT COULD'VE CAUSED IT?
RMM RMM RMM RMM
SKASHOOSH
SHRROOM
WHAT THE... !?
THE CABLES !?
GYAAAH!
FWAM

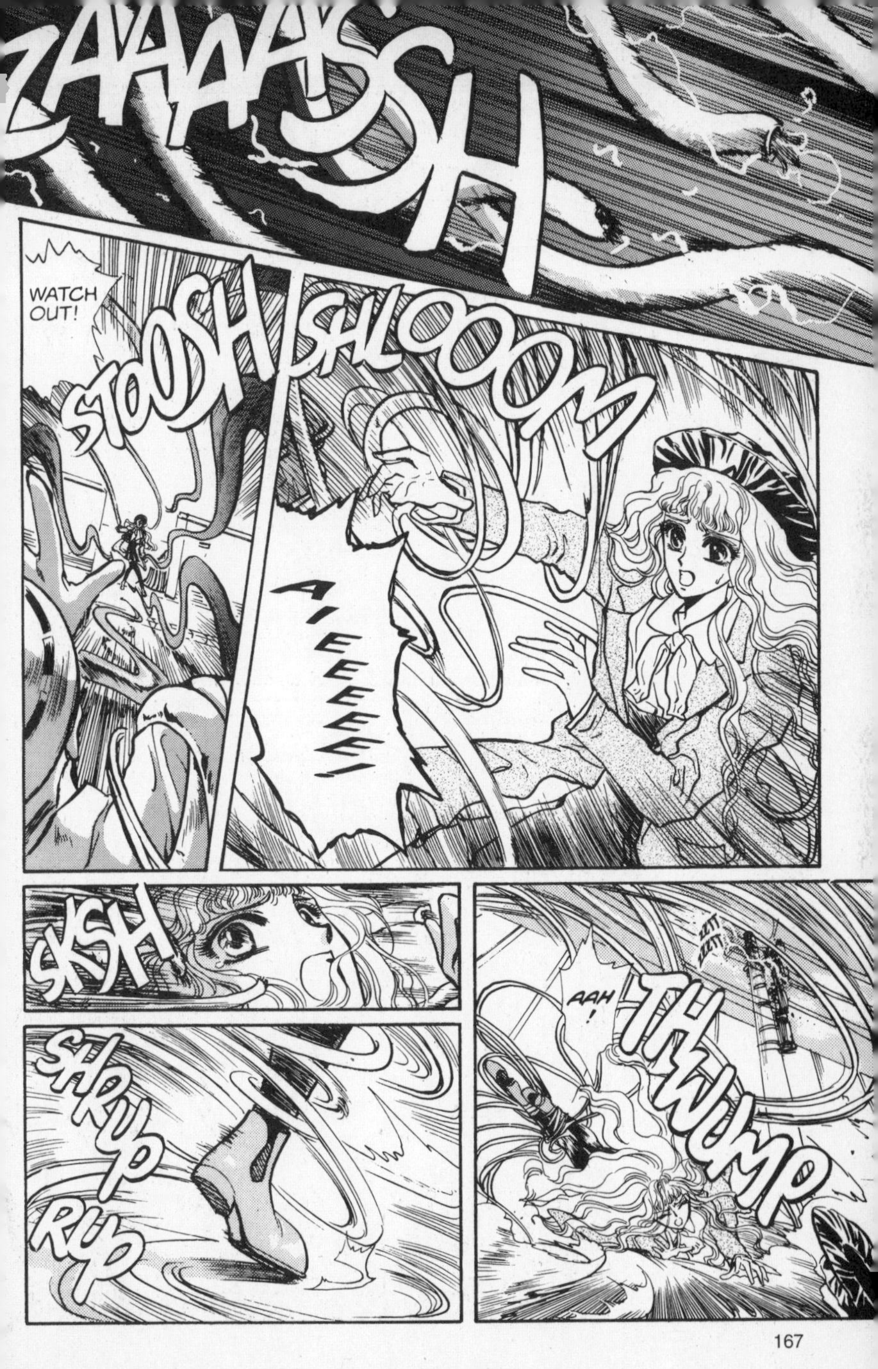
ZAAAASH
WATCH OUT!
STOOSH
SHLOOOM
AIEEEEEE!
SKSH
SHRUP RUP
AAH!
THWUMP

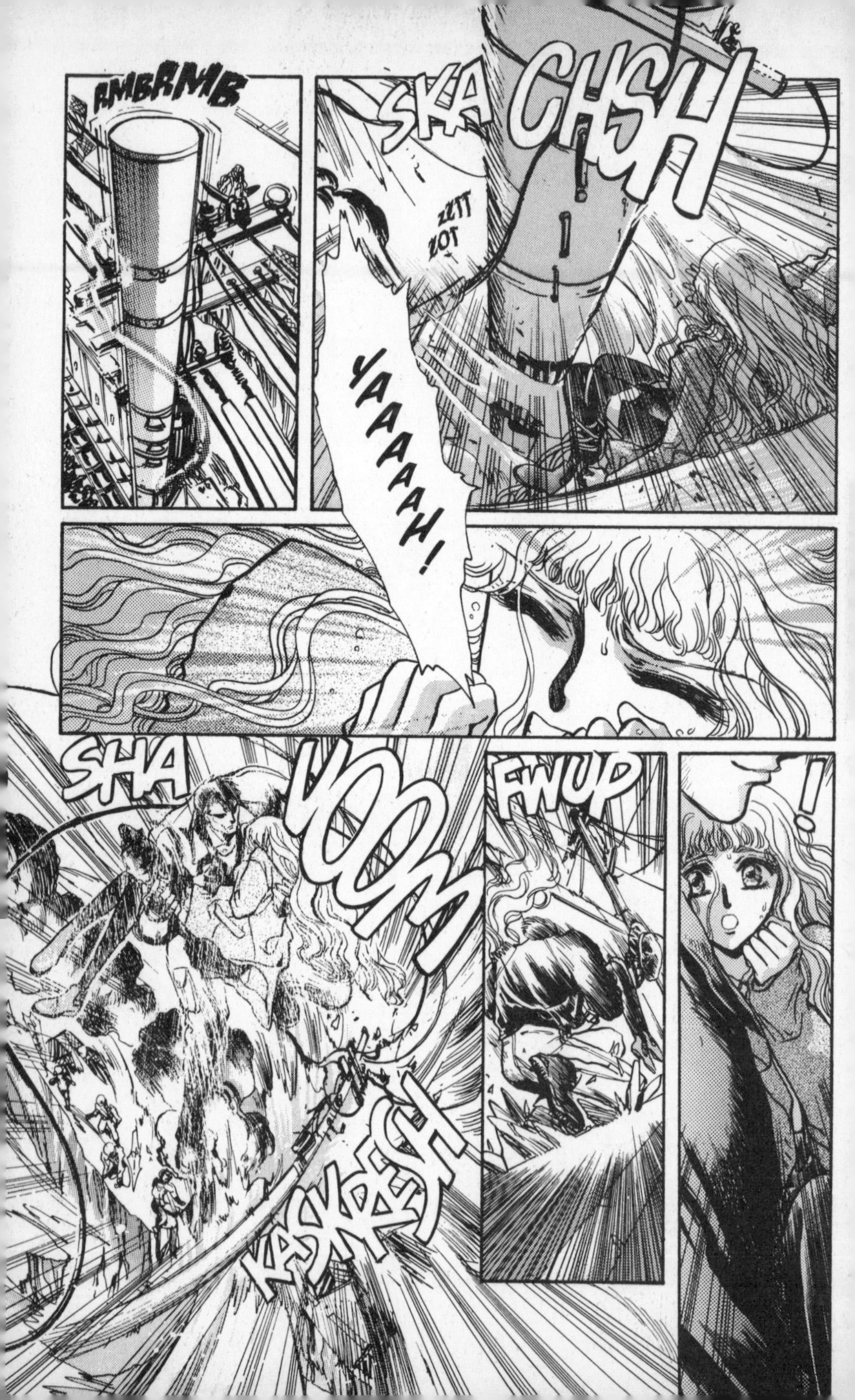
RMBRMB
SKA CHSH
ZZTT
ZOT
YAAAAAH!
SHA
VOOM
FWUP
!

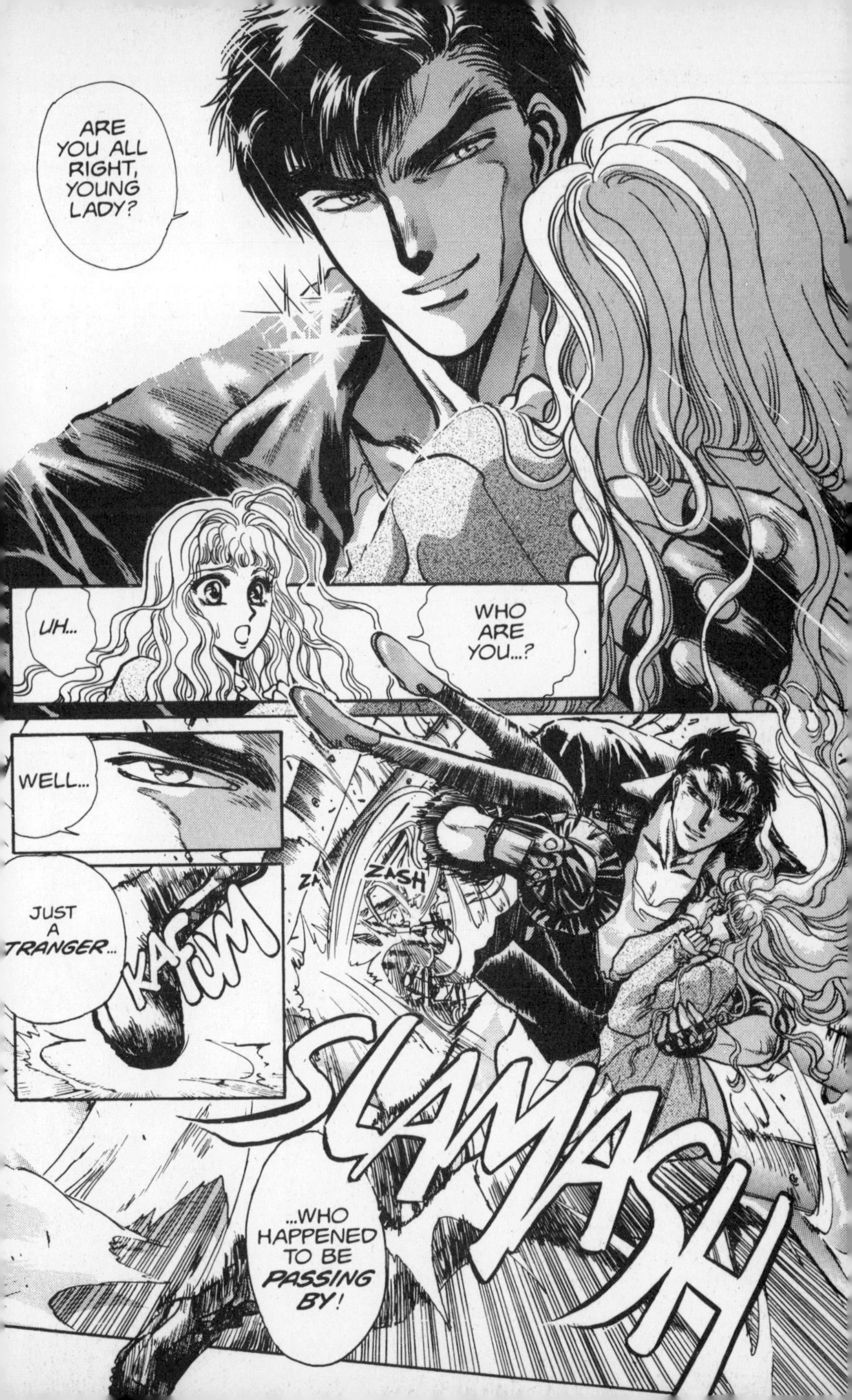
ARE YOU ALL RIGHT, YOUNG LADY?
UH...
WHO ARE YOU...?
WELL...
JUST A TRANGER...
KAFUM
ZA
ZASH
SLAMASH
...WHO HAPPENED TO BE PASSING BY!

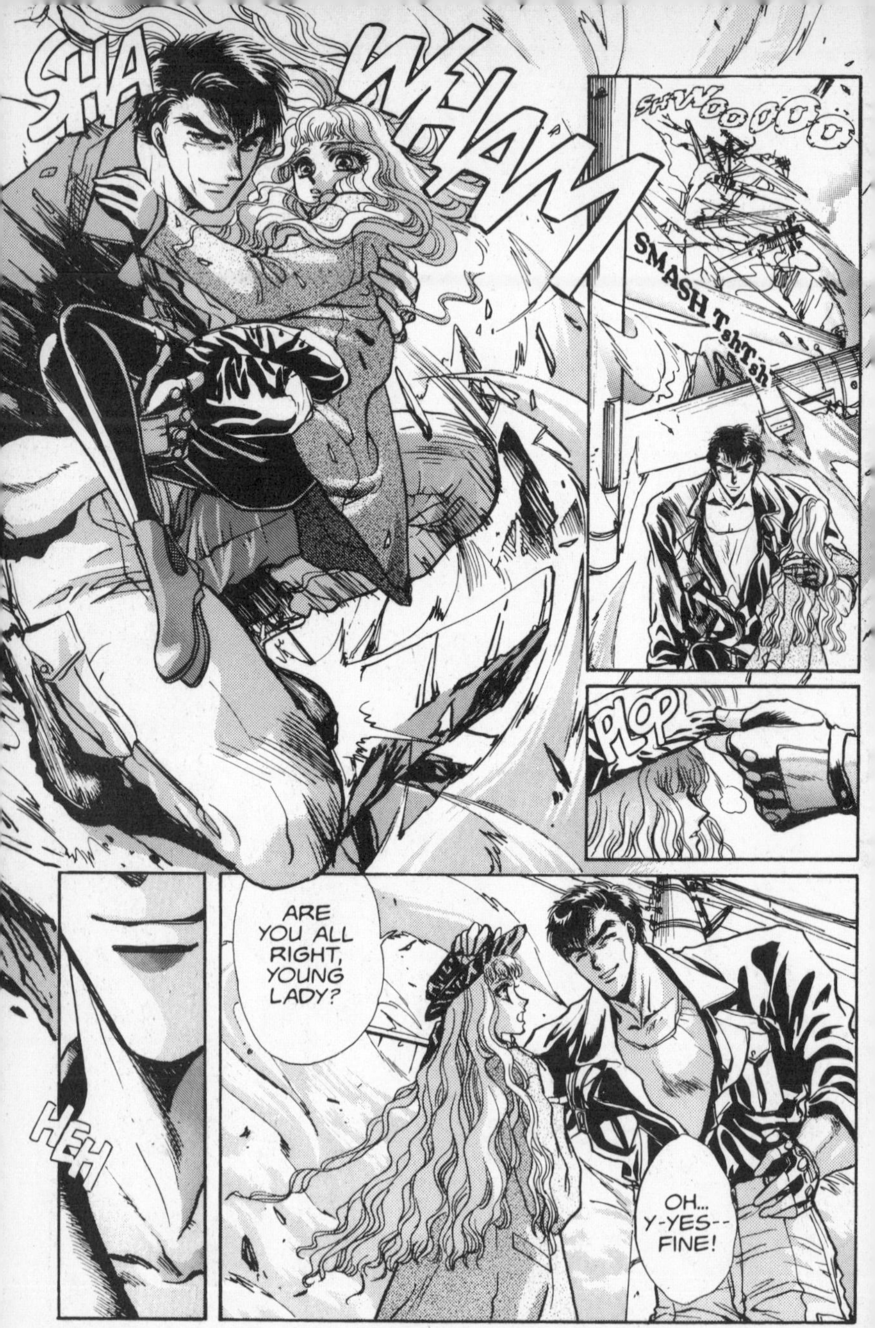
SHA
WHAM
SHVNOOOOO
SMASH TshTsh
PLOP
HEH
ARE YOU ALL RIGHT, YOUNG LADY?
OH... Y-YES--FINE!

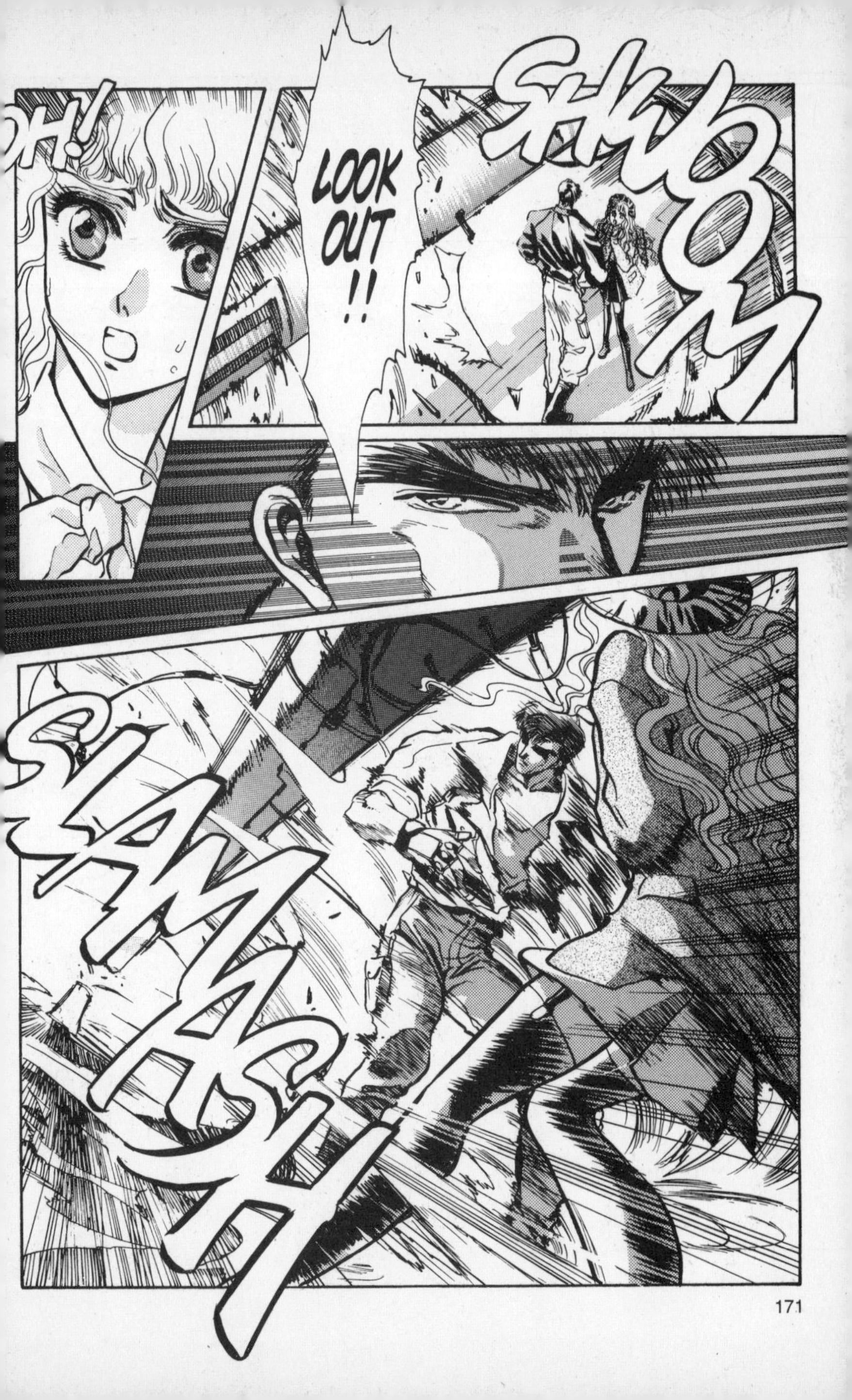
OH!
LOOK OUT !!
SHWOOM
SLAMASH

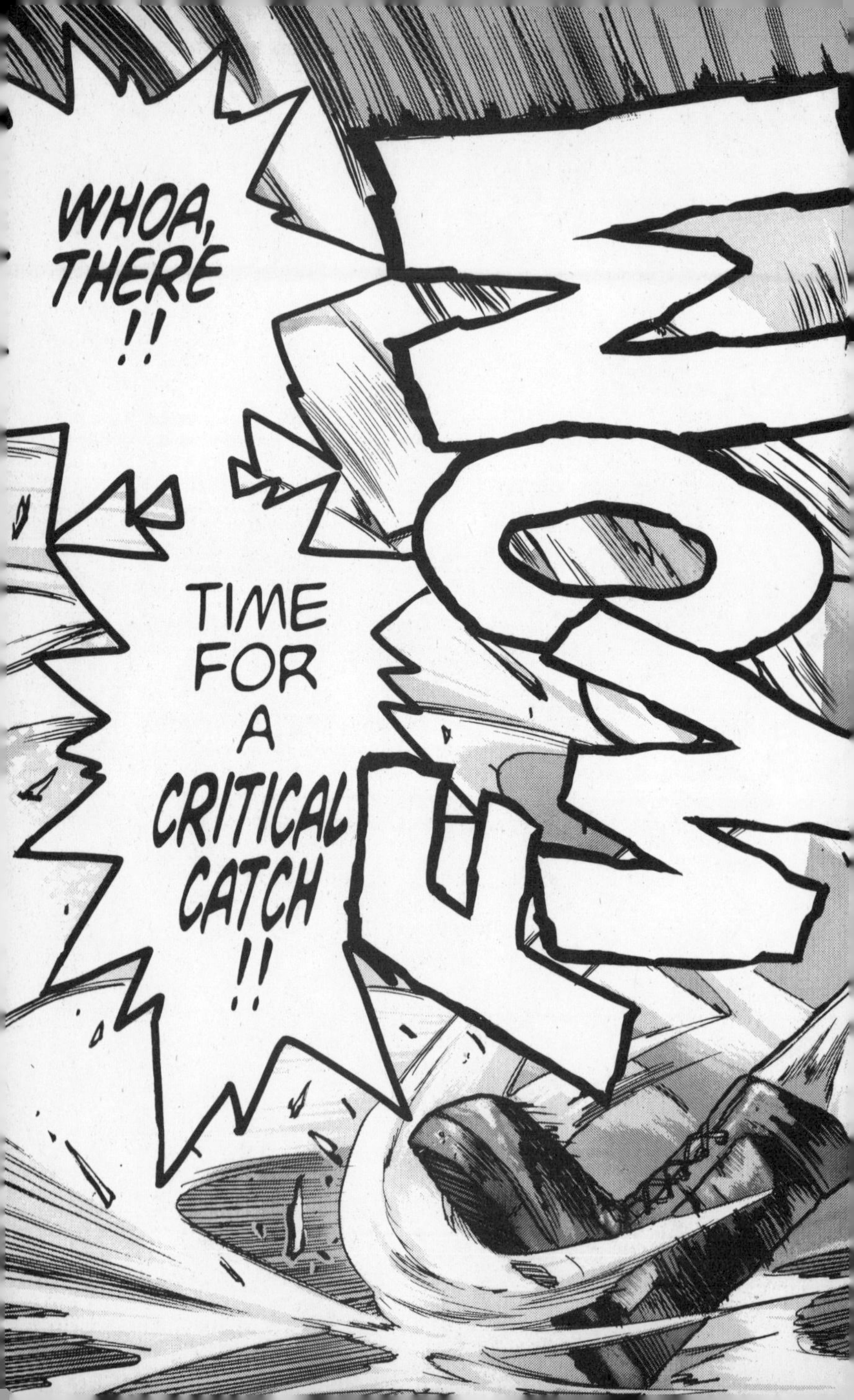
WHOA, THERE !!
TIME FOR A CRITICAL CATCH !!

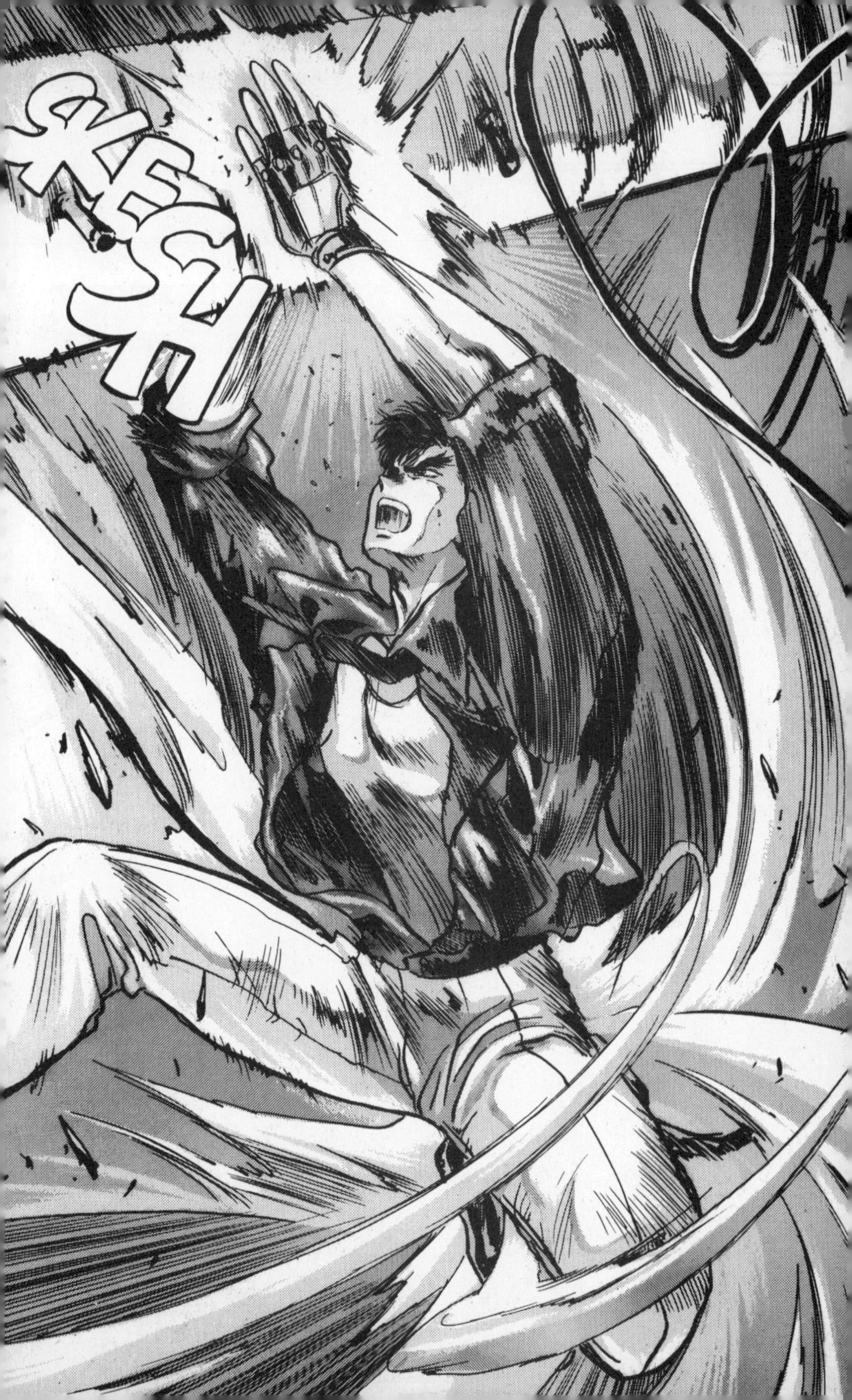

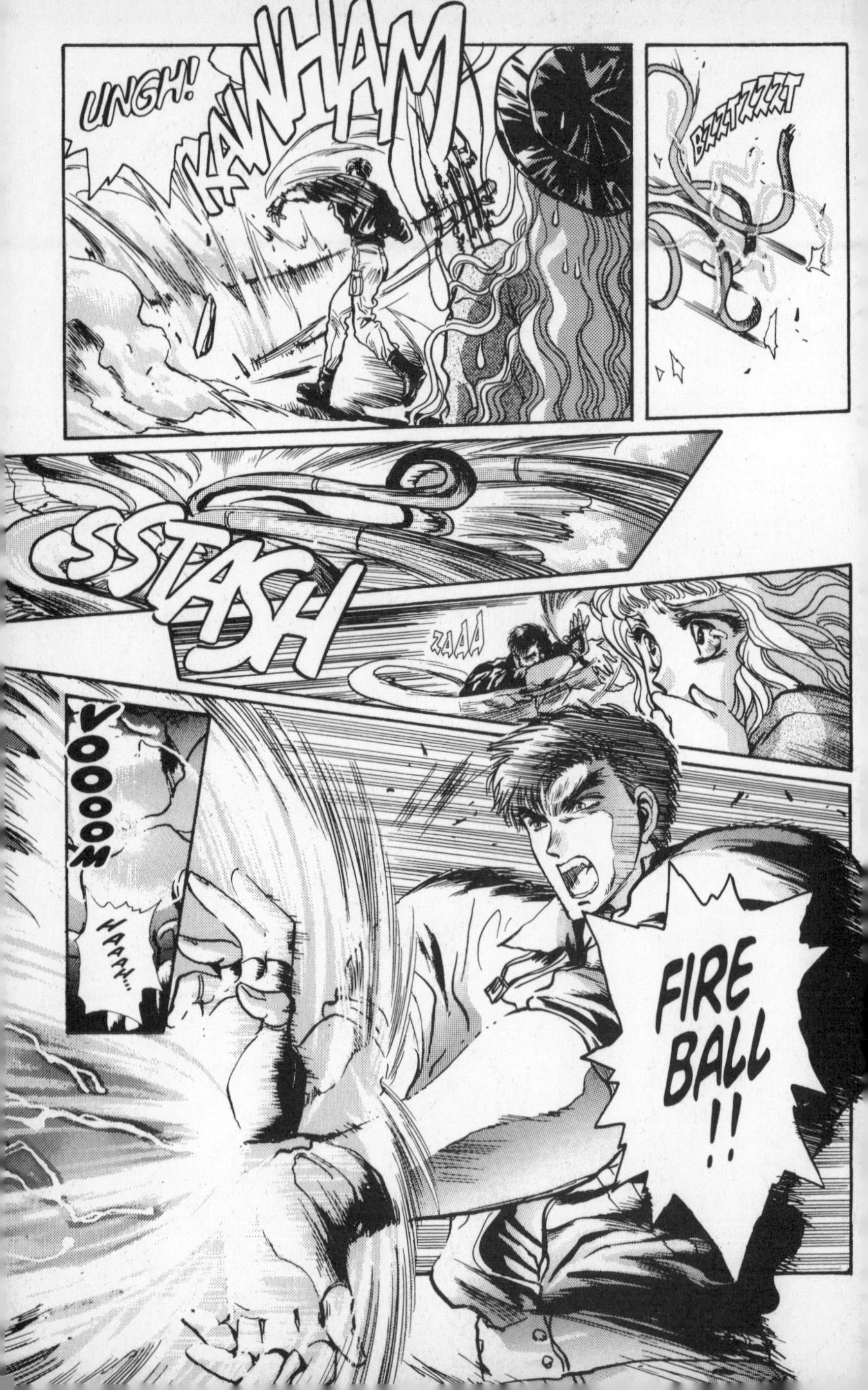
UNGH!
WHAM
BZZTZZZT
SSTASH
ZAAA
VOOOOOM
HAAAH...
FIRE BALL!!

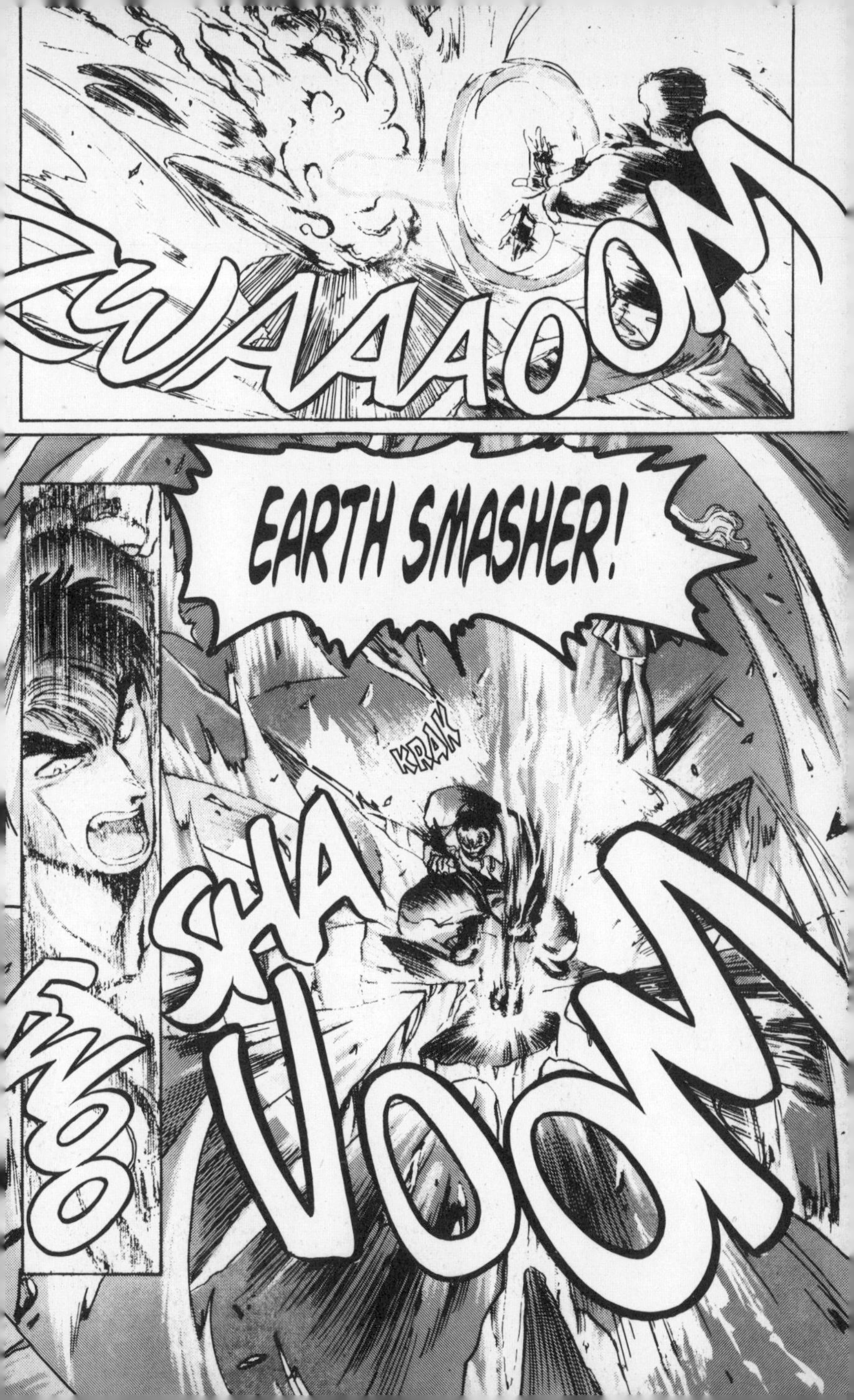
ZWAAAOOM
EARTH SMASHER!
KRAK
SHAVOOM

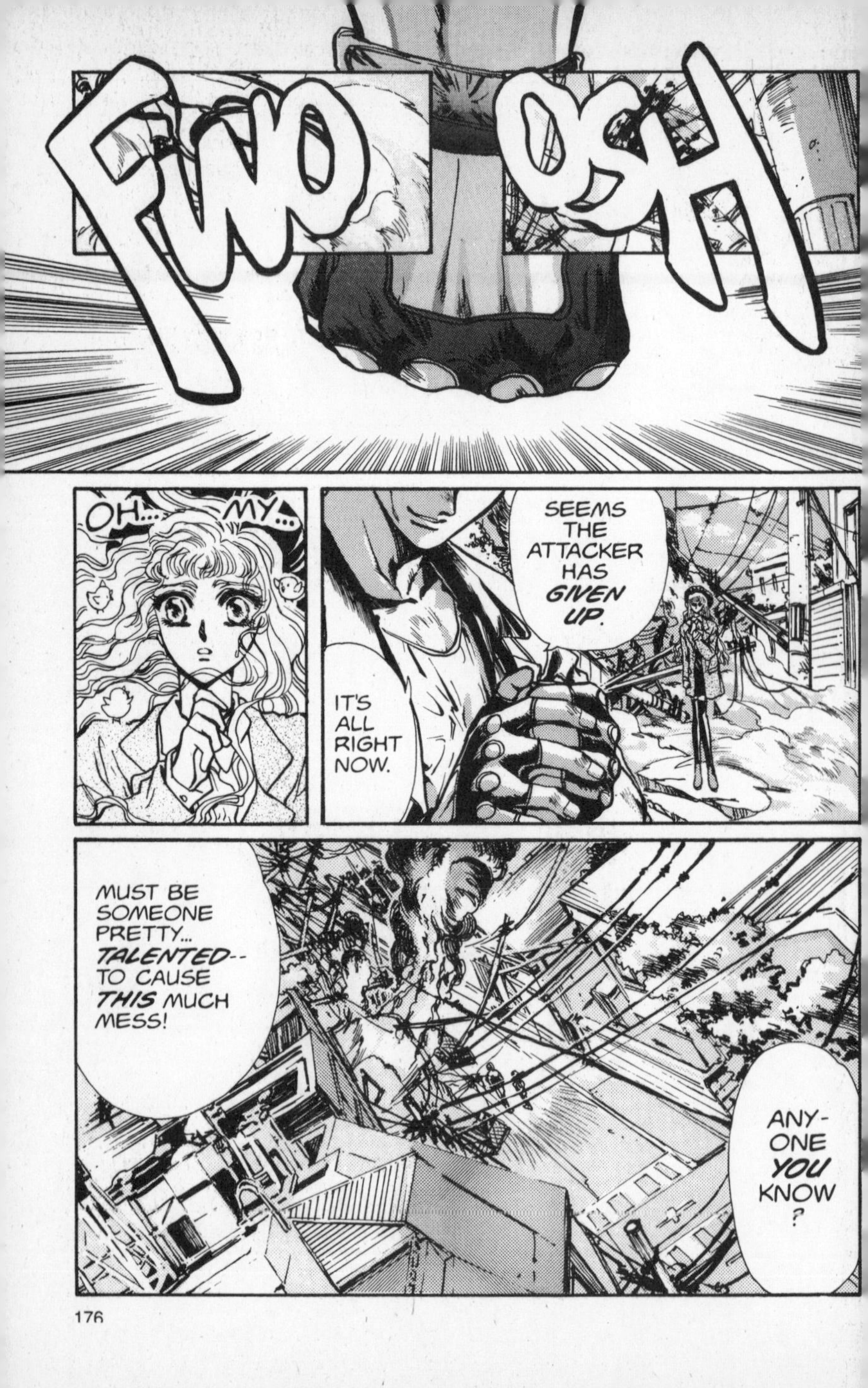
FWOOSH!
OH... MY...
SEEMS THE ATTACKER HAS GIVEN UP.
IT'S ALL RIGHT NOW.
MUST BE SOMEONE PRETTY... TALENTED-- TO CAUSE THIS MUCH MESS!
ANY-ONE YOU KNOW?

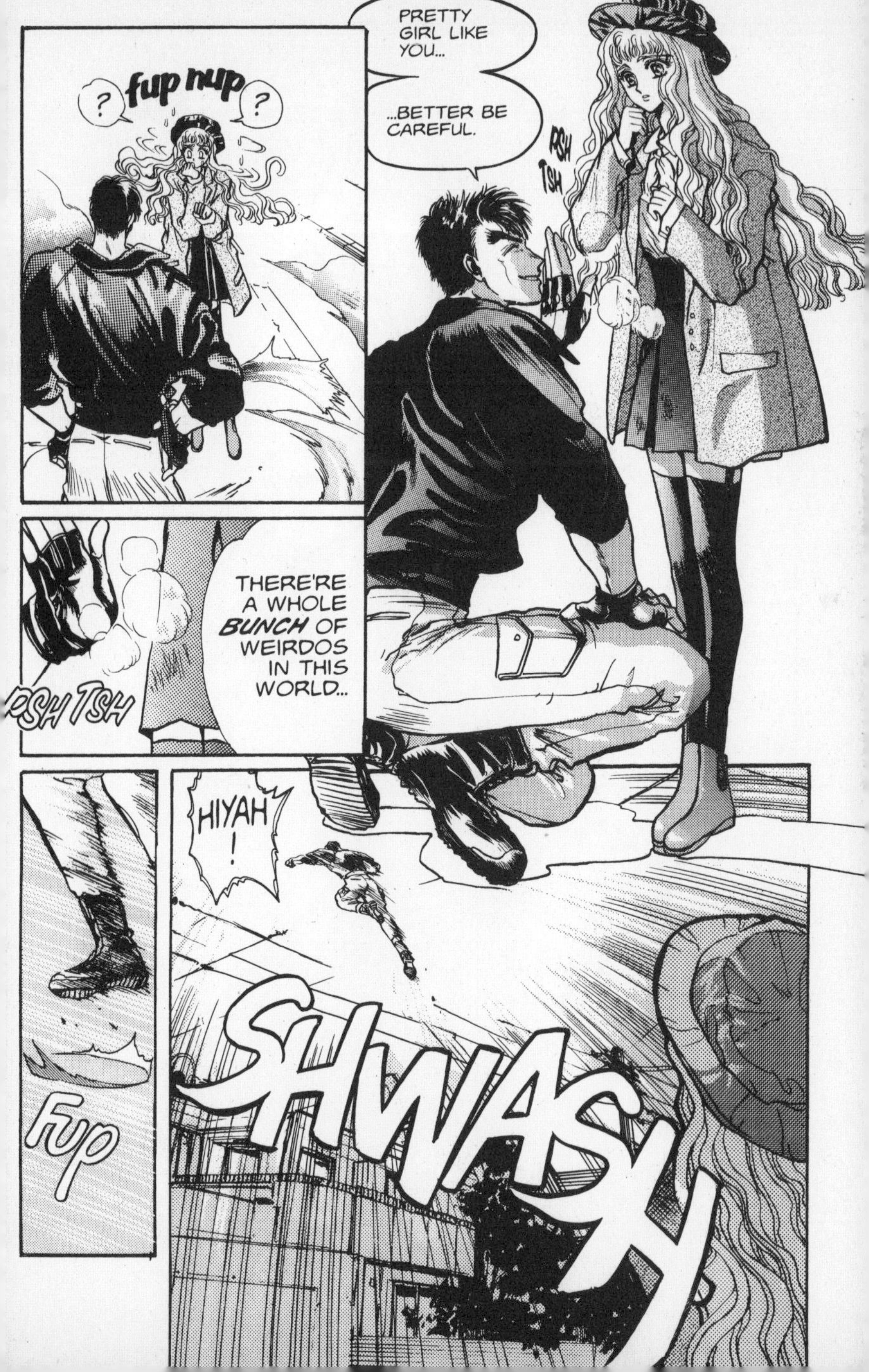

?
fup nup
?
THERE'RE A WHOLE *BUNCH* OF WEIRDOS IN THIS WORLD...
PSH TSH
PRETTY GIRL LIKE YOU...
...BETTER BE CAREFUL.
PSH TSH
Fup
HIYAH!
SHWASH

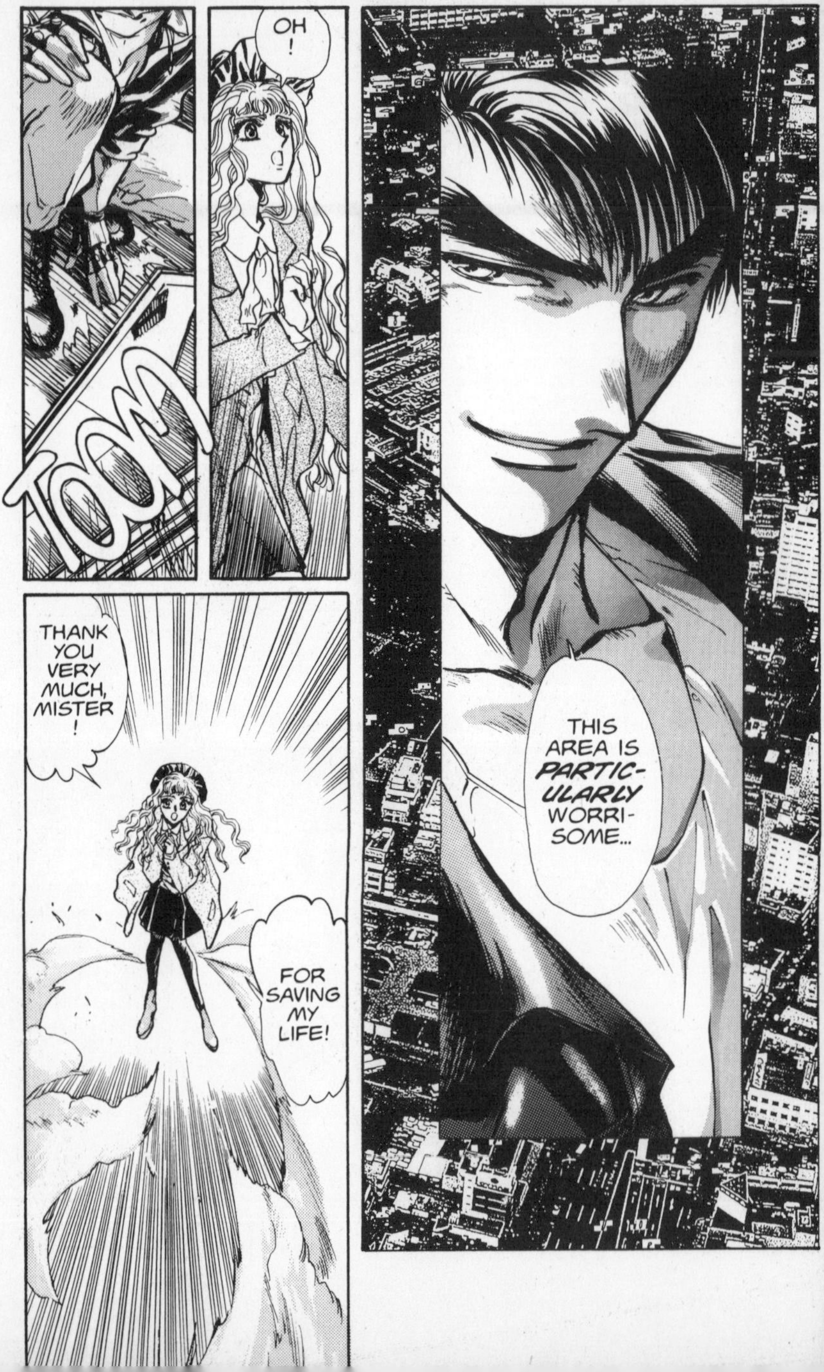
TOOM
OH!
THANK YOU VERY MUCH, MISTER!
FOR SAVING MY LIFE!
THIS AREA IS PARTICULARLY WORRISOME...

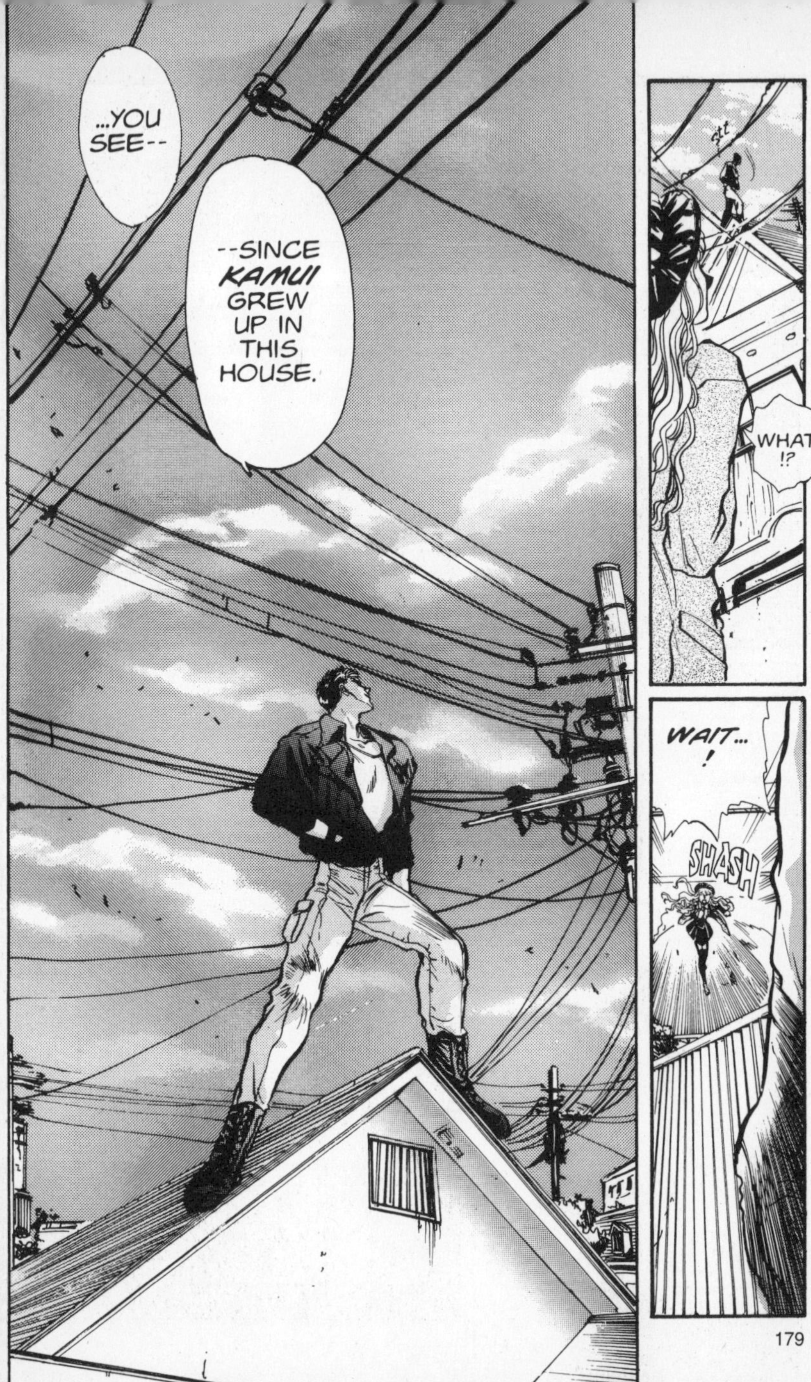
...YOU SEE--
--SINCE KAMUI GREW UP IN THIS HOUSE.
stt
WHAT !?
WAIT... !
SHASH

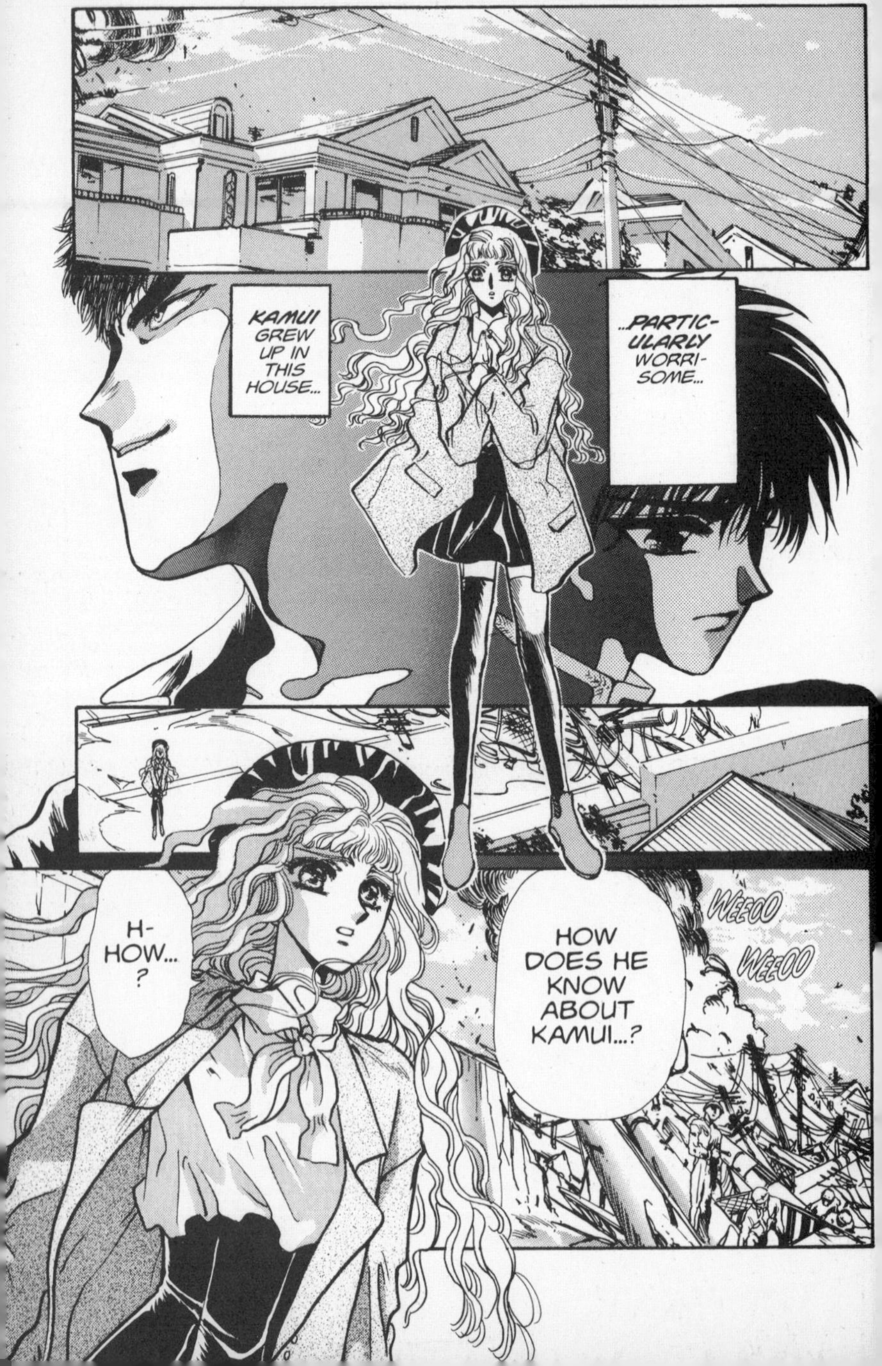
KAMUI GREW UP IN THIS HOUSE...
...PARTIC-ULARLY WORRI-SOME...
H-HOW...?
HOW DOES HE KNOW ABOUT KAMUI...?
WEEOO
WEEOO

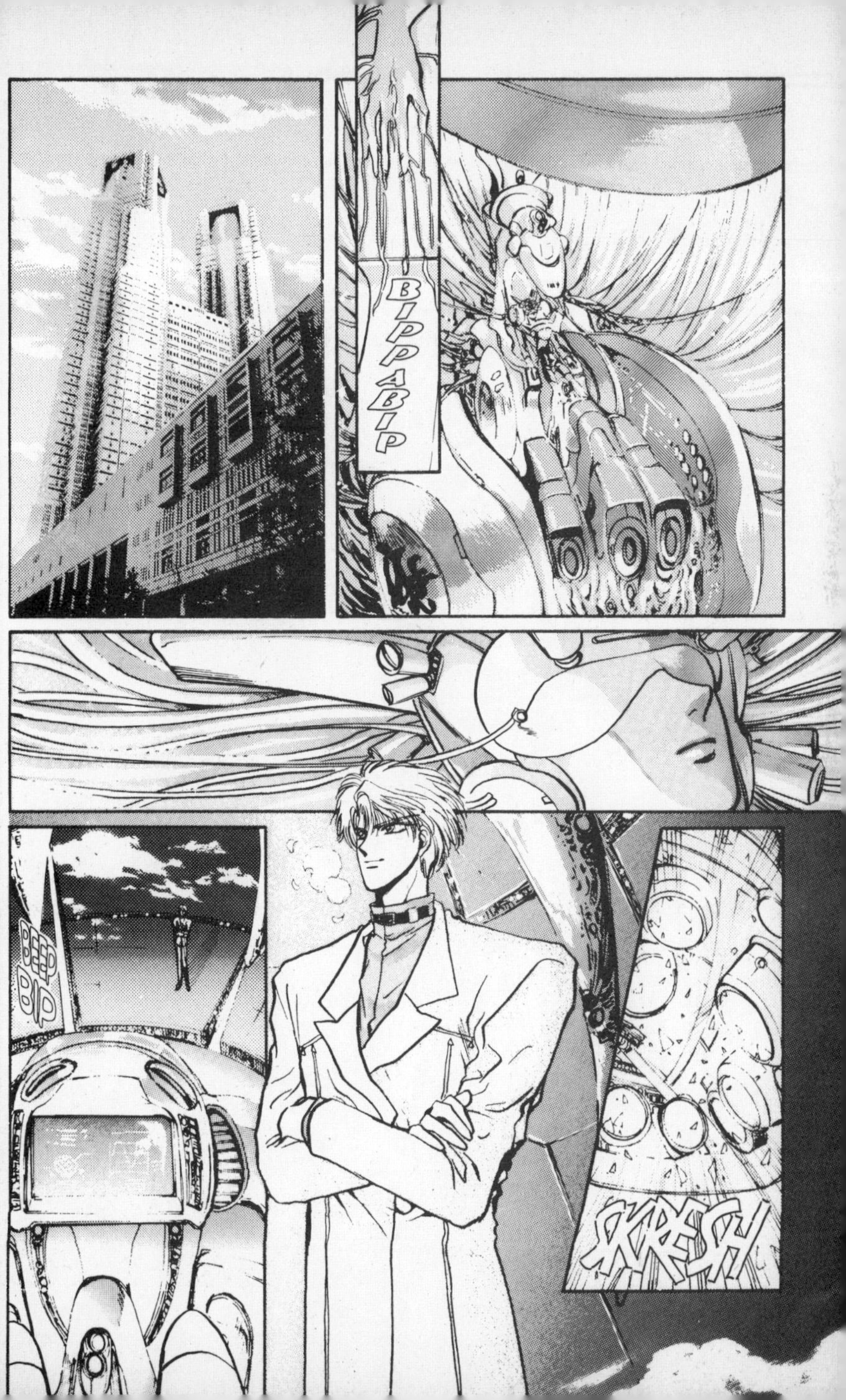
BIPPABIP
BEEP BIP
SKRESH

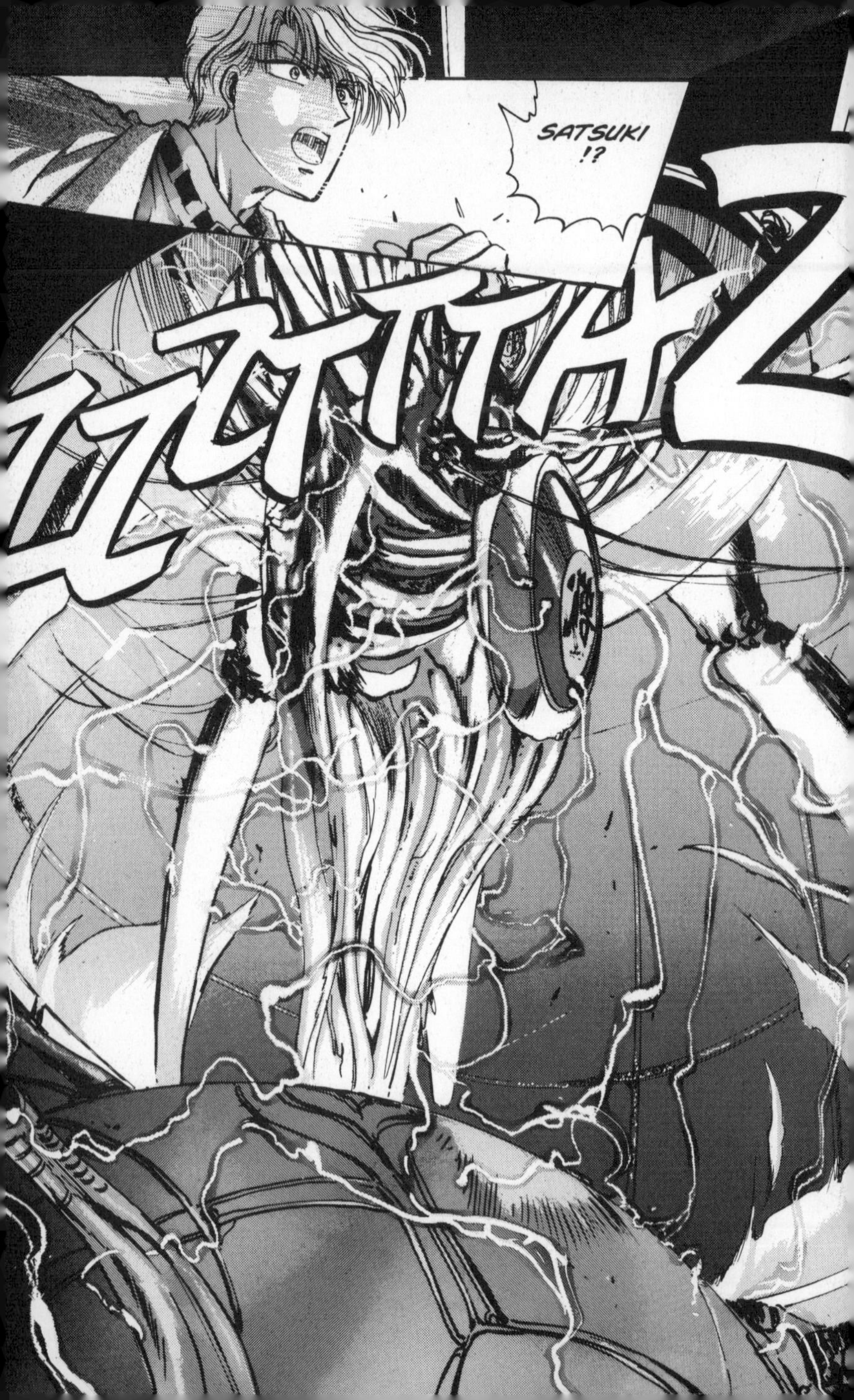
SATSUKI !?
ZZZTTTTTZZ

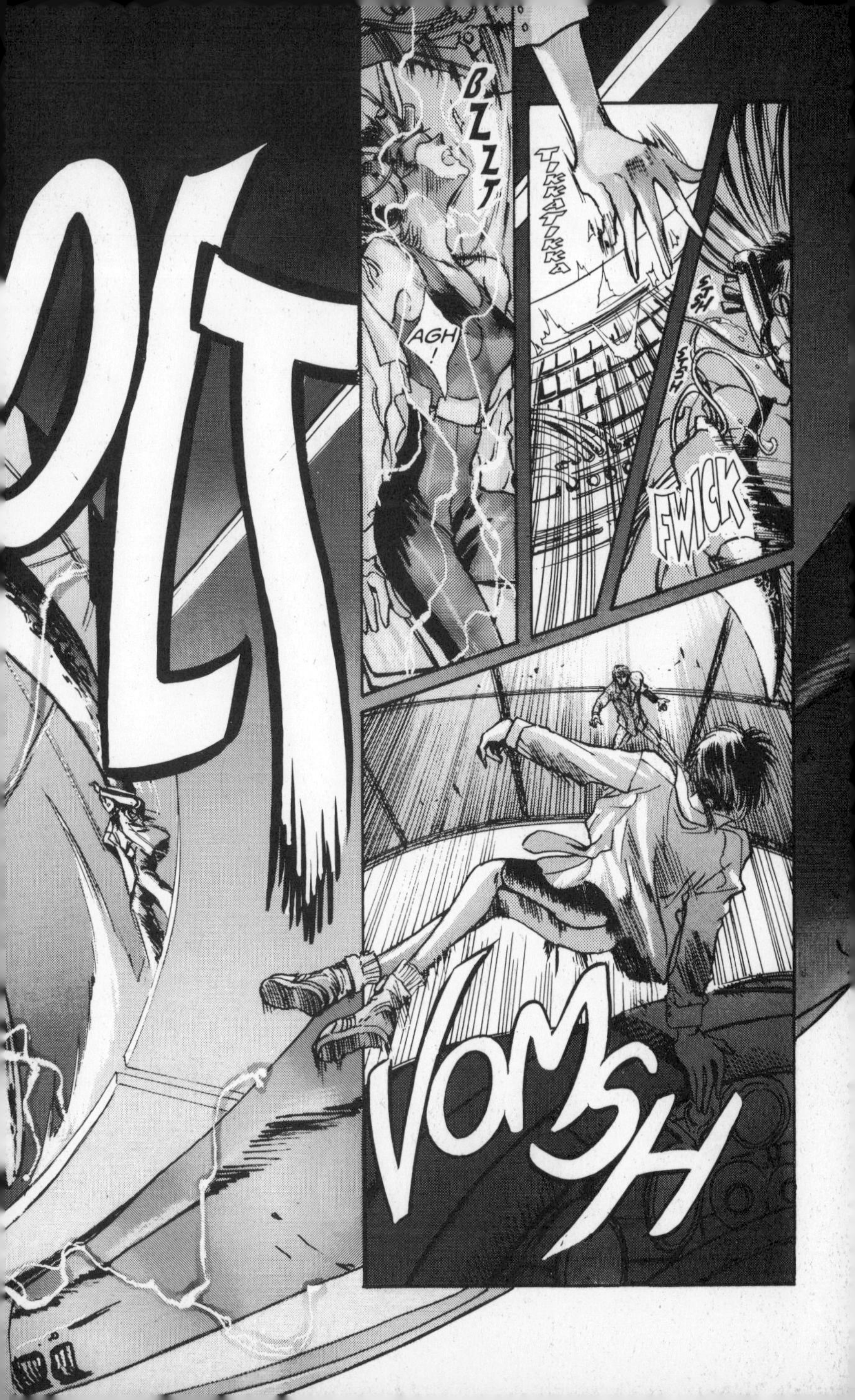
OLT
BZZT
AGH!
TIKKATIKKA
FWICK
VOMSH

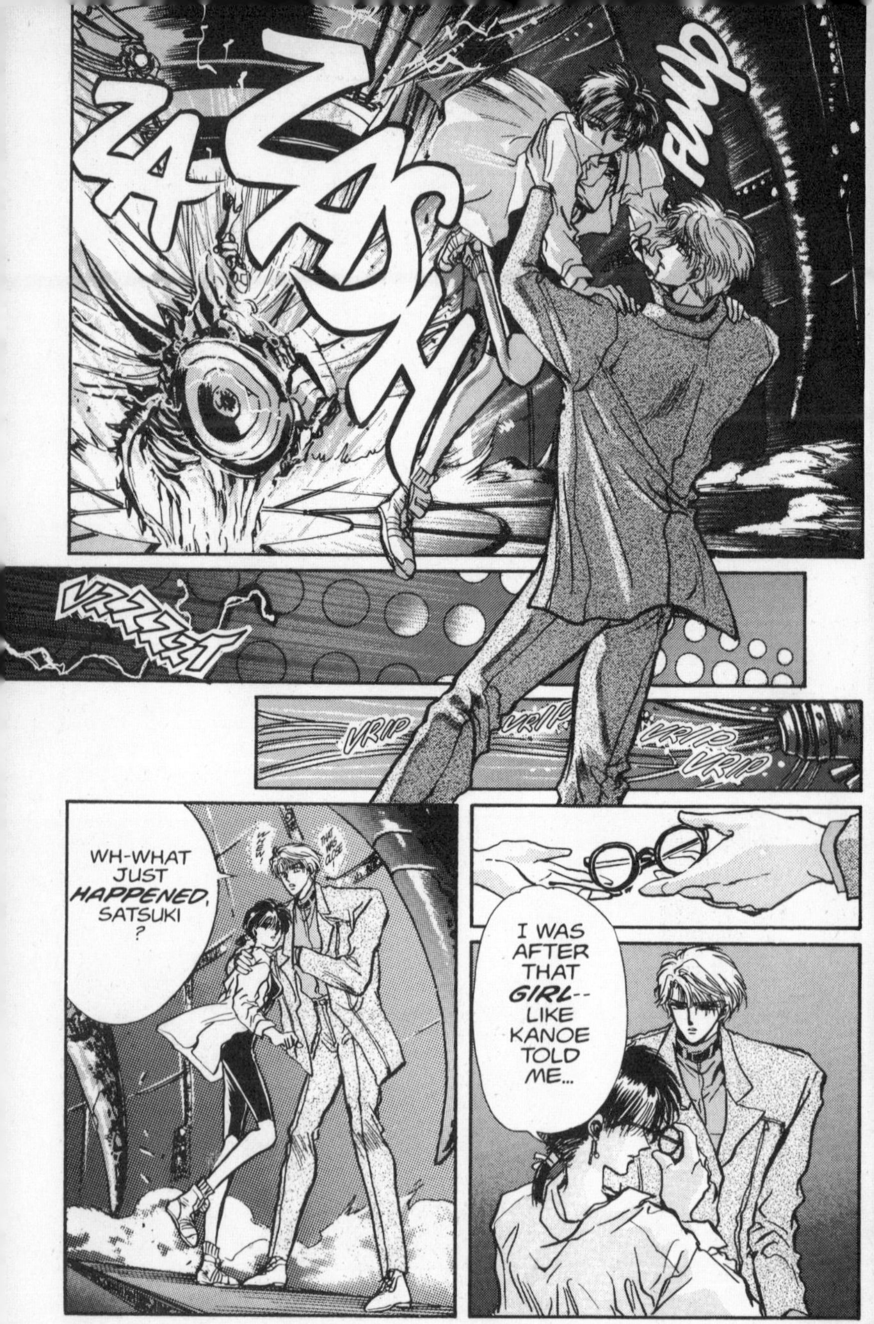
ZAZASH
FWUP
VRZZZT
VRIP VRIP VRIP VRIP
WH-WHAT JUST **HAPPENED**, SATSUKI?
WHEW!
THAT WAS CLOSE!
I WAS AFTER THAT **GIRL**-- LIKE KANOE TOLD ME...

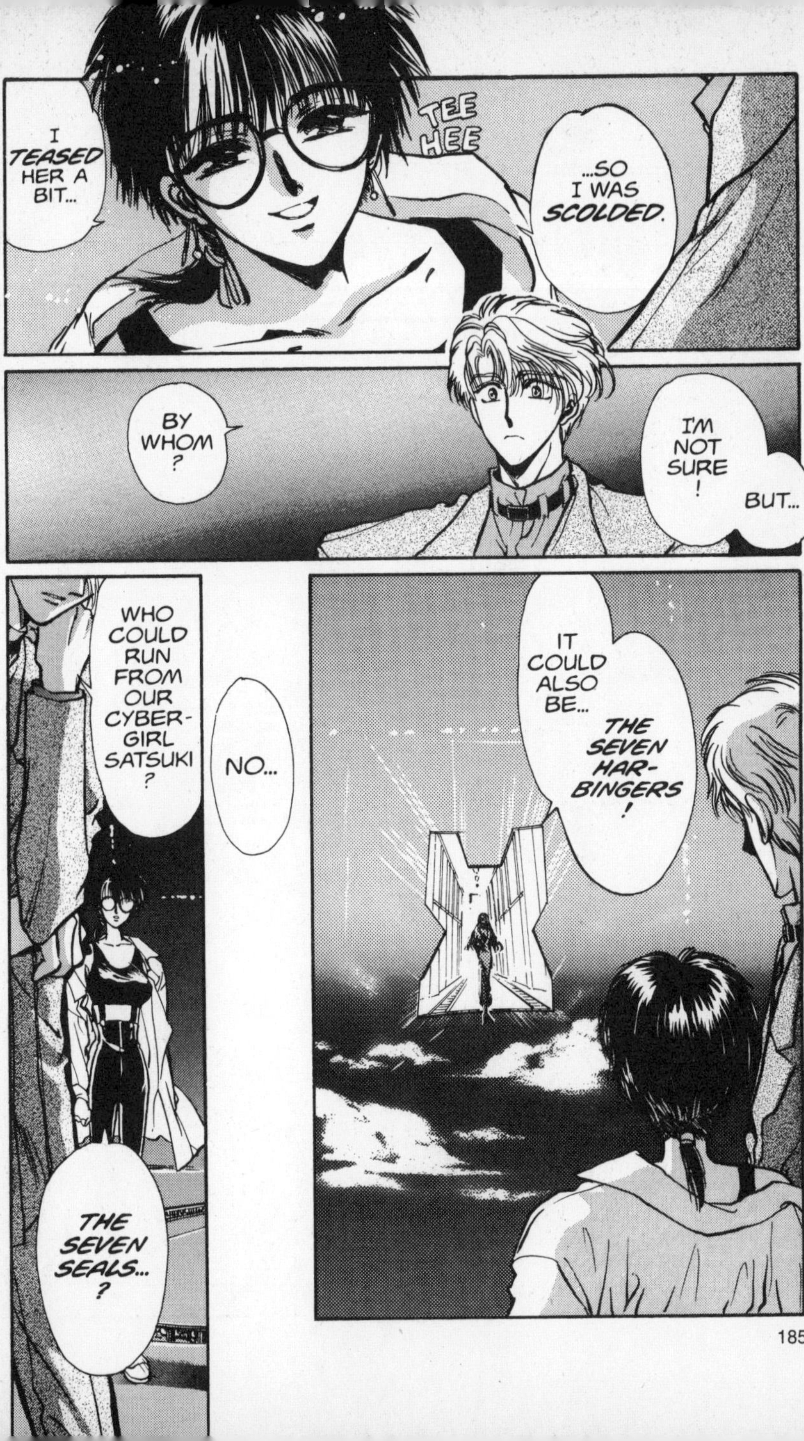
I *TEASED* HER A BIT...
TEE HEE
...SO I WAS *SCOLDED*.
BY WHOM?
I'M NOT SURE!
BUT...
WHO COULD RUN FROM OUR CYBER-GIRL SATSUKI?
NO...
THE SEVEN SEALS...?
IT COULD ALSO BE... *THE SEVEN HAR-BINGERS!*

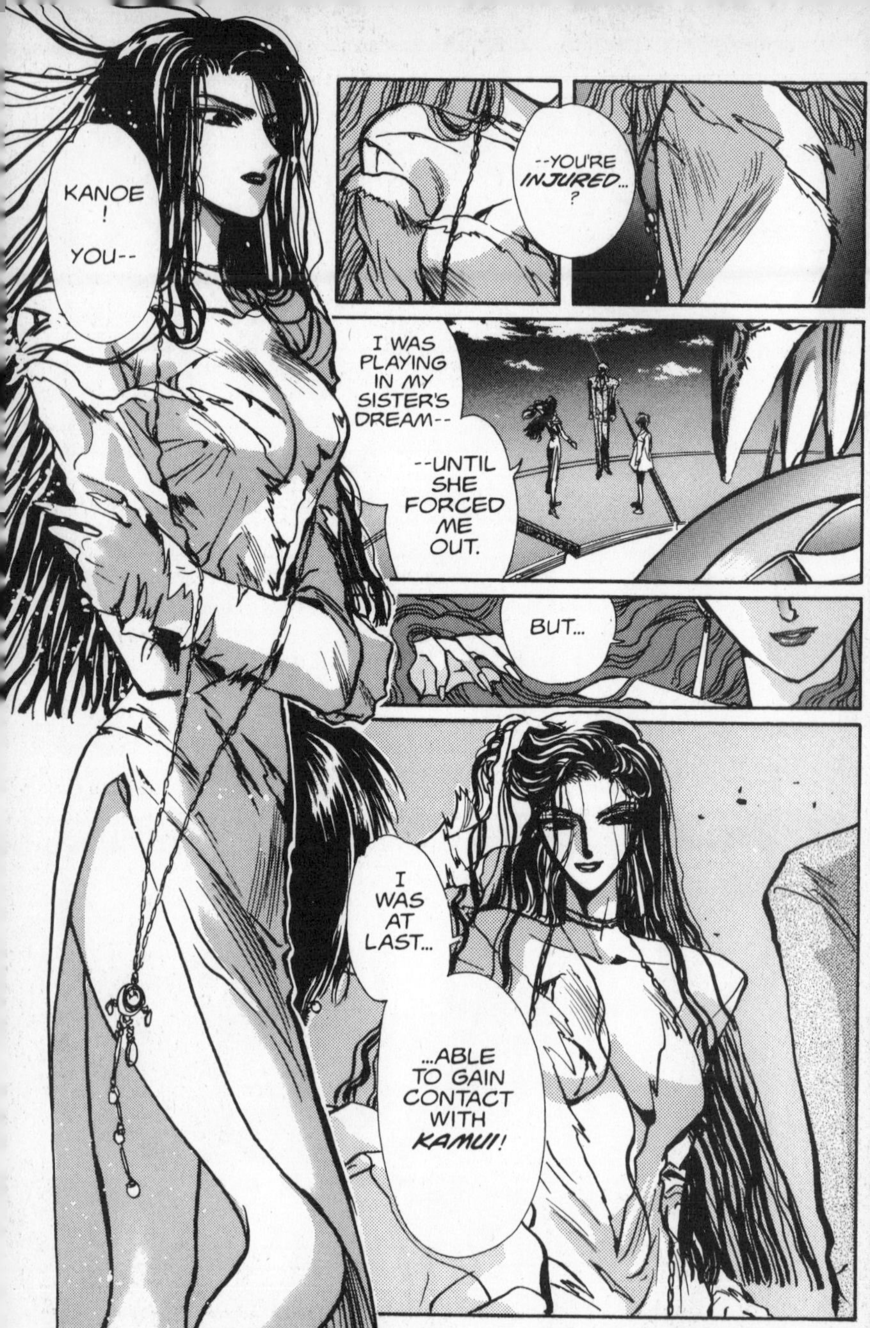
KANOE! YOU--
--YOU'RE *INJURED*...?
I WAS PLAYING IN MY SISTER'S DREAM--
--UNTIL SHE FORCED ME OUT.
BUT...
I WAS AT LAST...
...ABLE TO GAIN CONTACT WITH *KAMUI*!

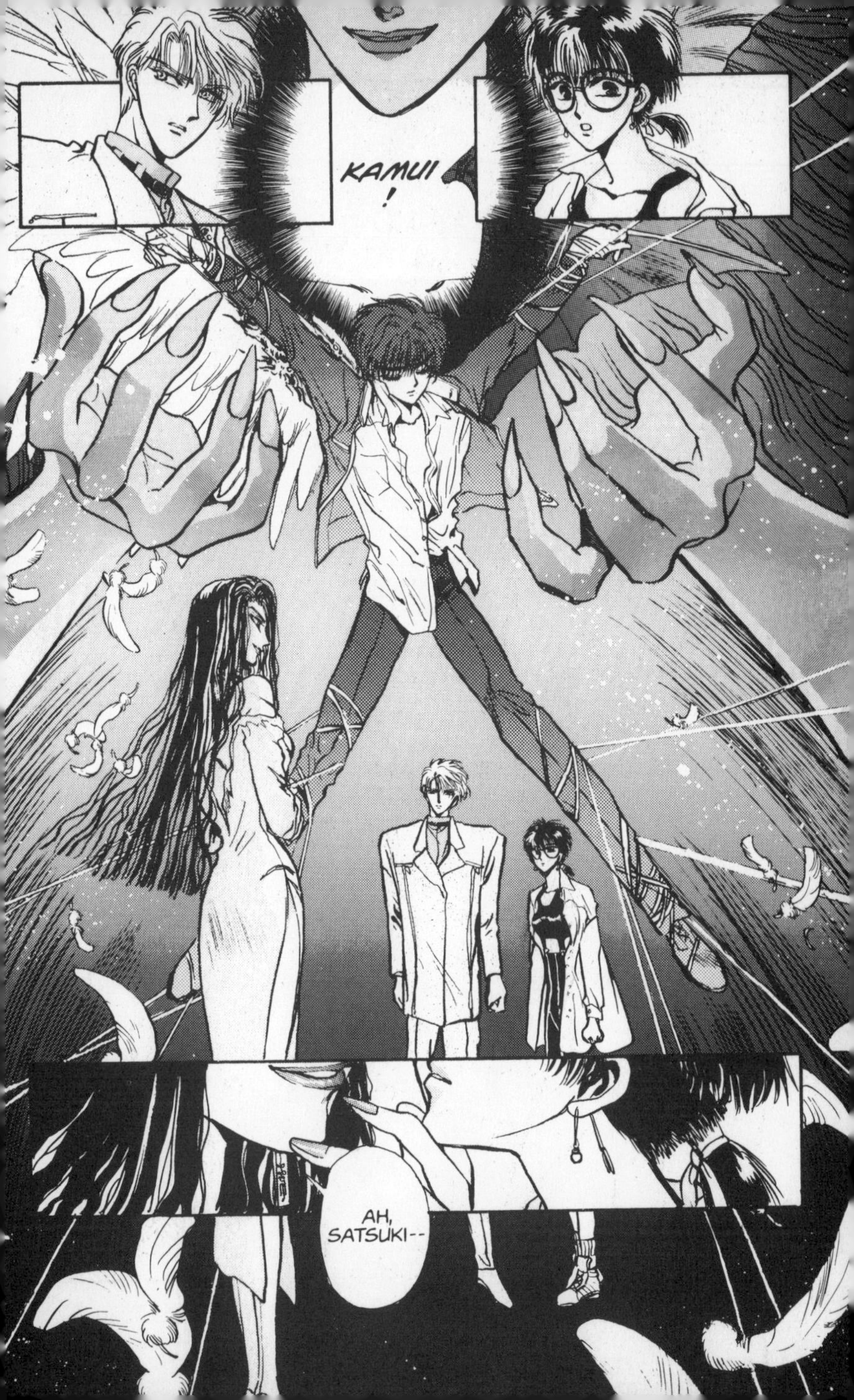
KAMUI!
AH, SATSUKI--

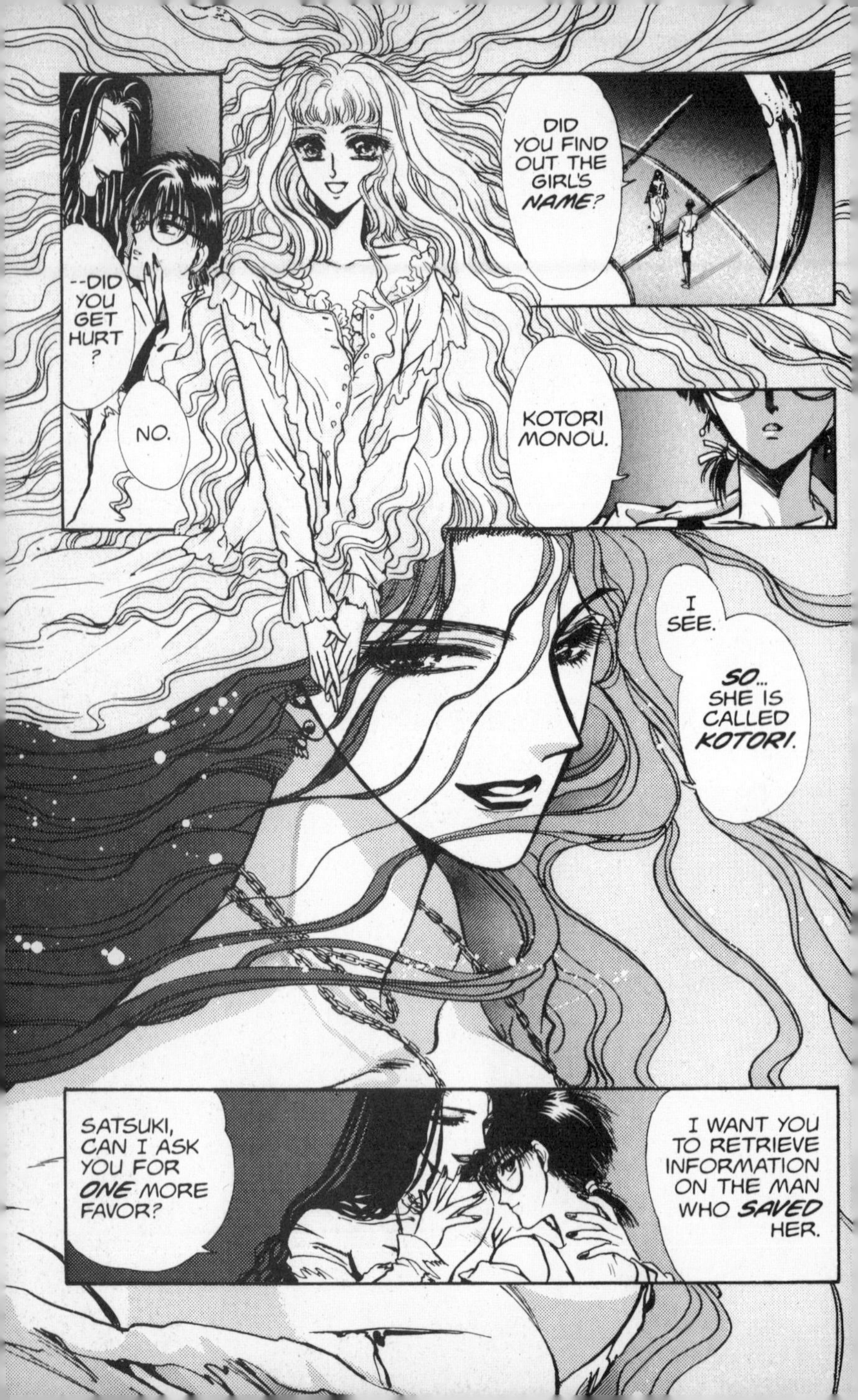
--DID YOU GET HURT?
NO.
DID YOU FIND OUT THE GIRL'S NAME?
KOTORI MONOU.
I SEE.
SO... SHE IS CALLED KOTORI.
SATSUKI, CAN I ASK YOU FOR ONE MORE FAVOR?
I WANT YOU TO RETRIEVE INFORMATION ON THE MAN WHO SAVED HER.

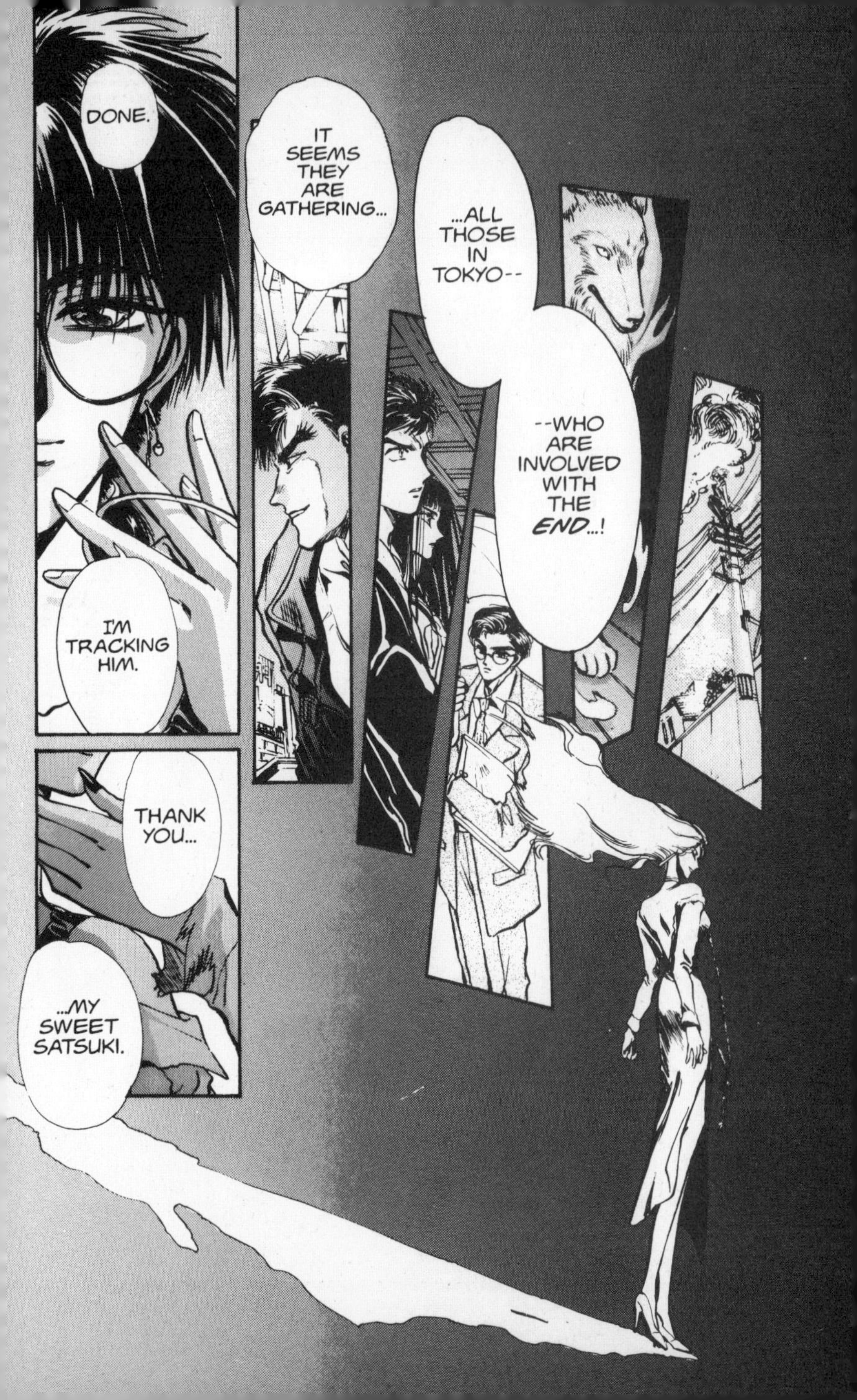
DONE.
I'M TRACKING HIM.
IT SEEMS THEY ARE GATHERING...
...ALL THOSE IN TOKYO--
--WHO ARE INVOLVED WITH THE *END*...!
THANK YOU...
...MY SWEET SATSUKI.

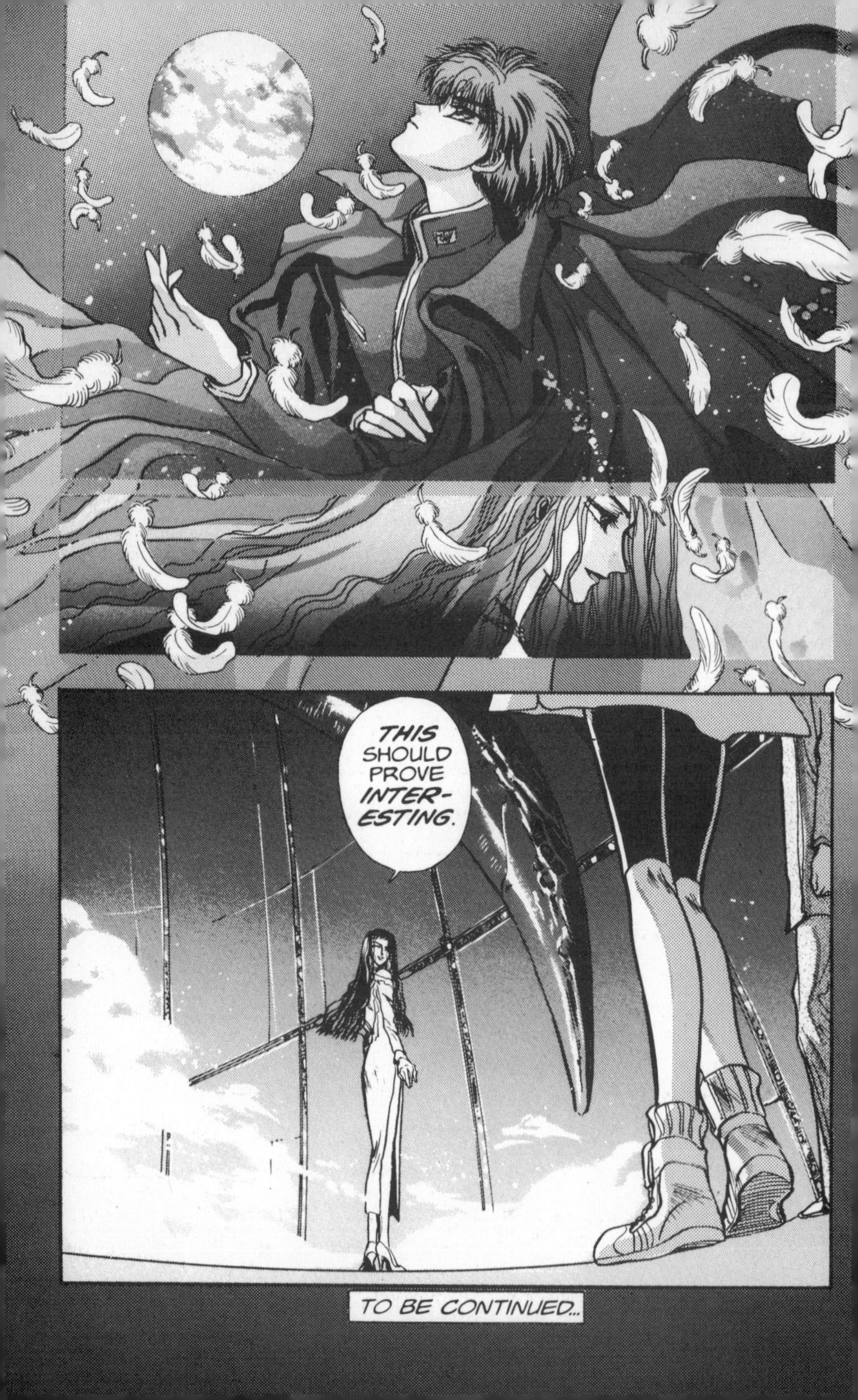
THIS SHOULD PROVE INTER-ESTING.

TO BE CONTINUED...

COMPLETE OUR SURVEY AND LET US KNOW WHAT YOU THINK!

☐ Please check here if you DO NOT wish to receive information or future offers from VIZ

Name: _____

Address: _____

City: _____ State: _____ Zip: _____

E-mail: _____

☐ Male ☐ Female   Date of Birth (mm/dd/yyyy): ___ / ___ / _____   (Under 13? Parental consent required)

What race/ethnicity do you consider yourself? (please check one)

☐ Asian/Pacific Islander   ☐ Black/African American   ☐ Hispanic/Latino

☐ Native American/Alaskan Native ☐ White/Caucasian   ☐ Other: _____

What VIZ product did you purchase? (check all that apply and indicate title purchased)

☐ DVD/VHS _____

☐ Graphic Novel _____

☐ Magazines _____

☐ Merchandise _____

Reason for purchase: (check all that apply)

☐ Special offer   ☐ Favorite title   ☐ Gift

☐ Recommendation   ☐ Other_____

Where did you make your purchase? (please check one)

☐ Comic store   ☐ Bookstore   ☐ Mass/Grocery Store

☐ Newsstand   ☐ Video/Video Game Store ☐ Other: _____

☐ Online (site: _____)

What other VIZ properties have you purchased/own? _____

_____

How many anime and/or manga titles have you purchased in the last year? How many we
VIZ titles? (please check one from each column)

ANIME
- ☐ None
- ☐ 1-4
- ☐ 5-10
- ☐ 11+

MANGA
- ☐ None
- ☐ 1-4
- ☐ 5-10
- ☐ 11+

VIZ
- ☐ None
- ☐ 1-4
- ☐ 5-10
- ☐ 11+

I find the pricing of VIZ products to be: (please check one)

- ☐ Cheap
- ☐ Reasonable
- ☐ Expensive

What genre of manga and anime would you like to see from VIZ? (please check two)

- ☐ Adventure
- ☐ Comic Strip
- ☐ Detective
- ☐ Fighting
- ☐ Horror
- ☐ Romance
- ☐ Sci-Fi/Fantasy
- ☐ Sports

What do you think of VIZ's new look?

- ☐ Love It
- ☐ It's OK
- ☐ Hate It
- ☐ Didn't Notice
- ☐ No Opinion

THANK YOU! Please send the completed form to:

NJW Research
42 Catharine St.
Poughkeepsie, NY 12601

All information provided will be used for internal purposes only. We promise not to sell or otherwise divulge your information.